RIVER CRUISING
IN EUROPE & THE USA

BY DOUGLAS WARD
THE WORLD'S FOREMOST AUTHORITY ON CRUISING

⊙ Walking Eye App

Your Berlitz River Cruising in Europe guide now includes a free Insight Guides app and eBook of the book, all included for the same great price as before. They are available to download from the free Walking Eye container app in the App Store and Google Play. Simply download the Walking Eye container app to access the eBook and app.

Multiple eBooks & apps available

Now that you've bought this book you can download the accompanying app and eBook for free. Inside the Walking Eye container app, you'll also find the whole range of other Insight Guides destination apps and eBooks, all available for purchase.

Events & activities

Free access to information on a range of local guided tours, sightseeing activities and local events in any destination, with the option to book.

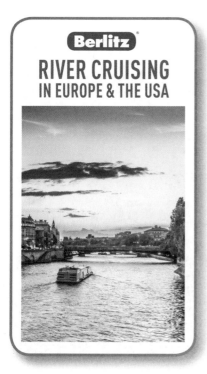

Berlitz River Cruising app

The app has been designed to give you quick and easy access to insightful ship reviews. The app search function makes it easy to find out which ships are best for you. You will be able to highlight your favourite cruise ships for future reference, and share with friends and family.

Rivership descriptions

The app also includes descriptions of the facilities and cruise experience on every one of the 332 riverships featured.

HOW TO DOWNLOAD THE WALKING EYE APP

1. Download the Walking Eye App from the App Store or Google Play.
2. Open the app and select the scanning function from the main menu.
3. Scan the QR code on this page – you will then be asked a security question to verify ownership of the book.
4. Once this has been verified, you will see your eBook and destination content in the purchased ebook and destination sections, where you will be able to download them.

Other destination apps and eBooks are available for purchase separately or are free with the purchase of the Insight Guide book.

TABLE OF CONTENTS

YOUR FREE WALKING EYE APP

When you buy this book, you get access to the free Insight Guides Walking Eye app, which contains an eBook version of River Cruising in Europe and the USA as well as all the ship listings in handy app form. Insight Guides is the sister brand of Berlitz Publishing, both owned by Apa Publications. See page 3 for more information on how to get your app.

FROM THE AUTHOR

Rivers were here eons before roads were created and have always been vital to human settlement and survival. Among the many of Europe's great cities that grew up on the banks of the river are London (Thames), Paris (Seine), Cologne (Rhine), Frankfurt (Main), Prague (Elbe/Vltava), Budapest (Danube) and Vienna (Danube). Rivers have long been used as lifelines by which nations conduct commerce and organise the transportation of goods. They are used for drainage, irrigation, water supply and the production of hydroelectric power. But they are also sources of adventure and romance. Note that rivers are natural entities, and Mother Nature can be unpredictable. Variable conditions mean that nothing – such as the depth, the current or flow of water – is guaranteed.

I have been travelling the world's oceans, rivers and inland waterways for more than 50 years and in this guide I have concentrated on the established river cruise companies, almost all of whose cruises can be purchased through specialist cruise booking agents and tour operators. This book is separated into two sections, covering river cruising in Europe (Part One) and the USA (Part Two). It covers the des-

tination highlights in both of those very distinct geographical areas before reviewing and rating over 320 riverships. Our Berlitz ratings of the riverships and steamboats are based on amenities, cuisine, service and the overall river cruise experience.

Part One: River cruising in Europe is all about visiting destinations and is very different from cruising aboard large ocean-going cruise ships, where passengers can number in the thousands, and embarking, disembarking and security queues can be an exercise in frustration. The maximum number of passengers per rivership is around 200, so any visits are done in much smaller groups, or individually, and on a personal scale.

River cruising in Europe has grown dramatically in recent years. In 2005 there were just over 22,000 beds available; in 2017 there were more than 45,000 beds, reflecting the rise in demand. Riverships vary from the equivalent of a waterbus to what some think of as *eau couture*. The hassles of ordinary travel are eliminated in one pleasant package, with someone else doing all the cooking and driving. Don't worry about motion sickness, either – it's all smooth sail-

ing. Budgeting is easy, too. Because you pay in advance, you know what you will spend on your holiday, without any hidden surprises. It's all low-key – there are no casinos, bingo, knobbly knees contests or other potentially irritating parlour games (unlike on an ocean cruise), and any events that are organised tend to be geared towards culture. And, when your rivership docks, you simply walk off. You never have to take a tender to go ashore, because most riverships dock close to the centre of a destination.

The biggest difficulty is deciding which river cruise, and which brand, to choose. They do, of course, vary in terms of quality, food and service, which is where this authoritative guide comes in.

Part Two: River cruising in the USA – which is a new section for this edition – takes place on the Mississippi River and its associated tributaries, and in the Pacific Northwest on the Columbia and Snake rivers. This is all about discovering the 'Americana' of yesteryear aboard the flat-bottomed steamboats that thrived in the era of that celebrated riverlorian Mark Twain.

Happy river cruising!

Douglas Ward

Why take a river cruise?

Here, we describe European river cruising and answer some questions that first-timers often ask before taking the metaphoric plunge.

The biggest challenge when considering a river cruise is deciding which river interests you the most, but all river cruises are aimed to be welcoming, scenic, comfortable, effortless, small-scale, mostly inclusive, unhurried, organised and memorable. Above all, there is a river cruise to suit every pocket.

CHOOSING A RIVER

Rivers/regions and highlights (in alphabetical order)

Bordeaux region (Gironde, Garonne and Dordogne) – for wine and food
Danube – for Budapest, Vienna and the Iron Gate
Douro – for riverbank vineyards and port wine
Elbe – for Prague, Meissen and mountain scenery

Uniworld's *River Countess* in Venice.

Moselle – for quiet and relaxation
Rhine (Rhein) – for Cologne, Heidelberg, castles, the Black Forest and the Lorelei
Rhône/Saône – for Lyon and Provence
Seine – for Paris and Normandy

River cruising provides an antidote to the pressures of life in a fast-paced world, in comfortable, unfussy surroundings, with decent food and enjoyable (often international) company. Riverships provide a harmonious blend of public and private space, and, once aboard, you only have to unpack once.

10 REASONS TO TAKE A RIVER CRUISE

1. The sights

River cruising is all about the sights (you get a 360-degree panorama from the open top deck of a rivership) and sightseeing, from the key highlights en route to villages and the countryside. Riverships provide ever-changing scenery ('riverscape') at eye level and up close, and offer the anticipation of waking up in a different place each day, usually in the heart of a city or town. They give a new take on a destination from the one you would experience on a wholly land-based tour and a totally different, too, from the coastal approach of an ocean cruise.

2. Almost everything is included

Upfront pricing means almost no unexpected additional costs, so budgeting is simple. Accommodation, all meals (usually including wine), snacks, destination talks, some (or all) excursions, light entertainment and perhaps transfers to get to and from your river cruise are all included.

3. They are small, friendly and comfortable

With their size governed by the length and width of the locks they need to negotiate, most riverships carry between 100 and 200 passengers. The atmosphere is friendly and informal, and never stuffy or pretentious, and the dress code is completely casual.

4. It's so easy

Simply embark, unpack and enjoy the scenery, as your floating inn takes you from one historic destination to the next. It's a single-currency world on board. There are no tenders to take to go ashore, no formalities, and you will no doubt learn something new every day.

Pont du Gard excursion in France.

5. There's always something to see and do
There will be talks by guest speakers, and perhaps wine- or beer-tasting sessions or cooking demonstrations.

6. You'll have a room with a view
Almost all cabins (except on *Primadonna* and *Rossini*) have windows with river views, so you'll be able to admire the scenery. Many cabins have a balcony, although this is most likely to be a 'French' (open-air) balcony, with doors or electrically operated windows opening onto a safety railing due to the size restrictions. (Some riverships have full balconies that you can sit out on.)

7. You don't have to look like a tourist on tours
Wireless receivers and earphones are provided, so you can hear what is being said without having to crowd around the guide.

8. It will all be smooth cruising
Don't worry about motion sickness – the gentle waters of rivers are different from those of the ocean, with no waves. Itineraries can, however, be affected by low or high water: not enough water and the riverships can't cruise; too much and they can't get under the bridges (in such cases, comfortable coaches take you to and from the key attractions).

9. Most riverships are surprisingly chic
The newest riverships are very different from those that previously dominated the market. You can have a balcony, various dining options (eg venues in different areas and possibly on an outdoor deck), Wi-Fi (usually at no additional charge) and a flat-screen infotainment system.

10. You don't have to cook
It's all done for you, and so is the washing up. You don't have to make the bed either! Or drive!

ARE RIVERS CALLED HE OR SHE?

This depends on their behaviour. The Rhône, for example, is almost always called he because it can be turbulent, bothersome and rough at times, whereas the Saône is a gentler kind of river – more beautiful and tranquil – and is referred to as she, as is the 'beautiful' Blue Danube (although Napoleon described it as the 'king of the rivers of Europe').

The Rhine is a he, as it is always referred to as 'Father Rhine' (although the adjacent Mosel/Moselle is a she – 'Mother Moselle', although supposedly actually the daughter of 'Father Rhine'). The Mighty Mississippi is called the 'granddaddy of all rivers', while the Volga is always referred to as the 'dear little mother', even though it is the mightiest river in Europe.

Rivers may also be colourful. The Danube is immortalised in music as being famously blue – although the reality is something different – whereas the Mississippi is brown (the 'Big Muddy'), there's a green river in Utah, a red river in Louisiana, a yellow river in China, and a black river in Brazil.

Taking in the view ahead.

THE DISADVANTAGES OF A RIVER CRUISE

The flow of water in almost all rivers cannot always be controlled by man, so there will be times when the water level is so low that even a specially constructed rivership, with its shallow draft, cannot travel. Occasionally, the water level can become so low (a depth of only a few centimetres) that it is impossible for riverships to move at all.

Conversely, the water level can be so high (after much rain) that riverships cannot fit under bridges. Multi-rivership companies such as Viking River Cruises may be able to transfer you from one side of a blocked waterway to an identical rivership on the other side, thus providing minimum interruption to your cruise.

If you are tall, note that the beds on board most riverships are usually less than 1.8m (5.9ft) long.

There is generally no room service – except in a few examples when breakfast may be available to occupants of the largest suites – as there aren't enough crew members to cope with this.

If your cabin is towards the aft (rear), there may well be the constant humming of a generator, which supplies power for air conditioning, heating, lighting and cooking, etc.

Cabin insulation may be poor, so you might hear noisy neighbours clearly, whether you want to or not.

Mealtimes are strictly followed (all passengers typically eat at one sitting), so there's no choice of dining times, as there is in the ocean-going cruise industry.

In some popular destinations such as Bratislava, Budapest and Passau, several riverships are often tied alongside each other. Passengers on the outermost vessel(s) must cross the others in order to disembark and embark, which is challenging for anyone with poor ambulatory skills. Also, if your cabin is on the side that is tied up alongside another rivership, not only will you not have a view, but you will need to draw your curtains if you want privacy.

Non-smokers should note that on the open deck you may find that smokers are right next to you. The only way to avoid this is for one of you to move.

RIVER CRUISING VS OCEAN CRUISING

So how does river cruising compare with its more established cousin, ocean cruising?

River cruises provide the kind of up-close inland cruising impossible aboard large ocean-going cruise ships.

The ride aboard riverships is typically silky smooth – there's no rolling about as there is on many of the ocean-going cruise ships.

On riverships, land is almost always in sight; aboard ocean-going cruise ships you may be sailing on open stretches of water for days to reach a destination.

The scenery is at eye level on a rivership; on an ocean-going ship it isn't, and you may need to take a lift to go up and out to see it.

On a rivership, you simply step on land almost as soon as the vessel ties up. Aboard ocean-going cruise ships, you can be waiting for up to two hours or more to go ashore in some ports when the ship is at anchor and you will need to take a shore tender. There can be long queues when you return to an ocean-going cruise ship. For rivership

passengers it's easy – you simply step aboard.

Aboard a rivership, you dock right in the centre of a city, town or village. Ocean-going cruise ships often have to dock in cargo terminals and other inconvenient places in insalubrious locations some distance from a city or town centre.

Riverships are more intimate than their ocean-going counterparts. They seldom carry more than 200 passengers. Ocean-going cruise ships can carry over 6,000 passengers.

Almost all cabins on a rivership have outside views; there are virtually no interior (no-view) cabins, as are typical on most ocean-going cruise ships.

With ocean cruising, the ship is the destination. In river cruising, the places visited are the destination!

On ocean-going cruise ships, most excursions are additional-cost items. Aboard most riverships excursions are usually included, although this does depend on the operator, so always check at the outset.

River cruising uncovered

Marketing brochures make river cruises look wonderfully appealing but they can't tell you everything about the experience on board. We cut through the hype to tell you what they don't.

Whether you look at printed brochures or go online and look at the claims made by the river cruise companies, you'd think that all were the best in the world (most of them say they are 'award-winning'). Well, surprise, surprise – they all aren't.

When companies describe their riverships as 'small and attractive' or 'comfortable,' you can rest assured that these will be older vessels, because companies with newer ones always describe them as 'the most luxurious', 'the most spacious' or 'the most innovative'. Naturally, some companies try to hide the fact that they are lagging behind in the design stakes.

And when operators talk about having the highest staff to passenger ratio, it should be noted that some riverships have more technical staff than others, while some have more staff on the hospitality side, depending on the requirements.

Of the river cruise companies operating in Europe, AmaWaterways, Viking River Cruises and Uniworld Boutique River Cruises deliver a product that is the closest to the one claimed in the brochures. AmaWa-

terways hits the spot for their excellent food and service, while Scenic comes close. Uniworld delivers opulent decor, while Viking is good for Scandinavian minimalism and uniformity, and for its large fleet (their 'Longships' have identical layouts, making it easier when low water problems necessitate swapping vessels) and choice of rivers.

To help you distinguish between companies and be better informed, here are some of the most commonly asked questions by potential river cruisers, with answers to the queries that the brochures gloss over.

Are river cruises taken aboard ships or boats?

To set the record straight, river cruises are taken aboard riverships. Ships are ocean- or sea-going. Boats are typically owned for pleasure, with the exceptions of lifeboats, of course, and steamboats (or replica steamboats), in the US. There are also cruise barges, which navigate canals. For more on this, see the 'What's in a name?' box.

Primadonna in Passau.

Are there differences between river cruise operators?

Yes, in terms of both hardware and software, in how their river cruises are packaged and in the pre- and post-cruise add-ons. Thus, the quality for which the company is known is provided through the whole experience, and is not dependent on third-party operators, drivers and guides. A-ROSA Cruises, Emerald Waterways and U by Uniworld, for example, offer a greater number of active excursions, such as mountain biking for younger passengers, than most.

Are there different classes aboard riverships?

No, everyone is treated equally. The only difference is in the size of the accommodation you choose.

Are there different cabin categories and prices?

Yes, but not many (unlike ocean-going cruise ships). Accommodation is priced according to size and location. Some suites/cabins have open-air balconies or opening windows; cabins on the lowest deck have opening or non-opening windows or portholes. Cabin sizes can vary from a dimensionally challenged 6 sq m (64.5 sq ft) to an expansive 82 sq m (882.5 sq ft).

Are excursions available?

Excursions are often included in the overall cruise price, depending on the operator. Optional excursions will also be available, although at extra cost. Arrangements can also be made for you to play golf or tennis.

Are meals included?

Yes. Meals include a self-service buffet breakfast and lunch (with hot food), afternoon coffee/tea, full waiter-service dinner and, sometimes, late-night snacks. In some cases, the chef purchases produce in local markets for consumption during the cruise. Some operators include beer, soft drinks and wine.

How about dining arrangements?

Breakfast (typically 7am–9am) and lunch (usually noon–2pm) are usually buffet-style, with open seating (sit where you want) and perhaps waiter service for a 'daily special' or other hot food order. Dinner, however, is at one seating, at a specific time (typically at 7pm), either at assigned tables, where you may or may not know the person next to you, or in an open-seating arrangement, so you can sit with anyone you want.

Do riverships have room service?

It's not standard, as there simply aren't enough crew members to be able to provide it. A handful of river-

WHAT'S IN A NAME?

There is considerable confusion among passengers, river cruise companies, cruise/tour packagers and travel journalists regarding the correct name for the different types of vessel, so here is a breakdown, from the largest to the smallest.
Ship
Ocean-going cruise ships can carry boats (lifeboats, search-and-rescue boats and shore tenders). Thus, a ship can carry a boat, but a boat can't carry a ship. Cruise ships sail on oceans and seas, generally have a deep hull and can carry between 50 and over 5,000 passengers.
Rivership
A rivership has a flat bottom and is designed for extremely shallow water. Riverships typically travel at speeds of between 10 and 18kph (6–11mph). On board, there is a captain (the driver) and crew, accommodation, all meals and some light entertainment. Riverships have two, three or four accommodation decks, and public rooms include at least a panoramic lounge/bar and a restaurant.
Cruise barge
A cruise barge (also referred to as a hotel barge) is a flat-bottomed craft that draws a shallow draft. They are typically about 30m (100ft) long and about 5m (16.5ft) wide.

Although a handful of them are custom built, most are converted cargo-carrying craft. Cruise barges travel slowly (between 3 and 10kph/1.8–6mph), slower than riverships. They normally have just one deck (a few have two decks), which houses cabins and a combination dining room/lounge, and they carry up to 12 passengers. Most cruise barges carry bicycles for you to use along the canal towpaths or for exploring the local towns and villages.
Boats
Boats are typically privately owned or rented for pleasure, with the exception of lifeboats or shore tenders carried by ocean-going cruise ships.
Steamboat
This term designates riverships powered by steam engines (and replica steamboats powered by diesel engines) that drive huge stern-mounted paddlewheels. They ply the rivers of the US, such as the Mississippi.
Narrowboat
These vessels are so named because the canals, waterways and locks they navigate are extremely narrow. They are usually only 2m (6.5ft) wide. Although there are exceptions, they are usually for use as charter or self-drive craft.

ships do offer this to occupants of suites for breakfast, however. You may also be offered it if you can't leave your cabin due to illness, for example.

Can I bring my own drinks on board?
Most river cruise companies allow you to bring your own drinks on board, but only for in-cabin consumption.

Are there any theme cruises?
Several theme cruises come to mind. You can experience theme cruises for classical and jazz music, fine food and wine tasting, shopping, Christmas markets and Christmas/New Year celebrations.

Music lovers might enjoy Danube cruises, while the green-fingered among you might enjoy the gardens of the Rhine, with visits to celebrated botanical gardens, arboretums, herbariums and castles and their grounds.

Are river cruise brochure ratings accurate?
No. Brochures are designed by marketing departments to attract you to take a cruise. According to cruise brochures, every rivership is the 'best in Europe'. Use the brochures to determine which itinerary and cruise attracts you most but take the ratings with a pinch of salt. I go beyond the brochure to bring you accurate, objective and totally independent Berlitz ratings.

Is the crew-to-passenger ratio important?
Not really (unlike ocean-going ships), because some riverships need more technical crew than hotel crew, depending on the configuration, technical requirements and other factors.

What about safety?
There are numerous regulations in Europe. Riverships built after January 2007 must have two compartments, and, in addition to the main propulsion system, a second, independent propulsion system (in a separate engine room).

Since 2010, riverships longer than 110m (360ft) must have a declaration of sufficient strength by one of three recognised classification societies: Bureau Veritas of France; Germanischer Lloyd; or Lloyd's Register of Shipping (London). Also, the rivership must remain in a floating condition, even if two watertight compartments are damaged and flooded. Most riverships have two or three fire zones, and some basic safety and life-saving equipment, but many older (pre-2000) riverships lack sprinkler systems.

Do riverships have to comply with any environmental regulations or restrictions?
Environmental regulation is the concern of authorities that control various rivers, or sections of rivers, under the auspices of the United Nations. In Europe, for example, the Central Commission for

A *Queen Isabel* junior suite (Uniworld).

the Navigation of the Rhine has strict emissions controls in force on the river (many are covered in EU directives).

Who takes a river cruise?
River cruises tend to appeal to the culturally aware and to those wanting to experience the heart of a country and its people, instead of simply travelling through it. They appeal, too, to anyone who prefers travelling in a small group environment.

Isn't it all very regimented?
As on any other packaged itinerary-based holiday, there are schedules. You don't have to go on an included tour if you'd prefer instead to have a relaxing day on board. And you can go sightseeing independently rather than in an organised group – just make sure that you're back on your rivership in time for sailing to the next destination.

How inclusive is all-inclusive?
Although river cruise companies state that their river cruises are 'all-inclusive', they are actually 'selectively inclusive', based on a packaging price, ie that their selected items (particularly when it comes to wine and other alcoholic drinks) are included, but there may well be exclusions to this. Depending on the country in which the rivership is marketed, there may be differences as to what is or is not included, so check carefully before you book.

Lower-priced 'all-inclusive' companies usually provide basic brand spirits for drinks and low-cost wines for lunch and dinner (not to mention miniscule wine glasses). Higher-priced 'all-inclusive' companies usually provide better-quality brand spirits for drinks and higher-cost wines for lunch and dinner.

What about the facilities?

Companies constantly try to outdo each other in terms of facilities and gimmicks to attract ever-more savvy travellers to the advantages of their products. Examples of this include small swimming pools with covers that can be added to convert the pool room into a cinema, 270-degree wrap-around windows on luxury suites or free iPads during the cruise.

Is it difficult to find one's way around a rivership?

No – two minutes should do it. Most riverships have only two or three accommodation decks plus a sun deck, so it's easy.

What's the dress code?

Strictly casual – river cruising is all about comfort, although you are more than welcome to dress more smartly for dinner if you want to.

Can I access the internet?

Yes. Aboard the newest riverships Wi-Fi will be available, subject to interrupted reception due to locks and bridges. Connections can be dropped as your rivership crosses borders between countries, when different telecom systems take over the transmissions. Some companies provide iPads or other tablets for passenger use.

Enjoying the sun and scenery.

Is canned music played on board?

Unfortunately, many riverships have music in the lounge, hallways and even the outside areas, because owners and operators seem to think it creates ambience (there are exceptions, however, such as the Swiss firm Excellence). What annoys many passengers, too, is being tied up alongside another rivership, which has music playing.

Is river cruising for solo travellers?

River cruising is really designed for couples. Solo travellers are an expensive afterthought, and only a few riverships have solo-occupancy cabins (examples include *Ariana, Camargue, Emerald Sky, Heidelberg, Inspire*). Although solos can occupy a double cabin, the fare will usually be higher. However, when river cruises are not sold out, opportunities can arise for solo travellers. The best advice is to keep checking.

Are river cruises for honeymooners?

Why not? Most arrangements will have been taken care of before your cruise, so all you have to do is show up. Some riverships have double-, queen- or king-sized beds, although you'll find that, in general, the cabins (and particularly the bathrooms) are compact, and the beds are short!

Are river cruises suitable for children?

Although a river cruise is educational, in general, river cruises in Europe are taken by the over 50s. A handful of riverships have family cabins (suitable for small families with small children). AmaWaterways and Disney started a partnership in 2017, and it is expected that more children and teens will start to enjoy river cruising. U by Uniworld has ships with black hulls, silent discos and a party atmosphere for ages 21 to 45.

Are river cruises suitable for mobility-challenged travellers?

Not really, although some riverships have lifts (elevators), typically between the main deck and the restaurant deck and/or stairlifts from the main to the upper (outside) deck. Only *AmaMagna* has a lift between all decks, and a few riverships have wheelchair-accessible cabins.

Many landing stages are linked to steps leading up to a city or town. In some locations, riverships berth side by side (this may also obscure the view from your cabin), and you may have to cross several to get to land.

It's on land where most problems arise, because many historic European cities have cobblestone streets, steps with no ramps and few facilities for the mobility-challenged.

Are there laundry facilities?

Not usually, although there are exceptions (such as The A and The B riverships of U by Uniworld). If your river cruise is part of a longer holiday, take some washing powder or liquid to clean small, personal clothing items in your cabin. Note that most suite/cabin bathrooms are dimensionally challenged and have little space to hang anything, although some have a retractable washing line in the bathroom. Only one or two riverships currently have ironing facilities.

Are there medical facilities on board?

Although riverships carry defibrillators and first-aid kits, they do not have a doctor or nurse on board (unlike ocean cruise ships). However, you are always close to land, so any emergency medical arrangements can be made relatively quickly.

How pregnant can I be when I take a river cruise?

River cruise companies don't allow mothers-to-be aboard past their 28th week of pregnancy. Pregnant women may need to produce a doctor's certificate, saying that they are fit to travel. Fortunately, you'll never be far from shore, so medical help can be summoned quickly. If you are taking any river cruise, make sure you have adequate medical insurance.

Is smoking allowed?

Most riverships are totally no-smoking inside but allow smoking on the open deck.

Won't I get bored?

No chance. There is always something to see on the river.

Do river cruise companies have frequent passenger (loyalty) clubs?

Some river cruise operators have a frequent cruisers club, where you collect points for discounts, upgrades or other benefits. Examples include: Avalon

A suite breakfast aboard Scenic's *Scenic Jasper*.

Waterways (Journeys Club), Excellence River Cruises (Excellence Travel Club), Scenic (Scenic Club), Transocean Tours (Columbus Club), Uniworld (River Heritage Club), Vantage River Cruises (Platinum Circle) and Viking River Cruises (Viking Explorer Society).

Are tips included?

Gratuities may or may not be included, depending on the company, so do read the fine print.

Where are riverships registered?

Most riverships are registered in France, Germany, Malta, The Netherlands, or Switzerland. A few (those owned/operated by non-EU companies) are registered in Bulgaria or Romania or the Ukraine.

What happens when riverships age?

Some rivership owners modernise or convert their vessels during the long winter months (and possibly rename them). One example of this is Tauck's *Esprit*, introduced in 2015; it is actually the modernised 2010-built *VistaPrima*. CroisiEurope is another example – its *Camargue* was nicely reconstructed from the same vessel, with the same name, but originally built in 1995. *River Ambassador* and *River Baroness* were converted to become the A and the B for U by Uniworld. I expect more modernisations will be made due to the lack of building space and the increasing cost of new riverships.

Some riverships are sold for use as 'floatels' (permanently moored and converted into floating hotels), because they no longer comply with the latest regulations, the engines are damaged or for other reasons (dissolved partnerships, for example).

Cruising past Boppard on the Rhine.

Booking and budgeting

Should you book directly with the river cruise company or through a specialist booking agent? Are there any hidden extras to look for when calculating costs? And what about insurance?

Booking direct

Whether booking direct or via a cruise booking agent, check thoroughly just what is included in any offers, particularly when enticing discounts catch your eye. Make sure, for example, that all port charges, government fees and any additional fuel surcharges are included in the quote.

The internet

The internet may be a useful resource tool, but it is not the best place to book your cruise, unless you know exactly what you want. You can't ask questions in the same way that you can with a cruise-booking agent sitting right with you, and information provided by some river cruise companies is pure marketing hype. Most sites providing cruise ship reviews have something to sell, and the information can also be misleading or outdated.

Many internet booking agencies are unlicensed and unregulated, so if you do book a cruise with one, confirm with the actual river cruise company that the booking has been made and that final payment has been received.

The internet vs travel agents

Perhaps you've found a discounted rate for your cruise online. Fine, but if a river cruise company suddenly offers special discounts for your cruising, or things go wrong with your booking, your internet booking service may prove very unfriendly. A physical cruise-booking agent, however, can probably work magic in making any discounts work for you. It's called personal service.

Most river cruise companies consider travel agents to be their distribution system (exceptions include Grand Circle Cruise Line and Saga Cruises, who only sell direct). Cruise booking agents do not charge for their services, although they earn a commission from the river cruise companies. Consider them to be your business advisor, not just a ticket agent. They handle all matters relevant to your booking and will have the latest information on any changes of itinerary and any other useful items.

When you have chosen an itinerary and river cruise company, look for an affiliated agency member of the Cruise Lines International Association (CLIA). This association has a full financial bonding scheme to protect passengers from failed river cruise companies.

Reservations

Riverships on Europe's waterways are small compared with ocean-going ships, carrying fewer than 200 passengers, and the most popular river cruises are often sold out a year ahead. With that in mind, book as far ahead as possible, and make any special dietary requests known, keeping any correspondence relating to the request.

After choosing a cruise, date and cabin type, you pay a deposit, typically followed by full payment within seven days (sometimes longer, depending on the river cruise company's conditions). You'll then receive a confirmation invoice. For a late reservation, you pay in full when space is confirmed (when booking via the internet, for example). River cruise companies reserve the right to change prices in the event of costs 'beyond their control'.

After the river cruise company receives full payment, your documents will be sent by post (examples include AmaWaterways, Emerald Waterways, Scenic, Uniworld), or possibly as an e-document (for example Crystal River Cruises). Check to make sure that everything is correct (date, itinerary, etc).

Embarkation documents for a Viking cruise.

Extra costs

Brochures boldly state that 'everything is included', but in most cases it's not actually true. In fact, for some less expensive cruises (usually with older vessels) 'all-exclusive' is a more appropriate term. Your fare usually covers the rivership as transportation, your cabin, all meals and snacks, and service on board, and, possibly, excursions and tips. Note that even if alcoholic drinks are included, there may be an extra cost for 'premium' brands.

Port taxes/handling charges

These are (usually) included in the cost your cruise.

Fly/cruise packages

If your river cruise price includes air transport, note that flights usually cannot be changed without paying a premium, because river cruise companies often book group space on aircraft to obtain the lowest rates.

If you arrange your own air/train/coach transport, the river cruise company is under no obligation to help you if you don't reach the ship on time. If you are flying overseas, allow extra time (particularly in winter) for possible flight delays or cancellations.

In Europe, fly/cruise packages generally start at a major metropolitan airport; some may include first-class rail travel from outlying districts. In the US, some river cruise companies include connecting flights from suburban airports convenient to the traveller.

Cancellations and refunds

Do take out full cancellation insurance. Otherwise, if you cancel at the last minute – even for medical

Approaching the Iron Gates Gorge.

reasons – you could lose the whole fare. Insurance coverage can be obtained from your booking agent or from an independent company (it may even be included), and paying by credit card makes sense (there's more chance of getting your money back, even if the travel provider goes bust).

River cruise companies usually accept cancellations more than 30 days before sailing, but all charge full fare if you don't turn up on sailing day.

Travel and medical insurance

River cruise companies and booking agents routinely sell travel cover policies that, on close inspection, appear to wriggle out of payment due to a litany of exclusion clauses, most of which are never explained. Examples include 'pre-existing' medical conditions – ignoring this little gem could cost you dearly – and 'valuables' left unattended on a tour bus, even though the tour guide says it is safe and that the driver will lock the door. To get the best travel insurance deal, shop around and don't accept the first policy you are offered. Read the contract carefully and make sure you know exactly what you are covered for. Ask for a detailed explanation of all exclusions, excesses and limitations. There may be exclusions for 'hazardous sports'. These could include things offered as part of an excursion, including horse riding or cycling.

Before you go, make sure you know what to do if you are the victim of a crime, for example if your wallet or camera is stolen while on an excursion. If anything does unfortunately happen, obtain a police report as soon as possible. Note that many insurance policies will reimburse you only for the second-hand value of any lost or stolen item, rather than the full cost of replacement, and you may be required to produce the original receipt for any items claimed.

If you purchase travel cover over the internet, check the credentials of the company underwriting the scheme. It is best to deal with well-established names and not necessarily to take what appears to be the cheapest deal offered.

QUESTIONS TO ASK A CRUISE BOOKING AGENT

What is included in the cruise price quoted?
If I need to make changes to my flight, routing, dates, and so on, will there be an extra charge?
Have you sailed on the rivership that I want to book or that you are purely recommending it?
What is the river cruise company's cancellation policy?
Does your agency deal with only one, or several different insurance companies?
Is your agency bonded and insured? If so, by whom?
Will I need a visa?

On the deck of the *Scenic Azure*, Douro Valley.

Design and layout

An overview of the different types of riverships
and what to expect to find inside followed
by a comparison of two different brands.

River cruise companies try to attract customers by adding bells and whistles to their newest riverships and constantly challenging designers to create new ways of providing practical and attractive cabins and suites, restaurants and lounge/bars.

Overview

Riverships are long and low in the water, with fold-down masts in order to negotiate low bridges. The navigation bridge can also be raised and lowered hydraulically, and all side railings can be folded down so that the uppermost (open) deck is completely clear of all obstructions.

Public areas common to all riverships include a restaurant, an observation lounge with a bar (the social hub of any rivership), which on newer vessels incorporates a bistro-style casual eatery at the front, and an outdoor 'Sun Deck' with chairs (some under shaded canopies). Some may also have a (tiny) shop and beauty room, a fitness room and a small sauna. Most have an excellent amount of outdoor deck space

A river-facing bed cabin on *Avalon Expression*.

for viewing the scenery and hosting food-and-drink-themed events such as a once-per-cruise, mid-morning 'Frühschoppen' (Bavarian-style brunch).

There is only so much that designers can cram into the hull of a rivership, but there has been a burst of creativity in recent years, particularly among industry drivers AmaWaterways, Crystal River Cruises, Emerald Waterways, Scenic and Viking River Cruises, compelled by the increased demand for premium (better than basic, or 'standard') facilities. The latest 135m (443ft) riverships (the maximum possible for the locks on the Rhine–Main–Danube system) for Emerald Waterways and Uniworld Boutique River Cruises, for example, also have a dual-purpose area aft containing a small heated indoor pool with a retractable glass roof; this converts the area into a mini-cinema by night. While Emerald places a pool/cinema aft and Uniworld has a small pool and bar aft, AmaWaterways has created a separate restaurant with a full galley, and Viking River Cruises places its two largest suites, each with a wraparound balcony, two chairs and drinks table, there.

Design

Depending on the river on which they operate, European riverships have two, two-and-a-half, or three accommodation decks. This is due to the restrictions placed on a vessel's dimensions by the locks and bridges on the various rivers.

There are two main types of rivership: mono-hull, and twin-cruiser. Riverships are traditionally built on a mono-hull, with or without a slightly modified split-front with bullnose (or 'Cadillac') front.

As a result of their long, low-slung design, riverships have a limited amount of space for public areas. There are just two principal public rooms: a restaurant and an observation lounge (main lounge). There are, however, variations and differences between riverships, such as the location and position of the bar (or food display counter) within the lounge, the addition of a small dance floor or a real or electric baby grand piano, and the degree of comfort provided. Many older riverships have tub chairs (with little or no back support), but newer vessels have more supportive seating.

Every centimetre of space aboard a rivership is utilised to the full, and innovative design thinking, such as that of Viking River Cruises for its Viking 'Longships', has created an increase in user-friendliness and comfort. The newest riverships are also 25m (82ft) longer than the older ones.

The two-deck high atrium aboard *Viking Delling*.

Unusual riverships

AmaMagna, a brand new, state-of-the-art, double-width, mono-hull rivership will enter service in 2019. *Primadonna* (1998) has two hulls, while *Crystal Mozart* (1997) has a double-width monohull with two sets of bows – giving the impression of having twin hulls. While the increased width provides more space, the monohull design needs to flex more to accommodate the strong currents encountered in some parts of the Danube. *AmaMagna, Crystal Mozart* and *Primadonna* are limited to that river, because the locks on the Rhine cannot accommodate double-wide vessels.

Twin-cruisers

The twin-cruiser was innovative when first launched in 2005 in the shape of the *Flamenco*. There are only eight of these in service. A twin-cruiser consists of two sections: a long accommodation block, including a restaurant, galley and lounge, built as a separate unit that is bolted onto a smaller aft section that houses the engines, engineering, propulsion and steering equipment plus a hydraulically operated navigation bridge that can be adjusted according to the height of any bridges encountered.

The rear power 'barge' pushes the front accommodation section. The captain has a forward view over the whole of the vessel, as aboard cargo ships. While this is neat in theory (the lack of power in the accommodation section at the front means that this part of the rivership is quieter), in practice it doesn't work well, because navigating around bends and docking are both especially challenging.

Atrium

Some riverships have a two-deck-high atrium-style lobby with abundant natural light (examples include the Viking 'Longships'), so they feel open and welcoming, as opposed to those of Uniworld, for example, whose two-deck high lobbies are cluttered with chandeliers and intrusive furnishings. Others have a single-deck height lobby that makes them feel more closed-in and clammy.

Uniworld's atriums are opulent but perhaps overwhelming for some. Scenic's and Emerald's are ultra-modern and open, as are those on Viking's 'Longships,' while Avalon's are plain, but open.

Observation lounge/bar

When observation lounges are positioned at the front of the vessel, they typically have large chairs, sofas and low coffee tables, and several pillars that obstruct sightlines (exceptions include *River Chanson* and *Royal Crown*), the result of outdated shipbuilding techniques. Although the pillars prevent the flexing that can occur in the longest riverships, designers and builders should re-think in terms of passenger comfort.

These lounges have large panoramic windows, which is important for sightseeing at the beginning and end of the cruise season in Europe, when it will

Life-sized chess board and bicycles aboard *AmaCerto*.

be too chilly to stay on the open deck for long. Within the lounge there is a bar, which is best placed at the back of the room to leave more space for prime river viewing in the front section. If the bar is towards the front of the lounge, as on the *Cezanne, Der Kleine Prinz, Emerald Sky* and *Excellence Royale*, for example, the bartender has good views, while anyone sitting on a bar stool faces inwards. The same is true of the Scenic vessels, where the front section has a bar, limiting the number of forward-facing (observation) seats.

Restaurants

Most riverships have one main restaurant, with large (often floor-to-ceiling) river-view windows, plus, sometimes an area outside for casual, alfresco eating. The principal difference in the present design of rivership restaurants lies in the layout of the buffet display counter. Note that tables located adjacent to the doors or open entrance to the galley can be noisy. Some newer riverships also have a second interior dining venue with its own galley. AmaWaterways, for example, has an aft restaurant whose galley is within a self-contained fire zone.

Other facilities

Some riverships may also have a small plunge pool (which, in practice, is hardly ever used), a diminutive sauna, massage room and a cabin-size fitness room, although there's hardly ever time to use these facilities on destination-intensive itineraries.

Some riverships, notably those of Emerald Waterways, have dual-purpose (heated) indoor pools that convert into comfortable mini-cinemas at night, plus a small bar. Uniworld's *SS Antoinette, SS Catherine, SS Josephine, SS Joie de Vivre* and *SS Maria Theresa* each have a small (heated) indoor pool aft, with an adjacent bar.

A number of riverships have squared-off fronts, which allows designers to accommodate a dining terrace. These usually have fully opening glass doors that allow a total alfresco option – the Viking 'Longships' incorporate this feature. And, for the well-heeled, one rivership – Uniworld's *Queen Isabel* – even has a small helicopter landing pad on the sun deck.

The top deck ('sun deck')

The most important area for viewing is the open top deck (sun deck). This runs almost the full length of the rivership. In, or close to, the front is the navigation bridge (except for the eight twin-cruisers), constructed so that it can be hydraulically lowered into the deck below to avoid low bridges. Canopies and railings are designed to be folded down, while chairs and sun loungers simply remain on deck.

The top deck may have real teak or hardwood decking, or rubberized covering, or faux turf (with or without decking stripes), but when it gets wet it is very soggy underfoot – and not nice to walk on.

Exterior stairways could be made from steel with a wood (polished or unpolished) step surface, or from perforated stainless steel (these are problematic for anyone in high-heeled shoes).

The top deck is also a social place for meeting your fellow travellers and enjoying drinks, barbecues and light bites. In terms of the quality of the seating and canopies on deck, there are differences between vessels.

Most riverships have a life-size chess game or small sunken plunge pool, or an area for mini golf. Viking River Cruises vessels each has a herb 'garden' on the top deck. The chef uses the fresh herbs, and also tends the garden.

White plastic patio-style deck chairs are typical of budget-priced river cruise operators. The more upmarket operators, such as AmaWaterways, Scylla and Viking River Cruises, provide better-quality – and more stable and comfortable – stainless steel or aluminium chairs.

RIVERSHIP DIFFERENCES

There are differences between the principal river cruise companies and their riverships. River cruise operators continue trying to outdo each other – all to the benefit of savvy passengers. While most travellers look at price, there are other things that the internet and river cruise brochures *don't* highlight, which can make a difference to your experience. For example, most river cruise operators provide personal headsets for shore excursions, but Scenic goes the extra mile by providing a hand-held or lanyard-mounted GPS smartphone-style unit, which is excellent for independent sightseeing.

If you wonder why some river cruises are more – or less – expensive than others, it's all in the details,

such as what is or isn't included, as well as the cost and quality of the food, and staff training. For example, on embarkation day, a formal dinner may not be served – from all the hype in the brochure, you may well be expecting a good meal when you first arrive, only to find instead a self-serve buffet, following a welcome aboard talk given by the Cruise Manager (Cruise Director).

All river cruise companies offer the same basic things, namely the rivership with a lounge, a restaurant, cabins and open top deck, and perhaps some excursions. The differences between them come in the finer details. Here are some examples:

Some companies have hallways with half-height wood panelling and artwork (Avalon, Excellence); some have plain walled hallways, usually with a little pieces of artwork (Emerald).

Most companies provide regular table salt (A-Rosa, CroisiEurope, Emerald, Feenstra, Grand Circle); the more premium operators provide sea salt or rock salt (AmaWaterways, Avalon, Scenic).

Some companies have cabins with a mini fridge, but many do not.

Some provide real wooden hangers (AmaWaterways, Avalon, Excellence, Luftner Cruises, Scenic, Uniworld, Viking), while others provide plastic hangers (CroisiEurope).

Only some provide bottled water.

Some provide a shaving/vanity mirror (AmaWaterways, Avalon, Scenic, Viking, for example); some don't (Emerald, for example)

A number provide just one electrical outlet in the cabin, but it's taken by the telephone (if there is one) or the charger for the personal receiver used for excursions.

A trio of Viking 'Longships'.

S.S. Catherine.

Viking Embla.

River Venture.

River Royale.

OLD AND NEW

River cruise operators think of their passengers mostly as 'one-time-only' guests, but in fact the number of repeat passengers is growing. So, there's now more interest in comparing river companies and riverships. There are substantial differences between vessels built before 2010 and the latest riverships.

Older riverships (pre-2010) typically have
Observation lounge with low ceiling, multiple pillars and uncomfortable tub chairs
Narrow hallways
Cramped cabins with little storage space
Ceilings made of metal 'planks'
Poor soundproofing
High noise level due to older type diesel engines and generators
No balconies
No Wi-Fi
No refrigerator
Poor (or no) bedside reading light
Small bathrooms
Tiny shower enclosures (most with shower curtains and fixed head showers)
One restaurant, with low ceiling and cramped seating
Very limited self-serve buffets for breakfast and lunch

Newer riverships (post-2010) typically have
Larger observation lounges with built-in facilities for light eating options
Wider hallways
Larger cabins and suites (with espresso machines)
Balcony-inclusive: full or French (i.e. that you can't actually walk out onto) or both
Creative, practical cabin design
Quiet-close drawers, closet doors and toilet seats
Good storage space
Mini-fridge
Wi-Fi
Dining options (main restaurant, plus a grill or another alternative)
Self-service espresso/cappuccino machines
Larger bathrooms
Larger shower enclosures (most with glass doors and flexible shower hoses)
One-piece cabin ceilings
Good soundproofing

Some provide a USB socket for charging digital devices; most don't.

Some have soft-close closet doors (Scenic, for example), cabinets and toilet seats, but most don't.

Some provide a washbasin in the bathroom that seems big enough only to wash your nose – but little else – and water may splash everywhere; some provide large washbasins.

The shower head may be fixed to the wall, but at navel height.

Most provide real soap, but others provide wall-mounted soap/shampoo dispenser (A-Rosa, for example).

Towels may be of different sizes and quality.

Toilets may be higher or lower, depending on the company, and outfitter. For example, the toilet aboard Emerald vessels is just 40.5 cm (16ins) above the floor, while aboard AmaWaterways vessels it is 53.5 cm (21ins) above the floor.

Some provide a retractable clothes line (Ama-Waterways, Scenic, Viking, for example). Some don't (Avalon).

Only some provide a vanity set, including cotton buds and make-up remover pads, nail file, etc.

Some have cabin ceilings made in one piece (AmaWaterways, Avalon, Scenic, Viking); others have (less desirable) 'planks' of metal and they are either unperforated or perforated (Emerald).

Some cruise brands carry a small number of bicycles either for individual passenger use or for guided excursions. For example, Avalon Waterways has folding bikes; Emerald Waterways has regular bikes; Scenic has e-bikes (power-assisted ones).

In-depth comparison

Using two brands – Scenic Waterways and Emerald Waterways – as an example, the below is a more in-depth look at how price differences manifest themselves. While both brands are owned by the same company, Scenic is more expensive, but more luxurious and more inclusive, while Emerald, the company's second brand is just that – second (but still good). Here are some of the differences between them:

Scenic Waterways: Each rivership has an outdoor dip pool on the open sun deck. The cabins *do* have a main light switch by the bed. The bathrooms are marble-clad, tiled and more lavish, with inward-opening doors, larger washbasins and towels, magnifying shaving mirrors and retractable clothes lines. Many cabins have bathtubs and a separate shower enclosure.

Drinks are included at any time (with a small extra-cost for premium drinks). There are more food choices and a higher food budget, plus a degustation 'Table La Rive'. There's also extra evening eatery Portofino (L'Amour on the French rivers).

The portable GPS receivers for (Taylor-Made) tours and self-guided excursions are excellent, and

Scenic has more included shore excursions than Emerald. Aboard the newer vessels (for example Scenic Amber, Scenic Jasper and Scenic Opal), Royal and Panorama suites have adjustable heated bathroom floors, and three-way push-button adjustable electric beds. Electric bicycles are available, and gratuities are included.

Emerald Waterways: Each rivership has an aft heated indoor pool that converts to a small cinema by night, and a retractable glass roof. There's no main light switch by the bed (they can only be turned off at the cabin entrance). The modular bathrooms are plain and have sliding doors (they are close to the bed) and a tiny washbasin. There are no bathtubs (even in the largest suites) or magnifying shaving mirrors, or retractable clothes lines.

Beer, wine and soft drinks are provided during meals; drinks consumed between meals cost extra (drinks packages are available). There are fewer food choices in the restaurant, and no extra evening alternative eateries with a different menu.

The personal 'Quiet Vox' receivers for excursions are small but heavy. Some excursions cost extra, and gratuities are not included, but (manual) bicycles are available.

The indoor-outdoor pool aboard *Emerald Star* at night.

Life aboard

From what to take with you to how to stay safe once on board, this A–Z gives the lowdown on all the practical basics that you need to be aware of during your cruise.

Air conditioning
The temperature is regulated by a thermostat inside your cabin, so you can adjust it to your liking; note, however, that you may not be able to turn the air conditioning off completely. At the beginning and end of the season – on Christmas market cruises, for example – heating, rather than air conditioning, is provided.

Bed linen
High-quality European duvets are usually provided. Anti-allergenic pillows may also be available. Suite occupants may have a choice of several different pillows.

Bicycles and walking accessories
On some riverships (examples include AmaWaterways, Emerald Waterways and Scenic), bicycles (either regular or electric ones) are provided for passenger use. Nordic walking sticks may also be available.

Captain
Most riverships have an open bridge (wheelhouse) policy, so you can visit at almost any time except during poor weather or in hazardous manoeuvring conditions.

Clothing
If you think you might not wear it, don't take it, as wardrobe space is really limited. In the summer, when the weather is warm to hot, pack clothes made of lightweight cottons and other natural fibres. Take a lightweight cotton jumper or windbreaker for the outdoor deck, plus sunglasses and a

Taking in the view of Durnstein, Austria.

hat. For river cruises in winter (those for Christmas markets, for example) take well-insulated clothing, including earmuffs and thick gloves, because it can be very cold, especially on deck when your rivership is moving.

The dress code is casual, but in the evening what you wear should be tasteful. Men might include a blazer or sports jacket. Comfortable low- or flat-heeled shoes are essential for women. Rubber soles are best for walking on deck.

Comment cards

At the end of the cruise you'll receive a comment card. Be truthful when completing it, as this feedback helps cruise providers to improve on their product. If there have been problems with other aspects of your cruise, say so.

Communications

Most riverships have direct-dial satellite telephones, so you can call anywhere in the world while on your cruise. Wi-Fi may be available in your cabin or selected areas such as the lobby or lounge, although reception can be patchy when going through locks or under bridges. Some companies provide iPads/tablets.

Daily programme

The daily programme is a list of any activities and social events plus destination arrival and departure times. It is normally delivered to your cabin the evening before the day that it covers. For a sample breakdown of a day on a river cruise, see page 38.

Departure time

At each destination, the vessel's sailing time will be posted at the gangway.

Disembarkation

This is straightforward. The night before disembarkation, place your luggage outside your cabin. It will be collected and off-loaded on arrival. Remember to leave out the clothes you intend to wear on disembarkation day and retrieve any items you have placed in the personal safe.

Drinks

Some companies provide free bottled water, which is replenished daily. For information on drinks provided with meals and what's covered in 'all-inclusive' packages, see page 36.

Electricity

The cabin voltage is usually 220 volts, but bathrooms may have both 110- and 240-volt (60 cycles) outlets for shavers only. Hairdryers are normally supplied in your cabin, but, if not, they will be available on request at the reception desk. Most European river-ships have a deeply recessed two-pin socket, so you may need an adaptor.

Emergencies

A few words about safety will be given by the captain or senior officer on embarkation day. Safety instructions – ie what to do in an emergency – are provided on the back of your cabin door, in the in-cabin info-tainment system, or in a documentation folder. Riverships also carry lifejackets.

Most door locks on today's riverships are operated by slide-in electronic key card or digital touch card. Aboard older riverships, an actual key may be required on the inside in order to unlock the door. It's best to leave the key in the lock, so that in the event of an emergency, you don't have to hunt for it.

Fires: Always make sure that you know the way from your cabin to the nearest emergency exit (typically aft and in the centre of the vessel), which will be identifiable by a green sign. Riverships have 'low location' lighting systems, of either the electro-luminescent or the photo-luminescent types, which will lead you to the exits.

In the unlikely event that a fire does break out, remain calm and think logically and clearly. If the fire is in your cabin, report it immediately, then leave your cabin and close the door behind you to prevent any smoke or flames from entering the passageway. If you are in your cabin and the fire is in the passageway, feel the cabin door. If the door handle is hot, use a wet towel to turn it. If there is smoke in the passageway, crawl to the nearest exit. Always assess the situation and act as you deem most appropriate for your safety.

Fitness facilities

A number of riverships now have small fitness rooms, typically with a couple of rowing machines, exercise bikes and a few weights, and possibly, although not always, a small infra-red sauna and a hot tub.

Identification cards/passports

When you embark, you hand in your passport (it is used for passport control, as you travel between various countries) and are given instead a personal boarding pass for identification purposes. This may include your photograph and other pertinent information and must be shown at the gangway each time you board. Your passport will be given back to you at the end of the cruise.

Laundry

Riverships do not generally have laundry facilities. You can always wash small items in your own bathroom, but be aware that there will be very little space to hang anything up to dry. Some riverships might offer a minimal laundry service, although this might be limited to passengers in suites (sometimes those in the Owner's Suite only).

Only a small number of riverships have ironing facilities.

Library
Any so-called 'library' will just be a few bookshelves, usually in the lobby. You'll find a few general-interest books, some destination reference material, and periodicals, as well as board games such as Scrabble, backgammon and chess.

Luggage
While there is generally no limit to the amount of personal luggage you can take on board, storage space is very limited. Towels, soap, shampoo and shower caps are provided, so you won't have to bring your own.

Medication
Although riverships carry first-aid kits, they do not generally have a doctor or nurse employed on board (unlike on an ocean cruise ship). However, riverships are always close to land, so any emergency medical arrangements can be made quickly, if necessary.

Take any medical supplies you need, plus spare spectacles or contact lenses and solution. In some countries it may be difficult to find certain medicines; others may be sold under different names. Ask your doctor for names of alternatives, in case the medicine you are taking is not available. Always take a supply of any medication in your carry-on luggage where flights are involved (eg if you are flying to the start point of your cruise), just in case your hold luggage goes astray. If you are diabetic, ask before you book whether your chosen rivership has an in-cabin refrigerator or mini-fridge to store medication in.

Mobility-limited travellers
River cruising is not ideal for travellers with disabilities. Some riverships have lifts (elevators) between the main deck and the restaurant deck and/or stairlifts from the main to the upper (outside) deck, and a few riverships have wheelchair-accessible cabins, but not all.

Many landing stages are linked to steps leading up to a city or town. In some locations, riverships berth side by side, and you may have to cross several of them to get to land. Anyone in a wheelchair will have to be carried across the riverships (possibly including steps) in order to be placed on the dockside.

Note that many historic continental European cities having cobbled streets, steps with no ramps and few facilities aimed at those with disabilities. Budapest and Esztergom, for example, are very hilly and cobbled, making wheeling bone-shakingly difficult and uncomfortable. Bratislava is one of several cities to have numerous steps between the docking place at river level and street level, which is much higher.

Money
European riverships operate in euros (€), but for the duration of the journey, it's cashless cruising on board, so you don't have to worry about carrying cash or cards with you. Your final payment at the end of the cruise can be made using major credit cards or cash.

Tipping: If gratuities are not included in the overall package price (check the small print or ask your booking agent to be sure), the accepted standard for gratuities aboard European riverships is €8–10 (£6–12) per person, per day. Tips are given as a lump sum at the end of your cruise and divided equally between all crew members.

Pets
With the exception of 1AVista Reisen, which operates an occasional cruise in Europe for owners and their dogs, pets are not allowed on board river cruises.

Reception desk
Centrally located and manned 24 hours a day, the reception desk is the nerve centre of the rivership for all information and help with any problems, plus ephemera such as postcards, stamps, river maps and items in the boutique. Your passport will normally be kept in a safe in an office behind the reception desk.

Room service
This is not generally available on riverships, as there simply aren't enough crew members to cope. Some riverships offer room service at breakfast to suite occupants. If you are unwell and confined to your cabin, you may also be offered help in the way of meals brought to your room.

Safety
Bridges: Riverships often pass under very low bridges. In some cases the space between the bridge overhead and the rivership can be so little that if you don't sit down, you run the risk of serious head injury. **Injury:** Slipping, tripping and falling can all unfortunately cause injuries on board riverships. This does not mean that vessels of this kind are unsafe, but there are some things that you can do to minimise the chances of injury.

In your cabin, there may be a raised 'lip' (typically between 15cm/6ins and 30cm/12ins) between the bathroom and the rest of the cabin. Watch out for this, as it's easy to trip over it. On deck, wear sensible shoes with rubber soles (not crepe) when walking on the open deck and don't wear high heels.

If you are injured aboard your rivership and want to take legal action against the company operating the cruise, note that you need to file suit in the country of registry – so for riverships registered in Switzerland, the lawsuit must be filed in Switzerland (this is known as the Forum Clause). For more details on this, check you ticket's small print, which will usually state at length the instances in which the cruise carrier will not be held responsible for injury. You may not be able to sue a river cruise company in the event of injury or accident on an included or optional excursion, since these tours are operated by independent contractors.

Security

All cabins aboard riverships can be locked. Old-style keys are made of metal and operate mechanical locks; most locks, however, are electronically coded and open with plastic key cards or touch cards.

Cruise companies do not accept responsibility for money or valuables left in cabins and suggest that you store them in a safe (see 'Valuables').

Shops

A small boutique on board, typically run by the reception staff, will offer a selection of maps, souvenirs, gifts and toiletries.

Smoking

Most riverships have complete no-smoking policies inside but they do usually allow smoking on the open deck. Smokers should not throw lighted cigarette or cigar butts, or knock-out pipes, over the side of the vessel. The water might seem like a safe place to throw them, but they can easily be sucked into an opening in the side or onto an aft open deck, and start a fire. It is also inconsiderate and environmentally unfriendly.

Swimming pools

Some riverships (those of Emerald Waterways, for example) have small swimming pools ('dip' pools), sometimes with retractable covers, so that the pool room can be used for other purposes in the evenings.

Television and film

Programming is obtained from a mix of satellite feeds and videos. Some riverships receive live international news programmes, for which river cruise operators pay a subscription fee. Satellite television reception is sometimes poor because riverships constantly move out of the narrow beam of a satellite and cannot track the signal as accurately as a land-based facility.

Films are shown on the in-cabin infotainment system and, on some of the most sophisticated riverships, in a combined pool/cinema room.

Valuables

Most riverships have a small personal safe in each cabin for storing valuables.

Chatting in the pool aboard an Emerald Waterways rivership.

Accommodation

Your cabin or suite is your home away from home, although it will most likely be much smaller than you expect.

Design

Accommodation has to be practical and functional, due to the limited space available. European riverships have either two or three accommodation decks, a result mostly of a vessel's dimensions, which are imposed by the many locks and bridges on the various rivers.

Note that cabins on the lowest deck have smaller (non-opening) windows or portholes than those on the decks above. Also, access may be via a narrow stairway or spiral staircase, with a handrail (often on one side) and very short steps. Anyone with concerns about mobility limitations should look closely at the deck plan when considering a cabin on the lowest deck.

It's not one size fits all, though. River cruise brochures list accommodation in different price levels, usually according to their size (pay more, get more space) and location – with a larger choice of accommodation types and sizes on the newer riverships.

Companies building riverships with less expensive materials, fitting modular bathrooms, for example, or low-quality soundproofing, large ceiling tiles (instead of more expensive, better looking one-piece ceilings) or Ikea-style closets instead of higher-quality units, do so to save building costs per cabin. They can then target a broader market, with more competitive pricing.

Cabins and suites

You may see different words used for what is simply a cabin, a large cabin or a suite. These include 'stateroom', which is often used by North American companies to describe a standard cabin. Then there are 'suites', which should comprise a lounge or sitting room separated from a bedroom by a solid door, not just a curtain. Smaller 'suites' may be termed 'junior' or 'deluxe', but they are still simply larger cabins.

Cabins can vary in size from a miniscule 6 sq m (65 sq ft) to around 82 sq m (883 sq ft). It's all about the management of space, and, if you've ever stayed or lived in a caravan, you'll know what I mean. Suitcases can often be stored under the bed, to save valuable cabin space.

A view of a suite (with divider open) aboard *Scenic Jasper*.

On a seven-day cruise, you probably won't spend much time in your cabin, so a suite (generally double the size of a cabin) may be a waste of money. However, it does allow you to spread out, and it will have a larger bathroom (perhaps with a bathtub, a separate glazed shower enclosure and one or two washbasins). If you take a longer cruise (for example 14 days or more from Amsterdam to the Black Sea), it may be worth the extra expense.

Try to avoid cabins located directly under or adjacent to the galley (kitchen), as these can be noisy, particularly early in the morning, when the chefs are preparing breakfast.

Although many cabins are small compared to most hotel rooms, they need to be functional. All have outside (river) views. Some riverships (examples include *Avalon Illumination II, Avalon Imagery, Avalon Poetry II*) have cabins placed in a sideways arrangement that allows for larger bathrooms. The advantage of this arrangement is that the bed faces the river, so you wake up each morning with a great view (unless the rivership is in a lock, in which case you may feel like you are in a darkened lift). This design was first employed in 2007 on the 104-passenger *Premicon Queen* (presently *Thurgau Ultra*).

Cabin ceilings (some are indented one-piece ceilings, while others are plain or perforated steel panels) tend to be rather low, and beds may be shorter and narrower than you have at home. Designers often place large mirrors opposite the bed to give the illusion of space (much to the horror of *feng shui* practitioners, for whom this means the reflection of negative energy).

Most cabins have a personal safe, a television and an alarm clock/radio (some may have a mini-fridge). Closets may or may not be illuminated, and with soft-close doors. If you have a suite, room service and 'butler' service may be included. Apart from this, and the extra space, there are few other advantages of paying more – you join the same excursions as other passengers, for example. Some suites, such as the two Owner's Suites aboard the Viking 'Longships', have a wrap-around outdoor balcony, although being located aft, these can be noisy when the vessels are underway.

Balconies, sliding windows and folding glass doors

Brochures lead us to expect floor-to-ceiling windows and doors that open (electrically, by pressing a button or by large sliding glass doors) on to some kind of balcony, but they don't tell us about the mosquitoes that can invade the Danube in the afternoon, or that riverships tie up alongside each other in busy ports (blocking the view), or that a balcony is fairly useless when a rivership moves up and down in the many locks. While a balcony of some sort may indeed be desirable, consider how much you will use it, given the extra cost. Since the main purpose of a river

cruise is to experience the destinations, a balcony may not actually be necessary.

A real (private) balcony – that revered bit of space that lets you step outside – costs more, of course. So, is a balcony – or floor-to-ceiling (or wall-to-wall) opening glass door desirable on a rivership? In practice, it is not so useful, because when in port, other riverships may be docked adjacent, meaning that you need to keep it closed. It's also best to keep it closed when in a lock. So, while a balcony is often useful just to 'feel' the air and temperature, and to know what clothing to choose, most people prefer to be outside on the sun deck (the top open deck) for scenery viewing. A balcony does, of course, provide a sense of exclusivity, but watch out for the mosquitoes.

Some passengers use their balconies to dry any items of clothing that they have washed – not a pretty sight, especially if you are docked next to it.

Glossary

Step-outside balcony: A real balcony is one on that you can sit outside to enjoy the scenery.

'Juliet' (or 'French') balcony: This is a floor-to-ceiling sliding glass door that opens (or folding glass panels that open) to safety railings. This design only allows you to stick out your nose (or toes) and smell the fresh air.

Twin balcony suites: In 2010, Viking introduced an innovative design, which became a series of over 50 Viking 'Longships'. These included several suites featuring both a real (step-outside) balcony *plus* a 'Juliet' (or 'French') open-air balcony, with floor-to-ceiling opening glass doors – made possible due to a double-width cabin layout. AmaWaterways also has some riverships with both real and Juliet balconies.

Panoramic opening windows: Wall-to-wall windows, such as those found aboard Emerald's *Emerald Belle, Emerald Dawn, Emerald Sky, Emerald Star, Emerald Sun* and some Scenic and Uniworld vessels (*Scenic Jasper, Scenic Opal, S.S. Catherine, S.S. Maria Theresa,* for example) are electrically operated by push button (it takes about 30 seconds to fully open or close the huge windows, which are around 2m/7ft across). Unfortunately, when you are seated in a chair, your view is blocked by the thick wood or steel frame of the window. Also, the weight of the huge windows can present a problem, because a rivership 'flexes' as it moves against currents, and the mechanism can cease to function.

The same is true of Avalon's vessels, whose large sliding glass doors (*Avalon Passion, Avalon Tapestry II, Avalon Tranquility II*) open on to a 'French' balcony, but these are really just large windows that open. They are, however, better than those of Emerald or Scenic because there is no viewing obstruction, other than the required safety railing. Placing the bed opposite the window is a bonus, because there's always a river view.

Uniworld's S.S. *Antoinette,* S.S. *Catherine,* S.S. *Joie de Vivre,* S.S. *Josephine* and S.S. *Maria Theresa* have push-button electric windows plus a mosquito screen (as do all the Scenic riverships, while those of Emerald Waterways have electric windows but no mosquito screen), while almost all CroisiEurope's riverships have small sliding windows and only a few balconies (such as aboard the nicely refurbished *Camargue and Symphonie II*).

Cabin carpeting: Some riverships have plush carpeting with thick underlay; some have good carpeting without underlay. Others have caravan-quality thin carpeting with no underlay.

Ceilings: AmaWaterways, Luftner, Scenic, Uniworld and Viking have one-piece cabin ceilings; others have ceilings made of metal 'planks' (Avalon, CroisiEurope), as on so many ocean-going cruise ships, or large ceiling 'tiles' (Emerald). One-piece ceilings are more attractive.

Infotainment systems

Riverships vary considerably regarding in-cabin infotainment systems – flat-screen units that are positioned opposite bed(s) and can be viewed from almost any angle. They typically include a shipboard information channel, television channel (including news from one of the major providers), movies channel and possibly an audio channel.

Note that when watching a movie, the picture could be interrupted when the rivership goes under a bridge or into a lock, if it's a GPS-based system. Those aboard Emerald's vessels (but not those of sister company Scenic) are like this.

Electrical sockets

The latest vessels have several (220v) electrical sockets for your digital devices, but they may not always be visible. Some companies put extra sockets at floor level under the beds; others hide them in the cupboards or wardrobes; some have several on the vanity/writing desk unit or shelf, although they may be taken by the telephone and rechargeable personal receivers used for tours. Older riverships simply don't have enough sockets – you may be lucky to find just one.

Beds and bedlinen

Most riverships built after 2010 have twin beds that can be placed together to form a double (or queen-sized) bed. However, aboard many older (pre-2000) riverships, cabins have two beds or twin beds that are fixed and can't be pushed together. This may not be good for romantics, but might be useful for providing 'snoring' and 'no-snoring' beds. Examples of the latter arrangement include *Bijou, Der Kleine Prinz, River Adagio, River Allegro, River Ambassador, River Aria, River Concerto, River Harmony, River Melody, River Rhapsody* and *Swiss Ruby*.

Some riverships (such as *Amsterdam, Bellevue, Bizet, Cezanne, Prinses Juliana, Rigoletto, River Harmony, River Rhapsody, Select Explorer* and *Serenity*) have fold-down beds, one or both of which can con-

vert into a sofa for daytime use, giving extra space in a dimensionally challenged cabin in the daytime. Being practical and space-efficient, these are good for couples who prefer separate beds.

Some riverships have two beds in an 'L'-shaped configuration (so you sleep head to head or toes to toes), which is definitely not for honeymooners! Note that beds in cabins for solo occupancy might be lower and/or slimmer than a standard single bed.

Some beds have mattresses *inside* a bed frame instead of on top of it, with square, not round, corners. The challenge is that there is very little room to move in, and legs can easily be knocked against the sharp corners. Aboard some riverships (*River Voyager, Scenic Amber, Scenic Jasper* and *Scenic Opal,* for example), mattresses have controllable tilt-up mechanisms. European down duvets, high-quality bed linens and plush mattresses are what fine sleeping environments are all about. The bed linen aboard most riverships is 100 percent cotton, but on the less expensive ones it may be a 50 percent cotton/50 percent polyester mix.

Pillows

While some companies provide a choice of pillows, such Tauck's hypoallergenic pillows, other companies (CroisiEurope, for example) have only a standard pillow (usually with a cotton cover and inside of polyester). Some companies (such as AmaWaterways and Scenic) provide a pillow menu with a choice of several different types, while others (including Emerald) have a pillow menu only for the top suites. Pillow choices might include hop-filled or hypoallergenic, goose down, Hungarian goose down (considered the best), isotonic, Tempur-Pedic or copycat memory foam.

Bathrooms

Bathrooms come in various sizes, shapes and fittings, and comfort levels. Some are marble-clad; some have tiled walls and floor; some have plain modular walls (like caravan units). Some have space to sit comfortably on the toilet, while others are really cramped; some have good lighting; others have modest lighting, and a number are so dim that you can't see your hands in front of you!

Expect them to be functional rather than sumptuous – there simply isn't room to accommodate the touches of luxury you would find in a hotel suite or in the best suites aboard ocean-going ships. A typical bathroom includes a washbasin, toilet and shower enclosure, while bathtubs are available in some suites.

Some suites, such as the Owner's Suites aboard the Viking 'Longships', have large wet rooms, with a wooden seat in the shower enclosure. You may find little extras (Emerald's vessels have tiny blue nightlights, for example), vanity kits including cotton buds and make-up removal pads, and other niceties. All riverships provide towels, soap and

Cabin infotainment system aboard *Emerald Sky*.

shampoo (sometimes in bottles, sometimes in wall-mounted dispensers).

Most riverships built before 2010 have shower curtains; newer vessels have more stylish – and hygienic – glass doors. Some bathrooms have fixed-head showers, but most have flexible shower hoses. One challenge, particularly for taller passengers, is that the ceiling height is limited. Some riverships may have high-power showers with changing colours (examples include *Scenic Gem, Scenic Jade*).

Some of Uniworld's newest riverships have heated towel rails. Scenic's vessels and Tauck's *Grace, Inspire, Joy* and *Savor* have heated bathroom floors. My own frequently stated irritant is bathroom mirrors that steam up, an all-too common complaint. Well, Viking's 'Longships' and Vantage's *River Voyager* have anti-steam mirrors. Long may the trend continue.

Towels are normally supplied on board, so you don't have to bring them with you. Sizes vary considerably – examples include 142 x 102cm (56 x 40ins) on Viking, 132 x 71cm (52 x 28ins) on AmaWaterways, and 102 x 71cm (40 x 28ins) on Scylla/Tauck vessels.

Toilets, too, can vary in height, from a low of 41cm/16ins (Emerald) to a high of 53cm/21ins (AmaWaterways).

Bathroom amenities

Personal amenities are provided aboard most riverships. AmaWaterways, Emerald, Scenic and Viking supply individual bottles of shampoo, conditioner and shower gel. Aboard A-Rosa vessels wall-mounted

dispensers for shower gel and shampoo are fitted. Uniworld provides a combined shampoo/conditioner, although suites have individual items.

L'Occitane toiletries (from Provence) are often provided. Some will be in fixed dispensers on the wall of the shower (Avalon), while suite occupants may receive premium products (Hermès in suites aboard Uniworld vessels, for example).

Items including illuminated make-up/shaving mirrors, cotton make-up pads or cotton balls, nail files, sewing kits and other personal amenities may be supplied aboard some riverships, such as those of AmaWaterways and Scenic, but not aboard the vessels of the low-priced operators. As is so often the case, the more you pay, the more you get.

Cabin numbering

Maritime tradition aboard ocean-going ships dictates that even-numbered cabins should be on the port side (the same as the lifeboats). However, aboard some riverships (CroisiEurope's and Tauck's, chartered from Scylla, for example), odd-numbered cabins may be found on the port side of the vessel. Even within the same company, some riverships may have even-numbered cabins on the port side, while others may have odd-numbers. It's all a little confusing, if you're used to the traditional system. In addition, some riverships have no cabins with the number 13 (*Crystal Mozart, Danubia* and *Prinses Christina*, for example), which could be reassuring for superstitious travellers.

Cuisine

Food is a major part of any successful river cruise. Here, we lift the lid on what the dining experience is really like.

Companies put maximum effort into telling you just how fabulous their food is. What is closer to the truth is that you'll be served agreeable food in comfortable surroundings. Just don't expect the variety you get on the ocean-going cruise ships.

River cruise cuisine compares favourably with the kind of 'banquet' food served in a decent hotel. Riverships cannot offer a full-on gourmet experience in the restaurant – despite what the brochures might claim – because the galley ('kitchen' for landlubbers) is small, with batch cooking used to turn out up to 200 meals at a time. At almost any time of the day or night, there is activity in the galley, whether baking fresh bread at night, preparing meals and snacks for passengers and crew around the clock, or decorating a special birthday cake. And things are starting to change with rivership cuisine.

The restaurant

All riverships have one 'main' restaurant. Many new riverships also offer a 'healthy-eating' corner as a bistro-style section (some with an indoor/outdoor option)

A section of the lunch buffet aboard *A-ROSA Stella*.

as part of or in front of the lounge. Occasionally, small buffets or barbecues may be offered on the 'Sun Deck' (weather and temperature permitting, of course).

Most tables are for four, six or eight persons; tables for two can be found on the newer vessels. When tables are unassigned – called 'open seating' – you can sit with whomever you wish. This means that you can change your dinner table partners each evening if you wish. Aboard riverships where tables are assigned, it may be difficult to change tables once the cruise has started.

Alternative eateries

Many of the largest 135m (443ft) riverships may also have an alternative dining venue aft, which allows you to eat in a more intimate setting. All AmaWaterways riverships, for example, have a separate 'Chef's Table' venue aft, with a show galley (kitchen), where chefs prepare a high-quality multi-course (dégustation) menu, where everything is cooked individually, beautifully presented and paired with some excellent wines.

Meanwhile, Scenic has 'Table La Rive', a single curtained-off table in the restaurant, with a set dégustation-style menu and wine pairings. Swiss company Excellence River Cruises has a steakhouse (extra cost) for its passengers, as does Phoenix Reisen aboard *Alina* and *Amelia*.

In some riverships the forward section of the lounge may become an 'alternative' eatery in the evening, so access to the exterior forward deck may be restricted. For example, Avalon has Sky Bistro (with tablecloths and youthful wine pairing). Scenic has Portofino (aboard its riverships on French rivers its name is L'Amour), located in the forward section of the main lounge (the staff serves from a connecting stairway to the main galley area).

Several companies (Emerald and Scenic, for example) also have a 'Healthy Choice' or 'Vitality' corner for breakfast and lunch.

Note that there's no extra charge to eat in any alternative area, and spreading diners out like this also helps to manage demand in the main restaurant from an operational point of view.

The nitty gritty: It's often the case that the little details all combine to create a greater or worse end product. For example, the restaurants of *A-ROSA Stella*, *Amadeus Silver*, *Avalon Expression*, *Belle de Cadiz* and *Excellence Royale* have chairs without armrests, which are less comfortable than those with armrests. Aboard *AmaCello*, *Crystal Mozart*, *S.S. Antoinette* or *Viking Embla* (as aboard all other Viking

River Royale buffet.

'Longships'), for example, most of the chairs in restaurants do have armrests.

Some riverships have a restaurant with alcove-style seating booths (examples include: *AmaSonata* and *AmaSerena*), which means that leaning over fellow passengers is necessary to serve.

Some companies (A-ROSA, for example) only have placemats and no tablecloths on restaurant tables for dinner. Emerald Waterways features placemats for breakfast and lunch, but has tablecloths for dinner. AmaWaterways and Scenic have tablecloths for breakfast, lunch and dinner. Ama, Scenic and Uniworld provide linen napkins, whereas some operators provide only paper napkins for dinner. Some companies provide paper napkins for breakfast and lunch, and linen napkins for dinner.

Some companies provide fish knives (AmaWaterways, Emerald Waterways, Scenic and Viking River Cruises, for example), but most vessels catering to North Americans – such as those of Grand Circle Cruise Lines and Vantage River Cruises – do not, nor does A-ROSA.

Meanwhile, AmaWaterways, Emerald Waterways, Scenic and Viking River Cruises also provide proper steak knives, but most others do not. The cuisine is generally international, often with some typical dishes that represent the country or region you are visiting. Gravies and salty cream sauces are often used to mask less-expensive cuts of meat or defrosted ingredients. Portions tend to be small, however.

On budget-priced riverships you can expect portion-controlled frozen ingredients that are modified with flavour enhancers and simply reheated and plated. On more expensive vessels, you can expect to be served more freshly prepared ingredients, especially fish, better meat cuts and higher-quality fruit and vegetables. Food quality and ingredient costs vary considerably, with the general rule being the more you pay, the better-quality food you can expect.

River cruise operators work generally closely with their food suppliers to identify and remove any products that contain genetically modified food, with the exception of packages of cereal. Some owners (such as Scylla) and operators may have different maritime caterers and suppliers for various riverships in their fleets in order to create healthy competition and maintain standards.

On European rivers, galley standards, food supply, handling and hygiene all come under the auspices of HACCP Certification (Hazard Analysis Critical Control Point).

Breakfast: The first meal of the day, taken between around 7am and 9am, is usually a self-service buffet with a variety of cold cuts of meat and a decent range of French and other European cheeses laid out on a central display table. There may also be an omelette station (some riverships use an industrial 'egg' mix

SPECIAL DIETS

If you have a vegetarian, vegan or macrobiotic diet, are counting calories or want salt-free, sugar-restricted, low-fat, low-cholesterol food, or indeed have any other dietary restrictions, tell the river cruise company or your cruise booking agent before you book, and ask the cruise operator to confirm that it can handle your dietary requirements. Note that food on many riverships tends to be liberally dosed with salt, and vegetables are often cooked with sauces containing dairy products, salt and sugar.

Politely hidden on the back page of menus aboard AmaWaterways' riverships is a list of possible food intolerance items (nuts, dairy items, for example) that you should make the chef aware of.

The bar aboard *Avalon Expression*.

and not real eggs). Hot food items can also be ordered from your waiter. Some riverships (including those of AmaWaterways, Scenic Cruises and Viking River Cruises) may additionally feature a 'special of the day' or other menu options.

Aboard a few riverships bread and bread rolls may be made on board (AmaWaterways, for example); but aboard most, these items are produced from frozen dough, or purchased ashore. Many rivership croissants have no taste, for example, because they are made from frozen starter dough and low-quality butter.

Note that 'fresh' fruit juices are almost always of the pre-packed supermarket variety (and definitely not 'fresh'), due to lack of preparation space in the galley. Fruit 'smoothies' are also often featured, but note that these can contain up to 50 percent white sugar.

Lunch: This is usually a self-service buffet. The selection will include a choice of fresh green salad items with dressings (typically unimaginative) and a range of oils (olive, basil, sesame, pumpkin, walnut, etc) that can liven up your salad. The omelette station from breakfast will probably have been converted into a pasta or meat-slicing station for lunch. Requests for à la carte or 'always available' hot food items are taken by a waiter and cooked to order.

Dinner: Dinner, at about 7pm (when everyone rushes to the restaurant to find a seat if it's an open seating arrangement) is typically normally a sit-down (plated) meal served at either assigned or unassigned (open-service) tables, although the self-service buffet of A-ROSA Cruises is one exception to this. Served dinners normally consist of a choice of cold or hot starter (appetizer), a choice of two or three main courses (entrées) – one fish, one meat, one vegetarian – plus dessert and cheese (usually in that order, although cheese might be available at any time throughout the meal). You can expect river fish (other than shrimp/prawns, there may be little in the way of shellfish), and dark red meats such as venison, beef and ox, as well as lighter fare including chicken and other fowl. AmaWaterways uses fresh fish – the only river cruise company to do so (at present).

Drinks

River cruise companies often tout that all drinks, including alcoholic beverages, are included in the cruise price. Take a look at the selection in the bar, however, and you may notice brands you've never heard of before. Whiskies available will inevitably be of the blended variety – ask for a decent single malt whisky and you'll probably have to pay extra. ('It's not included in the included drinks, sir.') And, for that gin and tonic, you may be facing tonic, such as Royal tonic, that tastes incredibly sweet and artificial, or, alternatively, basic tonic from a hose. As for premium gins – not a chance, although I did experience a popular Black Forest gin called Monkey 47 aboard the riverships of AmaWaterways and Scenic.

Wine: Many river cruise companies tout their 'specially selected' wines, sometimes dubbing them 'fine wine' (Uniworld) or 'superb regional and international wines' (Scenic). If you enjoy good vintage wines, expect to be disappointed, however, unless you bring your own (most companies allow you to do this, but only for consumption in your cabin, so not during a meal).

In most cases the wines are very, very young table wines – on a par with the least expensive supermarket wines. And in terms of quantity, most river cruise operators only provide small wine glasses for both white and red wines, although a few (notably AmaWaterways and Scenic) provide large, proper glasses – by this I mean Bordeaux-sized glasses for red wines and Chardonnay-sized ones for whites – and their wines are of a better quality. Measures are up to the waiter. It's not truly unlimited, either: if you read the small print, you will find phrases such as: 'Unlimited beverages do not include premium wine and premium spirits' (Uniworld).

Of course, there are exceptions, such as the specialist wine-themed cruises of AmaWaterways, for example, which feature private tastings, exclusive vineyard visits and special brochures on the wine regions of Europe.

Coffee and tea: Riverships have self-service drinks corners, typically with a good-quality push-button espresso/cappuccino machine and a selection of teas. Most companies provide teabags rather than loose tea, although Uniworld is an exception to this. Premium riverships provide a range of teas from specialist brands such as Fauchon, Ronnefeldt, Tea Forté, Twinings or Whittard. Standard riverships in Europe may provide teas of a lesser quality by companies including Bigelow, Dilmah, Lipton or Pickwick. Coffee varies from the best Italian brands (illy, Lavazza, Sagafredo) to the little known.

Some riverships provide only white sugar for hot beverages – a choice of white or brown at least is preferable.

Water: This is usually provided in jugs. These are towel-wrapped aboard some of the premium riverships, but aboard most, they are not.

Excursions

Excursions on a river cruise offer everything from helicopter rides and hot-air ballooning to wine tasting, horse riding and musical recitals in historic venues.

Excursions on a river cruise are a highlight for most passengers. If you are visiting new destinations and want the value of good local guides, it's best to choose a company where excursions are included. These will be full- or half-day excursions and sometimes evening events, such as concerts, too. Also, optional (extra-cost) excursions may be available for private tours, special events or culinary experiences.

When river cruise operators plan excursions, they assume that passengers have not visited a place before and aim to show them its highlights in a comfortable manner.

Buses or minibuses are usually the principal choice of transport. This cuts costs and allows tour operators to narrow the selection of guides to only those most competent, knowledgeable and fluent in whatever language the majority of passengers speak, while providing some degree of security and control. Some river cruise companies have their own buses (whether owned or chartered), so the seating and comfort level are consistent.

Learn to read between the lines about excursions: the term 'visit' should be taken to mean actually entering the place or building concerned, whereas 'see' should be taken to mean viewing from the outside (perhaps even just from the bus, for example).

Excursions are timed to be most convenient for the greatest number of participants, taking into account the timing of meals on board (these may be altered according to excursion times). Departure times are listed in the descriptive literature and in the daily programme (delivered to your cabin and posted at the reception desk), and may or may not be announced over the vessel's public address system. There are no refunds if you miss the excursion. If you are hearing-impaired, make arrangements with the excursion staff to assist you in departing for your excursions at the correct times.

Excursions for large cities are basically superficial, although they do provide a useful introduction. On most excursions, Audiovox or Quietvox headsets are provided. These enable the tour guide to communicate by talking into a microphone and passengers to listen wirelessly using in-ear headphones, so you don't look so much like a tourist and you can hear the commentary clearly.

To see specific sights in more detail, or to get to know a city in a more intimate fashion, go alone with a guidebook or with a small group and a private guide. (Scenic provides excellent sat nav-style devices packed with information for self-guided visits.) Go by taxi or bus or walk directly to the places that are of most interest to you.

Going solo? When hiring a taxi for sightseeing, negotiate the price in advance and do not pay until you get back to the vessel or to your final destination. If you are with friends, hiring a taxi for a full- or half-day sightseeing may make sense, particularly if the driver speaks your language, and has a comfortable, air-conditioned vehicle.

Some river cruise companies have their own buses.

A day in the life of a rivership

To give you a flavour of life on board a rivership, here's a sample daily programme. There's also a summary of who's who among the crew.

After arrival at your rivership (usually mid-afternoon), you simply step aboard and check in at the reception desk, where you are given your digital touch card (or cabin key). A steward or stewardess then takes you to your cabin and explains everything about it. Your luggage will already be inside the cabin, ready to unpack. While you have dinner in the dining room, your vessel will probably depart.

Each day, when you wake up, your rivership is probably on its way to the next destination or else has already arrived and is tied up at the landing stage; alternatively, it may be in a lock. Note that the excursions are completely optional – you can always just stay on board and relax, if you want to, or go ashore independently.

A TYPICAL DAY ON A RIVER DANUBE CRUISE

6.30am: Fresh coffee and pastries in the lounge for early risers.
7–9am: Breakfast in the dining room.
9am: Arrival at the first destination.
9.15am: Leave for the morning excursion – coaches will already be outside, as close to the gangway as possible.
12 noon: Return from the morning excursion (unless you are in a major city, in which case you could be out and about independently).
12 noon–1.30pm: Lunch in the dining room or a small bistro lunch on the open sun deck (weather permitting).
2pm: Arrival at the second destination.
2.15pm: Departure for the afternoon excursion or walking tour with a licensed local guide with in-depth knowledge of the locality.
4pm: Afternoon tea, cakes and sandwiches for anyone not on the afternoon excursion.
5pm: Return from the afternoon excursion.
6pm: Short briefing on the following day's programme (plus information on any changes to the schedule or docking times) in the lounge; pre-dinner cocktails and conversation.
7pm: Dinner of four or five courses is served in the dining room. Passengers typically linger and enjoy table conversation.
8pm: In the lounge, the resident musician (typically a pianist or accordionist) plays music for dancing or listening to. Occasionally, there might be some additional entertainment from ashore (perhaps a mini-concert). There may also be an evening excursion (such as a private concert in Vienna).

Continental breakfast options aboard Viking's *Aquavit Terrace*.

Gather round for lounge entertainment.

10pm: Late-night snacks in the lounge or, if it's warm weather, perhaps outside on the sun deck. The lounge/bar won't close until after midnight.

BEHIND THE SCENES: HOW IT WORKS

Riverships are small, and teamwork makes it all happen. Whether you are on or off a rivership, the crew works constantly, both on the technical side (engines, air conditioning, heating and electrical items, etc) or the hospitality side – eg the reception staff dealing with paperwork, acting as the main contact point for passengers, keeping track of who is on board or off the vessel, etc.

Even on the latest riverships, the maximum number of crew carried will usually be under 50. Some crews are much smaller than this – older-style riverships typically have as few as 18 staff members. They work closely together, and multi-tasking skills come in handy in such a confined environment.

Captain

The captain is the ultimate authority on board: driving the rivership, responsible for navigation, and licensed and insured for the river(s) the vessel sails on. A deputy (second captain) is licensed and able to take over at any time – there is sometimes a lot of night sailing to do, so they take turns.

Chief engineer

The chief engineer is responsible for all things technical, including air conditioning, lighting, heating systems and, of course, the engines and generators.

Hotel manager

The hotel manager is in charge of the overall hotel operation (and all department heads), including all things relating to passenger comfort and satisfaction, the provision of food and drinks (these may be provided by an outside maritime catering company), placing orders for supplies and generally communicating with the river cruise company's headquarters.

Cruise manager

Aboard riverships, the cruise manager makes sure that the route plan is followed, does evening recaps in the lounge, hosts social events, handles all the excursions, plans the timing for the next day's programme, and takes care of any other details such as entertainment and library books

Housekeeping

In the early morning, the cabin stewards and stewardesses will count out the number of fresh towels needed for the cabins in their sections. They will have a stock of sheets and pillowcases available in case any need changing, as well as any personal amenities that need changing.

Executive chef

The executive chef typically heads up a team of up to eight people in the galley – a small space no larger than a standard-size hotel room. At almost any hour of the day, chefs are busy preparing, cooking, grilling, sautéing or making sauces. During the night, a pastry chef prepares cakes and sweet items.

What to do if...

Here are some tips to ensure the best river cruise experience possible, and, just in case it doesn't quite go to plan, advice on what to do if you do have a problem.

...you fly internationally to take a cruise.

If your cruise is a long distance from your home, it makes sense (if time and budget allow) to fly to your cruise embarkation point and stay for at least a day or two before the cruise starts. This way you will be better rested and adjusted to any time changes. You then step aboard your rivership relaxed and ready for your holiday. As a bonus, you will get to know the departure city/town.

...your luggage does not arrive.

If your river cruise includes flights, the airline is responsible for locating your luggage and delivering it to the next destination. If you have arranged your own flights, you are responsible for collecting your luggage at the airport and transporting it to your cruise. Remember to place easy-to-read name and address tags both inside as well as outside your luggage, to identify it if it is delayed or missing. Also, give your airline your itinerary and any local representative contacts (included with your cruise documents), so that luggage can be forwarded to you. (Keep this list – and contact details for insurance purposes – in your hand luggage, for fast access.)

...you miss your rivership.

If you miss the departure at the port of embarkation due to late or cancelled flights or connections and you are travelling on an air/cruise package, the airline will make alternative arrangements to get you to your rivership. If you are travelling 'cruise-only' and have arranged your own flights, then it is your responsibility to arrive on time. If you miss the sailing, contact the emergency number included in your documents.

...a destination is deleted from the itinerary.

This can easily happen on a river cruise. Remember to read the small print in the brochure before you book. A river cruise operator is under no obligation to perform the stated itinerary if they have noted otherwise in the brochure.

Dinner time aboard a rivership in Lyon.

Ready for passengers to embark.

...you miss the rivership in a port of call.

The onus is on you to get back to your rivership before its appointed sailing time. Miss it and you'll need to get to the next destination at your own cost. In Europe, the train network is fortunately so good that this is usually possible.

...you accidentally leave personal belongings on a tour bus.

If you unintentionally leave something on a tour bus, and you are back on board, tell the staff at the reception desk. They will contact the excursion operator to ascertain whether any lost property has been found.

...your cabin has no air conditioning or it has heating or plumbing problems.

If there is anything wrong with your cabin, including problems with the plumbing in the bathroom, tell your cabin attendant immediately. If things don't improve, complain to the cruise manager.

...you are unwell aboard your rivership.

Riverships do not carry their own designated medical team or unit, unlike ocean-going cruise ships. Land, however, is always accessible, so arrangements can quickly be made to access medical assistance. Almost all river cruise companies offer insurance packages that include medical cover for most eventualities. It is wise to take out this type of insurance when you book (see page 17).

Members of European Union/European Economic Area (EU/EEA) countries or those of Swiss nationality should get a free EHIC, which entitles the bearer to state health care at a reduced cost or sometimes for free. It is valid in all EEA countries, including Switzerland. You can apply online at www.ehic.org.uk. Note that EHICs do not cover repatriation.

...the food is definitely not 'gourmet' cuisine, as stated in the brochure.

If the food is not as described – for example, it promises 'whole lobster' in the brochure, but you only see cold lobster salad once during the cruise, or the 'freshly squeezed' orange juice on the breakfast menu is anything but – inform the maître d' (restaurant manager) of the problem.

...you have a problem with a crew member.

Contact the hotel manager (via the reception desk) and explain the situation. It's their job to resolve issues of this kind, although they are rare.

...you're unhappy with your cruise experience.

If the cruise doesn't meet your expectations or performs less well than the brochure promises, let your booking agent and the river cruise company know. Be certain to read the small print, however – after you've done so, it'll probably seem as if passengers don't have many rights after all.

Cruising past Marksburg Castle on the Rhine.

European Rivers

0 _____ 200 km
0 _____ 200 miles

───── Featured river

N

NORTH
SEA

DENMARK

Edinburgh

Belfast

IRELAND   *Irish Sea*

Dublin

UNITED
KINGDOM

Kie

Ostfriesische Inseln   Hambu

Groningen   Brem

NETHERLANDS   Hannover
Amsterdam
Den Haag   Nijmegen
(The Hague)
Rotterdam   Essen
Duisburg   *Thür*
Bruxelles   Düsseldorf   *Wa*
(Brussels)   Köln
BELGIUM   (Cologne)
Liège   GERM
LUXEM-   Frank
BOURG
Luxembourg   Mannheim   Heide
Reims   Metz   Stutt
Strasbourg

ATLANTIC

OCEAN

English Channel

Roubaix

Amiens

Le Havre
Caen   Rouen
Normandie
Paris

Seine

Marne

Channel
Islands

Brest

Bretagne

Rennes

Angers   *Loire*   Orléans

Nantes   Tours

Dijon   Besançon   *Rhein (Rhine)*   LIECHTEN-
STEIN
Vosges   Basel   Vaduz
(Basle)
Zürich
Bern   SWITZERLAND   *Donau (Da*

Genève
(Geneva)

FRANCE   E

La Rochelle

Île d'Oléron

Limoges

Clermont-Ferrand

Bay of Biscay

Bordeaux   *Dordogne*

Massif   Lyon
St-Étienne
Central

Lot

Garonne

Mont Blanc   Milano
4808   (Milan)
A   Grenoble
L
Genov
Torino   (Geno
(Turin)
Provence   *Riviera*

A Coruña   *Costa Verde*
Santander

Vigo   *Miño*   *Cordillera Cantábrica*

Bilbao

Pamplona

PYRÉNÉES

ANDORRA
Andorra la Vella

Perpignan

Toulouse

Nîmes   Avignon   Nice   Monte Carlo
MONACO
Marseille   Toulon
Côte d'Azur

Bastia

Corse
(Corsica)

Ajaccio

Porto   *Douro*

Valladolid   *Duero*

Salamanca

Cordillera

Ebro

Lleida   Zaragoza   Barcelona
Costa Brava

Tarragona

PORTUGAL   *Cordillera Central*

Madrid

Lisboa   *Tajo (Tagus)*
(Lisbon)

Evora   *Guadiana*
Badajoz

SPAIN

Ibérica

Valencia   *Costa del Azahar*

Islas Baleares   Menorca
Palma
Ibiza   Mallorca

Sinisc

Macomer

Sardegna
(Sardinia)

Cagliari

Albacete   *Júcar*

Sierra Morena   Córdoba

Algarve   Huelva   Guadalquivir   Jaén

Faro

Sevilla

Cádiz   *Sierra Nevada*   Granada

Málaga   *Costa del Sol*

Algeciras   Gibraltar
(UK)
Tanger   Ceuta
(Tangier)   (Spain)

MOROCCO

Segura   Alicante   *Costa Blanca*

Murcia
Cartagena   *Costa*
Calida

MEDITERRANEAN SEA

Alger
(Algiers)

ALGERIA

The Douro Valley (a Unesco World Heritage site), Portugal.

Europe's rivers and waterways

A guide to the main river cruise routes and ports of Europe, accompanied by diagrammatic maps. Major ports of call come with our list of top sights.

Europe is the world's most developed and best-organised region for river cruises, and it is the heart of the European continent that is in most people's minds when they consider a river cruise. The earliest European river cruises were on the Rhine (Rhein), and later the Danube, and it isn't hard to see why. Accessible and wonderfully scenic, a trip on these great waterways instantly transports the passenger into old Europe, providing a constantly changing perspective on its history and landscapes.

A river cruise provides a unique perspective on the historic landscapes through which these waterways wend their way, past historic cities, medieval towns, fabled villages, forbidding castles, soaring cathedrals, monasteries, churches, romantic châteaux, forests, hills, gardens, vineyards and industrial backdrops (commerce is still conducted along these rivers and waterways, so the scenery, while often magnificent, can also be industrial at times). River cruises can be combined, too, with other interests, from music – in the shape of an evening concert, attendance at a festival – to tasting events for food and wine aficionados to film nights and more.

MAJOR EUROPEAN WATERWAYS

But on to the rivers themselves... The Rhine is justly famous for the fabulous scenery along its middle course between the German cities of Mainz and Koblenz, an utterly romantic riverscape of brooding castles perched atop steep hills covered in vineyards. Its major tributaries – the Mosel (Moselle in English), Neckar and Main – are also well-established cruise rivers. Most Danube cruises concentrate on the stretch between Passau on the German/Austrian border via Vienna and Bratislava to the Hungarian capital, Budapest – although there is also plenty of interest along the upper course in southern Germany (now linked to the Rhine via the Main–Danube Canal), as well as the lesser-known lower reaches that traverse the Balkans en route to the Black Sea. The Elbe, running from the Czech Republic through eastern Germany to the North Sea, is the other popular river of Central Europe, and itineraries along it typically explore the beautiful cities of Prague and Dresden.

OTHER WATERWAYS

Away from these major rivers, there is a variety of lesser-known waterways to explore, including the Douro in northern Portugal, and the Rhône and Seine in France. A wide range of barge cruises and other trips are also possible – barge cruising is especially popular in France.

KEY HIGHLIGHTS AND KILOMETRE MARKINGS

Along most (although not all) European rivers, you'll notice white marker boards with black numbers at every navigable kilometre. These generally mark the distance from the river's source to the estuary, although on the Danube it is the other way round.

What follows in this section of the book is an overview of the key highlights you'll see on your cruise, by river, with kilometre details included, if they are likely to be marked.

LOCKS

On a river or waterway these are chambered structures that are closed off with gates to raise or lower the water level within the lock chamber so that vessels can move from one elevation to another along the river or waterway.

A kilometre marking board along the Rhone.

River Danube

Winding its way from the foothills of the Alps to the distant shores of the Black Sea, this majestic waterway has long been a powerful transportation route and is a perennial favourite for river cruises.

The Danube has shaped the history of central Europe over many centuries, as an important transportation route and economic lifeline between the heart of Europe and the Balkans, although, commercially, it is less busy than the Rhine (Rhein). It has halted armies at its banks and been the inspiration for musical serenades, interludes and waltzes. Yet despite Johann Strauss's famous *Blue Danube* waltz, the river, its bed thick with sediment, is actually a murky brown, not blue – although some claim that it can have an azure sheen in the spring and autumn sunshine.

Europe's second-longest river after the Volga, the Danube flows through a range of scenery on the long journey from its source in the Black Forest to the vast delta on the Black Sea, cutting through the wooded hills of Bavaria to the steep terraces and castles of the wine-growing country of Lower Austria, then on to the edge of the Hungarian steppes and into the Balkans. The river has carved deep gorges across ancient mountain ranges, while in other places, meanders across broad, marshy plains. Sightseeing opportunities are numerous, from medieval monasteries to castles, fabulous museums and unspoilt national parks.

Towns and cities of particular interest include Regensburg and Passau in Germany; Linz and Vienna in Austria; Bratislava in Slovakia; Budapest in Hungary, and Vidin in Bulgaria. Other highlights include Dürnstein and Melk in Austria's alluring Wachau Valley and historic Esztergom in Hungary. Most cruises spend at least one night in Vienna and Budapest.

Visitors have a huge choice of itineraries, but the most rewarding is to cruise the river's entire length. There's something fascinating and addictive about the Danube, a promise of discovery and mystery as it flows eastwards through ever-more exotic lands. For many passengers, it is a first into the former Eastern Bloc. Take a shorter voyage as far as Budapest, and you'll find yourself looking longingly at the barges and cruise vessels continuing their journey through the Balkans towards the Black Sea, and vowing to come back and explore Serbia, Romania and Bulgaria.

Riverships on the Danube at Passau.

THE COURSE OF THE DANUBE

The source of the mighty Danube is marked by an ornate fountain and ornamental pool in the gardens of the Fürstenberg Palace at Donaueschingen in the hills of the Black Forest in southwestern Germany, where the two source streams, the Breg and the Brigach, unite. From here to its marshy delta on the distant Black Sea coast of Romania, the river flows through six countries and forms the border with three more, covering a distance of around 2,890km (1,795 miles). Along the way, some 300 tributaries join the river to bolster its flow. This lengthy course can be divided up into three sections.

The Upper Danube runs for approximately 1,000km (620 miles), stretching from its source to the 'Hungarian Gate', the point near the Slovakian border at which the river crosses into the wide Carpathian Basin. Along this section of the river there is considerable inclination of the river bed, and a rapid current. The first navigable point is at Regensburg.

The Middle Danube is approximately 940km (584 miles) long. From the Hungarian Gate it courses east across the plain until, at the Great Bend, it runs into the hard granite of the Börzsöny and Cserhát Hills, and swings suddenly south to Budapest. The Danube then meanders across the Great Hungarian Plain, clipping the northeastern corner of Croatia before surging across the plains of Vojvodina in northern Serbia to reach the dramatic Iron Gates Gorge on the Serbia-Romania border. Here, it cuts through the southern spur of the crescent-shaped Carpathian mountain range.

The Lower Danube is approximately 950km (590 miles) long. The river here is broad, shallow and marshy as it forges across the Wallachian Plain (forming the border of Romania and Bulgaria) to the large delta by the Black Sea.

MAIN-DANUBE CANAL

In 793, Charlemagne had the vision of establishing a navigable waterway between the Danube and Main rivers, to be called the 'Fossa Carolina'. Thousands of Charlemagne's workers began to dig a navigable trench between the Rezat and Altmühl rivers. But the project failed due to incessant rain and the resulting 'invasion' of water. One section, now called the Karlsgraben, still exists today.

Charlemagne's vision was finally realised on 25 September 1992, when the 170km (106-mile) Main-Danube Canal was opened, providing the means for larger craft of up to 3,300 tons to navigate all the way from the North Sea to the Black Sea. The construction of the canal, linking the Rhine, Main and Danube rivers, is one of Europe's largest transport-engineering projects.

Costing 4.7 billion German marks at the time to build, the canal runs through rural Bavaria and rises

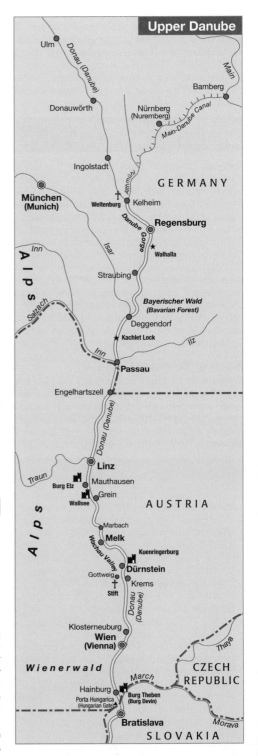

406m (1,332ft) via 16 locks, which vary from 5.29m (17.4 ft) to 49m (160.8ft) in water height difference. It was cleverly constructed to blend with the surrounding landscape, and it looks more like a river than a canal. Some 75 million German marks were invested in nature reserves and conservation projects. The canal is 55m (180ft) wide and 4m (13ft) deep, and flows into the Danube at Kelheim in Germany.

HIGHLIGHTS FROM BAMBERG (GERMANY) TO THE BLACK SEA (ROMANIA)

There are many permutations of river cruises on the Danube, but the main destinations are summarised below – cruising downstream, from Bamberg to the Black Sea. Note that, along the Danube, distances are measured not from the source to the estuary, as is customary in Europe, but from the estuary to the source.

One thing to note is that the water level of the Danube can be too low for navigation, particularly during the warm, dry summer months, so do check with your travel provider to make sure that the water levels are sufficient for your cruise. Conversely, the water level can be too high for vessels to pass under the bridges of the upper section of the Danube beyond Passau. Normally, after the melting winter snow and spring rain, there is sufficient top-up to carry the river through the summer.

Bamberg, Germany (Km 3–6.4)
Known for its symphony orchestra and tasty smoked beer (Rauchbier), this medieval city has narrow, winding streets lined with Baroque patrician houses. The old town, the 11th-century cathedral and the Bamberg Reiter (Bamberg Horseman) statue were declared a World Heritage Site by Unesco in 1993.

The River Regnitz runs through the middle of the city, joining up with the Main 3km (2 miles) downstream.

The tombs of the Holy Roman Emperor Heinrich II and Pope Clement II are housed in the magnificent cathedral. The old Town Hall, or Rathaus, sits in the middle of a twin-arched bridge over the river and is a most impressive sight, and old fishermen's cottages can be seen close by on the river bank. In Schillerplatz, you can see E.T.A. Hoffmann's House, dedicated to the poet, musician and caricaturist, author of The Tales of Hoffmann. Bamberg is also known as the home of several well-known breweries.

The scenery as you head south towards Nuremberg is craggy and forested, giving the area the name 'Fränkische Schweiz' (Franconian Switzerland).

Nuremberg (Nürnberg), Germany (Km 67.8–72)
Half-timbered houses, cobbled streets and Gothic churches with intricate spires and grand gateways are all part of the architectural heritage of Bavaria's second-largest city, as is the almost intact 5km (3-mile) city wall with its 80 defensive watchtowers. Most of the sights are contained within the walls and are easy to find on foot, although you'll need to take a taxi, public transport or the ship's shuttle service for the 15-minute drive from the suburban dock to the old town.

One of the best views of the city and surroundings can be had from the medieval Kaiserburg (Imperial Castle), an imperial residence for 500 years. The famed post-World War II trials of Nuremberg took place at the Palace of Justice.

Peter Henlein invented the world's first pocket watch in Nuremberg in 1510, and the world's first globe was also made here. You can see examples of

DID YOU KNOW...?

...that the Danube is the only major European waterway to flow from east to west?
...that the Romans called the Danube the Danuvius, from which its present name is derived?
...that the Greeks sailed up the Danube, in the 7th century? They got as far as the Iron Gates, where the rapids prevented them from further progress.
...that the Danube delta is a paradise for birdwatchers, with over 250 species including the last ibises and pelicans in Europe?
...that in 1989 an unprecedented 50,000 people assembled outside parliament in Budapest? They were part of the environmental movement protesting against plans for the construction of a hydro-electric dam on the River Danube.
...that in 1812, in Vienna, a vessel named Caroline became the first steam-driven vessel on the Danube? Its introduction was significant, and meant that, for the first time, vessels could move upstream under their own power. Prior to this date, all riverships moving upstream could only do so by being towed

– first by men, then by horses, then by locomotives; hence the term 'towpath'. Many towpaths still exist along both sides of the Danube, and today provide excellent pathways for cycling and walking.
...that the great wine route of the Wachau spans some 32km (20 miles) along the banks of the Danube, in Austria? The steep, terraced vineyards soak up the summer sun, yet the nights are cooler, making an ideal climate for a balanced wine, although the work of harvesting the grapes is a tortuous one. Many growers own small parcels of land – a hectare or two – and so making wines from the variety and quality of grapes provided is not an easy task for the region's wine makers.
...that in 2013, in Passau, the Danube reached its highest level in over 500 years? The flood marking can be seen on the town hall, by the river.
...that only about 30 percent of the Danube is truly free flowing?
...that sailing between Bamberg and Kelheim in Bavaria takes you over the Continental Divide?

The pretty town of Melk, Austria.

early watches on display at the German National Museum of Art and Culture (Germanisches Nationalmuseum), the largest museum of its kind in the German-speaking world. Another highlight is the Albrecht Dürer House (Albrecht-Dürer-Haus), with its multimedia show depicting the life of the German painter, printmaker, draughtsman and art theorist, generally regarded as the greatest German Renaissance artist.

In 1835, Germany's first railway line was opened between Nuremberg and Fürth. Today, the Transport Museum (DB Museum) houses many locomotives, wagons and railway accessories.

It's also worth visiting the Schöner Brunnen, a fountain on the Hauptmarkt. This towering, ornamented treasure was carefully covered during World War II to protect it from Allied bombing. A wrought-iron fence encloses it, and a bronze ring is looped around one part of the fence. Turning this ring three times is supposed to grant the turner's wish. Needless to say, there is usually a line of visitors waiting to be photographed doing just that.

Nuremberg gained notoriety during the 20th century, first as the site of the Nazi party rallies, but later when the famed post-World War II trials took place (from 20 November 1945 until 1 October 1946) at the Palace of Justice. Nuremberg was chosen because the Palace of Justice was spacious (it had 22,000 sq m/236,806 sq ft of space, with about 530 offices and about 80 courtrooms; war damage to it was minimal; and a large, undestroyed prison was part of the complex) following agreement between the four major powers at the time, although Russia had initially wanted the trials to be held in Berlin.

Aschaffenburg, Germany (Km 86–88)

Johannesburg Castle, set almost within touching distance right on the river bank, is simply stunning. It was the palatial residence of the archbishops of Mainz. Built of local red sandstone, it comprises four wings with corner towers and a central, square courtyard.

Miltenburg, Germany (Km 124–125)

Miltenburg is one of the best-preserved medieval towns on the River Main (its long main street, Hauptstrasse, runs parallel to the Main) and is characterised by beautifully preserved or restored half-timbered houses. The town centre features a fountain dating from 1583. Miltenburg castle, built by the archbishop of Mainz around 1200, predates the first documented mention of the town, in 1237. Somewhat more recently, the town gained notoriety when Elvis Presley stayed for one night.

Regensburg, Germany (Km 2381–2377)

Founded by Marcus Aurelius over 2,000 years ago, Regensburg is one of the best-preserved of all European medieval cities, having escaped the bombing of World War II, and is the oldest city on the entire length of the Danube; the first Roman camp here has been dated by historians to AD 70, and parts of the original Roman wall can still be seen. The city's 12th- to 14th-century Patricians' Houses are architecturally fascinating, and are reminiscent of the medieval tower-houses of San Gimignano in Tuscany. Riverships dock close to the centre, within walking distance of the main sights, and tours are usually a half-day, with free time afterwards.

Visit the Stone Bridge, built between 1135 and 1146 and, with 16 arches, a masterpiece of medieval engineering. The cathedral, regarded as the best example of Gothic architecture in Bavaria, has some superb stained-glass windows in its twin towers, which were added between 1859 and 1861 at the request of King Ludwig I of Bavaria, and a tranquil 15th-century cloister.

The heart of the city is Neupfarrplatz, which presents Regensburg's history in microcosm. Over the years it has been the home of Roman officers, the Jewish quarter, the marketplace, the scene of riots and protests, and of the mass burning of books by the Nazis. Between 1995 and 1998, massive excavations revealed Gothic and Romanesque synagogues, remains of the old Jewish houses and a treasure trove of gold coins.

Some 11km (7 miles) downstream from Regensburg, just outside Donaustauf, look out for a white classical temple with Doric columns on the hillside, approached by a grand staircase. This is Valhalla (Walhalla), home of the gods in German mythology – in this case, built by Ludwig I in the 1830s as a kind of Teutonic Hall of Fame, and a copy of the Parthenon in Athens.

Passau, Germany (Km 2210)

The starting point for many cruises on the Danube, Passau, located 290m (950ft) above sea level, marks the border between Germany and Austria. Ships dock right in the centre, although new berths for four riverships have been constructed at Landau, about 2km (1.25 miles) downriver from Passau, to ease the congestion that occurs at weekends, when many passengers embark and disembark.

Somewhat fancifully dubbed 'the Venice of the Danube' because of the three rivers that converge here (it is also sometimes called Dreiflüssestadt – the city of three rivers) and the Italianate style of the architecture, Passau has been a bishopric for 1,200 years. St Stephen's magnificent Baroque-style cathedral – considered to be the most important Baroque style church in Germany, with an especially fine ceiling – houses the world's largest cathedral organ; it has 17,774 pipes in three banks, and 233 registers, or stops. Liszt wrote his *Hungarian Coronation Mass* for this cathedral in 1857.

Passau's location as the confluence of the three rivers, the Danube, Ilz and Inn, means it often suffers from flooding. The tower of the town hall shows the high-water marks, the highest recorded being in 1501, 1595 and 1954.

Linz, Austria (Km 2139–2127)

Although the Renaissance and Baroque centre of the city, which is the provincial capital of Upper Austria, is attractive (Linz was designated a 'European Capital of Culture' in 2009), Linz is an industrial city, known for its chemical and metallurgical industries. The classic *Linzer Torte*, with a pastry base, redcurrant jam filling and crisscross pattern on the almond-encrusted top, was invented here by Bavarian baker Konrad Vogel in 1822. You can taste the real thing in one of the many street cafés in the beautifully preserved Old Town.

The cobblestoned main square is also the site of the Trinity Column – a 20m (66ft) -high white marble Baroque-style sculpture by Sebastian Stumpfegger to a design by Antonio Beduzzi; erected in 1723,

Regensburg's Cathedral Square.

it is dedicated to commemorate the dangers of war (1704), fire (1712) and the plague (1713).

Riverships dock next to the Lentos Art Museum – a magnificent glass structure housing a superb art collection.

Linz is also known for its connections with the composer Anton Bruckner, who was born at Ansfelden (now a suburb of Linz) in 1824, and died in 1896 in Vienna. Mozart also lived here for a while in 1783 as a guest of Count Thunn, during which time he composed his *Linz Symphony*. Alterdom, the magnificent baroque cathedral is where Anton Bruckner served as organist.

Melk, Austria (Km 2037.5–2037)

The mustard-yellow Benedictine Abbey of Melk, perched on a steep hill overlooking the river and visible from afar, is one of the highlights of a Danube cruise. It was founded in the year 1089 by Leopold II and dominates the town, though at the same time blending in beautifully with the surrounding landscape. It was completely reconstructed in Baroque style in the early 18th century by its architect, Jakob Prandtauer, who died before its completion. The imposing abbey was completed by Prandtauer's relation and assistant, Joseph Mungengast.

The imperial rooms of the abbey once accommodated such renowned figures as Emperor Charles VI and Maria Theresa, Pope Pius VI and Napoleon – all

CHRISTMAS MARKET CRUISES

There's nothing quite like a river cruise in Europe at *Christmas*, when the twinkling fairy lights and the seasonal aromas of cinnamon, gingerbread, roasting chestnuts and *Glühwein* (mulled wine) at Christmas markets in most cities and towns along the Danube, Rhine and Elbe really put you in the mood for the holiday. Many river cruise companies operate cruises to the Christmas markets of Europe.

Along the Danube, Vienna has a number of Christmas markets, and the window dressing of the stores along the wide Kärntnerstrasse is among the best in the world. The city's Christmas decorations are beautiful, too. Nuremberg hosts perhaps the most famous festive market of all. Located in the old walled section of the city, it is the oldest in Germany, dating back to the 17th century. Rows of specially constructed stalls provide the old-world setting and a magical atmosphere.

Along the Rhine, Cologne's magnificent Gothic cathedral provides an impressive backdrop to that city's Christmas market. Rüdesheim's Christkindlmarkt (Christmas market) is one of Germany's largest, with more than 100 stalls. Regensburg, often a starting or finishing point for several riverships, has its Christmas market in the town's delightful square.

presently immortalised in a permanent wax museum. Paul Troger frescoes can be found in the library, which houses over 2,000 manuscripts. A Gutenberg Bible, which was on display here for many years, has since been sold, and can now be viewed in the Yale Library in the US. The balconies command sweeping views of the Danube. A short organ concert is typically held for anyone on a shore excursion. The organ, built by Gregor Hradetzky (born in Krems), has three keyboards, 45 registers (stops) and 3,553 pipes.

Dürnstein, Austria (Km 2008)

Beyond Melk, the Danube carves its way through the beautiful, Unesco-protected Wachau Valley, a 30km (19-mile) section of steep, terraced slopes of vineyards and forested hills, which turn incredible shades of red and gold in the autumn. It is regarded by many as one of the most scenic stretches of the river. In its midst is Dürnstein, discernible from some distance away because of the jagged outline of the ruined castle on the hilltop, and the unusual Wedgwood blue-and-white Baroque monastery tower squatting like a giant pepperpot on the river bank.

A steep one-hour walk/climb from Dürnstein itself leads to the Babenberg Duke Leopold's Kuenringerburg Castle. Richard the Lionheart was incarcerated here for more than a year in the 12th century. He was released after paying an incredible 100,000 marks – truly a king's ransom in those days. There's not much of the castle to see nowadays, but the views along the Wachau Valley and over the town below are breathtaking.

Krems, Austria (Km 2003–2002)

This university town, together with its former sister town of Stein (both are located close to Dürnstein at the eastern end of the Wachau wine-growing district), grew wealthy as a result of trade in iron, grain, wine and salt. The town is an important example of successful restoration work and the centre has been a Unesco World Heritage Site since 2000. Krems was the home of the painter Martin Johann ('Kremser') Schmidt, who created numerous works in the churches of Austria.

One nearby attraction is the Stift Göttweig, an abbey set on a hillside. Its playful Benedictine architecture – its corner towers, onion domes and pastel-coloured facade – has earned it the title of 'Austria's Monte Casino', after the Italian abbey where the Benedictine Order was first established.

Vienna (Wien), Austria (Km 1933–1928)

Vienna, located 170m (558ft) above sea level (it used to flood regularly in the winter), is built in a very strategic location, at the junction of routes from both east to west and north to south.

For centuries, the city was the seat of the mighty Habsburg dynasty, and is also the birthplace of Schubert, and of much of the music of Mozart (he composed his greatest operas and symphonies here), Beethoven and Strauss. The city exudes romance at any time of year, with its beautiful parks and Baroque palaces, elegant shops and legendary coffee houses. Most cruises spend at least one night here, giving plenty of opportunity to see the sights, attend a performance at the opera, listen to the Vienna Boys' Choir or admire the white Lipizzaner horses at the Spanish Riding School.

The Danube does not pass through the centre of Vienna – instead it runs through the northeast part of the city. Most river cruise vessels stop at the Vienna Shipping Centre (Schiffahrtszentrum), about 3km (2 miles) from the old centre. The compact, historic centre is encircled by the Ringstrasse, inside which most of the main sights are located. The following is a list of the city's top attractions:

Stephansdom: St Stephen's Cathedral, with its distinctive roof, is one of Vienna's most famous landmarks and one of the greatest Gothic structures in Europe. The interior is rich in woodcarvings, altars and paintings. Climb the steps of the south tower for a breathtaking view of the city.

Museums Quarter: This is a giant cultural complex including the Museum of Modern Art (MUMOK) and the Leopold Museum, with its wonderful collection of 19th- and 20th-century art, including work by Egon Schiele, Gustav Klimt and Oskar Kokoschka. At the centre of the complex, the Kunsthalle holds temporary exhibitions.

Staatsoper: Vienna's magnificent opera house was constructed in the 1860s, and rebuilt in 1945 after suffering a direct hit in a bombing raid. It was inaugurated in 1869 with Mozart's *Don Giovanni*. The main facade is elaborately decorated with frescoes depicting *The Magic Flute*. Once a year the stage and orchestra stalls turn into a giant dance floor for the Vienna Opera Ball. If your rivership stays overnight in Vienna, you could

consider an evening out at the opera, although you may need to reserve well in advance for this.

Secession Building: The Secession Building was built as a 'temple of art' to plans by Joseph Maria Olbrich in 1897. Gustav Klimt designed the *Beethoven Frieze*, on display on the lower floor, a visual interpretation of Beethoven's *Ninth Symphony*. The cubic foyer is crowned by a dome of 3,000 gilt laurel leaves. Over the entrance is the motto 'To Each Time its Art, to Art its Freedom', a riposte from the Secession artists to the conservative Academy of Fine Arts.

Schloss Schönbrunn: A short distance from the inner city lies the Schönbrunn Palace, the imperial summer residence. Leopold I wished to build a palace to rival Versailles, but financial difficulties stalled his plans. It was not until 1743 that Empress Maria Theresa employed Nikolaus Pacassi to build the fabulous palace we see today. In the formal grounds are the Baroque zoo, the Palm House and the graceful Gloriette, a neoclassical colonnade perched on the crest of a hill.

Prater: The Prater, an open fairground and amusement park, is a favourite place of relaxation for the Viennese. Its main attraction is the Riesenrad, the giant Ferris wheel that was immortalised in the 1949 film *The Third Man*. This extensive stretch of parkland and woodland extends for almost 5km (3 miles).

Karlsplatz: Otto Wagner's two wonderfully elegant entrance pavilions for the Stadtbahn on Karlsplatz date from 1894 and are prime examples of Jugendstil (Austrian Art Nouveau). For the designs of the pavilions, he combined a green iron framework with marble slabs and gilded sunflower decoration, and pioneered a new form of architecture in which functionality and simplicity of ornament were the priority.

Vienna at night.

Bratislava's 16th-century castle with earlier fortifications.

Kunsthistorisches Museum: Several famous artists helped create the interior of the Kunsthistorisches Museum. A huge number of art treasures amassed by the Habsburgs are on display, including a fine collection of ancient Egyptian and Greek Art, and works by many of the great European masters.

Belvedere: The Belvedere, a palace of sumptuous proportions, was built between 1714 and 1723 for Prince Eugene of Savoy. It is in fact two palaces, the Upper and Lower Belvedere, joined by terraced gardens. Today it houses three museums containing works of Austrian and European art and sculpture.

Hofburg: The Hofburg was the winter residence of the ruling Habsburgs. Within the confines of this vast and impressive imperial palace are the Spanish Riding School and the sleek Lipizzaner horses, and the Burgkapelle, where the Vienna Boys' Choir sing Sunday Mass. Notable collections housed here are the Collection of Court Porcelain and Silver and the Imperial Treasury, containing crown jewels and ecclesiastical treasures. The palatial National Library, also in the complex, contains more than 2 million manuscripts, printed books, maps and musical scores.

Bratislava, Slovakia (Km 1869)

Located right at the heart of central Europe close to Slovakia's borders with Austria and Hungary, Bratislava has changed its identity, and its name, more times than it cares to remember. In Habsburg times, the city was Pressburg to the Germans and Pozsony to the Magyars. Renamed Bratislava after the creation of Czechoslovakia following World War I, it emerged from the communist years to become capital of the new state of Slovakia in 1993. An ambitious rebuilding and restoration programme has transformed the city. The picturesque old town is clustered around a low hill on the left bank of a broad stretch of the river. The Danube is wide here – about 300m (984ft) across.

Highlights include the castle, built in the 16th century on top of earlier fortifications (it was destroyed by fire in 1811 and painstakingly restored, although not until the 1960s), the picturesque Old Town with fabulous Baroque palaces, St Martin's Cathedral, with an unusual spire topped by a tiny Hungarian crown, St Michael's Gate, the city's only surviving medieval gateway, and Pálffyho Palace, where, in 1762, the six-year old Wolfgang Amadeus Mozart gave a performance. This distinguished building now houses the Academy of Fine Arts.

Esztergom, Hungary (Km 1718.5)

Formerly the Roman settlement of Gran, Esztergom is located in the foothills of the Pilis Mountains, right on the border with Slovakia. Esztergom is famous for its vast, neoclassical cathedral, flanked by a red-brick castle, which towers over the city. The giant dome is one of the world's largest and can be seen for miles around. The castle itself was the seat of government for Hungary's kings and queens for more than 300 years when the Hungarian lands further south were held by the Ottoman Turks, while the town was the centre of the Catholic Church in Hungary, which flourished during the reign of Louis I (1342–82), a role it retains today. The Gothic-style cathedral was built in the 19th century to replace its

predecessor, ransacked by the Turks in 1543 after they pushed northwards, although the red-marble Bakócz Chapel inside survived. Both Beethoven and Liszt performed here.

Vac, Hungary (Km 1680)

The site of a Roman fortress in the 9th century, Vac was rebuilt and destroyed many times, until shipping traffic flourished and the town recovered from its destructive past.

Budapest, Hungary (Km 1647)

Budapest is the perfect destination for river cruises, because the Danube flows right through the heart of the city for some 10km (6 miles), with Buda (and Obuda) on the west bank and Pest on the east bank connected by eight bridges.

Often referred to by the local inhabitants as the 'Pearl of the Danube', Budapest goes beyond the attractions of its fabulous, romantic setting. It is the cultural heart of the nation and a city of international standing that still possesses some of its late 19th-century flair and romance. Nostalgia can be found in the sumptuous spas offering the simple pleasure of bathing in thermal waters, and in the grand old coffee houses.

Riverships dock in a superbly convenient (and also picturesque) location. If your one leaves at night, you'll see the city's historic buildings in all their illuminated splendour – a real treat, especially if you stand outside on deck with a glass of Champagne in hand.

Budapest also marks the starting point for the second half of river cruises (typically of 14 days or more) that travel all the way to the Danube Delta at the Black Sea.

City highlights include the following:

Parliament Building: Strongly reminiscent of the Palace of Westminster in London, the Parliament Building (Országház) is one of Budapest's most famous sights. The neo-Gothic pile, which was completed in 1902, extends along the Danube for some 268m (879ft).

Chain Bridge: When it was completed in 1849, the Chain Bridge (Széchenyi Lánchíd) linked the two halves of the city, Buda and Pest, for the first time (there are now eight Danube bridges in the Hungarian capital, as well as more on the outskirts). Count István Széchenyi, the 19th-century reformer and innovator, brought in engineers from Great Britain to construct the graceful span, which is beautifully floodlit at night.

Gellért Hill: Rising steeply from the Buda riverfront, the craggy, wooded heights of Gellért Hill (Gellért-hegy) can be seen from almost anywhere in the city (not least from where the riverships dock). Naturally, the views are tremendous, extending as far as the distant Matra mountains on the Slovak border on a clear day.

Heroes' Square: At the end of Andrássy út, one of Pest's major thoroughfares, is the wide open space of Heroes' Square (Hősök tere), with its 36m (118ft) Millennium Monument, erected in 1896 to mark 1,000 years of the Magyar state. The square is flanked by the Palace of Art and Museum of Fine Arts and behind the former is the world's largest hourglass, the Timewheel, unveiled in May 2004 to mark Hungary's admission into the European Union. Some 8m (26ft) in diameter, the structure 'turns' once a year to send the sand running anew.

Váci utca: Long, narrow and pedestrianised for much of its length, Váci utca (pronounced vah-tsee ooh-tsa) is a busy and fashionable shopping street, which also has a range of bars, cafés and restaurants. At its northern end is the square of Vörösmarty tér. At No. 7 is one of the city's main meeting places and home to Gerbeaud, doyen of the city's prosperous café society since 1884 and a major tourist attraction in itself.

Museum of Fine Arts: Hungary's pre-eminent art gallery, the Museum of Fine Arts (Szépművészeti Múzeum) has a huge collection, focusing on European art from 1300–1800. Highlights include works by the Spanish school including El Greco, Goya and Velázquez.

Budapest's Chain Bridge and Parliament Building.

VIENNESE COFFEE HOUSES

The Viennese coffee-house tradition is deeply rooted in the country's culture and history, dating back over 300 years. Gentry and intellectuals mingled in the shady and fashionable *Kaffeehaus*. People take their coffee seriously here, and there are names for every shade, from black to white. More than 30 different coffee types are served as part of the Viennese coffee culture, often with the addition of alcohol or whipped cream, though always with an obligatory glass of water. Here are some of the most popular types found in the huge number of Viennese coffee houses – often run by families and handed down through generations.

Einspanner: Black coffee served in a glass with whipped cream (Schlagobers)

Fiaker: Black coffee in a glass, with a tot of rum (good in the winter months)

Franziskaner: Coffee mixed with chocolate chips

Großer/kleiner Brauner: Large/small cup of black coffee with just a splash of milk

Großer/kleiner Schwartzer: Large/small cup of black coffee

Kaffee Verkehrt: Coffee, but with rather more milk than coffee

Kaisermelange: Coffee with egg yolk and alcohol

Kapuziner: Black coffee with a small blob of whipped cream. (Note that it is not a cappuccino.)

Turkisher Kaffee: Strong coffee that is prepared in a small copper coffee pot. It is served hot in very small cups.

Verlängerter Schwartzer: Schwartzer/Brauner coffee, diluted with water

Matthias Church: The focal point of the old town of Buda, high above the river, the Matthias Church (Mátyás-templom) is named after Hungary's most popular medieval king, Mátyás Corvinus Hunyadi (1458–90). The Habsburg emperor Franz Josef I was crowned king of Hungary here in 1867. The unusual geometric patterns on the roof, the stained-glass windows and other details date from the 19th century, but parts of the building are far older. Outside the church in Trinity Square (Szentháromság tér) is the mighty equestrian statue of St Stephen.

Fisherman's Bastion: Overlooking the Danube and just in front of the Matthias Church, the fairy-tale spires and turrets of the Fisherman's Bastion (Halász-bástya) afford the classic view of Budapest. Built onto the castle walls in the early 20th century purely for ornamental reasons, the monument's name is a reference to the fishermen who heroically defended the ramparts here against invaders in the 18th century.

Hungarian National Museum: The large Hungarian National Museum (Magyar Nemzeti Múzeum) is the most important museum in the city. St Stephen's Crown, the symbol of Hungarian sovereignty, was returned here in 1978, having been stolen by the Wehrmacht in World War II. Inside, amid monumental architectural and ornamental details, the whole story of Hungary unfolds – from prehistory right up to the 21st century. On display are prehistoric remains, ancient jewellery and tools, Roman mosaics, a 17th-century Turkish tent fitted out with grand carpets, and a Baroque library. There are some notable royal regalia, although the crown, orb, sceptre and sword have been moved to the Parliament Building.

Lower Danube

Central Market Hall: A good place for souvenirs is the upstairs section of the cavernous Central Market Hall (Nagy Vásárcsarnok) at the Pest end of Freedom Bridge.

Gellért Baths: At the southern edge of Gellért-hegy, the Gellért Baths (Gellért gyógyfürdő) comprise medicinal baths as well as regular swimming pools, all decorated in opulent Art Nouveau style. The unisex indoor pool has a vaulted glass ceiling and Roman-style carved columns, while the thermal baths feature marble statues, fine mosaics and glazed tiles.

Kalocsa, Hungary (Km 1515.4)

Kalocsa is a pretty town in the middle of the Puszta region, located on a terrace overlooking the Danube, 10km (6 miles) from the river itself (passengers are taken by coach) and famous for growing the paprika that gives Hungarian goulash its distinctive flavour. It's an important agricultural and tourism centre, surrounded by pepper fields, and the shops are packed with paprika souvenirs, from painted eggs to colourful pottery and embroidered linen.

Some 1,000 years ago, Kalocsa was the seat of the archdiocese, and the Archbishop's Palace, whose permanent exhibition of ecclesiastical relics and treasure is open to the public. The House of Folk Art Museum and the Károly Viski Museum feature the colourful local painting for which the region is famous, while for something different, the world's only Paprika Museum documents the history of paprika production in Hungary, from growing to different pepper types and the processing technique.

Vukovar, Croatia (Km 1333)

The former Baroque city of Vukovar – Croatia's largest river port – is located on a picturesque bend in the Danube at the confluence of the Danube and Vuka rivers in the country's eastern section. The city was fiercely defended during the 87-day siege in 1991 – known as the 'Battle of Vukovar' – and a white cross on the river bank commemorates the many lives lost in the war. Unfortunately, much of the city was destroyed, and many buildings have still not been repaired or rebuilt.

Novi Sad, Serbia (Km 1255)

Originally called Neoplanta (Latin), Serbia's second-largest city was renamed Novi Sad by the Serbs. It is very international in character and much loved by artists and writers. Albert Einstein first met his wife here. The city's centre's wide pedestrianised streets are full of cafes and casual eateries. If you like food shopping, it's worth visiting the outdoor market stalls, close to the river.

Built on a large rock outcrop (often referred to as the Danube's Gibraltar) on the opposite bank of the river stands the Petrovaradin Fortress (it is now a hotel). After the fortress became Austrian in 1699, Prince Eugen commissioned a French architect to make it 'invincible'. It was further fortified by Empress Maria Theresa. Marshall Tito was imprisoned there between 1921 and 1928.

Belgrade (Beograd), Serbia (Km 1170)

Belgrade, capital of Serbia (and of the former Yugoslavia), is strategically located on the southern edge of the great Carpathian Basin, at the confluence of the River Danube and River Sava, and has a turbulent history. It is one of the oldest cities in Europe and nowadays forms the largest urban area in southeastern Europe after Athens. The ravages of communism and damage from the war in 1999 are still visible (the city has been destroyed and rebuilt over 20 times over the centuries), and it is noticeably less colourful (and wealthy) than Budapest, but vibrant nonetheless, with a busy, pedestrianised centre.

Iron Gates Gorge (Km 949.7)

The Iron Gates (Porţile de Fier) are a highlight of any itinerary on the eastern section of the Danube. The river cuts through the southern spur of the Carpathian Mountains where they meet the northern foothills of the Balkan ranges, forming an emphatic natural boundary between Serbia and Romania. The 'true' Iron Gates are in fact a single narrow gorge, which boats enter at Km 949, but the name is generally given to the entire stretch of river between Km 1,059 and Km 942 – a series of gorges linked by wider stretches of river. There are towering cliffs on either side, although these are less impressive than they were before the river level was raised in the 1970s. Parts of the river bed here are among the world's deepest, with depths up to 60m (197ft).

At the eastern end of the Iron Gates, at Km 942, is the enormous Djerdap hydro-electric power station complex. There are actually two power stations (one belonging to Serbia and the other belonging to Romania), two double-level locks, and a barrage supporting a railway and road bridge. The whole project involved much re-siting of infrastructure, the reconstruction of 13 river harbours and the relocation of many inhabitants (8,400 within Serbia and 14,500 within Romania) at the time of its construction, which, when completed in 1972, had cost an estimated $500 million. The dam raised the Danube's water level by some 33m (100ft), and removed the treacherous currents and whirlpools at a stroke. On the negative side, the higher water has hugely diminished the grandeur of the landscape, obliterated a number of historic towns and villages (notably the Turkish island enclave of Ada Kaleh, a short distance down-

MUSIC

Music is inextricably linked to the River Danube. Johann Strauss and Franz Schubert were born in Vienna. Brahms, Beethoven, Haydn, Mahler and Mozart were all inspired by this culturally rich city. Vienna's huge *Zentralfriedhof* (cemetery) has a Musicians' Corner, where Beethoven, Brahms, Gluck, Schubert, Strauss (The Younger), Strauss (The Elder), Franz von Suppé, Arnold Schoenberg and Antonio Salieri are buried. The following composers all have connections with this area:

Béla Bartók was born on 25 March 1881 in Nagyszentmiklós, Hungary. He died on 26 September 1945 in New York, US.

Ludwig van Beethoven was baptised on 17 December 1770 in Bonn, Germany. He died in Vienna on 17 July 1787.

Alban Berg was born on 9 February 1885 in Vienna, Austria. He died on 24 December 1935 in Vienna.

Johannes Brahms was born on 7 May 1833 in Hamburg, Germany. He died on April 3, 1879 in Vienna

Josef Anton Bruckner was born on 4 September 1824 in Ansfelden, Austria. He died on 11 October 1896 in Vienna.

Franz Josef Haydn was born on 31 March 1732 in Rohrau, Lower Austria. He died on 31 May 1809 in Vienna. The Haydn Museum, located at Haydengasse 19 is open to the public and highlights the places that were important in the composer's life. This is the house where he composed *The Creation* (1796–8) and *The Seasons* (1799–1801).

Zoltán Kodály was born on 16 December 1882 in Kecskemét, Hungary. He died on 6 March 1967 in Budapest, Hungary

Franz Liszt was born on 22 October 1811 in Raiding, Hungary. He died on 31 July 1886 in Bayreuth (Germany). Budapest is where you'll find many of his pianos, in the Liszt Museum (Vörösmarty u. 35).

Wolfgang Amadeus Mozart was born on 27 January 1756 in Salzburg, Austria. He died on 5 December 1791 in Vienna.

Antonio Salieri was born on 18 August 1850 in Legnago, Italy. He died on 7 May 1825 in Vienna.

Arnold Franz Walter Schoenberg was born on 13 September 1874 in Vienna. He died on July 13, 1951 in Los Angeles, US.

Franz Peter Schubert was born on 31 January 1797 in Vienna. He died on 19 November 1828 in Vienna. The house where he was born and where he spent the first four years of his life has been restored and now has a museum on the first floor.

Johann Strauss ('The Younger'), composer of *The Blue Danube* waltz, was born on 25 October 1825 in Vienna. He died on 3 June 1899 in Vienna.

Johann Strauss ('The Elder') was born on 14 March 1804 in Vienna. He died on 24 September 1849 in Vienna.

Richard Georg Strauss was born on 11 June 1864 in Munich, Germany. He died on 8 September 1949 in Garmisch-Partenkirchen, Austria.

The Iron Gates Gorge.

Nicolae Ceaușescu's truly monumental Parliament Palace, the world's second-largest administrative building (after the Pentagon), may be included on your excursion itinerary. Just a handful of the 3,000 rooms can be visited. You will probably also see Revolution (formerly Royal Palace) Square, where the famous riots started that led to the collapse of the communist dictatorship in December 1989.

Rousse (Ruse), Bulgaria (Km 495)

Rousse is the largest and most important river port in Bulgaria, set in gorgeous, rolling countryside brilliant with sunflowers in summer and golden wheatfields in autumn. The city itself was once the garrison of the Roman Danube fleets and was known as Sexaginta Prista – 'Sixty Ships'. Today, it's an industrial centre, and across the river you can see the grim-looking factories of Giurgiu in Romania.

Most of the attractions are outside the centre. A short drive away is the Rusenski Lom National Park, where a tributary of the Danube has carved a sheer-sided gorge through the uplifted limestone. Tours include a visit to the imposing Basarbovo Monastery, sprawling across a steep hilltop.

Giurgiu, Romania (Km 493)

Capital of Giurgiu County, southern Romania, the city is located about 65km (40 miles) south of Bucharest. Romanian crude oil is loaded here for shipping, via a pipeline that connects it with the oil fields of Ploesti. A bi-level, combined highway and railway bridge, the 2,224m (7,297ft) -long Friendship Bridge (Km 489), one of the longest bridges in Europe, which connects Romania with Bulgaria, was opened in 1954.

Cernavoda, Romania (Km 483)

Almost on the Black Sea, this is the starting point of the Danube-Black Sea Canal, which was completed in 1984. It is about 64km (40 miles) long and 80m (262ft) wide, and passes through the vineyards of Murfatlar, the best-known wine-growing area of Romania. The town's railway bridge, built in 1895, is stunning. It has 68 arches and rises up to 40m (131ft) above the surface of the water. When built it was one of the most modern and largest bridge installations in the world.

Oltenița, Romania (Km 430)

This little town is home to a building yard for riverships. In former times, however, it was a quarantine station.

The Chilia Arm

The most northerly of the three branches of the Danube, the Chilia also transports more water than the other two. Approximately 120km (75 miles) long and as much as 990m (3,250ft) wide for most of its course it marks the border between Romania (right bank) and Ukraine (left bank). For the last 17.5km (11 miles) before reaching its Black Sea confluence, it flows exclusively through Ukraine.

stream from Orșova), and the river's diminished flow is no longer sufficient to flush pollution – chemical toxins and other waste – downriver and out to sea.

The first gorge is the Golubac, 14km (9 miles) in length. The town of Golubac was flooded by the power-station project, but nine massive towers – the ruins of a castle that was, for more than two and a half centuries, a base for the Turks for their raids to the north and west until they left in 1688 – can still be seen on the Serbian side. After a broader section, the second gorge – the Gospodin Vir – extends for a further 15km (9 miles). Beyond is the famous Kazan gorge, 19km (12 miles) long, where the river flows between towering cliffs soaring 700m (2,300ft) through a chasm only 150m (492ft) across.

Vidin, Bulgaria (Km 790)

Vidin, on the Bulgarian side of the river, occupies the site of an old Celtic settlement and is one of the country's oldest towns, dating back to Roman times. The dramatic fortress of Baba Vida, built in the 14th century and formerly surrounded by a moat, is the best-preserved example of medieval architecture in the country and looms impressively on the bank of the Danube as you approach. In fact, the whole town used to be famous for its fairy-tale minarets, towers and domes, although its skyline suffered from the building of ugly concrete apartment blocks during the communist era. Most tours combine Baba Vida with a visit to the amazing village of Belogradchik, cut directly into sandstone rock.

Bucharest (București), Romania

There is no kilometre marking for Bucharest, the capital of Romania, but that's because the city is actually located somewhat inland from the river (about a one-hour coach journey from Rousse). A visit to

Izmail, Ukraine (Km 80)

This port city was designed and built from scratch during the Soviet era. Its highlight is the sumptuously decorated cathedral.

Kilija, Ukraine (Km 40)

Ukraine is on the left bank, and Chilia-Veche (formerly Chilia, in the province of Odessa Oblast), Romania, is on the right bank. Chilia is thought to be one of the oldest settlements on the Danube, and, at earlier times, was only about 5km (3 miles) from the Black Sea. Today, the river must run about 40km (25 miles) to reach the sea.

Vilkovo, Ukraine (Km 15.5)

Located on the left bank, this fishing village has quite a number of houses built on stilts. With its many canals and small islands, it is often referred to as the 'Venice of the East'. The residents are fiercely religious, and its two churches (the Nikolaevskaya Church of the Orthodox, and the Nikolaevsakaya Church of the Old Believers) are lavished with care and attention. Along the shoreline, the houses have beautifully attended, colourful gardens.

The Sulina Arm

The shortest of the three branches of the Danube, the Sulina (often called the Sulina Canal) is the most important for commercial shipping. The depth of the arm is maintained to enable commercial ships to reach Tulcea (and its shipyards) on the Black Sea.

Sulina, Romania

Formerly named Porto Franco, Sulina was the headquarters of the Danube Commission during the 19th century. No longer an important seaport, today it is a minor town, seemingly abandoned by the modern world.

The Sfantu-Gheorghe Arm

This 104.5km (65-mile) -long arm forks off to the south just a few kilometres east of Tulcea, but it is not traversed by Danube passenger riverships.

Constanța, Romania (Km 0)

The official end of the River Danube, this port city, whose original name was Tomis, of Jason and the Argonauts fame, is the capital of southeastern Romania, and located about 200km (125 miles) east of Bucharest. Reached via the 64km (40-mile) -long Danube–Black Sea Canal, which starts in Cernavoda, it is the country's principal seaport and its most important commercial centre, which is slowly being modernised. At journey's end in Constanța, riverships tie up at the Gare Maritime in the heart of the city.

THE DANUBE-KOSOVO CONNECTION

Since 1992, the 10 countries connected to the Danube had built up trade in shipping goods from the Black Sea to the North Sea. However, the Kosovo war in 1999 had devastating effects. Several bridges, including the three principal ones in Novi Sad, the capital of Vojvodina in northern Serbia, were blown up by NATO. The network of pipes to carry purified water from the west bank to homes on the opposite side of the river was also destroyed. Mines were also laid in the riverbed.

River cargo vessels, tugs ('pusher' vessels) and barges were trapped on either side of Serbia. Under the rules governing the Danube Shipping Convention, companies with riverships, tugs and barges can trade only with another country belonging to the convention. About 10 percent of the 700 or so regular trade vessels on the Danube were put out of work by the war, and many maritime employees were laid off.

Economically, ports along the river lost about $1 million per day in revenue and shipping. Bulgaria and Hungary probably suffered most from the effects of the war, which had nothing to do with them. Much of the agricultural and mineral exports had to go by road and rail, adding to shipment costs and time, and this made some products uncompetitive.

The Kosovo War also affected several river cruise operators, who were forced to cancel all voyages scheduled to start downriver (the Danube flows east to west) in Passau or other cities, to cross the region of conflict and end up at Black Sea ports.

After the war, a temporary pontoon (built in September 1999) was placed across the river, using disused barges. It prevented the use of the river as a through traffic point, reportedly done deliberately in order to obtain UN funding to rebuild the three bridges, although sanctions against the Milosevic regime also provided reasons for the delay.

In August 2001, the Danube Convention officially declared the river open again for through traffic – once each week, following the removal of bridge debris, mines and other ordnance, and the rebuilding of the three principal bridges. The three principal bridges are: Sloboda Bridge, opened in 1981 for road traffic; Zezeli Bridge (formerly called Marshall Tito Bridge), completed in 1961 for pedestrians and light traffic; and the Petrovaradin Bridge, built in 1946 for railway traffic). Three replacement bridges have been constructed and opened (one is a permanent structure).

The Rhine and its tributaries

The Rhine (Rhein) is a magnificent river for cruising, with its vineyard-clad slopes and romantic castles. The Mosel, Neckar, Main and Saar tributaries hold plenty of interest too.

'Old Father Rhine', as the Germans lovingly call it, is Europe's most important commercial waterway, flowing for some 1,320km (820 miles) from source to estuary. The Rhine has long been Europe's busiest river, with some of the densest shipping traffic in the world, yet its waters and turbulent past have inspired poets and romantics for centuries. The mystery of the river comes alive in the folklore tales of Lorelei and the Nibelung, the music of Wagner and Beethoven, and in the countless legends surrounding the fairy-tale castles and fortresses that line its banks.

Although it is essentially seen as a German river, the Rhine crosses several international boundaries, passing through no fewer than six countries – Austria, France, Germany, Liechtenstein, the Netherlands and Switzerland – on its journey from the Alps to the North Sea. Although the stretch known as the Middle Rhine, or the Romantic Rhine, with its towering cliffs, castles, vineyards and dense forests, is the best-known section, the river has many other faces as it flows along the German–French border, or cuts a course across the flat, agricultural landscapes of the Netherlands in the final stages of its journey north. The most scenic section is the 65km (40-mile)-long gorge between Bingen and Koblenz, which is almost always part of a Rhine river cruise.

Together with the Bodensee (Lake Constance), the Rhine forms a reservoir of drinking water for approximately 30 million Germans. It irrigates kilometre upon kilometre of vineyards. It has been an essential transport route through Europe since prehistoric times and has given rise to a string of prosperous towns and cities along its banks. A cruise on the Rhine is rarely without something to draw the eye. Heavily laden barges chug their way north or south, pleasure cruisers ply the waters from one beauty spot to the next, and hikers, swimmers and cyclists enjoy the river's banks and beaches. In parts, there is abundant birdlife to spot, spectacular castles to identify and bridges, statues and monuments all charting the river's history.

THE COURSE OF THE RHINE

The source of the Rhine is a mountain brook that trickles out from the craggy Gotthard Massif in southeastern Switzerland. This is where two small streams, the Hinterrhein and Vorderrhein, unite to form the Alpine Rhine (Alpenrhein). The waters then flow along the borders of Liechtenstein and Austria and into the beautiful sweep of Lake Constance, emerging from the other side of the lake to tumble over the Rhine Falls, Europe's biggest waterfall, near Schaffhausen in Switzerland, where the river plunges 21m (69ft). The river is joined here by the Aar, doubling its volume.

The next stretch, known as the High Rhine (Hochrhein), forms the Swiss–German frontier. At Basel, the river executes a sharp right turn, the 'Rhine Knee', to head northwards, cutting a course through a broad valley along the French–German border. Close to the city of Karlsruhe, the French border is left behind, and the river enters its German heartland. After holding a northerly course for some distance, it twists to the west between Mainz and Bingen, an area known as the Rheingau, before forcing its way through the Binger Loch (Hole of Bingen), a steep gorge that marks the beginning of the Middle Rhine (Mittelrhein), or Romantic Rhine. The river then flows northwest through the Uplands (Rheinisches Schiefergebirge) along its most scenic stretch with steep vine-clad slopes, deep gorges and dramatic castles towering over the water.

On the Rhine at Cologne.

Below Bonn the river becomes the Lower Rhine (Niederrhein). It then travels through the flat territory of Germany's heavily industrialised Westphalia and the neighbouring Netherlands, where it divides into a number of delta arms, the principal ones being the Lek and the Waal, before finally disgorging into the North Sea.

The Rhine is fed by a number of tributaries, the most important being major rivers in their own right, such as the Main and the Mosel. River cruises operate on both of these, usually in conjunction with the Middle Rhine, and also on the pretty Neckar, which flows through one of Germany's biggest tourist attractions, the city of Heidelberg.

CASTLES ON THE RHINE

The Rhine is home to the highest density of castles in Europe. Most date from the Middle Ages or earlier, and legends, deeds of chivalry, internment and torture of every kind are connected with almost every one of them. Many were built by the feudal lords to protect their land; others were built to take advantage of the views of the traffic on the Rhine and later became toll-collection points. Between Mainz and Bonn, especially in the narrow slate gorge between Bingen and Koblenz, a distance of only 56km (35 miles), there are more castles than in any other river valley in the world.

The following castles can all be clearly seen from a rivership as it motors quietly along the Rhine. Many are in excellent condition and have been converted into hotels, although some have fallen into ruin.

Bonn to Koblenz

Km 647.6 (right): Godesburg Castle
Km 645.3 (left): Königswinter Castle
Km 643.7 (left): Drachenburg Castle and Drachenfels Castle (ruin)
Km 640 (right): Rolandseck Castle (ruin)
Km 623.9 (left): Arenfels Castle (now a hotel)
Km 621.9 (right): Rheineck Castle (now a hotel)
Km 618 (left): Hammerstein Castle (ruin)
Km 592.3 (left): Ehrenbreitstein Castle (now a youth hostel)

Koblenz to Bingen

Km 585.2 (left): Lahneck Castle
Km 585.2 (right): Stolzenfels Castle (now a hotel)
Km 580 (left): Marksburg Castle
Km 566.5 (right): Sterrenberg Castle and Liebenstein Castle
Km 556.9 (right): Rheinfels Castle
Km 555.9 (left): Katz Castle (now a hotel)
Km 549.1 (right): Schönburg Castle
Km 546.5 (left): Gutenfels Castle
Km 543.1 (right): Stahleck Castle (with a water-filled moat and inner wall)
Km 541 (right): Fürstenberg Castle (ruin)
Km 539.8 (left): Nollig Castle (ruin)

Rheinstein Castle.

DID YOU KNOW...?

...that the name 'Rhine' comes from the Celtic word *renos*, meaning 'raging flow'?

...that there are more castles in the Rhine Valley than in any other valley in the world?

...that the Middle Rhine Valley (an 80km/50 mile stretch) became a Unesco World Heritage site in 1992?

...that since 1855 there has been a signal-box for river shipping at the top of the Mice Tower (Mäuseturm) near Schloss Ehrenfels (Ehrenfels Castle) on the Rhine, just downstream from Rüdesheim?

...that the composer Schumann (1810–56) attempted to drown himself in the Rhine in 1854? He lived in Düsseldorf for four years and was appointed conductor of the municipal orchestra in 1850.

...that the Roman Emperor Caracalla used to go to the spa at Baden-Baden to cure his rheumatism?

...that salmon once thrived in the Rhine? Sadly, dams and industrial pollution have all but killed the salmon population here. In 2001, despite €20 million having been spent on breeding wild salmon, only 60 fish were detected in the river; some €50 billion was spent in cleaning up the polluted river. Compare this with the more than 250,000 wild salmon recorded caught on the Rhine in 1885, and you can see why wild salmon (so much better tasting than the farmed variety) is now a rarity.

...that the first stone bridge across the Mosel was built in 1363 for pilgrims on their way to Rome?

...that in Switzerland, 25 percent of all freight arrives by water?

...that the German for 'lock', as in watergate, is *die Schleuse*?

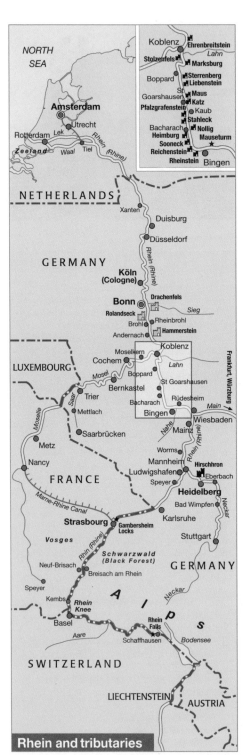

Rhein and tributaries

Km 539.4 (right): Heimburg Castle
Km 537.4 (right): Sooneck Castle
Km 534.4 (right): Reichenstein Castle (in use today
as a hotel)
Km 533 (right): Rheinstein Castle
Km 530.4 (left): Ehrenfels Castle (ruin)

Principal tributaries

The Main: Some 524km (325 miles) long, the Main
starts at Kulmbach from the confluence of the brooks
known as the White and Red Main, which have their
sources in the Fichtel Mountains and in the Franconian Alb. The riverships typically cruise on the section
between Frankfurt and Würzburg, passing forested
hills, lush meadows and historic towns.

The Mosel (Moselle, in English): At 535km (332
miles) long, the Mosel is the longest of the Rhine's
tributaries. It is narrower and, some say, prettier or
more intimate than the Rhine. It rises in the Vosges
Mountains at some 735m (2,410ft) above sea level.
Mosel means 'little Maas' in French, a reference to
the fact that, in prehistoric times, its bed joined that
of the Maas. The river was only developed into a navigable waterway as recently as 1964, an event made
possible by the signing of a contract between France,
Germany and Luxembourg, following which a system
of 14 locks was constructed.

The Mosel twists and turns in a series of sharp
bends as it cuts its way through a deep valley, the
sides lined with steeply terraced vineyards, before
merging with the Rhine at Koblenz, at an altitude
some 676m (2,218ft) lower than its source. On its
journey it forms the border between Luxembourg
and Germany for a distance of 36km (22 miles). The
Mosel is navigable from Thionville in France to Koblenz, a distance of 270km (165 miles).

The Neckar: This is one of the longest tributaries to
flow into the Rhine. Its source is in the Baar in a region between the Black Forest and the Swabian Alb
(the region in which the Danube also has its source),
to the east of the Rhine in Baden-Württemberg, north
of Lake Constance. The river is 367km (228 miles)
long and navigable for 203km (126 miles), although
some stretches have canals that enable cargo vessels to make their way through the 26 sets of locks
as far upstream as Plochingen.

The Neckar flows through some of Germany's
most beautiful countryside, castles guarding every
curve of the river, and vines and forests sloping
right down to the banks. The whole valley is one of
Germany's great summer playgrounds, with pleasure boats, canoes, punts and dinghies out on the
water, and cyclists and hikers enjoying the scene
from the banks.

After a journey of 367km (228 miles) past great
towns and cities including Stuttgart and Heidelberg,
the river cuts briefly across the flatter, more industrialised Rhine plain and disgorges its contents into
the major river at the city of Mannheim.

The Saar: Another of the Rhine's longest tributaries, the Saar flows through France and Saarland on its way from the Vosges mountain range to the Mosel. Some 246km (153 miles) long, it is navigable from Dillingen to the confluence in Konz. It was integrated in 1989 into the European waterways network with additional locks and canals. One of these canals cuts off a magnificent horseshoe-shaped loop of the river near Mettlach. The hill (called Cloef) adjacent to the river provides an excellent vantage point for photographs of this spectacular bend.

Amsterdam, The Netherlands (Km 0)

At the start of the Rhine Canal is cosmopolitan, easy-going Amsterdam. The city lies near the sea on the narrow land strips between Lake IJssel and the North Sea. The River Amstel runs through the centre of the city, which consists of a horseshoe-shaped network of over 100km (62 miles) of man-made canals that connect about 90 islands and 400 stone bridges. Whether you arrive by air, or by train, the riverships berth close to the central railway station, along the Oosterdokskade or Ruijterkade Oost (ocean-going cruise ships sail from a different terminal in Oostelijke Handelskade).

The city is one of Europe's most enjoyable destinations, unique in many ways – not least for its balance of past and present. Perhaps no community has ever had such a glorious explosion of wealth and culture as Amsterdam during the 17th century, the city's Golden Age, yet this is a place that has always looked

forward rather than back. The modern city is exuberant, with a tremendous range of cultural life from world-class art galleries to wacky street theatre.

Here are its highlights:

Canal ring: Amsterdam's horseshoe-shaped network of canals is the city's most distinctive feature and a must-see for visitors – lined with tall, elegant mansions from the 17th and 18th centuries. The canal ring (Grachtengordel) encompassing the three parallel waterways of Herengracht, Keizersgracht and Prinsengracht is the most scenic stretch.

Maritime Museum: This excellent museum (Het Scheepvaartmuseum) documents and celebrates Amsterdam's illustrious maritime history.

Rijksmuseum: Home to arguably the greatest collection of Dutch art in the world, the Rijksmuseum is housed within a magnificent Victorian Gothic building that has recently undergone a vast renovation programme.

The collection is varied, but most visitors come to see the works of the Dutch masters from the 15th to the 17th centuries. Highlights include the world's largest collection of works by Rembrandt, spanning his whole career and including *The Night Watch*. Johannes Vermeer is well represented, as is Frans Hals, the founding artist of the Dutch School, along with a collection of Dutch artists who were influenced or schooled by the masters. The museum also has a collection of work by non-Dutch artists, including Rubens, Tintoretto and El Greco, along with porcelain, furniture, sculpture and decorative arts, and Asiatic art.

Van Gogh Museum: The world's largest permanent collection features a selection of paintings by Van

One of Amsterdam's many canals.

Gogh hung in chronological and, to a degree, thematic order – though the location of individual works may change from time to time.

Royal Palace: Dominating Dam Square in the heart of Amsterdam is the 17th-century Koninklijk Paleis (Royal Palace). The rather heavy exterior belies an elegant series of rooms inside with some notable works of art. The square itself is a hub of activity and meeting point.

Anne Frank House: A staircase leads into the backrooms where Otto Frank, his family and friends hid for two fraught years, from 1942 until August 1944. The house is a monument to all the victims of Fascism and anti-Semitism and something of a place of pilgrimage.

De Looier antiques market: A vast indoor antiques market selling anything from memorabilia to handmade pottery, and old dolls and toys.

Utrecht, The Netherlands (Km 31)

The fourth-largest city of the Netherlands is also the capital of Utrecht Province in the country's central section. Magnificent churches abound here (Domkerk, or St Martin's Cathedral, St Jacobuskerk, St Janskerk and St Pieterskerk), and there's also a large, historic university, founded in 1636.

Amsterdam–Rhine Canal (Km 913.4)

The canal, which opened in 1952 and is 72km (45 miles) long, connects the city and port of Amsterdam with the Lek River, making Amsterdam an important port for the trans-shipment of cargo. Considered to be the most heavily used canal in Europe, it has four locks. *(Start of the Rhine kilometre markings).*

Düsseldorf, Germany (Km 744.2)

The capital of North Rhine-Westphalia and its administration centre, Düsseldorf is best known for its iron and steel production and as a centre for banking. It is also famous for its beer, with a number of microbreweries and some hundreds of pubs in the atmospheric Altstadt (Old Town), and for its shopping, particularly along the Königsallee.

The Fine Arts Museum is worth a visit, as is the Ceramic Museum, and the Lambertus Basilica, begun in 1288 (its spire is twisted), and the Castle Tower, which houses a museum of navigation. The city has long been famous for its Christmas market. Bolkerstrasse, one of the city's liveliest streets, was the birthplace of the poet Heinrich Heine, author of *Die Lorelei* (see page 70).

Cologne (Köln), Germany (Km 688)

Cologne is one of the most important traffic junctions and commercial centres in Germany and the most important economic centre on the Rhine. Riverships berth at landing stages in the heart of the old town centre, with its fine riverfront promenade and views along the Rhine.

It's a busy modern city with a strong sense of historical heritage. Already established as an important centre in Roman times and resurgent in the Middle Ages, today it has a city centre still dominated by its glorious twin-towered cathedral. Repeatedly bombed in World War II, Cologne preserved its historic street pattern when it was rebuilt and, although most buildings are modern, much of its traditional atmosphere survives. It's a lively place, best experienced for those with stamina during the merrymak-

Katz Castle and Lorelei rock (visible on the right).

ing of Karneval (Lenten Carnival) time. The historic core of Cologne is large, bounded by the semicircular boulevard of the Ring running along the line of the old city walls, although the epicentre of city life is to be found in the busy squares around the cathedral. Shoppers will enjoy walking the Hohe Strasse, close to the docking area.

Cologne is also noted for its very own 'Original' Eau de Cologne toilet water (its brand name is 4711, which was the maker's former address).

Dom: With its awesome dimensions, the cathedral (Dom) is the unmistakable landmark of the city, its two mighty towers the defining symbol of Cologne's skyline. Construction began in 1248 and resumed in 1880, the final result remaining true to the original plans. A winding staircase of 509 steps leads to a viewing platform 95m (312ft) up in the south tower, where the view amply rewards your efforts.

Fischmarkt: There are few reminders today that the people of Cologne once bought and sold fish, but adjacent to the river is the city's old harbour area and the former fish market. The late-Gothic buildings surrounding the square, now lined with bars and restaurants, have been preserved in their distinct, original style.

Römisch-Germanisches Museum: Containing treasures from over 2,000 years ago after the Romans had established their camp of Colonia here, the city's Roman-Germanic Museum was built over the famous Dionysus Mosaic.

Wallraf-Richartz-Museum: Cologne's oldest museum showcases art from the 14th to the 20th centuries. The collection represents every period and school, from Dutch and Flemish masters to French Impressionists, with works by Dürer, Rembrandt, Rubens, Degas and Cézanne, among many others.

St Gereon's Basilica: This medieval church is known for its intricate floor mosaic of David and Goliath and its unique decagon-shaped dome. It contains the tomb of St Gereon and other martyrs.

Bonn, Germany (Km 654.8)

The Rhine flows through the suburbs of Bonn, the former German capital. The Romans named it Castra Bonnensia 2,000 years ago, when it formed part of their Rhine Valley defences, although its real development did not begin until the Middle Ages. The city became the residence of the electors and archbishops of Cologne in the 17th century and was the capital of West Germany before reunification and the eventual reinstatement of Berlin as the home of government in 1999. Today, Bonn is a university town, with several museums on the riverbank in the 'Museum Mile', including the Kunst- und Ausstellungshalle (Art and Exhibition Hall), with exhibitions of art, technology, history and architecture, and the Kunstmuseum (Museum of Art).

Beethoven was born in Bonn in a house that, since 1890, has been a museum (Beethovenhaus). You can

Cologne at night.

see original manuscripts, his instruments (including a piano complete with amplified sound to allow for his deafness), listening horns and life and death masks.

Drachenfels Castle, Germany (Km 643.7)

According to legend, it was at the foot of the sheer Drachenfels (Dragon's Rock) cliff that Siegfried, the hero of the *Nibelungen Saga*, slew the dragon and then bathed in its blood in order to render himself invulnerable. The castle is now a ruin, and is reached by funicular from Bad Godesburg. The view is magnificent.

Rolandseck Castle (Km 640)

Rolandseck was originally a fortress that also served as a customs station. It is now in ruins, but old archways can still be found on the grounds, the principal one being Rolandsbogen (Roland's Arch). The Rolandsbogen got its name from the legend of the young knight Roland, who is said to have looked yearningly down from this window at the Nonnenwerth convent, on an island in the middle of the Rhine, where his beloved was incarcerated. She had taken her vows because she had believed that he would not return from the Crusades. He did come home, but she was not allowed to leave the nunnery, and the couple died apart, their love unfulfilled. It is said that a tunnel led from the castle to the Nonnenwerth convent, but the castle was destroyed in the 17th century, and the last remaining archway of the ruin collapsed in 1839. The poet Ferdinand Freiligrath had the idea that the Rolandsbogen should be restored – and it was, in 1840. It now rests some 150m (492ft) above the Rhine, covered in a thick growth of ivy.

Andernach, Germany (Km 613.3)

This place was known as 'Bäckerjungenstadt' ('city of baker's apprentices'), because legend has it that it was once under siege, and baker's apprentices threw bees' nests on the attackers from the city walls. Its historical town hall, with its Jewish baths, can be visited.

The curious Pfalzgrafenstein Castle.

Ehrenbreitstein Castle, Germany (Km 592.3)

Located opposite the mouth of the Mosel, where it flows into the Rhine at Koblenz, this squat, solid-looking fortress was built around 1100 on a site that is 116m (380ft) above the water, with incredible views over both rivers, the Eifel Hills and the city of Koblenz. It was acquired in 1152 by the Electorate of Trier and expanded, becoming a fortress around 1500 with the addition of more fortifications. By 1750, after several breaches by the French, the fortress was made impregnable by the brilliant architect Balthasar Neumann. Today, the castle houses the National Collection of Monuments to Technology, and also serves as a youth hostel. Ehrenbreitstein Castle is also one of the sites for the annual Rhine in Flames celebration (see page 69).

Koblenz, Germany (Km 591.5, Rhine/Km 0.30, Mosel)

A former Roman trading settlement, Koblenz grew up at the confluence of the Rhine and the Mosel and lies on the massif of the Middle Rhine Highlands. It is bordered by North Rhine-Westphalia to the north, Hesse to the east and Saarland to the south. The Rhine cuts it diagonally from southeast to northwest.

Stolzenfels Castle, Germany (Km 585.2)

Located just south of Koblenz and surrounded by thick forest, this handsome, imperial yellow castle was originally built in the 13th century to defend the

nearby silver mines. The castle was destroyed by the French but rebuilt in 1852 by the Prussian Crown Prince Friedrich-Wilhelm IV, in neo-Gothic style. In the castle's chapel, important works from the period of High Romanticism can be found in the murals. It is one of the best-known castles along the Rhine.

Marksburg Castle, Germany (Km 580)

This beautiful, mystical castle is the only one in the entire Rhine Valley never to have been destroyed, and is easily the most visited, as it gives the best insight into medieval life. It dates back to 1150, towering majestically 170m (557ft) above the town of Braubach. The original founder, one of the nobles of Braubach, named it after St Mark. A successor, Eberhard von Eppstein, had the castle extended and further fortified in 1219, and it was occupied after 1220 by vassals of the Counts Palatine. In 1283, the castle was acquired by the counts of Katzenelnbogen.

At the end of the 19th century it passed to the German Castles Association, which has its headquarters and archives here. The library houses over 12,000 volumes. A tour of the castle will take you through not only the citadel itself, but also the impressive kitchens in the Gothic Hall building. There is a gruesome torture chamber in the cellar of the older hall building, where a great assortment of grisly instruments of torture can be viewed.

A complete replica of the castle can be seen today in an amusement park in Japan. It appears that the Japanese offered to buy the original ruin, have it dismantled and shipped to Japan, for the price of 250 million marks, but were refused by the German Castles Association – hence the replica.

Boppard, Germany (Km 570.5)

A charming riverfront city, Boppard (of Celtic origin) is located at one of the bends in the Rhine. It has a medieval town hall, Roman castle (eight of the original 28 towers still exist, as do the medieval town gates), several convents, stylish villas and half-timbered houses. Grapes (mostly Riesling) are grown on slopes that are among the steepest in Germany – these are used by 14 full-time cooperatives that obtain more than 500,000 litres (approximately 110,000 imperial gallons) from the cultivation.

Liebenstein Castle and Sterrenberg Castle (Km 566.5)

Not far from Boppard are the ruins of two 12th-century castles, Sterrenberg and Liebenstein, built close together. These were inhabited by two brothers who hated each other so much that they erected a wall between the castles. The story goes that they made up their differences, and for fun, decided to wake each other with an arrow shot every morning. Inevitably, one killed the other by mistake with a badly aimed arrow.

Lorelei, St Goarshausen, Germany (Km 554.6)

Nobody can pass through the medieval wine-growing village of St Goarshausen without learning the legend of the Lorelei (see box). Here, the river

RHINE IN FLAMES

Time it right and you could be part of the fabulous 'Rhein in Flammen' (Rhine in Flames) celebration, which typically takes place in August each year. There are, in fact, three such celebrations, but by far the best is on the section of river between Boppard and Koblenz. Almost 100 riverships take part each year, strung one behind the other in convoy, like a string of sausages (the river police organise this), and measuring over 3km (1.8 miles) in length.

As the convoy moves from Boppard to Koblenz, past numerous towns and villages along the way, fireworks light up the night sky, with all the local towns and villages vying to create the best display. On reaching Koblenz, the convoy stops and turns round to face Ehrenbreitstein Castle (see page 68), the magnificent fortress across from the mouth of the Mosel River. The castle is gloriously lit in red spotlights, with smoke rising all around it, so that it seems to be on fire. It is an unforgettable sight. For more information, see www.rhein-in-flammen.com.

carves its way through a steep, narrow gorge, with its bed descending to 25m (82ft) in places, winding around jagged rocks and creating powerful whirlpools, which have sucked many a ship below the surface. The gorge, with its 132m (433ft) cliffs, is so narrow that the railway line that runs alongside the river has been cut into rock tunnels. A bronze statue of the maiden Lorelei looks down on the river from where, as related by the poem by Heinrich Heine in 1824, the mysterious nymph would once appear, captivating sailors with her beauty and her hypnotic singing before luring them onto the rocks to their death. The poem *Die Lorelei*, set to music in 1837, is seen as the epitome of Rhine Romanticism. A visitor centre stands on the top of the rock today, although the entrance fee is hardly worth it, as there is little inside (it's much better to cruise past the rock).

Pfalzgrafenstein Castle (Km 545)

This is undoubtedly one of the most curious castle creations in the world, a six-storey tower clinging to a tiny island in the middle of the swirling waters and resembling a ship. The castle was erected in 1326 by King Ludwig I of Bavaria purely for collecting customs duties from passing vessels on the Rhine. Anyone who couldn't pay would be sent down a rope to the 'dungeon' – a platform floating at the bottom of a deep well. Since 1946 it has been the property of the state of the Rhineland-Palatinate. Although it has been repaired and restored, purely for tourism purposes, the castle was in use as a signal point for Rhine shipping until the 1960s.

Reichenstein Castle, Germany (Km 534.4)

In the 19th century, Reichenstein was called Falkenburg Castle. It was erected to protect the property of Kornelimünster Abbey near Aachen in the 11th century. It has been destroyed and rebuilt several times, the last time in 1899. Nowadays, it is in use as a hotel.

Rheinstein Castle (Km 533)

Originally constructed as an imperial castle for customs and toll collection, Rheinstein also protected the surrounding estates. One of the oldest castle buildings on the Rhine – it dates back to the 9th century – it has an astounding position: the steely-grey castle appears to be part of a huge, jagged slab of rock high on the hillside.

Rheinstein belonged to the archbishops of Mainz, who named it after their patron saint, Bonifatius, although its original name was Vogtberg. It fell into ruin in the 16th century, and in 1823 Prince Friedrich of Prussia paid 100 Reichsmarks for what was left of it, renaming it Rheinstein. His great-granddaughter sold it in 1975, in an advanced state of dilapidation, to an Austrian singer from the Tyrol. It is now preserved thanks to donations from tourists, a society founded by the singer and income from its rental.

Mäuseturm, Germany (Km 529)

Below the mouth of the Nahe, close to Rüdesheim and Bingen, a slender red-and-yellow tower looking like something out of a Disney cartoon perches on a small island. The legend relates how the original tower was built by the evil, hard-hearted Archbishop Hatto of Mainz in 1208 as reinforcement for the customs castle, Ehrenfels, which stands in ruinous state on the opposite hillside. The tower's strategic position allowed the archbishop to fleece passing traffic on the Rhine. To bolster his income, peasants were levied a corn tithe, which he collected in a large barn in Mainz. After a bad harvest, the hungry populace went to Mainz and asked for grain. Archbishop Hatto, having promised to help, then proceeded to lock them up in his tithe barn and set fire to it.

Everyone inside perished, but the story goes that some mice escaped. The archbishop departed to his castle on the island by boat from Bingen, opposite Rüdesheim, but the mice followed him... and then ate him alive, even though he had had his bed suspended by chains from the ceiling, so that it was well above the floor.

The edifice thus became known as the Mice Tower (Mäuseturm), although its actual title was once Mautturm (Customs Tower). Under France's King Louis XIV, the castle was burnt down, although fortunately it was restored by the King of Prussia in 1855 and used as a signal tower for shipping, to warn ships of the treacherous whirlpools and rocks of the so-called Hole of Bingen (Binger Loch). It remained in this manner until 1974, when the channel was deepened, and since then it has been inhabited only by bats, and, so the legend goes, the ghost of the evil archbishop.

Rüdesheim, Germany (Km 526.7)

This was the terminal point of the old 'Merchant Road' that originated in Lorh and circumvented the waterfalls that once made this stretch of river treacherous. It is famous for its wine-growing districts on the Rüdesheim Hills, located at the foothills of the Niederwald Forest and Taunus Mountains. A cable car will take you to the top of the Rheingau hills, where the famous Niederwalddenkmal (Niederwald Monument) – a statue of Germania built to commemorate the founding of the German Empire in 1871 – is located.

Four castles were constructed to protect this important merchant centre and traffic route, one of which, Bromserburg, belonged for a while to the Knights of Rüdesheim; today it is a wine museum. A number of taverns and drinking houses line its narrow streets, particularly Drosselgasse.

One fascinating attraction in Rüdesheim is Siegfrieds Mechanisches Musikkabinett (Siegfried's Mechanical Instrument Museum). This unusual museum, located in the Bromserhof (parts of which date back to the 15th century), is famous for its outstanding collection of priceless mechanical musical instruments. All 250 instruments have been collected from the period

THE LORELEI

Near St Goarshausen, at one of the most notorious bends in the Middle Rhine Valley, the Lorelei is a large, almost perpendicular slate rock 130m (427ft) high that produces an echo. In days of old, so it is told, noblemen occupied the area in order to squeeze taxes from passing traffic – from every vessel and merchant needing to travel beyond its grasp.

Back then, Lorelei herself, a siren, could be seen occasionally on the hilltop. Echoing through the landscape, a mysterious voice belonging to the maiden chanted the now-famous poem, as fishermen passed within her grasp. She lured them on to the craggy rocks, and to a fate unknown.

The charming maiden's beauty and reputation spread throughout the land, until one day it reached the ears of the son of the Count Palatine. Yearning for passion, the young man left his father's palace in secret and journeyed by boat to win the maiden's heart. It is said that at sunset he and his followers reached the gorge and were spellbound by the singing of the Lorelei. He caught a glimpse of her hair and enchanting figure at the top of the steepest cliff.

Magically, the strength to row vanished from their arms as they stared at the figure. It seemed as if the boatswain had lost memory of his duties. The young prince, somewhat impatient, jumped into the waters to reach the lovely maiden and take her hand. With a cry of 'Lorelei', he sank into the busy, swirling waters, never to be seen again.

The Count ordered his son's betrayer to be captured. The rock, soon surrounded by the Count's revengeful soldiers, became a silent witness. One captain took the bravest of his soldiers with him to the top of the hill. 'Unholy woman, now you can pay for your sins,' he commanded, blocking the monster's path to her grotto. 'That does not lie with you,' she replied and cast her pearl necklaces into the floods below. They rose out of the water – as high as the cliff top – and carried the fairy away into the grey evening night. Lorelei was never seen again, but if you go today to the rock and stare at it, a manifold echo may taunt you.

The Lorelei has been the subject of a number of literary works, including, most famously, Heinrich Heine's 1824 poem, which has been set to music by more than 20 composers. Although Heine made the poem so renowned, he was not its creator. That honour goes to the German romantic poet Clemens Brentano, who, in 1801, included the ballad of Lore Lay in his novel, *Godwi*.

Christmas market in Düsseldorf's Altstadt.

spanning 150 years prior to 1930 and have all been re-stored. Siegfried Wendel, the museum's owner, is always on hand and frequently plays some of the instruments for visitors. It is open from March to December.

Mainz, Germany (Km 498.5)

Mainz, located on the west bank of the Rhine opposite the mouth of the river Main, is over 2,000 years old (it was founded as the Roman camp Moguntiacum). It is the capital city of Rhineland-Palatinate (Rheinland-Pfalz) and has a history as seat of electors and bishops. Much of the city was devastated by bombing in World War II and has been rebuilt. In the Old Town, visit the six-towered cathedral, originally constructed in AD 975 and a highlight of ecclesiastical architecture in the Upper Rhine region.

Mainz is also home to the Gutenberg Museum, which tells the history of printing. The city is also one of the main centres of the Rhine wine trade. There are several museums and palaces to explore, but one sight not to miss is St Stephen's Church, with its stunning stained-glass windows by the French painter Marc Chagall.

Worms, Germany (Km 443.2)

One of the oldest cities in Germany, Worms was originally inhabited as an imperial residence on the banks of the Rhine and the centre of the Burgundian Empire that was destroyed by the Huns. Today, the city is known as a wine-trading centre. The vineyards surrounding the city produce the grapes used for making 'Liebfraumilch', a trade name for the much-maligned semi-sweet white wine that is from the Palatinate, Rhine-Hesse (Rheinhessen), Nahe and Rheingau wine-growing regions. Passengers typically disembark at Worms to take a tour (by bus) to Heidelberg (see page 74).

Mannheim, Germany (Km 415–425)

The city was founded in 1606 in a circular layout that covered only the peninsula at the strategic confluence of the Neckar and the Rhine. The city, which developed from the fortress that is aligned with the Rhine, was created by the Palatine Elector Frederick IV and has grown into a modern finance and insurance centre. It also has a university.

Speyer, Germany (Km 400)

This is typically used as a short stop so that passengers can leave the vessel to take a tour to Heidelberg (see page 74), although Speyer has a few noteworthy sights, including an immense Unesco-protected cathedral, one of the most important Romanesque buildings from the time of the Holy Roman Empire, and the Jewish baths. The city was burned down on the order of Louis XIV in 1689. After it was returned to Germany in 1816, it became the government seat of Bavaria Palatinate until 1845.

Gambersheim Locks, France (Km 309)

The Gambersheim locks are a relatively recent construction, put into operation in 1974. They are op-

The Rhine in Flames celebration.

erated from Strasbourg and are the largest inland waterway locks in France. There are two chambers, each with a length of 270m (885ft), and the locks are in operation 24 hours a day, all year round (it takes about 15 minutes to pass through them). About 20 million tons of goods pass through the locks each year, as well as numerous riverships.

Strasbourg, France (Km 294.3)

The medieval city of Strasbourg is the seat of the Council of Europe, the European Commission on Human Rights and the European Science Foundation, and is also capital and cultural centre of the Alsace region of France. The port is the largest on the Upper Rhine, and a large network of docks provides freight and other services.

Strasbourg's centre is surrounded by the River Ill, and is mainly pedestrianised, particularly the area known as Petite France, where the river splits into a number of canals. At the end of Petite France, look out for the Ponts Couverts, a series of wooden footbridges dating back to the 13th century (but no longer covered).

The focal point of it all is place Gutenberg, named after Johannes Gutenberg, the inventor of the printing press, who lived here during the 15th century and whose statue stands at the centre of the square. A highlight of any visit is the massive hulk of the Cathédrale de Notre Dame, the tallest medieval building in Europe, its viewing platform reached by a wearying 332 steps up inside the tower. It's worth the climb for the vista of the Black Forest (and, in the other direction, the Vosges Mountains) beyond the colourful roofs of the old town. At noon, crowds are drawn to the astronomical clock inside the cathedral, adorned with a Parade of the Apostles, which dates from 1838.

Many river cruises start and end in Strasbourg, and the Gare Fluviale is located adjacent to rue du Havre, a short walk from the heart of the city on an arm of the Ill.

Basel, Switzerland (Km 165–169)

Basel, the navigable limit of the Rhine, is the starting point for many cruises. The city has grown up either side of the river, with the industrial Kleinbasel section to the north and the lovely old part, Grossbasel, on the south bank. Basel has a very international flavour; it is, after all, where three countries – France, Germany and Switzerland – meet. Situated at the 'knee' of the Rhine, it is the location of the oldest university in Switzerland, together with some 30 museums and an inviting old town – a jumble of medieval buildings along the hilly river bank (a short walk from the cruise boat landing stage). Basel is also steeped in Roman history.

The focal point of the city is the Rathaus (Town Hall) and marketplace, around which are several late Gothic, Renaissance and Baroque guildhalls. The 13th-century Romanesque Münster (Cathedral) is an unusual shade of red, its slender towers built from sandstone quarried from the nearby Vosges Mountains.

There are several museums worth visiting, including the Kunstmuseum, where you can view two Picasso paintings (The Seated Harlequin and Two Brothers), purchased by the people of the city in 1967, together with four others the artist donated.

Basel is famous for its music festivals and industrial trade fairs, the most famous being the Autumn Fair, which has been held each and every year since 1471.

HIGHLIGHTS ON THE MOSEL

Moselkern, Germany (Km 34)

This small, sleepy hamlet provides a stopping point for riverships, so that passengers can take a tour to Burg Eltz, a castle set not on a hillside but deep in the forest. The castle is unusual in that it is really a collection of three houses. A drawbridge-like entrance from a steep, winding forest road helps to add to the atmosphere.

Cochem, Germany (Km 51.3)

One of the loveliest and most picturesque of all the towns along the Mosel, Cochem is located at the beginning of a 20km (12-mile) bend in the river. The walled Old Town is laced with narrow alleys. The skyline is dominated by the Imperial Castle, which has a rectangular keep *(donjon)* and numerous small towers. Worth a look is the Capuchin monastery, built in 1623 and restored for use today as a cultural centre. The Baroque Town Hall is also of note, as are the old gabled houses overlooking the Market Fountain. The Mosel Wine Week takes place here in mid-June each year, and the wine taverns along the river front have 'green wine' (very young wine) available all year round. Behind the waterfront are more taverns, which are recommended for their friendly atmosphere.

Bernkastel-Kues, Germany (Km 129.4)

Bernkastel-Kues is comprised of two villages (Bernkastel and Kues), one on each side of the Mo-

sel (and joined by a bridge) at the confluence of the Tiefenbach (meaning 'deep stream'). The riverships dock on the Kues side. This is big wine-growing country, and the Middle Mosel Wine Festival is staged here in the first week in September. There is also a Wine Museum in the town. The ruins of a fortress called Lanshut dominate the town, which is filled with gorgeous half-timbered houses; the lowest floor of many houses is typically smaller than the upper floor because taxes used to be charged based on the amount of ground the house covered. During winter Christmas market cruises, the picture-postcard setting is magical.

Trier, Germany (Km 181.5–191.4)

Trier is the principal city of the Mosel Valley and the oldest in Germany; growing up around a ford used by the Germanic-Celtic Treveri tribe before being officially founded in 16 BC by the Roman Emperor Caesar Augustus, who named it Augusta Treverorum. Trier, which lies in the Middle Rhine Highlands, is bordered by Luxembourg and Belgium to the west, North Rhine-Westphalia to the north and Saarland to the south.

One of the best-preserved and most important Roman edifices in Germany is the 2nd-century, four-storey Porta Nigra (literally 'Black Gate'), the Town Gate, built of sandstone – originally without mortar – and today protected as a Unesco World Heritage Site. You can visit the Constantine Baths, and other remaining Roman relics such as a 20,000-seat amphitheatre and Roman bridge. A cross dating from AD 958 can be found in the Stadtmuseum (town museum); there is a replica in the

Sunset in Petite France, Strasbourg.

market square, while close by is the Petrus Fountain, constructed in 1595. It is also famous as the birthplace of Karl Marx (1818–83), whose house still stands in Bruckenstrasse.

Trier is at the heart of the Mosel wine-producing region and close to one of the area's largest breweries: Bitburger. It is also known for its Christmas markets.

Nancy, France (Km 149.2)

Five palaces, two fountains, a triumphal arch, a cathedral and a grand square are among the attractions backdrop of this delightful town, which is located in an important manufacturing region of France. At its heart is place Stanislas, a vast, impressive square with splendid iron gateways, gilded lanterns and a huge fountain with wrought-iron screen (features that were introduced by the former, exiled King Stanislas of Poland). On one side of the square is the Musée des Beaux-Arts, home to a collection of paintings from Old Masters to the 20th century. Other highlights include the rose-filled Parc de la Pépinière.

HIGHLIGHTS ON THE NECKAR

Heidelberg, Germany (Km 22.7)

Heidelberg, located just over 20km (12 miles) upstream on the Neckar from Mannheim, is the epitome of German Romanticism, nestling on the south

MUSIC

Several composers were born or died in the region of the River Rhine.

Johann Sebastian Bach was born on 21 May 1685 in Eisenach, Germany. He died on 28 July 1750 in Leipzig, Germany.

Ludwig van Beethoven was baptised on 17 December 1770 in Bonn, Germany. He died on 26 March 1827 in Vienna, Austria. The house in which he was born is close to his statue, which is located in front of the post office.

Cristolph Willibald Gluck was born on 2 July 1714 in Erasbach, near Berching, Germany. He died on 15 November 1787 in Vienna.

Paul Hindemith was born on 16 November 1895 in Hanau, near Frankfurt-am-Main, Germany. He died in the same city on 28 December 1963.

Engelbert Humperdinck (the German composer) was born on 1 September 1854 in Sieberg, Hannover, Germany. He died on 27 September 1921 in Neustrelitz, Germany.

Georg Philipp Telemann was born on 14 March 1681 in Magdeburg, Germany. He died on 27 June 1767 in Hamburg.

Wilhelm Richard Wagner was born on 22 May 1813 in Leipzig, Germany. He died on 13 February 1883 in Venice, Italy.

side of the river and set against the forested hills of Oldenwald, and dominated by a sprawling red-sandstone castle complex. This venerable city is the old capital of the Electorate of the Palatinate, although its history goes back a good deal further than that – some 600,000 years, in fact: the jawbone of *Homo heidelbergensis*, the oldest human remains discovered in Europe, was found near here. Thousands of years later, Celts and Romans settled the area. Count Palatine Ruprecht I founded Germany's oldest university here in 1386, and for 500 years the Electoral College, which was responsible for electing the German kings, was based in the city. Heidelberg Castle, constructed with a moat and several keeps, is considered to be the most magnificent castle ruin in all of Germany, and attracts several million visitors a year.

The castle took 400 years to build and encompasses many different architectural styles. It was destroyed by the French during the Wars of Succession between 1689 and 1693, then subsequently rebuilt only to be destroyed again in 1764 when freak lightning struck and burnt it to the ground. Today, some parts lie in ruins, while other sections have been restored to be used for concerts and banquets or to house museums. The whole complex can be reached on foot by steps and walkways that lead up to it from the city, spread along the river below, or via a funicular railway. Highlights include the Friedrich Wing, with impressive statues of the German kings, and the Heidelberg Tun, one of the world's largest wine vats. The castle houses a fine restaurant with views over the castle courtyard. Try the local duck speciality – you'll receive a handwritten card from the chef showing the number assigned to the portion of duck you have just eaten.

Within the castle complex, the Otto Henry Palace is a richly decorated Renaissance building constructed in 1556. Although only the facade remains, it is a splendid reminder that this was the first such Renaissance building to be built in northern Europe. Inside is the Deutsches Apotheken-Museum, containing old medical instruments and medicine bottles.

The city below is full of wonderful Baroque and Renaissance buildings, and remains an important university town, with its population swelled by 28,000 students, so there's always a lively buzz during termtime. Other things to see include the Heiliggeistkirche (Church of the Holy Ghost), the wonderful Renaissance facade of the Hotel Ritter and the Old Bridge (the Karl Theodore Brücke) over the Neckar, which the writer J.W. von Goethe believed to be one of the wonders of the world, thanks to its breathtaking view.

Eberbach, Germany (Km 57.4)

This market town is home to one of the best-kept medieval monasterial establishments in all of Ger-

Romantic Heidelberg.

many, the Eberbach Abbey (Kloster Eberbach). It was built in two stages, from 1145 to 1160, then from 1170 to 1186. Architectural scholars will enjoy the remarkable monks' dormitory, which was built as a double-naved, ribbed vaulted room with a slightly rising floor; columns were shortened accordingly, and the finished article provides the illusion that it is much longer than it really is (approximately 85m/279ft).

Bad Wimpfen, Germany (Km 100)

Located at the mouth of the River Jagst, Bad Wimpfen is a saline health spa that is extremely popular with German health seekers. From the river, there is a superb view of the old Staufen Palace, with its spires, Romanesque arcades and red roof. The town itself is extremely pretty, with richly decorated half-timbered houses and narrow streets.

Stuttgart, Germany (Km 179–189)

Wealthy in financial and cultural terms, Stuttgart is the capital city of Baden-Württemberg. It is known as the spiritual home of Mercedes-Benz, the building of which was started here by two remarkable pioneers, Gottlieb Daimler (1834–1900) and Karl Benz (1844–1929). At night, the famous trademark of Mercedes – a three-pointed star within a circle – can be seen illuminated high above the city.

Worth a visit for automobile-lovers is the Mercedes-Benz Museum, with over 100 vintage and veteran cars on display. Also worth seeing is the Linden Museum, with its many sections displaying ethnological collections from around the world, and the Staatsgalerie, one of Germany's finest art collections. The city itself has a handsome centre with many 16th-century buildings.

HIGHLIGHTS ON THE SAAR

Mettlach, Germany (Km 37)

Mettlach is best known as the home of the ceramics manufacturer Villeroy & Boch, whose offices are housed in the former Benedictine Abbey of St Peter. The abbey was completely rebuilt from 1728 onwards, but earlier excavations at the site revealed buildings that date from AD 700. Some of the scenery along the river around the town is spectacular, notably adjacent to Cloef (see page 65).

Saarbrücken, Germany (Km 90.6)

Saarbrücken, the capital of the Saarland, lies on the River Saar at the mouth of the River Sülz. Dating back to Celtic and Roman times, it was first mentioned in the record books in AD 999. The city is the centre of the Saar coal-mining region, and iron- and steel-making are important industries, as are food processing and brewing and other industries. Architectural highlights include the Protestant Baroque-style Ludwigskirche, built in yellow and red sandstone from the region, and the grand, harmonious Ludwigsplatz on which it stands.

River Elbe

From the Czech Republic to Germany's sandy North Sea coast, an Elbe cruise offers a range of landscapes and some fascinating cities, most notably Prague, Dresden and Berlin.

The Elbe runs for 1,165km (724 miles) from its source in the Czech Republic to the North Sea coast of Germany, passing through a wide range of scenery en route. From the highlands of Bohemia it curves west then north to the dramatic sandstone massif south of Dresden, continuing through the hills and vineyards of Saxony to reach the marshy woodlands of the Lüneburg Heath and the flatlands of the North European Plain. The history of the river is inextricably linked with division. In earlier days, it divided the Slavs and the Germans; later, a stretch of the river separated the former East and West Germany. From the Czech border to beyond Wittenberg the Elbe flows through the heart of the erstwhile German Democratic Republic (East Germany), its towns and villages still perceptibly less prosperous than those ones further west.

Great cities have grown up along its banks, including beautiful Baroque Dresden, and Hamburg, Germany's most important sea and river port. An Elbe cruise may also travel a short distance along the Vltava River to the fairy-tale Czech capital, Prague,

Elbe Princesse on the Elbe.

and much further north, along the Havel tributary to Berlin, until 1990 the city divided between East and West and now the united country's cosmopolitan capital. Fascinating historic towns along the river's course include Wittenberg, where Dr Martin Luther began the Protestant Reformation, Dessau, heart of the Bauhaus movement, and Meissen, world-famous for its fine porcelain.

Elbe cruises are available in a variety of permutations, usually between Berlin and Prague but also, for example, Magdeburg, Germany and Mělník, near Prague in the Czech Republic). Some continue north all the way to Hamburg; some even take in the coast and islands of the North Sea. All offer an opportunity to spend a couple of days in both Berlin and Prague, which is highly recommended.

KIEL CANAL

At Brunsbüttel, near the estuary, the Elbe passes the mouth of the Kiel Canal (also known as the Kaiser Wilhelm Canal), a 98km (60-mile) man-made waterway connecting the North and Baltic seas. It was constructed by the German government in the late 19th century across the northwest of the state of Schleswig-Holstein, from Brunsbüttelkoog to Holenau, on the Kieler Bucht of the Baltic Sea, and be-

DID YOU KNOW...?

...that the longest inland beach is on the River Elbe? Well, sort of. On 14 July 2002, between 80,000 and 100,000 people took part in the first International Elbe Swimming Day. The celebration was organised in 52 towns from the source of the Elbe in the Czech Giant Mountains to the mouth of the river in the North Sea. It was run by 'Project Living Elbe', together with the German organisation Deutsche Umwelthilfe, among other partners. The event, a swimming success, was designed to bring people's attention to the river, which, only a few years previously, had been extremely polluted. What was a sewer has been turned into a river in which one can swim, with the addition of more than 200 water treatment plants along its length.
...that in 2002 the Elbe reached its highest level since 1845?
...that both the Czech and German names for Elbe derive from Indo-Germanic *albi* or the Latin *albus*, meaning 'shining' or 'white'?

came an international waterway following the signing of the Treaty of Versailles in 1919.

Major tributaries

The 440km (273-mile) -long Vltava (known to the Germans as the Moldau) is a Czech tributary of the Elbe, although its source lies in the Bohemian Forest in Germany. It joins the Elbe at Mělník, a short distance north of Prague, the Czech Republic's capital and the most important city along its shores.

Another tributary is the 343km (213-mile) -long Havel, which originates in the Mecklenburg lakes in northern Germany. It flows through Berlin to Potsdam and Brandenburg and enters the Elbe near Havelberg.

The Oder–Havel Canal is reached via the Berlin Lakes. Because the lakes and the Oder have a height difference of 36m (118ft), in 1934 a special vessel lift (Niederfinow) was completed in order to raise rivership the required height in under five minutes.

HIGHLIGHTS ON THE ELBE FROM HAMBURG (GERMANY) TO PRAGUE (CZECH REPUBLIC)

On a river cruise between Hamburg (on the River Elbe) and Prague (on the River Vltava, a tributary of the Elbe), you are likely to visit some of the following towns and cities:

Hamburg, Germany (Km 623)

Best known, somewhat unfairly, for its raunchy nightlife, Hamburg is actually a very dignified and elegant city, the notorious Reeperbahn red-light district aside. It is Germany's main seaport, despite the

fact that it is some 110km (70 miles) inland, on the right bank of the Elbe where it meets the River Alster.

The city is crisscrossed by canals and has numerous green squares and corners, with lively street cafés. Exploring the canals and waterfront on a boat tour is one of the most restful ways to get around. Otherwise, things to see include the Rathaus (Town Hall), built in neo-Renaissance style in 1887 and set in one corner of the Binnenalster, an inland lake.

On Sunday mornings, head for the Fischmarkt, a noisy, atmospheric marketplace where everything from fish to household clutter is sold. The city has numerous museums, including the Kunsthalle, which houses one of Germany's finest collections of art, with exhibits from the 13th to the 20th centuries. Hamburg is also good for shopping; there are a lot of high-quality boutiques, while the major department stores are located in Jungfernstieg, Mönckebergstrasse and Spitalerstrasse.

Berlin, Germany (River Havel, no km marker)

Germany's capital actually lies on the River Havel, which passes through a complex system of lakes and locks, so river cruisers usually berth at Potsdam, and passengers are brought by coach to the city centre. Highlights in Potsdam include the Cecilienhof Palace, where the last meeting of the three main allies (led by Churchill, Stalin and Truman) took place at the end of World War II. Sanssouci Palace, the summer palace of Frederick the Great, is another highlight here.

But on the capital city of Berlin, which has metamorphosed since the fall of the Wall in 1990 into a buzzing, thriving metropolis, drawing artists and entrepreneurs, movers and shakers into its midst. Innovative architecture, ultra-chic shopping along the Kurfürstendamm, grand boulevards and lavish monuments collectively create one of Europe's most exciting capitals – and the nightlife is legendary, too.

Most itineraries allow a couple of days in Berlin. It's worth it to take in the grand neoclassical buildings along Unter den Linden, the Brandenburg Gate and the Reichstag, and the Museuminsel (Museum Island), now a Unesco World Heritage Site. Slightly more off the beaten track are some of the multicultural suburbs such as Kreuzberg, arty and newly gentrified Prenzlauer Berg, the patrician Charlottenburg, or the nearby lakes and forests.

Brandenburger Tor: The Brandenburg Gate has played varying roles in the history of Berlin. Napoleon marched through here on his triumphant way to Russia, and when the Berlin Wall fell in 1990, the gates came to symbolise freedom and unity. The sandstone structure is based on the gateway to the Acropolis in Athens.

The Reichstag: The Reichstag, restored to prominence with the return of the government to Berlin in 1999 and crowned by a spectacular glass dome designed by Norman Foster, was originally built in the late 19th century in Italian Renaissance style. A broad spiral ramp enables visitors to watch parliamentary proceedings from above.

Museuminsel: Between the River Spree and Kupfergraben lies Museum Island, which ranks as one of the world's finest museum complexes. The stunning diversity of displays includes everything from ancient archaeological artefacts to early 20th-century German and European art.

Kurfürstendamm: Inspired by the Champs-Elysées in Paris, Ku'damm (as it's usually known) is the most popular boulevard in Berlin, and is flanked by a series of exclusive hotels, department stores and cafés. In the 1920s it became the meeting-place for Berlin's intellectuals.

Checkpoint Charlie: From 1961 until 1989, Checkpoint Charlie was the only crossing point between East and West Berlin. Today, the former border crossing has become a shrine to the Berlin Wall's memory. Nothing remains of the actual military installation today, although a small guardhouse was rebuilt in the middle of the street. For more information on the general history of the Wall, visit the nearby Museum Haus am Checkpoint Charlie 5 at Friedrichstrasse 44.

Tangermünde, Germany (Km 388)

Tangermünde is a former Hanseatic League town with many fine examples remaining of Gothic brick architecture and half-timbered houses.

Magdeburg, Germany (Km 326–333)

Magdeburg is located about mid-way on the Elbe, southwest of Berlin, positioned at a natural crossroads on the river at the junction of six railway lines and seven arterial roads. The city is linked with Berlin and the lower River Oder by a system of canals, and to the River Rhine by the Mittelland Canal. It was

---

THE ODER

Renowned as a sanctuary for birdlife, the Oder is a little-cruised river that forms the border between Poland and Germany for a distance of 186km (116 miles). This isolated river valley is green and lush, lined with meadows and ancient forests, as well as expanses of grass and moorland. Apart from the occasional sleepy hamlet, the only signs of human life are cyclists and hikers. But this was also the region in which the Russians broke through the German lines in World War II to commence their final assault on Berlin, and it is rich in history.

Cruises operating on the Oder usually start in Berlin, travel east along the Havel to join the Oder, and then sail either south to Wroclaw (Breslau) or north to Szczecin, close to the river's mouth on the Baltic Sea.

---

almost destroyed in 1945, but is now a superb example of a traditional German town, albeit reconstructed. The town's museum houses the *Magdeburg Rider*, Germany's oldest equestrian statue, created in 1240. There is a replica of it in front of the town hall. Other notable city sights include the world's third-tallest wooden structure, a 60m (197ft) -high Millennium Tower (Jahrtausendturm), constructed as an exhibition centre in time for the beginning of the 21st century. Famous former residents of Magdeburg include the composer Georg Philipp Telemann.

Wittenberg, Germany (Km 215)

Not to be confused with another town with almost the same name (Wittenberge – located further along the Elbe), Wittenberg is a sleepy town, brought to life by hordes of visitors who come here to see where the Protestant Reformation began. The mooring is some distance from the town, so it's best to take a coach tour.

Dr Martin Luther, an Augustine monk and university lecturer, famously nailed 95 theses to the door of the Palace Church on 31 October 1517, an act that is defined by historians as beginning the Reformation. Three years later, Luther was excommunicated by the Pope. Luther's house can also be visited, as can St Marien's Church, where he preached. An oak tree marks the spot where he burnt the papal bull condemning his doctrines. Nearby is Luther Hall, a museum dedicated to the Reformation.

Meissen, Germany (Km 80–83)

Meissen is a lovely old town, dominated by the slender Gothic spires of its cathedral and the hulking Albrechtsburg Castle, built in 1525. There has been a settlement since AD 968, but the town really rose to fame in 1710 with the advent of porcelain manufacture.

Augustus the Strong, Elector of Saxony (where he was known as Frederick Augustus I) from 1694 to 1733, had earlier employed the renegade alchemist Johann Friedrich Böttger to make gold, partly in order to raise much-needed funds for the state, and partly (of course) out of personal greed. Not surprisingly, this scheme had failed, but in 1709 Böttger realised that valuable white porcelain could be made from nacrite, of which there were large deposits nearby, and the castle was quickly turned into a factory. The famous blue-glaze technique was discovered in 1740, and the porcelain soon became known all over the world. The castle houses an art collection today, with a number of early Meissen pieces.

Dresden, Germany (Km 50–61)

The Elbe runs for 25km (16 miles) right through the middle of this venerable German city, the capital of Saxony once again since 1990 and world-renowned for its fabulous art treasures, which have given it the epithet 'Florence on the Elbe'. There are water meadows and green parks close to the centre giving

Meissen at night.

a marvellous feeling of open space. The river cruise landing stage is right in the centre of the city, and most boats spend the night here, a good opportunity to see the beautiful sandstone buildings illuminated by dramatic floodlights.

Dresden will always be remembered for the devastating bombing in 1945, which flattened the city centre and cost some 35,000 people their lives. For years, the Frauenkirche (Church of Our Lady) was left ruined, as a reminder of the destruction, but it has now been rebuilt as an exact replica of its former self. The city centre is now a Unesco-protected site and has almost been fully restored, thanks to a 50-year rebuilding project.

Dresden is a very attractive city and, for many, is a highlight of an Elbe cruise. The Town Hall tower, standing at 100m (330ft), will always by law be the tallest building. The 13th-century Kreuzkirche, meanwhile, rebuilt in 1764 after the Seven Years War, is said to contain a fragment of the Holy Cross, and is a superb example of Baroque architecture.

Another beautiful Baroque building is the meticulously restored 18th-century Zwinger Palace, a superb collection of graceful pavilions on the south bank of the Elbe, known for its superb art collection of Old Masters, including pieces by Raphael and Rembrandt.

Music-lovers should see the incredible Semper Opera House, in which performances are given from September to May. On the opposite side of the river (the left bank) is the quadrilateral Japanese Palace, built to display Augustus the Strong's superb collection of Meissen porcelain and tableware.

Pillnitz Palace, Germany (Km 50)

One of Saxony's architectural treasures, Pillnitz Palace – built to rival Buckingham Palace and Versailles – houses an impressive collection of fine jewellery and porcelain.

The River Moldau starts at Km 0. Note that the kilometre marking systems in Germany and the Czech Republic are different.

Saxon Switzerland

Between the city of Dresden and the Czech border, the scenery is dramatic, the river having carved its way through sandstone for about 48km (30 miles). This has resulted in bizarrely shaped cliffs and rock outcrops that protrude from the dense forest. There are numerous rare plants and wildlife (with over 50 varieties of birds) in this rare habitat, much of which was declared a national park in 1991. In the quieter sections when there are few trains (the tracks run alongside the river), the sound of birds twittering away is delightful.

Bad Schandau (Km 6)

This spa town, on the edge of the Saxon Switzerland National Park and about 6km (4 miles) from the Czech border, is a stopping point for some Elbe riverships.

It is an ideal base for excursions to the Lichtenhain Waterfall in the Kirnitzsch Valley, the Kuhstall rock formations, and the towering Schrammsteine cliffs. Another excursion will take to nearby Bastei Rocks – a towering, jagged teeth-like rock formation. From this high vantage point you get a superb, sweeping view of the Elbe. It's well worth a visit (note that there are 117 steps to a viewing platform some 135m/443ft above the Elbe), this unworldly limestone rock formation, worn away millions of years ago by the Elbe, was the setting for a spectacular fortification that overlooked the river. Bastei is one of two sections of one of the 14 national parks in Germany (the second section is actually in the Czech Republic).

Königstein, Germany (Km 17)

Once you've passed the spa town of Rathen, set against a natural amphitheatre of cliffs, the dramatic medieval Königstein Fortress comes into view, 360m (1,180ft) above the river. Riverships usually stop here for a brief visit, taking passengers by coach to the fortress. Königstein has been rebuilt and strengthened several times, and in its day was considered impregnable; a well was dug 150m (490ft) into the rock in case of siege. Inside, you can see the living quarters and workshop of Johann Friedrich Böttger, the alchemist who discovered the secret of making true porcelain in 1709. Prior to this, Böttger was incarcerated here from 1706 to 1707, when the castle served as a jail – the Elector of Saxony, Augustus the Strong, had held him in 'protective custody' in order to be the beneficiary of the alchemist's quest to manufacture gold. Other prominent prisoners included the social democrat August Bebel and the poet Frank Wedekind.

Prague and its many bridges.

Děčín, Czech Republic (Km 98)

The town of Děčín is situated on both sides of the river. While the old town centre is worth visiting, the rest is unfortunately rather grey and dismal.

Litoměřice, Czech Republic (Km 792)

With buildings that span the Baroque, Gothic, and Renaissance period, and a large, delightful market square, the royal city of Litoměřice is one of the prettiest in the Czech Republic. One of the loveliest towns in the Czech Republic, Litoměřice (Leitmeritz in German) has an abundance of historic houses built between the 15th and 18th centuries. Notable are the 16th-century 'Chalice' (the former named for the shape of its chalice roof) and 'Black Eagle' houses. Underground passageways link several sections of the town's defence system (the Gothic tower of All Saints Church was originally part of the town's fortifications). Two other churches – St Wenzel's and St Mary's – are built in the Baroque style, while the Diocesan Museum contains a wonderful collection of paints of religious significance.

The fortified garrison of Terezín (Theresienstadt), just 3km (2 miles) south of Litoměřice, became renowned as a concentration camp established by the Nazis. Excursions here are often offered.

Mělník

Located at the confluence of the Elbe and the Vltava (Moldau) rivers, about 35km (22 miles) or about one hour by train north of Prague in an area of undulating hills, Mělník – in the Bohemian region of the Czech Republic – is an important container port. Hop plantation and vineyards are plentiful. In fact, high above

the town itself, the largely Renaissance castle (albeit with some Baroque additions) has vast wine cellars. Numerous cafes adorn the Market Square. The Town Hall dates from the 14th century, while dotted around the square are numerous houses built between the 16th and 18th centuries.

Prague, Czech Republic (Km 45–55)

The starting or finishing point for most Elbe/Vltava cruises (although the vessel actually docks at Ústí, 70km/43 miles to the north), the romantic city of Prague is located on a curve of the winding River Vltava, a tributary of the Elbe, and known to Germans as the Moldau. Graceful bridges span the river, including the famous Charles Bridge, the Lesser Quarter clinging to one side and the Old Town to the other, surveyed from above by the 10th-century Hradčany (Prague Castle). The city has inspired composers including Mozart, Smetena and Dvořák, as well as poets, writers, revolutionaries and intellectuals. It's still a great university city and seat of learning, with nightlife to match in the legendary bars and pubs.

If your river cruise ends in Prague, try to stay for at least a couple of days, so that you have plenty of time to visit the highlights, which include the following:

Charles Bridge (Karlův most): Slightly curved and spanning the Vltava between the Old Town and the hill leading up to the castle, Charles Bridge is a Gothic masterpiece, with the added impact of some fine Baroque sculpture. The first stone bridge was constructed here during the second half of the 12th century, in place of the wooden structure that was situated further to the north. The 30 statues adorning the bridge were added over a period of 250 years. The oldest and most significant statue is that of St John of Nepomuk, which was installed in 1683. Many are now replicas, and the valuable originals can be seen in the Lapidarium of the National Museum. The bridge is usually very crowded with sightseers; for a more atmospheric experience visit early in the morning or late at night.

Prague Castle (Hrad): With its commanding position high above the river, the castle has been key to every epoch in the city's history. It is the most extensive complex of buildings in the city, containing St Vitus Cathedral, the Royal Palace and many other monuments. It also serves as the seat of the president of the republic.

St Vitus Cathedral (Katedrála sv. Víta): Prague's magnificent Gothic cathedral contains not only chapels and tombs, but also some fine stained glass, including the window designed by Art Nouveau artist Alphonse Mucha. The main attraction inside the cathedral is St Wenceslas's Chapel, built by Peter Parler in which the national saint, Wenceslas, was interred. The saint's sacred place is exceptionally ornate; walls are decorated with polished jasper, amethysts, agate and emeralds, as well as fine gilding and frescoes.

Jewish Quarter (Josefov): The Jews of Prague suffered persecution from the Middle Ages, but found some freedom in their ghetto, now preserved as the Jewish Quarter and a memorial to their tenacity. The earliest mention of Prague's Jewish community comes from a document by the Jewish merchant Abraham ben Jakob, dated 965. The ghetto, built in about 1100 and surrounded by a wall, soon became one of the largest Jewish communities in Europe. Major sites include the Old-New Synagogue, the oldest remaining synagogue in Europe in which services are held. Nearby, the Old Jewish Cemetery is both a moving and fascinating place and was the last resting place for Jews between the 15th and 18th centuries. The number of graves is much greater than the 12,000 gravestones would suggest – this was the only place where Jews could be buried, so graves were layered one above the other. The Jewish community was destroyed in World War II, when thousands were sent to their deaths. Today there are around 1,500 people of Jewish descent in Prague.

Loreto Church: The Loreto Church is dedicated to the Virgin Mary and is the most famous pilgrimage church in Prague. The ornate facade and frescoes in the cloister date from the 18th century. In the tower is a glockenspiel with 27 bells, which play a Czech hymn to the Virgin Mary every hour. The highlight is the Treasure Chamber, which contains the remarkable Diamond Monstrance, a gift from a Bohemian nobleman. It was made in 1699 by Baptist Kanischbauer and Matthias Stegner of Vienna and is studded with over 6,000 diamonds.

Old Town Square (Staroměstské náměstí): Prague's picturesque Old Town Square is the natural midpoint of the Old Town, and the heart of Prague. Memorial tablets on the Town Hall Tower are reminders of various important events that have taken place here over the centuries. In the 12th century the Old Town Square was a central market place and a major crossroads on central European merchant routes. Over the next few centuries many buildings of Romanesque, Baroque and Gothic styles were erected. The Jan Hus monument in the centre of the square is in honour of the 15th-century reformer who stood up against the corrupt practices of the Catholic Church.

Astronomical Clock: The astronomical clock on the Town Hall Tower dates from 1410. It consists of three parts. In the middle is the actual clock, which also shows the movement of the sun and moon through the zodiac. Underneath is the calendar, with scenes from country life symbolising the 12 months of the year, painted by Josef Manés (these have now been replaced with replicas). The performance of the upper part of the clock is what draws the hordes of tourists. On the hour the figures play the same scene: Death rings the death knell and turns an hourglass upside down. The 12 Apostles proceed along the little windows that open before the chimes, and a cockerel flaps its wings and crows.

Týn Church: The landmark pointed towers of the Týn are one of the icons of Prague, looming 80m (260ft) above the Old Town. The building was erected between 1365 and 1511, and features many noteworthy Bohemian Baroque works of art and the oldest baptismal font (1414) in Prague. To the right of the high altar is the tombstone of the famous Danish astronomer Tycho Brahe, who worked at the court of Rudolf II. The church is a source of great national pride, and the facade, particularly when floodlit at night, is one of the finest sights in the Old Town.

National Gallery (Národní galerie): In Sternberg Palace, within the castle complex, is the National Gallery, which houses a fine collection of European art. There are three levels; the ground floor houses German and Austrian art from the 15th to the 18th centuries; the first floor comprises the art of antiquity, icons and the art of the Netherlands and Italy of the 14th to the 16th centuries; the second floor has Italian, Spanish, French, Dutch and Flemish art of the 16th to the 18th centuries. Albrecht Dürer's large-scale *Feast of the Rosary* is perhaps the most famous exhibit.

Wenceslas Square (Václavské náměstí): Nearly a kilometre (two-thirds of a mile) long, Wenceslas Square is not really a square at all, but a wide boulevard. Nowadays, the former horse market is dominated by hotels, bars, restaurants, cafés, banks and department stores. It is a busy area, along which half of Prague seems to stroll. The historic square is crowned by the giant equestrian statue of St Wenceslas, erected by Josef Myslbek in 1912 after taking 30 years to plan and design.

National Theatre (Národní divadlo): This is the city's main cultural venue and a potent symbol of the Czech spirit. In 1845 the ruling Habsburgs turned down the request for a Czech theatre. In response, money was collected on a voluntary basis, and the building of the theatre was declared a national duty. Built in an Italian Renaissance style in 1881, the theatre was destroyed in a fire just before it was due to open. Under Josef Schulz's direction, using many notable artists including Vojtěch Hynais, it was quickly rebuilt with the aid of endowments and donations and opened in 1883. The auditorium is only open to the public during performances.

North German port cities

Some river cruises also visit sea ports that lie within protected areas of the coastline. In the 19th century, wealthy Berliners came to the region to recuperate in fashionable coastal bathing resorts.

Cuxhaven (Km 730): The citizens of Cuxhaven in Lower Saxony once controlled all shipping in and out of the River Elbe. Today, however, it is one of the largest fishing ports in Germany and the centre of its fish processing industry. It is also home to Germany's oldest lighthouse, built in the 14th century on the island of Neuwerk.

Lauterbach, Isle of Rügen, Germany: Although few people think of islands when Germany is mentioned, Rügen is, at 926 sq km (357.5 sq miles), Germany's largest island, separated from the mainland by a narrow channel, although joined to the mainland by a 2.5km (1.5-mile) -long bridge. It is the port for Putbus, an elegant, all-white city that formerly had a royal residence, although its castle was demolished in 1960. Today, you can stroll around the castle gardens. The popular bathing resorts of Baabe, Binz, Göhren and Sellin are located on the southwest of the island.

Wolgast, Isle of Usedom, Germany: Another 'island', Germany's second largest and its easternmost, lies near the mouth of the River Oder, and the border with Poland. It is a mix of old established verdant forests (part of the national park) and white sandy beaches. Wolgast itself lies on the mainland at the point where a road bridge connects it with the island.

Stralsund, Germany: Located on the Baltic Sea coast and surrounded by three lakes, this port city, founded in 1209, features some fine architecture of Gothic red brick buildings, similar to those of nearby Lübeck. Although it has been the subject of many battles in the past, this important centre of maritime navigation has today been restored to its former glory.

Zingst, Germany: Sitting on a small peninsula, much of which is a national park (Vorpommersche Boddenlandschaft), the town has the character and charm of a typical German village untouched by time. Nearby, there are long sandy beaches and forests.

MUSIC

Several famous classical composers lived and worked between Hamburg and Prague, and Lutheran chants were always heard throughout the region.

Antonín Leopold Dvořák was born on 8 September 1841 in Nelahozeves (then Bohemia, now part of the Czech Republic), between Usti and Prague. He died on 1 May 1904 in Prague.

Leoš Janáček was born on 3 July 1854 in Hukvaldy, Moravia (then part of the Austrian empire, now in the Czech Republic). He died on 12 August 1928 in Ostrava (now part of the Czech Republic).

Bohuslav Martinů was born on 8 December 1890 in Policka, Bohemia, Austria-Hungary (now in the Czech Republic). He died on 28 August 1959 in Liestal, Switzerland.

Felix Mendelssohn was born on 3 February 1809 in Hamburg, Germany. He died on 4 November 1847 in Leipzig, Germany.

Bedřich Smetana was born on 2 March 1824 in Litomyšl, then Bohemia (now in the Czech Republic). He died on 12 May 1884 in Prague.

Robert Alexander Schumann was born on 8 June 1810 in Zwickaw, Saxony (now Germany). He died on 29 July 1856 in Endenich, near Bonn, Prussia, Germany.

River Rhône

A trip along the Rhône incorporates the gastronomy of Burgundy and Lyon, the Roman ruins of Vienne and Arles, the magnificent historic papal city of Avignon and modern-day cowboys in the Camargue.

The evocative names of Burgundy, Avignon, Lyon and Mâcon conjure up all kinds of enticing images, from fields of yellow sunflowers and purple lavender to ruby-red wines, truffles, rich cheeses and plates of charcuterie, not to mention magnificent Roman antiquities and colourful market towns. The Rhône flows through the gastronomic heart of France, carving its way across some of the most beautiful wine-growing country, as well as handsome, historic cities such as Avignon and Arles.

The Rhône has always been an important trade route, linking northern Europe to the Mediterranean and forming a means for armies from the south to move north through the continent. It is 813km (505 miles) long, and starts its journey in the Swiss Alps, just upstream from Lake Geneva. It descends westward through a long valley between the Alps and the Jura Mountains to Lake Geneva, and then enters France. The final section is from Lyon to the Golfe du Lion and the Mediterranean, which it enters through a two-armed delta that begins at Arles and extends for approximately 40km (25 miles) to the sea. The arms are known as the Great Rhône and the Little Rhône, with the unnavigable salt marshes and lagoon of the Camargue between them.

A Rhône river cruise starts either from Lyon, the country's gastronomic capital, located in the heart of the country between the Saône and Rhône rivers, or from Chalon-sur-Saône. In the reverse direction your journey will start from Arles or Avignon in Provence. If you are a devotee of French cuisine, it is worthwhile considering a stay of at least an extra day or two in Lyon. A visit on the third Thursday of November is always lively, since that's the date that Beaujolais Nouveau, cultivated near Lyon, is released for sale each year.

HIGHLIGHTS FROM CHALON-SUR-SAÔNE TO THE CAMARGUE

Chalon-sur-Saône (Km 141)

This important inland port in the heart of Burgundy is located at the confluence of the River Saône and the Canal du Centre in a region famous for its wine. Chalon is often the start for excursions to Dijon, considered by many to be the underrated capital of Burgundy (Dijon has a wide range of restaurants, an excellent city museum and a stunning array of Flem-

River Royale on the Rhône.

ish-influenced architecture in its beautiful city centre). Chalon's town's heart is place St Vincent, with its colourful half-timbered houses and cathedral, the oldest parts of which date from the 11th century. It was also the birthplace of photography in 1822; Kodak still has a presence here. Nicéphore Niépce is credited for having invented photography in 1816, and the Musée Nicéphore Niépce, located on quai de Messageries, slightly downstream from the Pont St-Laurent, covers every conceivable aspect of photography, including cameras employed on the Apollo space missions.

Mâcon (Km 80)

Nestled neatly into the west bank of the River Saône at the end of a 14th-century bridge (Pont St-Laurent), Mâcon is located at the southern end of the Burgundy wine region and plays an important part in its wine trade. May is the month when Mâcon hosts the Burgundy wine sales. The Unesco-protected Benedictine Abbey of Cluny, 25km (15 miles) northwest of Mâcon, is the highlight of a visit to this area, although wine lovers could travel to the region to taste the local wines.

Lyon (Km 0–12)

The gastronomic capital of France, Lyon actually lies on a little peninsula between the Rhône and Saône rivers. It was founded more than 2,000 years ago and is today the second-largest city in the country, and its most important educational centre outside Paris. The city's reputation for wonderful food is completely deserved, and there are countless local specialities to try, among them *quenelles de brochet* (mousse of pike) and a huge array of magnificent charcuterie. Notable Michelin-starred chefs connected with the city include Paul Bocuse, Guy Lassausaie and Philippe Gavreau.

There's also an eclectic collection of museums in the city, including the Musée Historique des Tissus et des Arts Décoratifs – a wonderful textile museum with some rare exhibits – and the Musée des Beaux Arts, its collection ranked second in France only to that of the Louvre.

A visit to Lyon also usually includes a trip up Fourvière Hill, requiring either a clamber up steep steps or a funicular ride. At the top, you can visit the Basilique de Notre-Dame and gaze out over the city's rooftops, past the two rivers to the vineyards beyond. Riverships tie up close to some magnificent architecture, including one of the city's historic universities.

DID YOU KNOW...?

...that the Rhône is the only major river that flows directly into the Mediterranean?
...that the river has famously fierce currents? Climatic conditions (eg the mistral) and seasonal changes (eg bringing meltwater from the Alps) create extra navigational difficulties.
...that the French for 'lock' is *écluse*?

Vienne (Km 28)

This town's position, between the Beaujolais and Burgundy wine regions, makes it the gateway to the countryside around Lyon. Most notable, however, is the town's amazing Roman heritage: Vienne has one of the best-preserved Roman amphitheatres in France, on the slopes of nearby Mt Pipet, seating 13,000 and still used for theatrical performances. The Temple d'Auguste et de Livie in the town itself is also an arresting example of 1st-century Roman architecture. Vienne is well known for its jazz festival, which normally takes place in July.

Tournon-sur-Rhône (Km 91)

The scenery as the river carves its way south is rugged and mountainous, dotted with castles and jagged rock outcrops, although vineyards are still the main feature along the banks. Tournon is one of the region's most attractive cities, nestling on the left bank of the river (Tain-l'Hermitage is on the opposite bank) and overlooked by its 10th-century castle, built into a rock.

An excursion from here – not to be missed – is a 32km (20 mile) ride on a nostalgic steam-hauled train to the Ardèche region (between Tournon and Lamastre), a wild, limestone upland of craggy cliffs, gorges and caves in the Doux Valley, with red wine and lavender among its main products.

There are also excursions by coach to the Gorge de l'Ardèche: a road runs along the top of the red-rock gorge, the river a silvery ribbon hundreds of feet below, and there are various lookout points and peculiar rock formations. Between Tournon and the city of Valence, the Rhône is reinforced by the turbulent waters of the Isère, flowing in from the Alps to the northeast.

Tain-l'Hermitage (Km 91)

Tournon and Tain-l'Hermitage are connected by a bridge, created by the celebrated engineer Marc Seguin, in 1825. He used cables made from iron wires for the first time; the original bridge was taken down in 1965, but today you can still walk across a replica bridge, dating from 1849. A food market is located in the town centre on place du Tourobole (named after the sacrifice of the bulls in ancient times), while close by is the delightfully decadent Cité du Chocolat Valrhona, which is a haven for chocolate lovers. If your rivership docks overnight, take a stroll along the embankment – a favourite pastime for locals and visitors alike.

Viviers (Km 166)

This hilltop town – a Unesco World Heritage site and one of the best-preserved Medieval towns in southern France – occupies a strategically important position. It has a long history, dating to when the Celts occupied the location. It is divided into two parts, established when it became a bishopric in the 5th century. The Upper Town, which can only be accessed through the 40m (130-ft) -high Tower of St Michael,

View of Lyon from Fourvière Hill.

remained an ecclesiastical domain for over 1,000 years. It has outstanding views over the Rhône. The Lower Town includes the magnificent Maison des Chevaliers, built by an important government official in the mid-16th century. The Lower Part was the home of artisans and tradesmen, and is remarkably well preserved.

This quiet town retains its old-world charm today, with medieval houses and its impressive cathedral of St Vincent. Some riverships stay overnight, when the illuminated town is beautiful, and mysterious.

An excursion may be offered to Montélimar, known as the centre for nougat-making in France (it was created here in the 16th century). Almond trees were imported here Asia; nougat is made from ground almonds, mixed with local honey, sugar and egg whites, before being boiled and then allowed to set.

Some riverships may make a stop at Châteauneuf-du-Pape. The town is about 5km (3 miles) from the landing stage, from where an excursion to the town and its environs may be offered.

However, one thing not to be missed is a visit to the Pont du Gard, the 2,000-year-old aqueduct whose three tiers of arches were built without mortar. The awe-inspiring Roman-built structure stands 274m (900ft) long and is 49m (160ft) tall.

Avignon (Km 241)

The river broadens out as it enters Provence and nears the Mediterranean, although the scenery is still undulating and becomes rich with colour – yellow sunflowers all summer long, and ranks of purple lavender spread across the hilltops, scenting the air.

The beautiful university city of Avignon is totally encircled by medieval walls and known as the 'City of Popes'; in the 14th century, this was the residence of the papacy for 70 years. The ravishingly handsome medieval Palais des Papes at the centre is one of the great wonders of France, and was once considered the heart of the Christian world. Nearby are the remains of the famous bridge, Pont St-Bénezet – originally built in 1189 – which juts out across a branch of the river (only four out of the original 23 arches remain). It was reduced to its present condition by terrible flooding in 1667. It is the subject of one of the most famous French nursery rhymes, Sur le Pont d'Avignon ('On the bridge of Avignon'). The city has a terrific buzz on warm summer nights, with outdoor cafés and bars lining the streets and free entertainment provided by buskers and street artists, especially during the Theatre Festival in July.

Châteauneuf-du-Pape

Not far from Avignon (about 16 km/10 miles) is Châteauneuf-du-Pape. It was Pope John XXII of Avignon who planted the vines in the grounds of what was his summer home. Today, the cuvée red wines (a blend of the temperamental grenache and other grape varieties) are among the most respected in France. Some riverships may dock at the town itself.

Pont St-Bénézet and the Palais des Papes, Avignon.

Tarascon (Km 267)

Your rivership might stop at the fortified medieval town of Tarascon, from where you can visit Arles on an excursion. The river runs right through the centre of the commune, which is located between Arles and Avignon. Among the main attractions are the 15th-century Château de Tarascon, built on the edge of the Rhône, and a 12th-century collegiate church of St Martha. Provençal fabrics can be seen in a museum located in a 14th-century building in the town centre (the Charles Demery fabric factory is in the town). If your rivership happens to be in Tarascon on a Tuesday, it's worth visiting the market.

Arles (Km 282) and the Camargue

The Romans built their first bridge across the Rhône here, and this helped to create a vital link between Italy and Spain. The small town – one of the most attractive in Provence – is located on the banks of the river. It boasts many Gallo-Roman ruins, including Les Arènes, an amphitheatre that has a capacity of 20,000 and is still used for bullfights and plays. A visit to the animated place du Forum, in the heart of town, is a must. Vincent van Gogh, who lived here for 444 days between 1880 and 1890, immortalised in vibrant colours many of this city's highlights.

The river splits into two arms just before Arles; the Petit Rhône flows to the southwest, while the Grand Rhône continues south for about 48km (30 miles) and empties (after coursing through the Camargue's marshes and silt) into the Mediterranean Sea. From Arles, you can take an excursion (it may be included in the cost of your holiday) to the Camargue, the delta of the River Rhône and one of Europe's finest nature reserves, with its unspoiled landscape and wildlife (renowned for its wild, pink flamingos, black bulls and white horses). You may be able to see the *gardians*, modern-day Camargue cowboys who tend the bulls.

Just 32km (20 miles) from Arles is Nîmes, where denim (serge de Nîmes) was created. It was the 16th-century name given to the tough fabric produced in the city and used as material for making sacks. Transported to America via Genoa, it was chosen by a German immigrant in San Francisco – Levi Strauss – as a sturdy material for clothing for gold prospectors in the 'Gold Rush' in about 1850.

MUSIC

Several French composers were born or died in the region of the River Rhône.

Claude-Achille Debussy was born on 22 August 1862 in St-Germaine-en-Laye, France. He died on 25 March 1918 in Paris.

Clément-Philibert-Léo Delibes was born on 21 February 1836 in St-Germain-du-Val, France 1836. He died on 16 January 1891 in Paris.

Olivier Messiaen was born on 10 December 1908 in Avignon, France. He died 27 April 1992 in Clichy, near Paris.

Darius Milhaud was born on 4 September 1892 in Aix-en-Provence, France. He died on 22 June 1974 in Geneva, Switzerland.

Jean-Phillippe Rameau was baptised on 25 September 1683 in Dijon, France. He died on 12 September 1764 in Paris.

Edgard Victor Achille Charles Varèse was born on 22 December 1883 in Paris. He died on 6 November 1965 in New York, US.

River Seine

A voyage along the Seine offers beautiful scenery, from romantic Paris to bucolic Normandy and historic Rouen to the pretty port of Honfleur. Gastronomic delights and wine tours add to the appeal.

From the iconic French capital to Honfleur, one of the most picturesque of all French ports, the Seine has been witness to some of the most remarkable characters throughout history: Joan of Arc, Van Gogh, Seurat and Claude Monet. A cruise along this slow-flowing river is a gentle voyage through some of France's most mellow countryside, of farmland and meadows, historic towns and sleepy villages. It is also a gastronomic adventure, in the land of brie and camembert cheeses, Calvados liqueur and Normandy cider.

The Seine is is 780km (485 miles) long, and its source is 471m (1,545.2ft) above sea level on Mont Tasselot in the Côte d'Or region of Burgundy. It is the longest navigable waterway in France, and carries more commercial traffic and freight than any other river or canal in the country. It flows northwest of Dijon, Burgundy, through the dry chalk plateau of Champagne then through Paris, Giverny, Rouen and across Normandy before emptying into the English Channel not far from Le Havre. The estuary is wide and extends for 26km (16 miles) between Tancarville and Le Havre. The relatively flat Seine is slow-flowing and hence eminently navigable. On its journey, it is joined by the Aube, near Romilly, the Yonne, near Montereau, and the Marne, its greatest tributary, near Paris.

Riverships can go all the way to Paris all year round – the reason why the port of Paris trans-ships more than 20 million tons of cargo each year.

HIGHLIGHTS FROM PARIS TO HONFLEUR

Paris (Km 0)

The major highlight is, of course, Paris, perhaps the most romantic city in Europe.

It is cut through the middle by the slowly meandering River Seine and edged with gentle hills. The Seine is the capital's widest avenue; it is spanned by a total of 37 bridges, which provide some of the loveliest views of Paris. The fascination of the French capital is eternal, and the city has long been a magnet to artists, writers, philosophers and composers. Grand architecture, fine cuisine and haute couture combine to make Paris one of the most glamorous European capitals. Ile St-Louis, in the middle of the River Seine and at the heart of the city, is the official start of kilometre markings along the River Seine.

River Baroness cruising on the Seine.

There are too many city highlights to cover here in full, so what follows is a classic top-10 big sights. If you know the city already, less obvious delights include the Marais area, with its show-stopping place des Vosges, or the adjacent, more edgy, Bastille. Otherwise, head to the literary St-Germain, explore the city's other key waterway, the Canal St-Martin, or, if shopping appeals, the so-called grands magasins (department stores), including Galeries Lafayette and Printemps. Alternatively, if the weather allows, simply relax in the elegant Parisian parks, such as the Jardin du Luxembourg or the Tuileries or else just along the arty banks of the Seine itself.

KEY SIGHTS INCLUDE

Musée du Louvre: One of the largest palaces in Europe has assembled an incomparable collection of Old Masters, sculptures and antiquities. There are 380,000 objects in the collection, of which around 35,000 are displayed. It has three wings, and the superb collections are divided up into seven different sections, each assigned its own colour to help you find your way around. Highlights include Leonardo da Vinci's Mona Lisa.

Tour Eiffel: No visit to Paris would be complete without a trip to the Eiffel Tower, symbol of the city and of France herself. The metal giant looms over the area southwest of the centre. This icon of iron girders was chosen as the centrepiece to the World Fair of 1889. The first two floors are negotiated on foot or by lift, and then another lift goes up to the top. From here you will see a spectacular city panorama, best viewed one hour before sunset.

Notre-Dame: The cathedral's position on the banks of the Seine is an unforgettable setting. Just as Gothic cathedrals were considered symbols of paradise, so the entrance facade, with its series of sculptures, was considered to be the gateway to heaven. The stories of the Bible are depicted in the portals, paintings and stained glass of the cathedral. The scale exceeded all earlier churches – Paris became the capital only a few years before the foundation stone was laid, and the building was designed to reflect the power of the state and its church. Construction work on the cathedral began in 1163 and was finished around 1240. The exquisite 13th-century north and south rose windows are star attractions.

Arc de Triomphe: Built between 1806 and 1836, this triumphal arch is the epitome of French grandeur. The many statues on the main facade glorify the insurrection of 1792 and Napoleon's major victories.

Centre Pompidou: Made entirely of glass and surrounded by a white steel grid, the Pompidou Centre is the main showcase for modern and contemporary art in Paris. Now a much-loved city icon, Richard Rogers and Renzo Piano's 'inside-out' design was controversial when it was unveiled in 1977.

Sacré-Cœur: Perched on the Montmartre hilltop is the virginal-white Basilique du Sacré-Cœur, its Byzantine cupolas as much a part of the city skyline as the Eiffel Tower. It can be reached by walking up 250 steps or by taking a funicular cable car. When the lights are turned on at night, the Sacré-Cœur resembles a lit wedding cake.

Musée d'Orsay: France's national museum of 19th-century art is housed in the former Gare d'Orsay, an ornate Beaux-Arts train station, opened in 1900 to serve passengers to the World Fair. It's an immensely dramatic setting, worth visiting for its own sake. But the museum's contents are unmissable too: there is a major collection of paintings by the Impressionists, plus works by Delacroix and Ingres.

Musée Rodin: Housed in the Hotel Biron is the Rodin Museum. Auguste Rodin came to live here in 1908 and stayed until his death in 1917. Here you can admire Rodin's famous works, The Kiss and The Thinker, reputedly based on Dante contemplating the Inferno.

Sainte-Chapelle: This is a masterpiece of Parisian Rayonnant Gothic architecture on the Ile de la Cité. The beautiful 13th-century stained glass, magnificently displayed in 85 major panels, is without equal anywhere in Paris.

Versailles: Located southwest of Paris lies the grand Palace of Versailles. Take the RER line C5, which will drop you a short distance away. Allow a full day to visit the château and its magnificent formal gardens.

Conflans–Ste-Honorine (Km 68)

Situated on the confluence of the Oise and the Seine, the pretty town of Conflans became an important shipping centre from 1855 onwards, when a chain was laid along the bed of the Seine allowing barges to be hauled upstream to the capital. Highlights of the town include the Montjoie Tower (look out for the novel violin maker's shop tucked into the side walls) and St-Maciou church. A religious festival is held here for three days each June, and riverships flock to attend. Many riverships also moor here overnight, and tours may take you to Napoleon and Josephine Bonaparte's Château de Malmaison and its gardens, just outside Paris.

DID YOU KNOW...?

...that the name Seine comes from the Latin name 'Sequana', the goddess of the river?
...that the Seine is the third-longest river in France, after the Loire and the Rhône?
...that Joan of Arc's ashes were supposedly scattered in the Seine at Rouen?
...that the first steamboat on the River Seine was in 1816? However, it actually frightened the people along the river banks because the vessel's steam engine sprayed out smoke and sparks.
...that the composer Puccini set his 1918 opera Il Tabarro (The Cloak) aboard a barge on the Seine?
...that in 1991 the banks of the Seine in Paris were declared World Heritage sites? Unesco calls the French capital 'a river town', with banks 'studded with a succession of masterpieces'.

Melun (Km 110)

About 45km (28 miles) from Paris, Melun (the Romans called it Melodunum) is, like Paris, located on both banks of the Seine, on the northern edge of the forest of Fontainebleau. Its ancient church of Notre-Dame stands on an island between two branches of the river. The town is a centre of commerce for the agricultural district of southern Brie. The famous Brie de Melun is made here – quite different in texture and taste to the bries of Coulommiers, Meaux and Montereau.

Located about 6km (4 miles) from Melun is the 17th-century royal Château de Fontainebleau, home of French kings and emperors from François I to Napoleon and well worth a visit, if time allows.

Giverny (Km 147)

World-famous as the setting for the water-lily pond and graceful arched bridge immortalised by the Impressionist artist Claude Monet, who lived here for 43 years, Giverny is one of France's most-visited sights, receiving 500,000 tourists a year, some of them clutching easels and paint, hoping to recreate the master's work. You can visit the house and, of course, the garden, which is especially glorious, even if the throng of tourists does take a little of the shine off it. The Musée d'Art Americain Giverny, located just along the main road in the village and showcasing the works of Monet and some of the US-born Impressionists inspired by him, is also worth a visit.

Vernon (Km 150)

The delightful medieval town of Vernon is an alternative stopping point for riverships and excursions to Giverny. Vernon is home to the Collégiale Notre-Dame, built large in the Gothic style between the 11th and 16th centuries, with a large, flamboyant rose window, while the town is full of half-timbered houses, mostly from the 16th century. Cross the bridge and you can see the Château de Tourelles.

It's worth taking an excursion to the Château de Biz, built in 1740 and nicknamed 'Normandy's Versailles'. It has a magnificent courtyard and water garden, and is linked by a splendid lime-tree avenue

over a kilometre long to the town itself. The château houses an exhibition of horse-drawn carriages, as well as tapestries and momentos to Napoleon

Les Andelys (Km 174)

Delightful copper-topped street lights with twin hanging baskets of flowers characterise the charming village of Les Andelys, situated on a stunning scenic bend in the Seine. Located above the town itself is the imposing fortress of Château Gaillard, built in 1196 by England's King Richard the Lionheart. This masterpiece of medieval military architecture was built in just one year. Richard the Lionheart was killed just two years later.

Rouen (Km 238–245)

Rouen is known as the 'City of 100 Spires', and you can see its graceful skyline as you approach along the river. Until the 17th century, it was the second-largest city in France, and is still important today as France's fourth-largest port. Although badly damaged during World War II, the city has been extensively restored – in particular the 700 or so half-timber-framed buildings on the right bank of the river in the old quarter. The spot everybody wants to see, though, is the bronze cross in place du Vieux Marché, where Joan of Arc was burnt at the stake as a 'witch' in 1431.

Other sights include the magnificent Cathédrale Notre Dame, the western facade of which was painted by Monet (the work is housed in the city's Musée des Beaux Arts), and the medieval Eglise St-Maclou, which contains some superb wood carvings. Also look out for the Gros Horloge, a splendid, gold-faced clock mounted into an arch, which you would see as you leave place de la Cathédrale. Rouen is also home to some superb Michelin-starred restaurants, including the two-starred Gill and the one-starred L'Odas and Origine.

Caudebec-en-Caux (Km 309.5)

The medieval town of Caudebec-en-Caux is a short cruise downstream from Rouen, through pretty Nor-

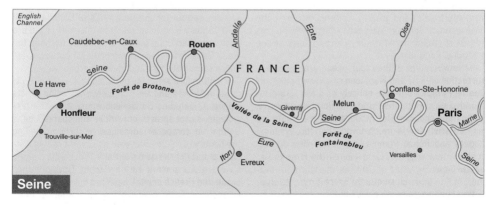

Monet's house and garden at Giverny.

mandy scenery of woods, orchards and fields. Its main attraction is the Eglise Notre Dame, the construction of which was started by the English when they conquered the town in the 14th century, but completed by the French in 1439 after they had won the town back. The church is in flamboyant Gothic style, with an abundance of intricate stone carvings, flying buttresses and graceful spires. Close by is the 13th-century Templar's House, which now houses the Biochet-Brechot Museum, which focuses on the history of Caudebec.

Most riverships offer a tour to the pretty seaside town of Honfleur. Some stay overnight and offer all-day tours to the Normandy beaches – the target for the greatest amphibious military operation in history. D-Day excursions typically visit the Pegasus Bridge and memorial museum, Omaha beach (the prettiest beach), possibly also Utah beach, and Pointe du Hoc. Another tour may include a view of the famous Bayeux Tapestry, which illustrates the Norman invasion of England and the Battle of Hastings, together with a taste of Normandy's cuisine.

Honfleur (Km 355)

The Seine broadens out into a wide estuary as it approaches the coast, and is busy with commercial traffic. Honfleur is a charming old port city on the southern shore of the Seine Estuary, opposite the port of Le Havre; most cruises turn around here and head back to Paris. It was from Honfleur that French settlers set out for the new lands of Canada in the 16th century. The town really is the stuff of picture postcards, particularly around the inner harbour, the Vieux Bassin, where narrow medieval houses overlook a colourful yacht and fishing harbour.

It's no surprise that the light, the space, the old coloured buildings and the boats have attracted artists for years, including Boudin and many of the Impressionists. You can see their work in the Musée Eugène Boudin, which has an ethnographic section detailing the history of the town as well as several rooms containing paintings, mainly from the 19th century, of the town, including some work by Monet. Buying French bread and cheese or duck pâté and having a picnic on a bench beside the river is highly recommended here.

Bordeaux Region Cruising

Think of wine, cognac, oysters, truffles, châteaux and grand architecture and you'll be in the heart of alluring Bordeaux

RIVERS DORDOGNE, GARONNE, GIRONDE

Just below the city of Bordeaux, the Dordogne and the Garonne rivers (the latter starts in southwest France and mostly flows northwest from the Spanish Pyrenees) meet to form the Gironde. This is actually an estuary rather than a river and is under the constant influence of the Atlantic tides in the Bassin d'Arcachon – Europe's largest estuary.

The area is renowned for its fish farming and oyster cultivation (up to 10,000 tons of oysters are harvested in the Bassin d'Arcachon each year). Special flat-bottomed boats – called *pinasses* – are used due to the shallow, marshy water and the remarkable profusion of bird life.

It is the Gironde (about 72km/45 miles long and 3 to 11km/2 to 7 miles wide, it includes Gironde Island) that provides the gateway to Bordeaux. The river divides the famed wine-growing region into two distinct sections: the Left Bank and the Right Bank. Strong tidal currents can be challenging for navigation, and there are numerous sandbanks, shallows and other obstructions to negotiate.

Bordeaux region cruises on the Garonne are relatively new, but itineraries include excursions to the stunning ancient commune of St-Emilion, and the châteaux and estates of one or more of the famous winemakers such as Pauillac. Both the Garonne (including the Dordogne) and Gironde wend their way through charming picture-postcard landscapes.

Graves and Médoc wines are made in the low-lying gravelly land to the south of the Gironde. The gently sloping right bank, which consists of limestone and clay, to the north, is home to some of the most famous wine districts such as Pomerol and St-Emilion.

About Bordeaux cruises

Cruising the tidal rivers Garonne, Gironde and Dordogne can prove challenging for river cruise operators because they are influenced by the sea, particularly by the huge estuary of the River Gironde, which has tides of up to 7m (23 ft).

Among the companies that feature Bordeaux region cruises include: AMA Waterways, Avalon Waterways, CroisiEurope, Grand Circle Cruise Line, Scenic, Uniworld and Viking River Cruises.

Bordeaux

The vineyards covering the rolling hills along the banks of the rivers of the Aquitaine region are renowned for their remarkable wines. The city of Bordeaux is at the heart of 'wineland'.

With over 8,500 châteaux in the region, it's no wonder that Bordeaux has become world renowned as the capital of the wine world. Bordeaux itself is the ninth largest city in France. It is situated on a bend in the River Garonne, and is the capital of Aquitaine and the Gironde *département*; it is also a major university city. Bordeaux was founded over 2,000 years ago, when it was known as Burdigala. Formerly known as *la belle au bois dormant* (Sleeping Beauty), Bordeaux is, today, the centre of the wine trade and home to the world's main wine fair, Vinexpro. The city is also famous for its *macarons* (macaroons), typically filled with buttercream, caramel or preserves.

Bordeaux has a population of about 250,000 and is an absolute delight since its park-like waterfront regeneration was completed in 2013. Riverships moor directly alongside the city centre, on a broad stretch of the river, close to the St-Michael basilica and magnificent Cathédrale St-André, charming pedestrian-only boulevards, and place des Quincones, one of the largest squares in Europe.

Blaye

The 17th-century citadel (small fortress) town of Blaye is situated on the right bank of the Gironde. It was built

Bordeaux by night.

Vineyard in St-Emilion.

to protect the Bordeaux region from invasion via the Bay of Biscay. Blaye lies opposite a small island named the Ile Paté, home to Fort Paté. These two fortress locations form part of a trio of fortifications known as the 'Fortifications of Vauban' group (Vauban was Louis XIV's outstanding military engineer), the other being Fort Médoc on the opposite side, the left bank – all were listed in 2008 as Unesco World Heritage sites.

The citadel of Blaye is a short walk from your rivership's landing place. Today the thick-walled moated fortress contains tunnels, a museum and a well-established market town. Over time, the town outgrew its walls, and then started to spread along the riverfront. Warehouses for wine storage, wine cellars, coopers' shops and wine-transportation agents sprung up to service the growth of the wine business. Blaye is not far from the vineyards of Pomerol and St-Emilion.

Libourne

This charming little fortified town was created in 1270 and originally named Leyburnia, after Roger de Leybourne (1215–71), of Kent, England. It is strategically located where the Isle and Dordogne rivers meet. Today, Libourne is a pretty and dynamic little town and the wine-making capital of the northern Gironde. Located close to Pomerol and St-Emilion, it is a sister (and often a rival) to Bordeaux as a distributor and exporter of the region's fine wines. Other attractions include the fish market, one of the largest in the region, held every weekend in the main square, place Abel Surchamp.

Bourg (Bourg-en-Gironde)

This lovely ancient town is located high on a hilly outcrop at the confluence of the Dordogne and Garonne rivers. It is enclosed by ramparts with streets that tumble down to the harbour front and marina.

Cadillac

Located on the Garonne, directly opposite Sauterne, the charming Aquitaine medieval bastide town of Cadillac was founded in 1280. Its attractions include the

imposing Château des Ducs d'Epernon, a horseshoe-shaped palace that dominates the town.

St-Emilion

This stunning Dordogne town, whose heyday was considered to be in the Middle Ages, was named after the monk Emilion. It is now a Unesco World Heritage Site, with highlights including numerous wine merchants and a remarkable subterranean church, hewn out of soft limestone bedrock. The largest of its kind in Europe, it measures 35m (115ft) long, 20m (66ft) wide and up to 11m (36ft) high. If you like wine, and have some spare time (perhaps if you are not on an organised tour), do visit the 14th-century Cloître des Cordeliers – a former Franciscan friary, where sparkling wine is made and aged in the labyrinth of underground passages.

River cruise companies provide an excursion that will take you to the cobblestoned town square, and include a visit to the Eglise Monolithe, whose tower is 52m (171ft) tall. Climb the 196 steps to the top to get some magnificent views over the town and its fortifications.

Arcachon

Long considered the jewel of France's western coastline in Aquitaine, Arcachon is located on the northern tip of Europe's longest coastal beach, some 55km (34 miles) southwest of Bordeaux. Its bay is known for hosting Europe's largest sand dune, the Dune du Pilat, which is almost 3km (2 miles) long and home to an array of nature habitats, as well as being an important oyster-growing area.

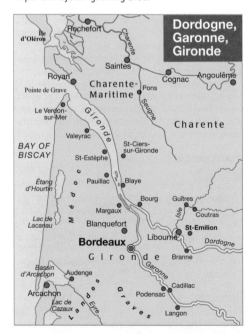

The Loire

Enchanting, but shallow and challenging, and with specialised vessels only able to navigate its extremes.

With a length of 1,012km (629 miles), the River Loire drains an area of 117,054 sq km (45,195 sq miles) – that's about one-fifth of France. The Loire flows from the Cévennes Mountains to St Nazaire, on the Bay of Biscay in the west. It forms the southwest border of Burgundy, and along its axis stand the main towns of the Nièvre *département*: La Charité-sur-Loire, Pouilly-sur-Loire and Cosne-Cours-sur-Loire. Like most rivers it has attracted settlements and trade since prehistory – when boats were fashioned from tree trunks to navigate the river.

A rich array of wildlife inhabits the River Loire and its sandbanks – so much so that a strip of 20km (12 miles) is now a protected nature reserve. The temperate climate along the river's valley is due to the influence of the Atlantic and this provides a remarkably diverse range of wildlife and fauna. The stretch between Chalonnes and Sully-sure Loire is also a Unesco World Heritage Site because of its 'outstanding cultural landscape'. But it is the glorious châteaux and their gardens that visitors come to admire.

The river's path through Burgundy begins in the Brionnais in eastern France, not far from the medieval village of Semur-en-Brionnaise, one of the most beautiful villages in France. The river carries on to Digoin, known as the 'town of water' with the rivers Arroux, Bourbince, Vouzance and Aronce converging on the Loire, making it a boater's haven. With a marina for 100 craft, the Canal du Centre, Canal Latéral à la Loire and Canal de Roanne à Digoin converge here.

One of the most interesting and scenic aspects is that of the Pont-Canal, which resembles a viaduct, except that it is a 'viacanal', which crosses the Loire and joins the Canal du Centre with the Canal Latéral at a great height. You can watch the activity from the 'Observaloire' centre on the river bank.

The inspiration for *Sleeping Beauty* came from the turreted castle of Ussé. Today, the big attractions are the storybook villages, historic towns and fortified châteaux, not to mention the wonderful array of wines that are produced in this beautiful environment (France's third-largest AOC region).

At present, among the river cruise companies, only CroisiEurope cruises the Loire, with the custom-designed, mid-ships side paddlewheel vessel *Loire Princesse*, built in 2015.

Taking in the view from the *Loire Princesse*.

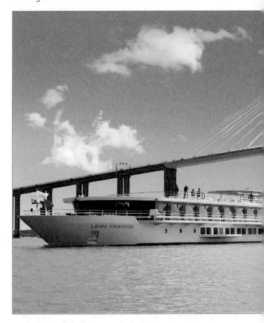

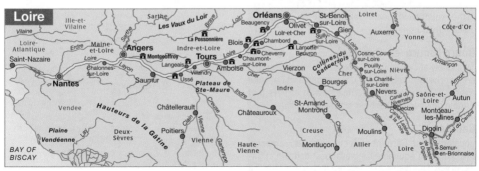

River Douro

Portugal's picturesque Douro Valley is a winning cruise destination between April and November. The journey is usually a round trip from Porto, taking in country estates and celebrated port wineries.

The Phoenicians and Romans mined gold in the Baixo Douro region and used the river to transport the ore to the coast – hence the name, which means 'of gold', although some poetically say that the name also derives from the golden sheen of the river as it reflects the sunlight, and the sand-coloured hills through which it flows.

The Douro region itself lies north of the river, while to its south is Biero Alto. The river starts small in the high hills of the Picos de Urbion, in Spain's Soria Province, to the north of Madrid (the river is called 'Duero' by the Spanish). It then flows west across to the border with Portugal, before turning southwest, delineating the border for approximately 97km (60 miles). It then flows west again, meandering though some enchanting countryside, including sleepy villages, castles, almond and olive groves, and vineyards that have remained remarkably unchanged and pastoral for hundreds of years, before hitting the Atlantic at Portugal's second city, Porto (Oporto).

The river serves as a transportation route for wine products of Portugal's Paiz do Vinho region; it also supports Portugal's fishing industry. The river is navigable within Portugal, although there are rapids and occasional flooding in its lower reaches. Only vessels with a very shallow draft can enter the river due to sandbars at its mouth.

From Porto, you cruise 'upstream' and cross five dams and locks, including the Crestuma-Lever Dam (14m/46ft), the Carrapatelo (35m/115ft – one of the hightest in the world), the Bauste Dam (28m/92ft), Valeira Dam (32m/105ft) and the Pachino Dam (20m/66ft). Excursions are made by motor coach to various *quintas* (country estates) and establishments that produce the region's favourite tipple – port.

The dams were constructed along the Douro in the 1980s for flood control and for electricity and hydro-electric power generation. Fortunately, the planners had the foresight to include locks within the dams, and these have enabled navigation right through Portugal and into Spain. The once fast-flowing river is now like a series of connected tranquil lakes with spectacular scenery.

In addition to the city highlights, you'll encounter almond and olive groves, fincas, and constant terraced hillside vineyards. The other attractions of a Douro cruise include the Portuguese cuisine, which is simple but full of taste. Fresh fish and seafood play an important part, as do ham and chicken, and fresh vegetables that are typically grown by small farms that do not use pesticides. Locally produced wines are plentiful, of good quality, and usually enjoyed with lunch and dinner. Events might include a *fado* (literally, fate) evening, a great chance to sample this unique Portuguese form of music that always tells a sad story.

Cruising from Porto.

Note that cruises along the Douro often include a coach excursion from the border town of Vega de Terrón to the historic Spanish university city of Salamanca.

HIGHLIGHTS ON A ROUND TRIP FROM PORTO

Riverships on the Douro are smaller in size than those sailing on the Danube/Rhine, due mainly to the size of the locks and dams built for flood control. Most are about 80m (262ft) in length vs 135m (443ft) for Danube riverships.

Only a handful of river cruise companies operate on the Douro, usually offering seven-night itineraries starting and finishing in Porto. Typical stops include Peso da Régua, Pinhão and Vega de Terrón (a jumping-off point for Salamanca, across the border in Spain). Apart from the joy of cruising the river as it carves its way through the steep hills, most of the excursions are a coach journey away from the various stops. Cruises can be combined with a stay in Lisbon and Coimbra, Portugal's former medieval capital and still an important university town, using local trains for transport.

Porto

Located on the Douro, Porto (Oporto) is Portugal's second-largest city, the heart of the port-wine trade and one of the most attractive cities on the Iberian Peninsula. It dominates the hillsides above the Douro, tumbling down the side of a gorge carved from granite by the fast-flowing water. The gorge is spanned by several graceful bridges, leading to Vila Nova de Gaia on the opposite bank, where all the great port lodges are located, including Cockburns and Sandeman – their English names reminders of the fact that British merchants controlled the industry from its inception. Cruise boats moor up in the heart of the city on the Vila Nova side, within easy reach on foot of the medieval town, the Ribeira district. On the banks of the river you'll see the colourful *rabelo* boats that were once used to transport port down from the vineyards.

Rabelo boats once transported port down from the vineyards.

The historic city has Unesco World Heritage status and was designated a European City of Culture in 2001. The city centre is a chaotic mix of medieval alleys, the old fisherman's quarter and a skyline of ornate Baroque towers, all crowned by a magnificent cathedral. Highlights include the Ponte Dom Luis I (the iron bridge), an impressive steel railway bridge that looms over the vividly painted houses of the Ribeira district and spans the river to the south bank. Built in 1886, the bridge has two decks, the upper one for the metro, and leads directly to port cellars in Vila Nova de Gaia.

The cathedral Sé crowns the highest point of the granite rock on which much of the old town stands. It was built as a defensive fortification in the 12th century, and despite extensive alterations it has retained its fortress-like appearance. The 18th-century Torre dos Clérigos is the tallest granite tower in Portugal and has become the emblem of Porto. Unless you really have no head for heights it is worth climbing the endless spiral staircase of 225 or so steps for a dazzling view over the city, the river Douro and its estuary. Another notable church is Santo Ildefonso, built in the 18th century and decorated with *azulejos* (glazed tiles) depicting scenes from the life of St Ildefonso and allegories of the Eucharist. Look out, too,

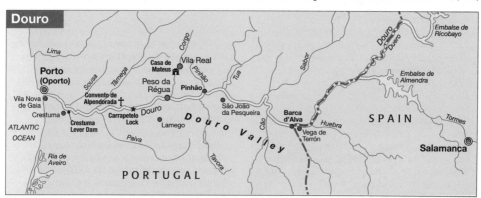

for the Stock Exchange, built on the site of a convent, which burnt down in 1832. It is noted for its opulent neo-Moorish reception hall. Finally, across the Ponte Dom Luis I, are the port-wine lodges of Vila Nova de Gaia. Many of the larger ones welcome weekday visitors to tour the installations and taste their wines. Most prominent is Sandeman, whose distinctive silhouette rises on the skyline.

Peso da Régua

From Porto the Douro snakes eastwards to Peso da Régua past wooded valleys, fields of almond trees and quiet villages. Shortly after leaving Porto, the rivership passes through the floodgates of the Crestuma-Lever Dam, one of several built over the last few decades to tame the river, which was previously difficult to navigate. Some cruises stop for the evening at Bitetos, with an excursion to the nearby 11th-century Convento de Alpendurada, which overlooks the river. The monastery hosts medieval-style banquets and wine-tastings, and provides an atmospheric setting for dinner. The Carrapetelo Lock, with a maximum lift/drop of 35m/yds, is also a highlight of this stretch of the river.

The port region proper begins at Peso da Régua. At this point, the river suddenly enters a region of steep hills covered with green vineyards, and the occasional lavish manor house set back from the river. Giant lettering on the hillsides denotes each grower's name. Peso da Régua is the home of the Port Wine Institute, and almost all its inhabitants have some connection with the port-wine trade; in the past, this was the starting point for the *rabelo* boats, laden with barrels, on their long and treacherous journey to Vila Nova de Gaia on the coast.

For passengers it's now a departure point for coach tours to Vila Real, 25km (16 miles) to the north, and notable as home to the Casa de Mateus.

Pinhão

This small, rustic Douro town, located at the end of the wine trail, is known for its picturesque setting and its proximity to the *quintas*, the country seats of the big names in port production. The railway station has some beautiful *azulejos* (ceramic tiles) on the walls, depicting local scenes and culture. The town also has a bridge by the French architect Gustave Eiffel (of tower fame). Riverships stop here to run excursions to the wine-growing estates, where visitors learn about grape crushing, fermentation and blending. Even if you don't drink port, it is worth the visit simply to admire the beauty of the estates, some of them with lavish gardens on the river banks.

Vila Real (Casa de Mateus)

The magnificent 18th-century Baroque house and gardens of Casa de Mateus (Mateus Palace, open daily June–Sept 9am–7.30pm; Mar–May & Oct 9am–1pm, 2–6pm; Nov–Feb 10am–1pm, 2–5pm) lies 3km (2 miles) outside the busy town of Vila Real. It houses a fine collection of historic books and manuscripts, together with the original printing plates of Portugal's national literary classic, the epic poem, Os Lusíadas – The Luciads – by Luís Vaz de Camões. Mateus Palace – first published in 1542. It belonged to the counts of Vila Real, and was the birthplace of the navigator Diego Cão, who discovered the mouth of the Congo River in central Africa. The estate has beautifully cool, shady formal gardens and a fine *allée* of cedar trees. The area is famous for its Mateus Rosé wine, and an image of the house appears on all Mateus Rosé bottles. Vila Real itself has little of interest, although it is the largest town in the region, and is on the edge of a dramatic gorge carved by the River Corgo (a tributary of the Douro).

Barca d'Alva

This gentle spot, inside the Douro International Natural Park, was once the upper navigation limit on the Douro. It is the closest point to the Spanish border (less than 2km/1.2 miles away), and 207km/130 miles from where the Douro enters the Atlantic Ocean, near Ports. Barca d'Alva itself sits among al-

PORTUGUESE CUISINE

Food in Portugal conjures up images of empire, with influences from its erstwhile colonies Brazil, Angola, Mozambique, Goa and Macau. Voyages of the explorer Vasco da Gama brought back cinnamon and curry powder, and both are still important flavourings in Portuguese cuisine. Common ingredients include fresh fish and seafood, ham, chicken, and fresh vegetables typically grown on small, organic farms. It is the quality of the produce that delights many visitors, whether the nutty, earthy potatoes or the juicy tomatoes that taste like an explosion of flavour to those accustomed to bland supermarket varieties. Pork is the dominant meat, and the wonderful charcuterie features in many soups and stews.

Some local specialities in Porto include tripe of veal with beans. The story goes that altruistic locals donated all their meat to the ships departing to conquer the New World, leaving only the tripe for their own consumption. More palatable are the local *sardinhas assadas* (grilled sardines), *bacalhau à brás* (salt cod), succulent roast lamb, slow-cooked lamb shanks, and the famous *caldo verde* (a soup of potatoes, cabbage and olive oil). Between spring and early autumn, sardines can be found as street food, cooked on small terracotta braziers. Sweet, egg-based puddings and tarts including *pasteis de nata* (custard tart) are also popular and go well with a glass of port.

Lamego's Nossa Senhora dos Remédios.

mond and olive groves. The sleepy village itself, with its abandoned railway, is usually just a stopping-off place for the night.

Vega de Terron

This is an alternative dropping off point for the excursion to Salamanca, or for an overnight stay, and is on the Spanish side of the river.

São João da Pesqueira

São João, usually offered as an excursion from Pinhão or Ferradosa (the latter is northeast of the Douro), is a sprawling wine-growing village famed for its town hall, which has stunning tiled murals depicting port-wine-making scenes. It is surrounded by port *quintas* on a plateau that overlooks the valleys and vineyards of the Douro in a delightful, picture-postcard setting.

Lamego

Lamego, 12km (7.5 miles) south of the river and often offered as a half-day tour from Peso da Régua on the return journey to Porto, is an important pilgrimage site, overlooked by the Sanctuary Church of Nossa Senhora dos Remédios (Our Lady of the Remedies). A fine Baroque-style staircase of some 600 steps reaches the church, by which point most visitors are in need of a blessing from the saint. The view from the top, though, is worth it – it is absolutely stunning. In September, thousands of pilgrims flock to the town.

Lamego was once the trading post of the Moors who journeyed across from Spain. They left their legacy in the 12th-century castle with an unusual vault-ed cistern. The town's museum houses an impressive collection of furniture, paintings, 16th-century Flemish tapestries, sculpture and jewellery from the Bishop's Palace within which it is situated.

Lamego (whose outer suburbs belong to the wine-growing region) is famed for its port wines, and for one of Portugal's favourite sparkling wines (Raposeira).

Vega de Terrón (for Salamanca, 128km/ 80 miles away)

Across the Spanish border, riverships berth for the day at Vega de Terrón. Passengers enjoy a full-day tour to Salamanca, a university town since the 13th century, where some 40,000 students live and study today, greatly expanding the resident population of around 160,000. The Plaza Mayor, a huge, elegant square surrounded by gracious sandstone buildings, is one of the most impressive and beautiful in Europe. The twin cathedrals, Catedral Nueva (16th-century Gothic) and Catedral Vieja (12th-century Romanesque), the latter with its spectacular silver Byzantine dome, are also well worth seeing, and are usually included in a walking tour of the old city.

Pocinho

This small area is typically used as a departure point for an excursion to the Côa Museum, near Vila Nova de Foz Côa. The museum is set in a delightful area between the Côa and Douro rivers and it displays rock art represented in the Côa Valley Archaeological Museum, which is home to the largest known open-air paleolithic rock art site in the world (closed on Mondays).

Barge cruising

A barge holiday offers a wonderful opportunity to sample life in the (very) slow lane in beautiful surroundings, both on board and off. This chapter covers all the essentials.

In this chapter, we answer some of the basic burning questions potential barge cruise customers might ask.

Why barge cruising?
Quite simply because barges let you de-stress completely by providing an antidote to the pressures of life in a fast-paced world, with their calming, slow speed. They have surroundings that are comfortable but not pretentious, plus you can expect fine food and, hopefully, enjoyable company. Barges are like little bed-and-breakfast places tucked away in some forgotten corner.

In addition, they provide a wonderful way to experience and explore new surroundings – effortless discovery, if you like.

Tell me more
As with riverships, there are no casinos, bingo or horse racing or other potentially unappealing parlour games, or art auctions or other revenue-generating events that are for many a negative aspect of the ocean-cruise experience. And once on board,

Cruising on the Canal du Midi, southern France.

you only have to unpack once, convenient when compared with touring by road or train and constantly having to pack and unpack, as you change hotels.

What's the difference between a river cruise and a barge cruise?
The main difference is that cruise barges travel much slower (up to 6kph/3.75mph) than riverships (up to 18kph/11mph). They are also smaller and typically cater to a maximum of 12 persons, as opposed to riverships, which can carry up to 200.

Are meals included?
They certainly are, as are wonderful cooks. Full board is included in the cruise fare, and everything is cooked to order. The chef purchases their own food in local shops and markets, so it's really fresh.

What about special diets?
If you are on a special diet, let your travel provider know when you book. The chef will be pleased to accommodate you. Fresh foods are purchased daily because the galley and storage space are tiny, so any special diets can be taken into account.

What about drinks?
All drinks (both alcoholic and non-alcoholic), including Champagne and wines with dinner, are included.

Won't I get bored?
Hardly! There is always something to see on the canals – it's like live armchair travel.

DID YOU KNOW...?

...that the Canal du Midi in the South of France was the incredible work of one man? It was the work of 17th-century engineer Pierre-Paul Riquet, who sacrificed a fortune to finance his dream of creating a waterway linking the Atlantic with the Mediterranean. The mammoth project took 14 years to complete, using 12,000 workers; it was finally finished in in 1681. There have been relatively few modifications since the canal was constructed, although the original wooden lock gates have been replaced with steel ones. The canal offers 386km (240 miles) of navigable waterway, skirting the sun-bathed shores of the Mediterranean and winding its way up towards the wine regions of Bordeaux.

Cycling alongside the Canal du Midi.

Apart from totally unwinding, you can also be active if you wish. You can walk (probably faster than the barge can chug along), go bicycling (almost all barges have bicycles), hill climb, go hot-air ballooning, go horse riding or play golf or tennis. You can go food shopping with the chef or learn some cooking tips from him or her. Or you could simply head into the nearest village to sample some local cheese or charcuterie.

What's the best season for a barge cruise?
Late spring or early autumn (fall) are when you'll get the best weather for a cruise of this kind, although each season brings its own attractions. Note that cruise barges do not operate in winter.

Is barge cruising for solo travellers?
The world of cruising is made for couples. Solo travellers are an expensive afterthought, and few barges have dedicated solo cabins. You can occupy a double cabin on your own, but the cruise fare will be higher.

Are barge cruises for honeymooners?
Possibly! Barge cruises in France provide an utterly romantic setting. Most arrangements will have been taken care of before you sail, so all you have to do is show up. Some cruise barges have accommodation in double-, or queen-sized beds, but, in general, cabins are tiny when compared to those in a typical hotel room.

Is barge cruising for families with children?
Some families have discovered the joys of chartering a barge (most accommodate between 4 and 12 people), which could cover one or two average-sized families. Meals and excursions can also be tailored

for all tastes and age ranges. Well-respected operators such as Abercrombie & Kent specialise in holidays of this kind.

Are barge cruises suitable for disabled passengers?
Unfortunately, they are too small and not well equipped for passengers with disabilities. Cruise barge cabins are not the only problem, but getting from shore to vessel and vessel to shore can prove extremely difficult. My advice is to try a rivership, rather than a cruise barge, as these are better equipped (many have lifts as well as larger cabins/suites that can better accommodate wheelchairs).

Are tips included?
In general, tips are not included. As a guideline, you should allow €8–10 (£7–9) per person, per day for gratuities. You give these to the barge master on the morning of disembarkation, and they will be shared among the crew.

Is airfare included?
Generally airfare is not included, although it may be included in packages available through specialist operators.

Is insurance included?
No. To summarise briefly, for health cover, travellers from within the EU are covered to some degree with EHICs, but you are well advised to take out travel insurance with full medical cover (including repatriation by air ambulance) before travelling. Passengers from the US will need to take out full medical cover.

Is there a difference between cruise barges?

The appointments and interior decor range from rustic but comfortable to unabashed luxury, with prices to match.

What is the electric current?

Almost all cruise barge cabins have European two-pin 220-volt electrical outlets. Take an adapter for any electrical appliance you use (hairdryers are usually provided).

Will I get seasick on a barge cruise?

No. The movement of water on the rivers and canals is so slight that it is extremely unlikely that anyone would suffer from motion sickness.

Are there medical facilities on board?

No. First-aid kits are carried, cruise barges are always close to land, and any necessary arrangements in the event of a medical problem can be made relatively quickly.

How pregnant can I be if I take a barge cruise?

A mother-to-be won't be allowed on a barge cruise past her 28th week of pregnancy. You may be required to produce a doctor's certificate in order to be allowed to travel. Fortunately, you'll never be far from shore, where medical help can be summoned.

Can I smoke on board?

Smoking on barges is usually restricted to the open deck area (as on riverships).

What about security?

Most barges have locking cabin doors, and there are always crew members on board.

WHAT IS A BARGE CRUISE?

It's about life in the very slow lane. Remember Simon & Garfunkel's 1966 song, 'Feelin' Groovy'? The lyrics 'Slow down, you move too fast' are perfectly apt here. There are just two speeds to a cruise barge: dead slow, and stop. So, slow down – way, way down – and simply pootle on your way. It is called the 'CD' approach – chug and drift, as you wind your way through some of the most tranquil landscapes in Europe.

Although there are some variations, a 'standard' canal barge cruise is six days long, with each cruise barge operating on fixed itineraries. (The seventh day can then be spent in cleaning and preparing the vessel again for the next set of passengers.)

Auxerre is the centre of barging in France.

Every cruise starts in a civilised manner with a glass of Champagne and moves gently through picture-postcard countryside. One of the first things to notice is the assortment of flowers and flower boxes that litter the uppermost deck – barge owners delight in trying to outdo each other.

There's nothing quite like pastoral countryside to take you back in time. Going more slowly than a person would on foot, cruise barges travel along the canal systems as well as the rivers. They cover very little in terms of distance but offer more time to get to know the countryside. You really can experience the colours of the blackberry bushes that overhang the path instead of speeding by them, as on a typical river cruise.

Taking a barge cruise is one of the best ways to experience part of a country in small doses. In Europe, barge cruises can be taken in Belgium, France, Germany, the Netherlands and the UK, although the most popular country is undoubtedly France, where barge cruising has been carefully packaged and practised for many years.

Cruise barges (the French word for barge is *peniche*, although the French also call it *la maison qui marche* – 'the house that walks') chug along slowly in the daytime and moor early each evening, giving you time to pay a visit to a local village, and get a restful night's sleep (no late nights or noisy overnight travelling).

The inland waterways of Europe all adhere to the CEVNI regulations (Code Européen des Voies de la Navigation Intérieure), which is a UN instrument with international authority and relevance.

French cruise barges have a reputation for excellent food and wine, and good conversation (no doubt the latter is to some degree the direct result of the former). As is typical in France, meals on cruise barges tend to be slow, sociable occasions. Locally grown fresh foods are usually purchased and prepared each day, allowing you to live well and feel like a houseguest. There is no mass dining here.

And you need to be as good at socialising as you are at eating when you join a barge cruise on your own (or as a couple), as you will be living in close quarters with a handful of others (most likely total strangers). A good sense of humour and an international outlook on life helps. Note, however, that most cruise barges can also be chartered exclusively, so you can just take your family and friends.

Design and layout

Many cruise barges have been skilfully converted from cargo- or munitions-carrying barges, most of which were built in either the Netherlands or Scotland (*L'Art du Vivre* is an example of a Scottish-built barge), while a handful of new ones have been constructed expressly for holidaying in the past few years. Most have the timeless appeal of a tiny country house.

The cruise barge *Anjodi* in Languedoc.

Cruise barges are typically between 30 and 50m (100–164ft) in length, with a beam (maximum width) of between 5 and 7.3m (16.5–24ft), although their actual size depends on the area of operation and the ability to manoeuvre in the many locks that line the canals.

A cruise barge almost always has a steel hull, with a flat bottom, and (with a few exceptions) will have been converted from a cargo-carrying vessel. Their cruising speed is generally up to 6kph (3.75mph). Most carry a maximum of 12 passengers (although a few carry up to 24 passengers), and they tend to be beautifully fitted out with rich wood panelling, carpeting, custom-built furniture and fine fabrics. Each barge has a dining salon/lounge-bar. Barge captains are often owner/operators and they take great pride in their vessel.

Some have air conditioning and heating. Most also have some kind of canopied sun deck. Barge interiors always have plenty of cosy cushions on lounge seats and armchairs. Most cruise barges carry bicycles for your use; others may have a minibus that tootles alongside, ready to take you on excursions, all of which are included in the cruise fare.

Many cruise barges that carry fewer than 12 passengers have their own idiosyncrasies and niceties.

Cabins: These tend to be compact and homely, while the overall look does tend to depend on the owner's preference in terms of decor. While most cruise barges are strictly for couples (with queen, double or twin beds), some also have single cabins.

The size of cabins varies considerably, from a tiny 6 sq m (64.5 sq ft) to a luxurious 24 sq m (258 sq ft). The 'Monet Suite' aboard *L'Impressioniste* measures 15.77 sq m (169.7 sq ft), for example, and the 'Nuits-St-Georges' Suite aboard *La Belle Epoque* measures 15.36 sq m (165.3 sq ft). Further down the scale, the three twin-bedded cabins (often erroneously called 'staterooms' by enterprising marketeers) aboard *Nymphea* measure 6.25 sq m (67.2 sq ft).

If you want more space in your 'bedroom', you'll need to check the details carefully with your booking agent or with the owner, if you book direct (not recommended).

Bathrooms: Cabins usually have en suites, with a toilet, basin and shower at least.

Design specifics: Let's look at some of the details that make cruise barges so distinctive. What makes one cruise barge more luxurious than the next – apart from the size of the cabins – is the use of space and the quality of its decor, cabinetry and furnishings (in addition to the specialised local knowledge of the captain and crew, plus the quality of the cuisine).

Anjodi has a hot tub and a skylight in the salon. *Anacolouthe* has a baby grand piano in its lounge, which has rich wood panelling and a red colour scheme. *Elisabeth* has a split-level dining room with oak beamed ceiling. *Fleur de Lys* has a grand piano in its lounge and some rare vintage wines in the cellar, while bathrooms have two washbasins, as well as romantic canopied beds.

Fleur de Lys is also the only cruise barge I know of with a lounge decorated with fine antiques and a grand piano, plus a heated (decent-sized) plunge pool. *Horizon II* is a split-level design with beautifully panelled interiors. *L'Impressioniste* has an exercise room and spa tub. *La Belle Epoque* also has richly panelled interiors, a fitness studio, hot tub and even a sauna. *La Nouvelle Etoile* has internet access in all cabins, tiled bathrooms and a lift (the only cruise barge to have one). *Napoleon* has one bedroom with a large, marble-clad bathroom – reminiscent of some of the bathrooms in the legendary Hotel Danieli in Venice – plus a sun deck measuring a spacious 75 sq m (807 sq ft).

Princess, built in 1973 by Daniel Ludwig, international shipping magnate and founder of Princess Hotels, has a canopied sun deck and cabin bathrooms with windows that open. *Quiétude* has an open fireplace. *Saroche* has a wood-burning stove in its split-level lounge, beautiful panelled interiors, satellite television and even its own washer/dryer (most unusual for a cruise barge). Meanwhile, *Sérenité* has lovely scrolled armrests on the dining room chairs, plus a very roomy dining room, with large, wood-trimmed picture windows.

Cuisine

The entertainment of any barge cruise is the food. How you dine will depend on which cruise barge you choose. Dining ranges from homely cooking to outstanding nouvelle cuisine with all the trimmings. Tables are set with fine linen and china, and dinner is usually a leisurely candlelit affair, accompanied by high-quality wines, some of which would be almost impossible to find outside the local producing region. Often, the owner of the barge, or his/her partner, is also the cook, and you can be assured that the ingredients are all fresh, and purchased almost daily.

A cruise barge crossing the Loire on the aqueduct at Briare.

BARGE CRUISING IN FRANCE

There are about 8,500km (5,280 miles) of navigable canals and waterways in France, and operators place their vessels in the best stretches, both for scenic beauty and architectural interest, as well as for ease of getting to and from your chosen cruise.

Locks

A barge cruise in France means going through a succession of locks, and nowhere is this more enjoyable and entertaining than on the Canal du Midi, with its numerous locks along the canal's 240km (149-mile) length, or in Burgundy, where, between Dijon and Mâcon, a cruise barge can negotiate as many as 54 locks during a six-day journey. Lock hours of operation are civilised – between 8.30am and 6.30pm, with an hour off for lunch. If locks are of the hand-cranked type, you can lend a hand to open or close the lock gates – it's good exercise, and you get to talk to the lock keepers. Some lock keepers have a stock of vegetables to sell to the cruise barges.

Sights

Medieval walled towns, sleepy villages, towering cathedrals and cloistered abbeys, wine châteaux, chic shops, summer festivals and romantic hamlets all await you in France, dependent, of course, on the region in which you are cruising. In general, cruise barge companies split the country into several regions, and barges usually operate regular itineraries for the complete season (with few exceptions).

The key regions include Burgundy, home to the Canal de Bourgogne, Canal du Centre and the River Saône, renowned for its fine wines and excellent cuisine. Highlights include the elegant historic city of Beaune, the vineyards of Meursault, Nuits-St-Georges, Santenay and Savigny, and the Unesco-

protected Basilica of Vézelay and Abbey of Fontenay. Other attractions in the region include Auxerre, the centre of barging in France, and Chablis, another wine-tasting hotspot. Popular barge cruises include Dijon to Pont Royal (from big city to tiny hamlet) along the Canal de Bourgogne or from Dijon to Lyon along the Saône – a trip that is particularly good for wine lovers, who can visit all five appellations in one cruise.

Then there's the Loire Valley, also great wine country, where attractions along the Canal Latéral à la Loire include crossing Gustave Eiffel's 19th-century aqueduct at Briare (it crosses the River Loire, and so does your barge with you on board), the longest canal bridge in the world. Other highlights in the Loire include a visit to Montargis, often dubbed the 'Venice of France'.

An eastern France barge cruise would include Franche-Comté, east of Burgundy, as well as Alsace-Lorraine, which borders Germany, while southwestern France is another popular region, with Bordeaux and the Dordogne the highlights here. Provence is another great region for barge cruising in France, with a plethora of attractions including the great Roman cities of Avignon and Arles, the Roman aqueduct at the Pont du Gard and cowboys of the Camargue.

The cost

Rates typically range from €1,650 to more than €10,000 per person for a six-day cruise, varying according to the season, with those in the spring and autumn being the least expensive and those in the peak summer season the most expensive. Rates include a (real) Champagne reception, a cabin with private facilities, all meals, good wine with lunch and dinner, beverages (including an open bar), use of bicycles, side trips and airport/railway transfers. Other activities, such as horse riding, golf or tennis can be arranged at extra cost.

At the beginning (March) and end of the season (November), the weather can be unreliable, so it's best to take clothing that can be layered, including sweaters, plus a waterproof windbreaker.

Arrival

If you are travelling by train, note that many European stations do not have porters, so travel light and use luggage with wheels. Note that not all stations have lifts, and at some you might have to cross a footbridge with lots of stairs to reach the exit, so make sure, too, that you can manage to carry your own luggage up the stairs.

Chartering a private cruise barge

Private 'whole barge' charters (often with special themes, such as a fine French 'dégustation' cuisine cruise) are the way to go if you want to travel with a few select friends or as a large family, although you'll certainly have to pay for the privilege. The cost for a private charter of a four- to eight-person luxury cruise barge would be anywhere between around €12,500 and €50,000 for one week.

FRENCH WATERWAY TERMS

barge *une péniche*
beam *une largeur*
embankment *une digue*
distance marker *un point kilométrique*
dock *une darse*
downstream *aval*
(lock) gates *les portes*
length *la longueur*
lock *une écluse*
lock keeper *un éclusier*
port (left side) *bâbord*
propeller *une hélice*
rudder *un gouvernail*
starboard (right side) *tribord*
towpath *un chemin de halage*
upstream *amont*
wheelhouse *une timonerie*

Emerald Star approaching Durnstein, Austria.

River cruise companies

This list of the main river cruise providers includes background information on each company, including whether it owns or charters riverships, plus essential characteristics of its cruises.

When you are choosing a river cruise, it can be useful to know a little about the companies that own and operate them. Here is a summary of the main providers, with background information and details of key features of their cruises.

Other companies that market and sell river cruises, but either charter, or part-charter, or sell into riverships of other owners and operators (such as UK-based Newmarket Travel, Riviera Travel and Shearings, and US-based companies including Abercrombie & Kent), are not listed here. The financial investment companies that own riverships and charter them to tour operators (often for language-specific markets) are not included here either, but their riverships may be found in the listings section of this book.

A-ROSA Cruises

German company A-ROSA Cruises (established in 1969 as Seetours, when it was one of the first companies to charter riverships – in Russia) began operating its own river cruises in 2002. Seetours was founded by (the late) Alf Pollak with financial back-

A-ROSA Stella at Chalon-sur-Saône, France.

ing from Holland America Line, for whom Pollak was the general sales agent in Germany. The company – which became A-ROSA Cruises in 2003 – is based in Rostock, Germany. It also operates spa resorts in Austria and Germany.

The onboard dining concept is different to most, in that there is no formal meal service – instead, meals are provided in a self-service buffet (no tablecloths). Extra-cost 'all-inclusive' drinks packages are available. However, aboard the riverships operated by A-ROSA Cruises exclusively for the English-speaking market – predominantly in North America – waiter service is provided for dinner, and other items are included, but this comes at a higher price point.

Children up to age 15 travel free (conditions apply) and a children's club is operated aboard the vessels that cater to the German-speaking market during the German school holidays.

AmaWaterways

Founded in 2002 by modern river cruise industry pioneer Rudi Schreiner, cruise industry executive Kristin Karst and the late former owner of Brendan Worldwide Vacations, Jimmy Murphy, as Amadeus Waterways (the company changed its name in 2008), AmaWaterways has helped to redefine European river cruising. The company fully owns, operates and markets its own riverships, all of which are new builds (not refits or renamed older vessels).

The company's riverships have spacious cabins, 82 percent of which have French (open-air) balconies. Each passenger is provided with a large pocket-sized travel guide, with detailed information on the route, highlights, sights and historical information.

The company features self-serve buffet breakfasts and lunches, while dinner is a served meal. AmaWaterways spends considerably more on high-quality food ingredients and wine and on hotel crew service training than any other river cruise company. The company is also known to offer the highest levels of customer care and friendliness in the river cruise industry.

APT (Australian Pacific Touring)

Founded by Bill McGeary in the 1920s in Melbourne, Australia, APT River Cruises is part of the APT Group. Still a family-owned company, run by Rob and Lou McGeary, it added European river cruises to its portfolio for its mainly Australasian clients in the 1990s, although its offering has really taken off in the last few years or so. APT is a partner of

AmaWaterways, some of whose riverships are used for its European river cruise programmes, and it maintains the same very high standards. APT may also purchase space on the riverships of other companies (in which case, the overall quality may be different). APT also owns the lower-priced brand 'Travelmarvel by APT'. The company features self-serve buffet breakfasts and lunches, while dinner is a served meal.

Avalon Waterways
Originally founded in 1928 by Antonio Mantegazza, who used his rowing boat to take passengers across Lake Lugano in Switzerland, the company became Avalon Waterways in 2004, under the umbrella of privately held company Group Voyages Inc., and it was run from Colorado. Now based in California, the company includes well-known tour operator brands Globus and Cosmos (the group consists of more than 30 tourism and aviation businesses).

Avalon operates, but does not own, its own vessels. Over half of all the riverships in the Avalon fleet have some cabins with beds that face the river. Gratuities and all drinks (except premium brands) are included in the cruise price, but there is a strong emphasis on extra onboard revenue generated by selling optional excursions and 'premium'-brand drinks. The company features self-serve buffet breakfasts and lunches, while dinner is a served meal.

Avalon Artistry II main lounge.

CroisiEurope
CroisiEurope was founded in France in 1976 by the late Gérard Schmitter as Alsace Croisières and originally ran lunch and dinner cruises (river cruising proper started in 1982). Alsace Croisières became CroisiEurope in 1997, in order to reaffirm its commitment to Europe. The company, which is presently run by Gérard Schmitter's four offspring, has its headquarters in Strasbourg, France; other offices are in Lyon (France), Brussels (Belgium) and Ft Lauderdale (US). The fleet consists of more than three dozen riverships, most of which are owned, with a few chartered.

The company specialises in river cruising, mainly for French-speaking passengers, but now markets to more international passengers. Most of its riverships have the same layout, cabin sizes, features and facilities in two grades: 'Prestige' and 'Excellency' (equivalent to 'standard' and 'standard-plus'). Negatives include the deck lounge chairs, which are white plastic patio-style ones and not particularly elegant (stainless steel or aluminium ones are generally more comfortable and stable as well as smarter). The company also runs gastronomic theme cruises several times each year, including dinners ashore with notable French chefs. The company features self-serve buffet breakfasts and lunches, while dinner is a served meal. Excursions and gratuities are at extra cost.

Crystal River Cruises
New entrant Crystal River Cruises is owned by well-known and respected parent company Crystal Cruises (founded originally in 1998 by NYK Line, but owned since 2015 by Genting Hong Kong). It operates two excellent mid-size ocean-going cruise ships and one boutique-size ship.

The river cruise division purchased the unusual, double-width, 1987-built *Mozart*, completely refitted it to the upscale standards of Crystal Cruises, and renamed it *Crystal Mozart*. It also ordered four new riverships, with the first pair for 2017, and a second pair for 2018. These are: *Crystal Bach*, *Crystal Debussy*, *Crystal Mahler* and *Crystal Ravel*. All accommodate 110 passengers. The company features self-serve buffet breakfasts and lunches, while dinner is a served meal. Gratuities are included, as is one meal in a Michelin-starred restaurant in one of the destinations.

DouroAzul
This private, family-owned company was founded in 1993 by Mario Ferreira to share the outstanding beauty of the River Douro. It has a fleet of several vessels, some operated by DouroAzul, and some under exclusive charter to other operators. DouroAzul's holding company, Mystic Invest, purchased Germany-based Nicko Cruises, which continues to operate low-cost river cruises throughout Europe. The company features self-serve buffet breakfasts and lunches, while dinner is a served meal.

Emerald Waterways
This company, which debuted in 2014 with two new riverships is a division of Scenic. It is a lower-priced

alternative to its parent company (about 20 percent lower, but with fewer choices included), and is aimed at a younger audience, with excursions that are more active. With rapid expansion, Emerald Waterways now has a good fleet of riverships. Each one features an indoor pool at the stern, which can be covered and converted into a cinema at night. The company features self-serve buffet breakfasts and lunches, while dinner is a served meal.

Gate 1 Travel

Gate 1 Travel, based in the Philadelphia suburb of Port Washington, was founded in 1981 with three employees, but is now a company with a workforce of over 200. It is a tour operator that charters, rather than owns, its riverships. The company states that its aim is to deliver high-quality travel experiences at affordable prices. Its riverships have a brand name of Monarch. The company features self-serve buffet breakfasts and lunches, while dinner is a served meal.

Grand Circle Cruise Line

Grand Circle Travel was founded in New York in 1958 by Ethel Andrus, a retired schoolteacher. She founded the American Association of Retired Persons (AARP – today an extremely large organisation for retirees and senior citizens) and served its members until 1982. Grand Circle Travel was purchased in 1985 by Alan Lewis, who moved the company to Boston. Its first privately owned rivership was *River Symphony* in 1998. The company was sold in 2007 to private equity firm Court Square Capital Travel.

Grand Circle Travel caters exclusively to North American retirees, with its own riverships in Europe under the Grand Circle Cruise Line brand. It also offers an extensive array of pre- and post-cruise optional stays and tours. The deck lounge chairs are of inelegant white plastic, which spoils an otherwise fairly decent product. The company features self-serve buffet breakfasts and lunches, while dinner is a served meal.

Lüftner Cruises

The Austrian family-owned company was founded over 30 years ago by Dr Wolfgang and Martina Lüftner (they are among the most respected pioneers of European river cruises). The company, based in Innsbruck, Austria, owns and operates its own fleet of modern riverships, some of which are chartered to other operators. Many travel agencies sell cruises aboard the Lüftner vessels because of their high standards. The company provides high-quality food and elegant, restrained and tasteful interior decor combined with superior-quality furnishings and fabrics aboard its riverships. The company features self-serve buffet breakfasts and lunches, while dinner is a served meal. Drinks and gratuities are at extra cost.

Nicko Cruises

Based in Stuttgart, Germany, this company was founded in 1992 by Eckkehard Beller to market and operate river cruises with chartered riverships. It first started with cruises in Russia, but added ones on the Rhine in 2002. In 2005, it launched the first 'twin-cruiser' rivership *(Flamenco)*, with French balconies for each cabin. Switzerland-based financial investment company Capvis became a major investor in February 2013.

Nicko Tours became insolvent in 2015. The company, including its fleet of riverships and the brand name, was purchased by Portuguese company Mystic Invest, which owners of the well-known brand DouroAzul, whose vessels operate Douro river cruises. The brand continues to operate as before, under the Nicko Cruises name, principally for the German-speaking market. Premium-brand drinks, optional excursions and gratuities are at extra cost. The company features self-serve buffet breakfasts and lunches, while dinner is a served meal.

Riviera Travel

Based in the UK, Riviera Travel was founded in 1984 by Michael Wright to operate tours for British campers going to the French Riviera. It is a tour operator that charters, rather than owns, custom-designed riverships from Swiss family-owned company Scylla, for its mainly British clientele. The company was sold in 2014 to equity company Phoenix (not associated with Germany's Phoenix Cruises). The company features self-serve buffet breakfasts and lunches, while dinner is a served meal.

Scenic

Founded in Newcastle, Australia, in 1986 by Glen Moroney, Scenic Tours began by operating coach tours throughout Australia. In 2008, the company began its European river cruise operations, marketing primarily to passengers from Australian and New Zealand. Growing rapidly, the company expanded by making its cruises available to British passengers. The company, which is still Australian owned, changed its name to Scenic in 2015. It now owns and operates several riverships in Europe, all of which feature 'butler'-style service.

The company provides good information about the included excursions, and each passenger gets an excellent GPS-based 'Tailor-Made' information system, which includes self-guided city tours. Also provided in each cabin are Nordic walking sticks, umbrellas, good bedside reading lights, and under-bed space for storing luggage. Cruises are fully inclusive, including gratuities and all onboard drinks (although some 'premium' brands cost extra). The company features self-serve buffet breakfasts and lunches, while dinner is a served meal.

See also Emerald Waterways (see page 107), a sister company that operates river cruises at a lower price point, but without some of the included items of Scenic.

Swiss Excellence River Cruises

Switzerland's well-known and respected Reisebüro Mittelthurgau is based in Winterthur, Switzerland, and founded in 1997. The company became part of the Twerenbold Reisen Gruppe of Baden-Rütihof, Switzerland, in 2001. The company owns its own riverships (its first new build debuted in 2006), and charters others from various owners, then reconstructs them to its own design tastes. It concentrates on the source markets of Austria, Germany, and Switzerland. Special culinary cruises (marketed as Excellence Gourmet Festival) feature Michelin-starred chefs, and are organized on designated sailings usually during the autumn/fall season. The riverships feature self-serve buffet breakfasts and lunches, while dinner is a served meal.

Tauck

Based in Connecticut, US, this company was founded in 1925 by Arthur Tauck as a tour packager and operator to take participants on life-enriching tours. The company charters its riverships from Swiss company Scylla but operates under the Tauck brand name. Tauck is known for its attention and care of clients and provides more staff from the US (at least three per rivership) aboard its vessels than most other operators, to the benefit of its mainly North American clientele. On excursions, sightseers are split into small groups, using the 'Quietvox' system (where you wear an earpiece into which tour information is conveyed) for guided tours. In 2017, Tauck plans to increase its family cruising capacity. The company features self-serve buffet breakfasts and lunches, while dinner is a served meal.

Travelmarvel River Cruises

A division of APT, this company has a small fleet of three chartered riverships for 'all-inclusive' river cruising at reduced prices for its mainly youthful, active Australasian passengers. The cabins (particularly the bathrooms) are small. The company features self-serve buffet breakfasts and lunches, while dinner is a served meal. The food is quite decent, but you won't find much in the way of between-meal snacks, and any premium drinks cost extra, as do most excursions.

U by Uniworld

In 2018 'U by Uniworld' was created for millennials (defined as being 21–45 years old), with two of Uniworld's oldest vessels refitted for the new brand, with fewer things included, for its urban party-style experiential cruises. The two riverships, named the A and the B are painted black (black on the 'blue' Danube?), have American Diner retro-style bistro (tablecloth-free) food. Tours, drinks and port charges

Crystal Mozart in Budapest.

Dining tables on Uniworld's *Queen Isabel*.

cost extra. Whether hipster and classical European culture work together (particularly during the winter season) remains to be seen.

Uniworld Boutique River Cruises

Uniworld was founded by former Yugoslavian travel entrepreneur Serba Ilich in 1976. The company started offering river cruises in Europe in 1994 and was one of the first companies to charter Russian riverships exclusively for American passengers.

Based in Encino, California, Uniworld has its own European river cruise line, Global River Cruises (which itself owns 75 percent of Holland River Line – established as a Swiss-owned company and based in Basel, Switzerland). While most of its riverships in Europe are nearly new, some features are a little basic – the plastic chairs on deck, for example. Also, dining room chairs typically have no armrests. The company's passengers are typically all English speakers.

In 2004 Uniworld was purchased by The Travel Corporation (founded by South Africa-born Stanley Tollman), parent company of Trafalgar Tours, Contiki Tours and several others, including Red Carnation Hotels. Its name is now Uniworld Boutique River Cruises. Some of the company's riverships are owned, while some are chartered from other owners. The company features self-serve buffet breakfasts and lunches, while dinner is a served meal.

Vantage Deluxe River Cruises

Vantage Deluxe World Travel was founded in 1983 by Gordon Lewis (river cruises started in 1999), whose son, Hank, is the present president (his brother Alan Lewis is president of Grand Circle Cruise Lines – a competitor – although some operational details are actually shared). The company headquarters are in Boston, US. The fleet presently consists of several owned and chartered riverships.

The company sells direct (via e-brochures) instead of marketing via travel agents. It caters exclusively to North Americans and specialises in trips for solo travellers. Dining is in an open-seating arrangement. Smoking is not allowed inside any of the riverships – only outside on the open decks.

The company features self-serve buffet breakfasts and lunches, while dinner is a served meal. Low-salt, low-fat, gluten-free and diabetic menu selections are available. However, the food is quite average, with little choice of main courses (entrées) for dinner and a limited choice of breads, pastry items and cheeses. The deck lounge chairs are white plastic ones. Gratuities and drinks (except for a Captain's Dinner evening) are not included, but some excursions are.

Viking River Cruises

Viking River Cruises is perhaps the best-known river cruise company. It was founded in 1997 by a Scandinavian and Dutch consortium and headed by Torstein Hagen (formerly connected with the long-defunct ocean-going Royal Viking Line) and Christer Salén (formerly of Salen Lindblad Cruising – the ocean-going expedition cruise company now called Quark Expeditions). The company has grown fast from small beginnings when it chartered a single Russian rivership. The company then purchased Aqua Viva, a French operator, with two vessels.

In 2000, in a brilliant strategic move, Viking purchased KD River Cruises, Europe's oldest established rivership operator, with the landing stages (a valuable asset) included in the purchase. The UK's Travel Renaissance, founded in 1977 by Graham Clubb (for many years Viking's UK general sales agent) was purchased by Viking in 2005.

Some riverships cater exclusively to North Americans; others cater to European and international passengers. An ambitious new-build programme saw several new vessels constructed specifically for North American passengers and introduced in just two years.

The company deservedly prides itself on the consistently high standard of its product, cuisine and service. Aboard the Viking 'Longships' the smart, comfortable deck lounge chairs are made of stainless steel or aluminium. An Aquavit Terrace casual eatery is a standard feature, as are pocket-sized travel guides, with information on the route, for each passenger. Tablecloths are provided for breakfast, lunch and dinner. Gratuities and most drinks cost extra.

THE VIKING 'LONGSHIPS'

Each Viking 'Longship' is named after a Norse god, and has been intelligently and tastefully designed and has an identical number of cabins. Some small decor and design modifications have been made as the series has progressed.

A solar panel-topped skylight sits above an uncluttered, two-deck-high atrium lobby, and natural light floods in through floor-to-ceiling windows, while a straight central glass and wood stairway connects the two decks. A lift provides accessibility for mobility-limited passengers (except for the open sun deck).

The forward observation lounge is both contemporary and comfortable, with a bar and bar stools in the back section, and an indoor-outdoor Aquavit Terrace at the front. The decor is imbued with many earth-tone colours. Two 24-hour self-help beverage stations are located at the entrance to the lounge. Although the lounge seating includes large armchairs and sofa seating, it unfortunately doesn't quite accommodate everyone at once (eg for talks) when the vessel is full, and thick pillars make it feel somewhat confined. However, there's natural light in abundance

An indoor-outdoor Aquavit Terrace occupies the front third of the lounge. The outdoor section has about 10 tables with chairs for three or four persons.

Polished wooden railings adorn the exterior Sun Deck, together with fold-down canopies and chairs, shuffleboard court and herb garden consisting of several wooden boxes of herbs, tended to by the executive chef, who uses the fresh herbs during food preparation.

Accommodation

Viking 'Longships' feature a clever, patented off-centre hallway through the Upper and Middle Decks, with the interior hallway positioned off-centre. This excellent arrangement allows for full balcony cabins on one side, and narrower cabins – some as suites with separate sleeping and living areas – on the other. Each hallway has an ice machine.

Aft are two large genuine suites (with a completely separate bedroom and large 'wet' room), measuring approximately 41 sq m (445 sq ft). These also feature a wrap-around outdoor balcony, as well as a separate French (open-air) balcony with floor-to-ceiling sliding glass doors.

There are 93 cabins in three categories (including 25 non-balcony cabins). Intelligently designed and highly functional, the cabins have square-edged limewood cabinetry (rounded would be nicer) and soft-close drawers. A floor-to-ceiling sliding glass door leads to a full or French (open-air) balcony; cabins on the lowest deck have windows only– by regulation. Full balcony cabins feature both a proper balcony (with two small mesh chairs and small drinks table), plus a French balcony, accessed by

floor-to-ceiling sliding glass doors.

The decor includes Nordic wood and earth tones and fabric-covered walls. The generously sized beds (200 x 160cm/79 x 63 ins) are very comfortable, with room underneath for luggage storage. Faux suede (or silky) headboards, excellent mattresses and white duvets complete the picture.

Facilities include a Sony flat-panel infotainment system, mini-fridge, hairdryer and ice bucket (self-help ice machines are located in hallways). Fresh fruit and bottled water are provided daily. There are 110v and 220v electrical sockets (for US and Euro plugs), light switches on both sides of the bed, as well as room dimmers (much thought has gone into the lighting). Wood or glass sliding-door closets have wooden hangers and a personal safe.

The bathrooms are tiled, have heated floors (and heated, non-steam mirrors – hooray!), circular washbasins and generously proportioned glazed shower enclosures. Bathrobes are available on request, and towels are of a generous size. Low-flush toilets with environmental design mean that you may have to push the flush button twice (their positioning is a little tight, but the best that could be made of the available space). The space for the toilet is rather tight, however. Individual bottles of L'Occitane products are provided.

Aboard Viking Freya and Viking Njord the shower enclosure's glass walls can be crystallised at the touch of a button. But, turning on the bathroom light also floods the sleeping area and can disturb a light-sensitive person.

Restaurant and food

The restaurant has floor-to-ceiling windows that let in abundant natural light, and is tastefully decorated. Many chairs do not have armrests. The cuisine is unfussy, but has plenty of taste and there's a decent variety of dishes (typically three main courses for dinner), which are very nicely presented. Vegetarian alternatives are available. The wines supplied during meals are young, and breakfast buffets are rather repetitious.

The alternative Aquavit Terrace (breakfast and lunch, and for a light dinner with a non-changing set menu) offers good, unfussy café food as well as an excellent alfresco setting, with some outdoor space.

Overall

Viking River Cruises appeals mainly to its single-language North American, British and Australasian clientele, to whom it caters extremely well. Even with the high-density of 190 passengers, the 'Longships' don't feel congested, except perhaps in the main lounge. However, the constant background music played – including open decks, hallways, and in the restaurant – is irritating and unnecessary. Although excursions port charges are included, gratuities are not.

How we evaluate the riverships

To help you differentiate between riverships, we have evaluated each one against a set of key criteria. This section explains how the ratings and Berlitz star system work.

Just as I have been evaluating and rating ocean-going cruise ships professionally since 1980, I have also been travelling extensively aboard Europe's riverships to construct an independent Berlitz rating system for the 300-plus vessels in service.

In our rating system, each rivership is graded out of a total of 500 points across five areas: hardware/facilities, accommodation, cuisine, service/hospitality plus any 'other' components, with a maximum of 100 points in each category. In each area, the little things – the extra touches that improve the quality of the overall experience – mean the addition or deduction of points on the great scorecard.

The 500 points have then been divided into ranges, to create our independent Berlitz star ratings from 1 to 5. Thus, any vessel awarded between 251 and 300 points is classed as a 3-star rivership; one gaining between 301 and 350 points is a 3-star plus rivership (I have assigned double categories for all except 5-star vessels to help differentiate within the categories); and a rivership with a total of between 351 and 400 points is classed as 4-star, etc.

My Story alongside.

In creating criteria for evaluating riverships, the qualitative differences, conveniences and comfort factors, together with the operating and product delivery standards are all taken into account. The resulting scoring system is fair and equitable for all, as in the Berlitz Cruising and Cruise Ships guide (in continuous publication for over 30 years).

Note that many riverships are of the same size and configuration. The subtle differences are in the onboard product, and, most notably, the food and service. It's all about the details (the size of wine glasses, towels and personal amenities, for example), staff training, service and presentation.

Scores also take into account nationality-specific factors, because some are dedicated to a single national market clientele, such as Australia, Germany, North America, etc.

Ultimately, there really is no world's best rivership or river cruise line – despite what the brochures might claim (they are, after all, written by marketing departments), only the one that is right for you. Hopefully our ratings will prove helpful to you.

Note that sometimes, companies change vessels between different areas, for operational or other reasons. So, although we list the riverships and the rivers they sail on at the time of going to press, always check with the cruise operator in case there are any changes.

CRITERIA

Hardware: This includes the general profile and condition of the vessel, its age, maintenance, decking material, pool and hot tub, furniture (such as deck lounge chairs – whether hardwood, stainless steel, or plastic, and with or without cushioned pads). It also covers interior cleanliness – eg the public bathrooms, lift (elevator), floor and wall coverings, stairways, passageways and doorways.

The score also reflects the quality of the facilities, public rooms (including the main lounge, library and shop), ceiling height, pillars, lobby layout, stairways, hallways, lifts, wellness facilities, public restrooms, lighting, air conditioning and ventilation systems, floor coverings, decor and artwork. It covers dining-room facilities including windows, chairs (with or without armrests), lighting and tableware including china, cutlery, linen and centrepieces (flowers).

Accommodation: For suites/superior grades, this includes the design and layout of all suites, balconies, lighting, beds/berths, furniture (placement, and

mattress quality), hanging space for clothes (including whether wooden or plastic hangers are provided), drawer space, bedside tables, vanity desks, lighting, mirrors, air conditioning and ventilation, artworks, soundproofing, soft furnishings, written information, tea- and coffee-making equipment, flowers, fruit, bathrobes and slippers (if any).

It reflects the bathroom facilities, notably the shower unit, washbasin, cabinets, storage for toiletries, and the size and quality of the towels.

NB: suites should not be designated as such, unless the sleeping room is completely separate from the living area.

For standard cabins this includes the design and layout of the space, furniture and fittings, clothes storage space, bedside tables, vanity unit, lighting, air conditioning and ventilation, artworks, plus bulkhead insulation and noise levels. It also covers soft furnishings and details such as the in-cabin information folder (list of services), flowers, fruit, slippers (if any), towels and bed linen, plus bathroom facilities, notably the shower unit, washbasin, cabinets, storage for toiletries and the towels.

Note that balconies can be described as 'full' (a full balcony, just wide enough for two small chairs) or 'French' (floor-to-ceiling glass doors opening on to railings, with just room enough to stick your toes out). Some vessels have both. Others have windows only, which may or may not open. Cabins on the lowest deck almost always have non-opening 'panoramic' windows instead (because they are too close to the water line).

Cuisine: The score covers the restaurant, informal dining/buffets, the ingredients used and tea/coffee/ bar snacks. Under 'restaurant' we have included menus (variety and presentation), culinary creativity, the appeal, taste, texture, freshness, colour and balance of the food, plus garnishes, fresh fruit and wine list and wine prices.

Informal dining/buffets covers the hardware (eg hot and cold display units, sneeze guards, tongs and other serving utensils) plus presentation, food temperatures and food labelling, the quality and consistency of the ingredients, plus portion size.

Tea/coffee/bar snacks covers the quality and variety of tea and coffee provided. This includes afternoon tea, cakes and sandwiches, whether mugs or cups and saucers are provided, whether cream and milk is provided, and bar snacks.

Service: This includes the restaurant staff (serving, taking from the correct side, etc), wine service, communication skills, approach, uniform and finesse.

In bars and lounges, this covers the ambience, communication skills (between bartenders, service staff and passengers), attitude, personality, flair and finesse, plus the glasses used.

With relation to cabins, it includes housekeeping, cleanliness, in-cabin food service (if there is any), linen and bathrobe changes, and communication skills.

Attractive cabin bed area on S.S. *Antoinette*.

Miscellaneous: This category embraces a range of elements that do not easily fall into the ones above. It includes such miscellaneous areas as the accuracy of the information in the brochure/cruise provider's website, any information on the itinerary and on destinations visited *en route*, airport/train station transfers and the standard of any excursions. It also covers lecturers, any entertainment provided and in-cabin infotainment systems.

THE STAR RATINGS

Points are then converted into star ratings, as follows:

★★★★★ = 451–500 points
★★★★+ = 401–450 points
★★★★ = 351–400 points
★★★+ = 301–350 points
★★★ = 251–300 points
★★+ = 201–250 points
★★ = 151–200 points
★+ = 101–150 points
★ = 1–100 points

The star categories, of which there are five, are broken down below. Note that riverships that have a plus sign (+) next to their rating are a little better than the number of stars awarded.

5 Stars (★★★★★)

The vessel must have finely appointed, excellently designed interiors and be spotlessly maintained. As for accommodation, suites (minimum size expected 25 sq m/270 sq ft) and large cabins (minimum 16 sq m/172 sq ft) should have the highest-quality fittings and furnishings. A choice of bed linen and pillows (regular goose down pillows or the non-allergenic type) should be provided, as should bathrobes for all passengers, plus high-quality personal toiletries. The cuisine must be the best available in a rivership, with at least three choices of main courses for dinner, plus pasta dishes for lunch. A full sit-down service must be provided by staff schooled in the art of service and hospitality. Other items, including lectures, entertainment, audio-visual equipment, etc, would be expected to be of an extremely high standard. This is as good as it gets for a rivership.

4 Stars (★★★★)

To reach this level, a vessel must have well-appointed, well-fitted interiors and be well maintained. As for accommodation, suites (minimum size expected 22 sq m/236 sq ft) and cabins (minimum 14 sq m/150 sq ft) must have practical, high-quality fittings. A very good dining experience must be provided, and there must be at least three choices of main course (entrée) for dinner, with vegetarian options available. A full, sit-down service must be provided by staff with professional food and drink service skills. Any components sitting within our 'other' category should be of a high standard.

3 Stars (★★★)

The vessel must have nicely appointed interiors, although the style, finish or layout will be less than elegant or sophisticated than on higher-rated riverships. The level of cleanliness must be of a standard well above basic. As for accommodation, suites (minimum size expected 20 sq m/215 sq ft) and cabins (minimum 11 sq m/118 sq ft) must be of a good standard and very comfortable. Under cuisine, there will be a choice of main courses for dinner, with vegetarian options available for all meals. Service

should be provided by staff with a good professional knowledge of serving food and drinks. Any components relating to our 'other' category should be well above the minimum required.

2 Stars (★★)

The vessel must have interiors that are decent, although they may well be made from average-quality materials (more basic than those of a higher star rating). Overall levels of cleanliness will be above basic. Suites (minimum size expected 18 sq m/193 sq ft) and cabins will be practical (minimum size 9 sq m/96 sq ft) but less luxurious and well equipped than higher-rated vessels. In terms of cuisine, there will typically be little or no choice. Breakfast and lunch will be self-service buffet-style. Waiters/waitresses will provide an acceptable level of service, with training a weak point. Miscellaneous items covered under our 'other' category may be acceptable, but no more.

1 Star (★)

At this level, the hardware will include utilitarian interiors that need some improvement. The accommodation will typically be tiny and simply equipped, with poor soundproofing. The cuisine will be at the most basic end of the scale, with little choice and low-quality produce. As for service, the staff is unlikely to have been trained in hospitality. Miscellaneous 'other' items will be at the most basic level.

Queen Isabel restaurant (Uniworld).

The Top 10 Performers

Having reviewed over 300-plus riverships in Europe and the steamboats/riverboats in the USA, Berlitz names them here.

Despite constant claims by river cruise companies that they have been named 'Best River Cruise Line' or 'Best Rivership' by this or that magazine or online readers' poll, there really is no such thing – there is only the rivership that is right for you. Few operators can really deliver a rivership, product, and crew worthy of the highest Berlitz star rating – it's all about excellence, passion, consistency, food and service standards. The previous chapter explains in detail the things that are taken into account when evaluating and scoring the riverships – many of which are identical in design and structure – but there are always subtle differences between them, and the scores reflect these accordingly. Whichever rivership and operator you choose, however, we hope that you have a very enjoyable river cruise experience.

For this third edition, the following 10 riverships have achieved the highest scores:

AND THE WINNER IS...

AmaKristina scores so highly because of the outstanding cuisine and service. Congratulations!

AmaKristina	427	★★★★+
AmaViola	425	★★★★+
AmaStella	424	★★★★+
Crystal Debussy	424	★★★★+
Crystal Ravel	424	★★★★+
AmaSerena	423	★★★★+
Crystal Mahler	423	★★★★+
Crystal Bach	422	★★★★+
AmaPrima	421	★★★★+
AmaReina	421	★★★★+

ALEMANNIA ★★+

THIS DATED RIVERSHIP IS BEST CHOSEN FOR THE ITINERARY, BUT LITTLE ELSE.

Operator .... Various tour operators
Built 1971
Length (m) 110.0
Number of decks (excluding sun deck) 3
Passenger beds 184
Sit outside (real) balcony .... No
French (open-air) balcony .... No
Approximate cabin size (sq m) 12.0–24.0
Lift (elevator) .... No
Rivers sailed .... Rhine

BERLITZ'S RATINGS		
	Possible	Achieved
Hardware	100	38
Accommodation	100	38
Cuisine	100	43
Service	100	46
Miscellaneous	100	47
OVERALL SCORE 212 points out of 500		

Many people choose a river cruise simply for the itinerary and destination experiences. If this is you, then *Alemannia*, with its high-density and dimensionally challenged cabins, tiny bathrooms and limited storage space, may be suitable. The lounge is pleasant enough, but the low-back seating is uncomfortable. The restaurant is modestly attractive, but don't expect fine food, because the small galley is only able to turn out basic dishes; the wines are young, and wine glasses are small. Overall, it's cheap and cheerful.

ALENA NYR

THIS CONTEMPORARY RIVERSHIP WITH STYLISH FEATURES WOULD MAKE A GOOD CHOICE.

Operator .... Phoenix Cruises
Built 2018
Length (m) 135.0
Number of decks (excluding sun deck) 3
Passenger beds 191
Sit outside (real) balcony .... No
French (open-air) balcony .... Yes
Approximate cabin size (sq m) 12.0–17.0
Lift (elevator) .... Yes
Rivers sailed .... Rhine, Main, Danube

BERLITZ'S RATINGS		
	Possible	Achieved
Hardware	100	NYR
Accommodation	100	NYR
Cuisine	100	NYR
Service	100	NYR
Miscellaneous	100	NYR
OVERALL SCORE NYR points out of 500		

The well-designed *Alena* (sister to *Asara*) is comfortable, with contemporary, but restrained decor. The cabins, although not large, are well designed, with good lighting and decent storage space. Two decks of cabins have floor-to-ceiling glass doors that open to a French (open-air) balcony. Bathrooms have large, glazed shower enclosures, and space for toiletries. The restaurant has large windows and comfortable seating. Highlights will include good food and friendly service. A second (aft) speciality restaurant is an alternative eatery.

ALINA ★★★★

THIS STYLISH RIVERSHIP PROVIDES A GOOD-VALUE RIVER CRUISE EXPERIENCE.

Operator ....Phoenix Cruises
Built 2011
Length (m) 135.0
Number of decks (excluding sun deck)................... 3
Passenger beds...216
Sit outside (real) balcony ....No
French (open-air) balcony ....Yes
Approximate cabin size (sq m) 14.0–16.0
Lift (elevator)..No
Rivers sailed............................. Rhine, Main, Danube

BERLITZ'S RATINGS		
	Possible	Achieved
Hardware	100	68
Accommodation	100	62
Cuisine	100	74
Service	100	75
Miscellaneous	100	73
OVERALL SCORE 352 points out of 500		

Alina is a high-density vessel with a panoramic lounge and restful (no glitz) interior decor. The cabins are reasonably large, and most have French (open-air) balconies. The bathrooms are well designed, with large, glazed shojwer enclosures. The two-deck restaurant is comfortable. There's also an aft bistro (an alternative venue, with an outdoor terrace), for more casual fare. The cuisine itself is varied, of good quality and the service is also good, from a well-trained crew.

AMABELLA ★★★★+

A TIP-TOP CONTEMPORARY RIVERSHIP KNOWN FOR ITS HIGH-QUALITY CUISINE.

Operator ....AMA Waterways
Built 2010
Length (m) 135
Number of decks (excluding sun deck)................... 3
Passenger beds...161
Sit outside (real) balcony ....Yes
French (open-air) balcony ....Yes
Approximate cabin size (sq m) 13.0–32.5
Lift (elevator)..Yes
Rivers sailed............................. Main, Rhine, Danube

BERLITZ'S RATINGS		
	Possible	Achieved
Hardware	100	80
Accommodation	100	82
Cuisine	100	84
Service	100	80
Miscellaneous	100	85
OVERALL SCORE 411 points out of 500		

AmaBella is a comfortable vessel with delightfully warm, welcoming interior decor. Most of the cabins have floor-to-ceiling, slide-open French (open-air) balconies, ample storage space and spacious, nicely appointed bathrooms with large shower enclosures and more storage. The cuisine and service is what most passengers remember after their cruise, because this company spends more on food and wine than most, with an emphasis on fresh fish and regional vegetables. Overall, this would be a good choice for anyone seeking excellence.

AMACELLO ★★★★
EXPECT HIGH STANDARDS AND FINE CUISINE ABOARD THIS EXCELLENT RIVERSHIP.

Operator .... AMA Waterways
Built 2008
Length (m) 110.0
Number of decks (excluding sun deck).................... 3
Passenger beds...150
Sit outside (real) balcony ....No
French (open-air) balcony ....Yes
Approximate cabin size (sq m) 13.0–23.5
Lift (elevator)...Yes
Rivers sailed..Rhone, Saone

BERLITZ'S RATINGS		
	Possible	Achieved
Hardware	100	74
Accommodation	100	74
Cuisine	100	85
Service	100	79
Miscellaneous	100	83
OVERALL SCORE 395 points out of 500		

AmaCello is a high-quality, well-designed and spacious vessel with elegant interior decor. Most cabins have floor-to-ceiling, slide-open French (open-air) balconies, and all are generously sized, well laid out and very comfortable. Storage space is good, as is soundproofing. The spacious, marble-appointed bathrooms have large, glazed shower enclosures. Amenities include a fitness area with sauna, and a small open top deck pool is a bonus. The cuisine is excellent, creative, varied and accompanied by good-quality wines.

AMACERTO ★★★★+
THIS SUPERB CONTEMPORARY RIVERSHIP IS PRAISED FOR ITS HIGH-QUALITY CUISINE.

Operator .... AMA Waterways
Built 2012
Length (m) 135.0
Number of decks (excluding sun deck).................... 3
Passenger beds...164
Sit outside (real) balcony ....Yes
French (open-air) balcony ....Yes
Approximate cabin size (sq m) 15.0–32.5
Lift (elevator)...Yes
Rivers sailed............................ Main, Rhine, Danube

BERLITZ'S RATINGS		
	Possible	Achieved
Hardware	100	80
Accommodation	100	75
Cuisine	100	84
Service	100	80
Miscellaneous	100	85
OVERALL SCORE 404 points out of 500		

This very stylish, contemporary rivership will provide you with a first-class river cruise. It includes an excellent variety of high-quality food and very good wines. The cabins are well designed and practical; many have floor-to-ceiling slide-open French (open-air) balconies. The bathrooms are pleasing, and storage space for toiletries is good. With its well-orchestrated excursion programme and really good food (well prepared and with plenty of choice), *AmaCerto* is highly recommended for a fine river cruise experience.

AMADANTE ★★★★
THIS VERY COMFORTABLE RIVERSHIP DELIVERS A HIGH STANDARD AND FINE CUISINE.

Operator .... AMA Waterways
Built 2008
Length (m) 110.0
Number of decks (excluding sun deck).................... 3
Passenger beds...150
Sit outside (real) balcony ....No
French (open-air) balcony ....Yes
Approximate cabin size (sq m) 13.0–23.5
Lift (elevator)..Yes
Rivers sailed.............................. Main, Rhine, Danube

BERLITZ'S RATINGS		
	Possible	Achieved
Hardware	100	78
Accommodation	100	74
Cuisine	100	84
Service	100	81
Miscellaneous	100	83
OVERALL SCORE 395 points out of 500		

It's the cuisine and service that most passengers remember after a cruise aboard this rivership because the company spends more on food and wine than most of its competitors. The cabins are practical and well appointed. The open-seating restaurant is instantly comfortable, and has large picture windows. The cuisine is of a high quality, with ample variety, and accompanied by good wines. The excursion programme is good, and varied. Overall, this rivership is a winner for anyone seeking the best-quality river cruise experience.

AMADOLCE ★★★★
THIS IS A FIRST-CLASS RIVERSHIP WITH OODLES OF STYLE, COMFORT AND FINE FOOD.

Operator .... AMA Waterways
Built 2009
Length (m) 110.0
Number of decks (excluding sun deck).................... 3
Passenger beds...150
Sit outside (real) balcony ....No
French (open-air) balcony ....Yes
Approximate cabin size (sq m) 13.0–23.5
Lift (elevator)..Yes
Rivers sailed.................................... Bordeaux region

BERLITZ'S RATINGS		
	Possible	Achieved
Hardware	100	74
Accommodation	100	75
Cuisine	100	84
Service	100	80
Miscellaneous	100	82
OVERALL SCORE 395 points out of 500		

This is a high-quality, well-designed and spacious vessel with elegant interior decor. Most cabins have French (open-air) balconies, and all are generously sized, well laid out and very comfortable. Storage space is good, as is soundproofing. The bathrooms are marble-clad and have spacious shower enclosures and ample space for toiletries. The restaurant has half-height windows, and is quite comfortable. The cuisine is of a very high standard, with ample variety, good taste and presentation, with quality bread, cheeses, and wines. Aft is the alternative Chef's Table, for a degustation experience.

AMAKRISTINA ★★★★+

THIS IS A REALLY FIRST-CLASS RIVERSHIP WITH EXCELLENT CUISINE AND SERVICE.

Operator	AMA Waterways
Built	2017
Length (m)	135.0
Number of decks (excluding sun deck)	3
Passenger beds	158
Sit outside (real) balcony	Yes
French (open-air) balcony	Yes
Approximate cabin size (sq m)	15.0–32.5
Lift (elevator)	Yes
Rivers sailed	Rhine

BERLITZ'S RATINGS		
	Possible	Achieved
Hardware	100	87
Accommodation	100	83
Cuisine	100	86
Service	100	85
Miscellaneous	100	86
OVERALL SCORE 427 points out of 500		

AmaKristina has bright but elegant interior decor and a warm ambience, with some very comfortable panorama lounge furnishings. A small, open top-deck pool is a bonus. The cabins are quite spacious and have real sit-out balconies, good cabinetry and ample storage space. Lighting and soundproofing are also good. The marble-clad bathrooms are well designed and have large glazed shower enclosures. The open seating restaurant is instantly comfortable, with large picture windows. The food is really good: it has style and passion, it's well presented and there's plenty of choice.

AMALEA NYR

THIS CONTEMPORARY RIVERSHIP WITH THE LATEST FEATURES COULD BE A WISE CHOICE.

Operator	AMA Waterways
Built	2018
Length (m)	135.0
Number of decks (excluding sun deck)	3
Passenger beds	158
Sit outside (real) balcony	Yes
French (open-air) balcony	Yes
Approximate cabin size (sq m)	15.0–32.5
Lift (elevator)	Yes
Rivers sailed	Rhine, Main, Danube

BERLITZ'S RATINGS		
	Possible	Achieved
Hardware	100	NYR
Accommodation	100	NYR
Cuisine	100	NYR
Service	100	NYR
Miscellaneous	100	NYR
OVERALL SCORE NYR points out of 500		

The contemporary (but not brash) interior decor of AmaLea has a warm and welcoming feel in the lounge, and the soft furnishings are of a high standard. The cabins are well designed and have ample drawer and storage space; they include sit-out balconies (with two chairs), good cabinetry, and good lighting and soundproofing, plus excellent mattresses and high-quality bed linen. The marble-clad bathrooms have good storage space and excellent shower enclosures. The restaurant has attractive, warm decor and comfortable seating.

AMALYRA ★★★★

OUTSTANDING CUISINE AND GOOD SERVICE ABOUND ABOARD THIS STYLISH RIVERSHIP.

Operator .... AMA Waterways
Built 2009
Length (m) 110.0
Number of decks (excluding sun deck).................... 3
Passenger beds...150
Sit outside (real) balcony ....No
French (open-air) balcony ....Yes
Approximate cabin size (sq m) 13.0–23.5
Lift (elevator)..Yes
Rivers sailed.............................. Rhine, Main, Danube

BERLITZ'S RATINGS		
	Possible	Achieved
Hardware	100	74
Accommodation	100	75
Cuisine	100	84
Service	100	80
Miscellaneous	100	81
OVERALL SCORE 394 points out of 500		

AmaLyra is a spacious, high-quality vessel with an elegant, contemporary interior decor. Most cabins feature French (not full) balconies, but all are large and well appointed. Marble bathrooms have large shower enclosures and ample storage space for toiletries. Facilities include a small fitness area and sauna. The restaurant has large picture windows, and comfortable seating. The cuisine is excellent, varied and plentiful. Bicycles are available free.

AMAMAGNA NYR

THIS STUNNING, DOUBLE-WIDTH RIVERSHIP HAS OODLES OF SPACE, COMFORT AND PIZZAZZ.

Operator .... AMA Waterways
Built 2019
Length (m) 135.0
Number of decks (excluding sun deck).................... 3
Passenger beds...198
Sit outside (real) balcony .... NYR
French (open-air) balcony ....Yes
Approximate cabin size (sq m) 28.0
Lift (elevator)..Yes
Rivers sailed...Danube

BERLITZ'S RATINGS		
	Possible	Achieved
Hardware	100	NYR
Accommodation	100	NYR
Cuisine	100	NYR
Service	100	NYR
Miscellaneous	100	NYR
OVERALL SCORE NYR points out of 500		

NEW RIVERSHIP

AmaMagna has warm and welcoming decor, a large lounge and a library. The spacious cabins have plenty of storage space; marble-clad bathrooms have large, glazed shower enclosures and ample space for toiletries. The lift connects all decks. Facilities include an extensive pool, a hot tub, spa and wellness facilities, and an aft marina platform with canoes and kayaks. The main restaurant is located forwards, while a Chef's Table (offering a multi-course gastronomic dinner with paired wines), with its own galley, is aft.

AMAPRIMA ★★★★+

OUTSTANDING CUISINE AND HIGH STANDARDS CHARACTERISE THIS COMFORTABLE RIVERSHIP.

Operator	AMA Waterways
Built	2013
Length (m)	135.0
Number of decks (excluding sun deck)	3
Passenger beds	164
Sit outside (real) balcony	Yes
French (open-air) balcony	Yes
Approximate cabin size (sq m)	15.0–32.5
Lift (elevator)	Yes
Rivers sailed	Rhine, Main, Danube

BERLITZ'S RATINGS		
	Possible	Achieved
Hardware	100	85
Accommodation	100	81
Cuisine	100	86
Service	100	83
Miscellaneous	100	86
OVERALL SCORE 421 points out of 500		

AmaPrima is an extremely comfortable vessel with warm interior decor, well-designed, practical cabins – some have floor-to-ceiling, slide-open twin French (open-air) balconies, excellent beds and high-quality bed linen, with elegant marble-clad bathrooms that have large shower enclosures and plenty of storage space for toiletry items. Features include a small open-deck heated outdoor pool with 'swim-up' bar. The restaurant is very comfortable, and the cuisine is impressive, with plenty of choice. The wines are good, too. AmaWaterways knows how to do it right, and it shows.

AMAREINA ★★★★+

THIS FIRST-CLASS RIVERSHIP FEATURES REALLY FINE CUISINE AND SERVICE.

Operator	AMA Waterways
Built	2014
Length (m)	135.0
Number of decks (excluding sun deck)	3
Passenger beds	164
Sit outside (real) balcony	Yes
French (open-air) balcony	Yes
Approximate cabin size (sq m)	15.0–32.5
Lift (elevator)	Yes
Rivers sailed	Rhine

BERLITZ'S RATINGS		
	Possible	Achieved
Hardware	100	85
Accommodation	100	81
Cuisine	100	86
Service	100	83
Miscellaneous	100	86
OVERALL SCORE 421 points out of 500		

The vessel has contemporary interior decor, comfortable seating in the observation lounge, and a good ambience. A small, open top-deck pool is a bonus. The cabins are quite spacious and have sit-out balconies with chairs, good cabinetry, ample storage space, high-quality bed linen and good lighting. The marble-clad bathrooms are extremely comfortable and have large shower enclosures. The restaurant is attractive and comfortable. The taste-filled cuisine is excellent, exudes flair and variety, and is creatively presented.

AMASERENA ★★★★+

THIS VESSEL HAS REAL OPEN BALCONIES AND EXCELLENT FOOD AND SERVICE.

Operator .... AMA Waterways
Built 2015
Length (m) 135.0
Number of decks (excluding sun deck)................... 3
Passenger beds..164
Sit outside (real) balcony ....Yes
French (open-air) balcony ....Yes
Approximate cabin size (sq m) 15.0–32.5
Lift (elevator)..Yes
Rivers sailed............................. Rhine, Main, Danube

BERLITZ'S RATINGS		
	Possible	Achieved
Hardware	100	85
Accommodation	100	83
Cuisine	100	86
Service	100	83
Miscellaneous	100	86
OVERALL SCORE 423 points out of 500		

This well-designed rivership has contemporary but elegant interior decor. The spacious cabins (most with proper sit-out balconies with chairs and drinks table) are designed well, and have decent drawer and storage space, a minibar-fridge and good lighting and soundproofing. Marble-clad bathrooms have good storage space and excellent shower enclosures. Very comfortable but somewhat noisy restaurant provides excellent cuisine, with plenty of variety, and good wines.

AMASONATA ★★★★+

EXCELLENT CUISINE AND GOOD SERVICE IN A STYLISH, CONTEMPORARY RIVERSHIP.

Operator .... AMA Waterways
Built 2014
Length (m) 135.0
Number of decks (excluding sun deck)................... 3
Passenger beds..164
Sit outside (real) balcony ....Yes
French (open-air) balcony ....Yes
Approximate cabin size (sq m) 15.0–32.5
Lift (elevator)..Yes
Rivers sailed..Danube

BERLITZ'S RATINGS		
	Possible	Achieved
Hardware	100	84
Accommodation	100	82
Cuisine	100	86
Service	100	82
Miscellaneous	100	86
OVERALL SCORE 420 points out of 500		

AmaSonata is chic, with high-quality appointments and delightful, contemporary interior decor. A small, open top-deck pool is a bonus. Generously sized, well-appointed cabins (and double-sized suites) have sit-out or floor-to-ceiling slide-open French (open-air) balconies (the lowest deck cabins have fixed windows), ample storage space, mini-fridge, high-quality mattresses and elegant marble-clad bathrooms with large, glazed shower enclosures. The cuisine is excellent, varied and accompanied by good wines. Chef's Table (a second restaurant) features a fine dégustation experience.

AMASTELLA ★★★★+

FAMILY-FRIENDLY RIVERSHIP WITH STYLE AND REALLY FINE CUISINE.

Operator .... AMA Waterways
Built 2016
Length (m) 135.0
Number of decks (excluding sun deck).................... 3
Passenger beds..158
Sit outside (real) balcony ....Yes
French (open-air) balcony ....Yes
Approximate cabin size (sq m) 15.0–32.5
Lift (elevator)...Yes
Rivers sailed............................. Rhine, Main, Danube

BERLITZ'S RATINGS		
	Possible	Achieved
Hardware	100	86
Accommodation	100	82
Cuisine	100	86
Service	100	85
Miscellaneous	100	85
OVERALL SCORE 424 points out of 500		

High-quality furnishings and contemporary interior design abound aboard this vessel. The well-designed, practical, nicely furnished cabins have good drawer and storage space, excellent mattresses and high-quality bed linen. Some cabins are family-friendly, and have interconnecting doors. Delightful marble-clad bathrooms have fully glazed shower enclosures and space for personal toiletries. Very comfortable restaurant and high-quality cuisine with plenty of variety, choice and taste.

AMAVENITA ★★★★+

THIS RIVERSHIP WOULD BE AN EXCELLENT CHOICE FOR AUSTRALASIANS.

Operator .... APT Touring
Built 2016
Length (m) 135.0
Number of decks (excluding sun deck).................... 3
Passenger beds..164
Sit outside (real) balcony ....Yes
French (open-air) balcony ....Yes
Approximate cabin size (sq m) 15.0–32.5
Lift (elevator)...Yes
Rivers sailed............................. Rhine, Main, Danube

BERLITZ'S RATINGS		
	Possible	Achieved
Hardware	100	85
Accommodation	100	82
Cuisine	100	85
Service	100	82
Miscellaneous	100	84
OVERALL SCORE 418 points out of 500		

This fine vessel has extremely comfortable furniture and decor in its panoramic lounge, with contemporary design elements and cool but tasteful colours. The well-designed cabins are very practical, and have excellent beds and high-quality bed linen. They have good storage space and soundproofing, and the marble-clad bathrooms have large, glazed shower enclosures. The open seating restaurant has pleasant, warm decor and comfortable seating areas. Overall this will be a good choice for a first-rate cruise experience, and the food is very good indeed, with ample choice.

AMAVERDE ★★★★+

THIS EXCELLENT CONTEMPORARY RIVERSHIP IS KNOWN FOR ITS HIGH-QUALITY CUISINE.

Operator .... APT Touring
Built 2011
Length (m) 135.0
Number of decks (excluding sun deck)................... 3
Passenger beds...161
Sit outside (real) balcony.......................................Yes
French (open-air) balcony ....Yes
Approximate cabin size (sq m) 13.0–32.5
Lift (elevator)..Yes
Rivers sailed...Danube

BERLITZ'S RATINGS		
	Possible	Achieved
Hardware	100	82
Accommodation	100	81
Cuisine	100	86
Service	100	82
Miscellaneous	100	86
OVERALL SCORE 417 points out of 500		

AmaVerde has classy interior decor, fine furnishings and plenty of space per passenger. The cabins are well appointed and very comfortable; many have full balconies and good soundproofing. Bathrooms have large shower enclosures. However, it's the food (taste, creativity, variety) and service that most passengers remember. It's a winner for anyone seeking a high-quality cruise experience, especially those who enjoy good food with plenty of choice.

AMAVIDA ★★★★

A RIVERSHIP HIGHLY PRAISED FOR ITS FINE REGIONAL CUISINE AND HIGH STANDARDS.

Operator .... AMA Waterways
Built 2013
Length (m) 79.5
Number of decks (excluding sun deck)................... 3
Passenger beds...106
Sit outside (real) balcony..No
French (open-air) balcony ....Yes
Approximate cabin size (sq m) 15.0–30.0
Lift (elevator)..Yes
Rivers sailed... Douro

BERLITZ'S RATINGS		
	Possible	Achieved
Hardware	100	85
Accommodation	100	80
Cuisine	100	73
Service	100	74
Miscellaneous	100	77
OVERALL SCORE 389 points out of 500		

Specially designed for River Douro cruises, Ama-Vida features elegant interior decor. Two decks of very spacious cabins feature floor-to-ceiling slide-open French (open-air) balconies, while cabins on the lowest deck have windows only, but decent amount of storage space. The bathrooms are also well equipped, with a glazed shower enclosure. The restaurant itself is not particularly inspiring but it is comfortable. The cuisine is noteworthy, and there is plenty of choice, including several regional dishes.

AMAVIOLA ★★★★+

STYLISHLY DESIGNED FOR FAMILIES, THIS RIVERSHIP REALLY DOES HAVE IT ALL.

Operator .... AMA Waterways
Built 2016
Length (m) 135.0
Number of decks (excluding sun deck)................... 3
Passenger beds...158
Sit outside (real) balcony ....Yes
French (open-air) balcony ....Yes
Approximate cabin size (sq m) 15.0–33.0
Lift (elevator)...Yes
Rivers sailed............................ Rhine, Main, Danube

BERLITZ'S RATINGS		
	Possible	Achieved
Hardware	100	86
Accommodation	100	82
Cuisine	100	86
Service	100	85
Miscellaneous	100	86
OVERALL SCORE 425 points out of 500		

This very well-designed vessel has a really comfortable observation lounge and protected sitting area outside at the front, while a small, open top-deck pool is a bonus. Many cabins have open-air balconies (those designed for families with children have interconnecting doors), with good drawer and storage space; they are also tastefully furnished, and very good mattresses and high-quality bed linen. They also have well-appointed bathrooms with large shower enclosures and good space for personal toiletry items.

AMADEUS I ★★★

THIS WOULD BE A GOOD CHOICE FOR A DECENT MEDIUM-BUDGET RIVER CRUISE.

Operator ....Luftner Cruises
Built 1997
Length (m) 110.0
Number of decks (excluding sun deck)................... 3
Passenger beds...146
Sit outside (real) balcony ....No
French (open-air) balcony ....No
Approximate cabin size (sq m) 15.0
Lift (elevator)...No
Rivers sailed...Danube

BERLITZ'S RATINGS		
	Possible	Achieved
Hardware	100	52
Accommodation	100	52
Cuisine	100	54
Service	100	55
Miscellaneous	100	56
OVERALL SCORE 269 points out of 500		

The fairly smart, modern-looking *Amadeus I* is a comfortable vessel, with decor that is rather elegant but unstuffy. The cabins are really quite spacious and have mini-fridges, good-quality mattresses and bed linen and practical bathrooms, with space for toiletry items. The cuisine is pretty good and includes a decent amount of variety. Service, too, is good. You should have quite a pleasant experience aboard this rivership.

AMADEUS BRILLIANT ★★★★
THIS IS A GOOD CHOICE FOR A FIRST-RATE CRUISE IN COMFORTABLE SURROUNDINGS.

Operator	Luftner Cruises
Built	2011
Length (m)	110.0
Number of decks (excluding sun deck)	3
Passenger beds	150
Sit outside (real) balcony	No
French (open-air) balcony	Yes
Approximate cabin size (sq m)	10.0–22.0
Lift (elevator)	Yes
Rivers sailed	Rhine, Main, Danube

BERLITZ'S RATINGS		
	Possible	Achieved
Hardware	100	79
Accommodation	100	78
Cuisine	100	74
Service	100	74
Miscellaneous	100	76
OVERALL SCORE 381 points out of 500		

The smart, very nicely decorated, contemporary *Amadeus Brilliant* should provide you with a very comfortable cruise experience. Except for two singles, all cabins are extremely spacious (especially the nine suites, which double the size) and have decent storage space and elegant bathrooms. Some have French floor-to-ceiling slide-open (open-air) balconies. Lighting and soundproofing are also good. Dinners are served at your table, with full tablecloth and cutlery settings.

AMADEUS CLASSIC ★★★★
A GOOD-LOOKING RIVERSHIP BUT DATED WHEN COMPARED TO NEWER VESSELS.

Operator	Luftner Cruises
Built	2001
Length (m)	110.0
Number of decks (excluding sun deck)	3
Passenger beds	146
Sit outside (real) balcony	No
French (open-air) balcony	Yes
Approximate cabin size (sq m)	15.0–22.0
Lift (elevator)	Yes
Rivers sailed	Rhine, Main, Danube

BERLITZ'S RATINGS		
	Possible	Achieved
Hardware	100	72
Accommodation	100	72
Cuisine	100	72
Service	100	72
Miscellaneous	100	76
OVERALL SCORE 364 points out of 500		

This pleasant, very comfortable rivership features an interior decor that is quite understated and almost refined, if a little dated. The cabins are comfy and practical, but small by today's standards, with no balconies and with windows that are not particularly large. Storage space is a little tight, too. The restaurant is attractive and comfortable. The food is decent, but nothing really stands out.

AMADEUS DIAMOND ★★★★
THIS FIRST-CLASS RIVERSHIP COMBINES STYLE WITH REALLY GOOD HOSPITALITY.

Operator ....Luftner Cruises
Built 2009
Length (m) 110.0
Number of decks (excluding sun deck)...................... 3
Passenger beds..146
Sit outside (real) balcony ....No
French (open-air) balcony ....Yes
Approximate cabin size (sq m) 10.0–22.0
Lift (elevator)..Yes
Rivers sailed...Seine

BERLITZ'S RATINGS		
	Possible	Achieved
Hardware	100	75
Accommodation	100	75
Cuisine	100	81
Service	100	78
Miscellaneous	100	81
OVERALL SCORE 390 points out of 500		

The modern, smart-looking *Amadeus Diamond* is a very comfortable vessel, with decor that is really classy yet unpretentious. The cabins and bathrooms are both spacious and practical, with amenities including mini-fridges. The restaurant is pleasant and comfortable. It offers varied and very creative cuisine – a notch above many others – and the service is very good. A real first-class experience.

AMADEUS ELEGANT ★★★★
A FINE-LOOKING RIVERSHIP WITH EXCELLENT ITINERARIES, FOOD AND WINE.

Operator ....Luftner Cruises
Built 2010
Length (m) 110.0
Number of decks (excluding sun deck)................... 3
Passenger beds..150
Sit outside (real) balcony ....No
French (open-air) balcony ....Yes
Approximate cabin size (sq m) 10.0–22.0
Lift (elevator)..Yes
Rivers sailed............................. Rhine, Main, Danube

BERLITZ'S RATINGS		
	Possible	Achieved
Hardware	100	75
Accommodation	100	75
Cuisine	100	76
Service	100	75
Miscellaneous	100	78
OVERALL SCORE 379 points out of 500		

Amadeus Elegant has an interior decor that is understated and rather classic in style. The well-designed cabins – most have floor-to-ceiling slide-open French (open-air) balconies – have bathrooms with large shower enclosures; nine junior suites have bathtub/showers. The cuisine and variety of food offered is excellent, with service from a well-trained crew. Overall, this would be a good choice for anyone seeking a first-rate experience.

AMADEUS PROVENCE ★★★★+
HIGHLY COMFORTABLE, AND WITH THE RIGHT FACILITIES FOR FRENCH RIVER CRUISING.

Operator ....Luftner Cruises
Built 2017
Length (m) 110.0
Number of decks (excluding sun deck).................... 3
Passenger beds...140
Sit outside (real) balcony..No
French (open-air) balcony ....Yes
Approximate cabin size (sq m) 17.0–26.0
Lift (elevator)..Yes
Rivers sailed..Rhone

BERLITZ'S RATINGS		
	Possible	Achieved
Hardware	100	81
Accommodation	100	80
Cuisine	100	81
Service	100	80
Miscellaneous	100	80
OVERALL SCORE 402 points out of 500		

This first-class vessel is the first in the fleet to have a small pool and bar on the uppermost (open) deck – useful in the hot Provence sun. Inside, the decor is clean, warm and tidy. The cabins are nicely equipped, as are the bathrooms. Bedside reading lights and soundproofing are good. The restaurant is really comfortable, and the cuisine is excellent, with oodles of taste, artful presentation and variety. Overall, this offers an absolutely first-rate experience.

AMADEUS ROYAL ★★★★
THIS COMFORTABLE MODERN RIVERSHIP WILL DELIVER A WELL-ROUNDED CRUISE.

Operator ....Luftner Cruises
Built 2005
Length (m) 110.0
Number of decks (excluding sun deck).................... 3
Passenger beds...144
Sit outside (real) balcony.......................................No
French (open-air) balcony ....Yes
Approximate cabin size (sq m) 15.0–24.0
Lift (elevator)..Yes
Rivers sailed...Rhone, Saone

BERLITZ'S RATINGS		
	Possible	Achieved
Hardware	100	72
Accommodation	100	76
Cuisine	100	73
Service	100	73
Miscellaneous	100	76
OVERALL SCORE 370 points out of 500		

The contemporary, smart-looking *Amadeus Royal* is a very comfortable vessel, with decor that is elegant but unfussy. Most of the well-designed cabins have floor-to-ceiling slide-open French (open-air) balconies and nicely equipped bathrooms with large shower enclosures (four suites have bathtub/showers). The restaurant is both attractive and comfortable. The food is nicely varied, of a good standard and well presented.

AMADEUS SILVER ★★★★

THIS EXTREMELY COMFORTABLE RIVERSHIP DELIVERS A FIRST-CLASS RIVER CRUISE.

Operator ....Luftner Cruises
Built 2013
Length (m) 135.0
Number of decks (excluding sun deck).................... 3
Passenger beds..180
Sit outside (real) balcony ....No
French (open-air) balcony ....Yes
Approximate cabin size (sq m) 16.0–24.0
Lift (elevator)...No
Rivers sailed............................. Rhine, Main, Danube

BERLITZ'S RATINGS		
	Possible	Achieved
Hardware	100	81
Accommodation	100	81
Cuisine	100	75
Service	100	75
Miscellaneous	100	81
OVERALL SCORE 393 points out of 500		

The interior decor of *Amadeus Silver* has some very elegant, warm touches, and the public lounges are especially cosy. The generously sized cabins are attractively outfitted, and most have floor-to-ceiling slide-open French (open-air) balconies. Twelve suites also have full balconies, minibars, and bathrooms with bathtub/showers. This rivership has very good food, and there's plenty of variety; the wines are quite decent, too.

AMADEUS SILVER II ★★★★+

THIS WOULD BE A GOOD CHOICE FOR A VERY STYLISH, FIRST-RATE RIVER CRUISE.

Operator ....Luftner Cruises
Built 2015
Length (m) 135.0
Number of decks (excluding sun deck).................... 3
Passenger beds..168
Sit outside (real) balcony ....No
French (open-air) balcony ....Yes
Approximate cabin size (sq m) 17.0–26.0
Lift (elevator)..Yes
Rivers sailed............................. Rhine, Main, Danube

BERLITZ'S RATINGS		
	Possible	Achieved
Hardware	100	81
Accommodation	100	81
Cuisine	100	80
Service	100	77
Miscellaneous	100	82
OVERALL SCORE 401 points out of 500		

The observation lounge has relaxing, understated interior decor, with high-quality furnishings. The cabins are well designed and have ample storage space, and good lighting and soundproofing. The bathrooms are comfortable, and have glazed shower enclosures. The restaurant has a low ceiling, and can be noisy. The cuisine, however, is very good, and comes with plenty of taste and ample variety.

AMADEUS SILVER III ★★★★+
AN EXCELLENT CHOICE FOR A STYLISH, WELL-ORCHESTRATED CRUISE.

Operator ....Luftner Cruises
Built 2016
Length (m) 135.0
Number of decks (excluding sun deck)................... 3
Passenger beds...168
Sit outside (real) balcony ....No
French (open-air) balcony ....Yes
Approximate cabin size (sq m) 17.5–26.5
Lift (elevator)..Yes
Rivers sailed.............................. Rhine, Main, Danube

BERLITZ'S RATINGS		
	Possible	Achieved
Hardware	100	82
Accommodation	100	81
Cuisine	100	80
Service	100	78
Miscellaneous	100	82
OVERALL SCORE 403 points out of 500		

This rivership has warm, restrained (no bling) and refined interior decor in the lounge, and high-quality soft furnishings. The cabins – many have floor-to-ceiling slide-open French (open-air) balconies, while the suites have sit-out balconies – are really well designed, very comfortable, with practical bedside reading lights, good storage space and soundproofing, and high-quality bed linen. The bathrooms have large glazed shower enclosures and good lighting. The restaurant is comfortable and has open seating. The cuisine is really good, with taste and ample variety; the wines are quite decent, too.

AMADEUS SYMPHONY ★★★★
THIS FIRST-CLASS RIVERSHIP COMBINES STYLE, GREAT FOOD AND GOOD HOSPITALITY.

Operator ....Luftner Cruises
Built 2003
Length (m) 110.0
Number of decks (excluding sun deck)................... 3
Passenger beds...146
Sit outside (real) balcony ....No
French (open-air) balcony ....Yes
Approximate cabin size (sq m) 15.0–22.0
Lift (elevator)..No
Rivers sailed...Rhone, Saone

BERLITZ'S RATINGS		
	Possible	Achieved
Hardware	100	70
Accommodation	100	72
Cuisine	100	72
Service	100	73
Miscellaneous	100	73
OVERALL SCORE 360 points out of 500		

This very comfortable vessel has decor that is quite classy but unpretentious. The cabins are spacious and practical, have good soft furnishings, twin beds that convert to queen-sized beds, writing desks and mini-fridges. The bathrooms have decent-sized shower enclosures. The cuisine is varied and very creative, and the service is attentive. A real first-class experience.

AMELIA ★★★★

THIS RIVERSHIP PROVIDES GOOD CUISINE AND SERVICE IN A CONTEMPORARY SETTING.

Operator ....Phoenix Cruises
Built 2012
Length (m) 135.0
Number of decks (excluding sun deck)....................3
Passenger beds...216
Sit outside (real) balcony......................................No
French (open-air) balcony ....Yes
Approximate cabin size (sq m) 14.0–16.0
Lift (elevator)..Yes
Rivers sailed............................. Rhine, Main, Danube

BERLITZ'S RATINGS		
	Possible	Achieved
Hardware	100	79
Accommodation	100	79
Cuisine	100	80
Service	100	76
Miscellaneous	100	76
OVERALL SCORE 390 points out of 500		

Amelia is an extremely comfortable and well-proportioned rivership. Cabins on the lower deck have windows; all others feature floor-to-ceiling slide-open French (open-air) balconies. All cabins are reasonably spacious and well furnished, and bathrooms are practical with good-sized shower enclosures. The restaurant spans two decks, and an aft bistro provides an alternative. The cuisine is good, creative and nicely presented, and there's a decent variety of food.

AMSTERDAM ★★

THIS VINTAGE RIVERSHIP OFFERS A BASIC, NO-FRILLS, CHEAP AND CHEERFUL CRUISE.

Operator ....Various tour operators
Built 1948
Length (m) 78.0
Number of decks (excluding sun deck)....................2
Passenger beds...100
Sit outside (real) balcony...................................... No
French (open-air) balcony ....No
Approximate cabin size (sq m) 6.0
Lift (elevator)..No
Rivers sailed...Rhine

BERLITZ'S RATINGS		
	Possible	Achieved
Hardware	100	31
Accommodation	100	30
Cuisine	100	38
Service	100	40
Miscellaneous	100	40
OVERALL SCORE 179 points out of 500		

Amsterdam has pleasant, albeit very dated, interior decor, but the cabins and bathrooms are really tiny (having a shower is a squeeze). Storage space is very limited, and both the lighting and air conditioning (well, air flow) are poor. The food choice is likewise extremely limited, and lacking in green vegetables. Overall, it's a basic, no-frills river cruise at a low price, but fine if you are travelling for the itinerary – or on a very tight budget.

ANESHA ★★★★
CHOOSE THIS HANDSOME RIVERSHIP FOR A DELIGHTFUL CRUISE EXPERIENCE.

Operator ....Phoenix Cruises
Built 2016
Length (m) 135.0
Number of decks (excluding sun deck)....................3
Passenger beds...180
Sit outside (real) balcony.......................................No
French (open-air) balcony ....Yes
Approximate cabin size (sq m) 17.0–18.5
Lift (elevator)..Yes
Rivers sailed.............................. Rhine, Main, Danube

BERLITZ'S RATINGS		
	Possible	Achieved
Hardware	100	80
Accommodation	100	78
Cuisine	100	78
Service	100	76
Miscellaneous	100	76
OVERALL SCORE 388 points out of 500		

This fairly high-density vessel has contemporary, but restrained interior decor that is chic and very comfortable, and features high-quality soft furnishings in its almost pillar-free main lounge. The cabins are well designed, have good drawer and storage space, minibar, and high-quality mattresses and bed linen. The bathrooms are a decent size, and have a glazed shower enclosure.

ANTONIO BELLUCCI ★★★+
THIS FAIRLY MODERN VESSEL WILL PROVIDE YOU WITH A DECENT ALL-ROUND CRUISE.

Operator .... Feenstra Rhine Line
Built 2012
Length (m) 110.0
Number of decks (excluding sun deck)....................3
Passenger beds...140
Sit outside (real) balcony.......................................No
French (open-air) balcony ....Yes
Approximate cabin size (sq m) 13.0–32.0
Lift (elevator)..Yes
Rivers sailed.............................. Rhine, Main, Danube

BERLITZ'S RATINGS		
	Possible	Achieved
Hardware	100	71
Accommodation	100	68
Cuisine	100	56
Service	100	57
Miscellaneous	100	58
OVERALL SCORE 310 points out of 500		

This small, fairly modern rivership has attractive features including a comfortable panoramic lounge, and a top-deck hot tub. The interiors incorporate warm woods and marble. Cabins have twin beds that can convert to queen-sized ones, and many cabins have floor-to-ceiling slide-open French (open-air) balconies. The bathrooms are small but functional. The cuisine is good, but the variety is limited and underwhelming; however, the desserts are good. Overall, it's a decent all-rounder

ARIANA ★★★+

THIS MODERN RIVERSHIP PROVIDES A MODEST BUT DECENT-VALUE CRUISE EXPERIENCE.

Operator ....Phoenix Cruises
Built 2012
Length (m) 110.0
Number of decks (excluding sun deck)................... 3
Passenger beds...162
Sit outside (real) balcony ....No
French (open-air) balcony ....Yes
Approximate cabin size (sq m) 10.0–14.0
Lift (elevator)...Yes
Rivers sailed..Danube

BERLITZ'S RATINGS		
	Possible	Achieved
Hardware	100	74
Accommodation	100	71
Cuisine	100	62
Service	100	63
Miscellaneous	100	68
OVERALL SCORE 338 points out of 500		

This small, modern high-density vessel has a pleasant lounge, although the decor is nondescript, and the mainly tub-chair seating is uncomfortable. The cabins are very small, with plain decor, and there's not much storage space for clothing items. Many have floor-to-ceiling slide-open doors to access the French (open-air) balconies; the bathrooms are small and basic, but they are practical. The restaurant is fairly pleasant, but the seating is cramped and the ceiling is low. The cuisine is underwhelming, and there's limited choice. It's best to choose *Ariana* for the itinerary.

ARLENE ★★+

THIS SMALL, NO-FRILLS VESSEL IS ONLY FOR THOSE ON THE MOST MODEST BUDGET.

Operator .... Feenstra Rhine Line
Built 1986
Length (m) 91.2
Number of decks (excluding sun deck)................... 2
Passenger beds...106
Sit outside (real) balcony ....No
French (open-air) balcony ....No
Approximate cabin size (sq m) 8.0–10.0
Lift (elevator)..No
Rivers sailed...Rhine

BERLITZ'S RATINGS		
	Possible	Achieved
Hardware	100	42
Accommodation	100	43
Cuisine	100	40
Service	100	41
Miscellaneous	100	42
OVERALL SCORE 208 points out of 500		

Arlene is a small, older-style rivership with a lounge with uncomfortable tub chairs. The cabins are really plain, with two slim beds that fold down from wooden wall units. The upper-deck cabin windows slide open; lower-deck windows don't open. The bathrooms are extremely small. The restaurant is pleasant but ultra-cramped, and the steps to get to it are steep. The meal choices are limited, as is the quality. Go only for the itinerary and price.

A-ROSA AQUA ★★★+
MODERN HOTEL-STYLE RIVERSHIP WITH EXCELLENT FEATURES FOR A GOOD CRUISE.

Operator	A-ROSA River Cruises
Built	2009
Length (m)	135.0
Number of decks (excluding sun deck)	3
Passenger beds	198
Sit outside (real) balcony	No
French (open-air) balcony	Yes
Approximate cabin size (sq m)	14.5
Lift (elevator)	No
Rivers sailed	Rhine, Moselle, Main

BERLITZ'S RATINGS		
	Possible	Achieved
Hardware	100	66
Accommodation	100	60
Cuisine	100	61
Service	100	60
Miscellaneous	100	69
OVERALL SCORE 316 points out of 500		

This trendy rivership has very colourful interior decor and soft furnishings. Many cabins have floor-to-ceiling slide-open French (open-air) balconies, while others have small windows; all have angular cabinetry. Two slim beds can be converted into a double bed. Note that there's little storage space. The bistro-style restaurant is bright and cheerful, and the buffet-style food is decent enough, but there's no 'wow' factor, and the wine glasses are small. Facilities include a fitness area with a decent-sized co-ed sauna.

A-ROSA BELLA ★★★+
THIS IS A POPULAR MODERN RIVERSHIP IDEAL FOR YOUTHFUL, ACTIVE TYPES.

Operator	A-ROSA River Cruises
Built	2002
Length (m)	124.5
Number of decks (excluding sun deck)	3
Passenger beds	202
Sit outside (real) balcony	No
French (open-air) balcony	Yes
Approximate cabin size (sq m)	14.5–16.5
Lift (elevator)	No
Rivers sailed	Danube

BERLITZ'S RATINGS		
	Possible	Achieved
Hardware	100	58
Accommodation	100	58
Cuisine	100	61
Service	100	60
Miscellaneous	100	68
OVERALL SCORE 305 points out of 500		

The decor on this high-density vessel is colourful and bright, with minimalist furnishings. The cabins, some of which have French (open-air) balconies, are unfussy but practical (although storage space is minimal), and have two slim beds that can be converted into a double bed. A wellness area includes a large (unisex) sauna and fitness equipment. The bistro-style restaurant is bright and cheerful, and the buffet-style food is decent enough, but lacks 'wow' factor, and the wine glasses are small. A-Rosa operates well-orchestrated cruises, and bicycles are provided for active excursions.

A-ROSA BRAVA ★★★+

A WELL-RUN, CONTEMPORARY-STYLE RIVERSHIP FOR YOUTHFUL, ACTIVE TYPES.

Operator .... A-ROSA River Cruises
Built 2011
Length (m) 135.0
Number of decks (excluding sun deck)................... 3
Passenger beds..202
Sit outside (real) balcony ....No
French (open-air) balcony ....Yes
Approximate cabin size (sq m) 14.5
Lift (elevator)..No
Rivers sailed............................ Rhine, Moselle, Main

BERLITZ'S RATINGS		
	Possible	Achieved
Hardware	100	66
Accommodation	100	61
Cuisine	100	61
Service	100	61
Miscellaneous	100	71
OVERALL SCORE 320 points out of 500		

This high-density rivership has bright, upbeat decor and soft furnishings, with cabins – some with floor-to-ceiling slide-open doors to (open-air) balconies and bathrooms that are practical but unfussy, plain, lack storage space, and have poor soundproofing; the twin beds can convert to a double. The bistro-style restaurant is cheerful, and the self-service buffets are attractively presented, but the cuisine itself is underwhelming. One nice touch is that bicycles are provided for excursions. Overall, A-Rosa operates well-orchestrated cruises.

A-ROSA DONNA ★★★+

UPBEAT DECOR AND MINIMALIST STYLE ARE THE FEATURES OF THIS WELL-RUN RIVERSHIP.

Operator .... A-ROSA River Cruises
Built 2002
Length (m) 124.5
Number of decks (excluding sun deck)................... 3
Passenger beds..200
Sit outside (real) balcony ....No
French (open-air) balcony ....Yes
Approximate cabin size (sq m) 14.5–16.5
Lift (elevator)..No
Rivers sailed...Danube

BERLITZ'S RATINGS		
	Possible	Achieved
Hardware	100	60
Accommodation	100	57
Cuisine	100	61
Service	100	60
Miscellaneous	100	68
OVERALL SCORE 306 points out of 500		

One of the first A-Rosa vessels, *A-Rosa Donna* offers excursions including bicycle tours. The lounge has cheerful, modern decor. The brightly coloured, unfussy cabins are practical (but the cabinetry corners are square, so watch your legs, as it's easy to bump them); some cabins have floor-to-ceiling slide-open doors to French (open-air) balconies, and two slim beds that convert to a double. The bathrooms are small and functional but modular and plain. The bistro-style restaurant has open seating but the food, while colourful, has little flair. Go for the itinerary and destinations.

A-ROSA FLORA ★★★+
THIS CONTEMPORARY RIVERSHIP IS FOR A YOUTHFUL ACTIVE CRUISE EXPERIENCE.

Operator .... A-ROSA River Cruises
Built 2014
Length (m) 135.0
Number of decks (excluding sun deck)................... 3
Passenger beds...166
Sit outside (real) balcony.......................................No
French (open-air) balcony ....Yes
Approximate cabin size (sq m) 14.5–29.0
Lift (elevator)..No
Rivers sailed............................. Rhine, Moselle, Main

BERLITZ'S RATINGS		
	Possible	Achieved
Hardware	100	70
Accommodation	100	61
Cuisine	100	62
Service	100	63
Miscellaneous	100	72
OVERALL SCORE 328 points out of 500		

A-Rosa Flora is a funky vessel aimed at a younger market. It has bright, minimalist decor in rainbow colours. The cabins (think Ikea-style cabinetry) are bright and quite spacious; many have floor-to-ceiling slide-open French (open-air) balconies, but storage space is negligible. The bathrooms are practical enough, but they are small and plain. Facilities include a spa/fitness area. As for food, there's a self-service buffet, with daytime grilled food and tablecloth-service for dinner. Excursions include well-run bicycle tours.

A-ROSA LUNA ★★★+
A SMART, CONTEMPORARY RIVERSHIP WELL SUITED TO YOUTHFUL ACTIVE TYPES.

Operator .... A-ROSA River Cruises
Built 2004
Length (m) 125.8
Number of decks (excluding sun deck)................... 3
Passenger beds...174
Sit outside (real) balcony.......................................No
French (open-air) balcony ....Yes
Approximate cabin size (sq m) 14.5
Lift (elevator)..No
Rivers sailed...Rhine, Saone

BERLITZ'S RATINGS		
	Possible	Achieved
Hardware	100	66
Accommodation	100	58
Cuisine	100	61
Service	100	61
Miscellaneous	100	68
OVERALL SCORE 314 points out of 500		

The decor on this smart but high-density vessel is colourful and bright, with minimalist furnishings. The lobby spans two decks and is light and airy. The cabins, many with French (open-air) balconies, are plainly furnished but practical (although storage space is minimal), and have two slim beds that can be converted into a double bed. A wellness area includes a large (unisex) sauna and fitness equipment. The bistro-style restaurant is bright and cheerful, and the buffet-style food is good, but the wine glasses are small. A-Rosa operates well-orchestrated cruises, and bicycles are provided

A-ROSA MIA ★★★+
UPBEAT DECOR AND MINIMALIST STYLE FOR CRUISING FOR YOUNG-AT-HEART TYPES.

Operator	A-ROSA River Cruises
Built	2003
Length (m)	124.5
Number of decks (excluding sun deck)	3
Passenger beds	200
Sit outside (real) balcony	No
French (open-air) balcony	Yes
Approximate cabin size (sq m)	14.5–16.5
Lift (elevator)	No
Rivers sailed	Danube

BERLITZ'S RATINGS		
	Possible	Achieved
Hardware	100	66
Accommodation	100	57
Cuisine	100	61
Service	100	61
Miscellaneous	100	68
OVERALL SCORE 313 points out of 500		

The decor is bright and trendy in oranges and yellows, with minimalist-style furnishings. Cabins are plainly furnished but practical, with two slim beds that can be converted into a double; some cabins have floor-to-ceiling slide-open French (open-air) balconies. A fitness area includes a large (mixed) sauna. Self-service bistro-style buffets are what the cuisine is all about, and, while the selection is decent, there's no 'wow' factor. Also, the wine glasses are small.

A-ROSA RIVA ★★★+
PROVIDES AN UPBEAT, YOUTHFUL SETTING FOR A GOOD GENERAL RIVER CRUISE.

Operator	A-ROSA River Cruises
Built	2004
Length (m)	124.5
Number of decks (excluding sun deck)	3
Passenger beds	200
Sit outside (real) balcony	No
French (open-air) balcony	Yes
Approximate cabin size (sq m)	14.5–16.5
Lift (elevator)	No
Rivers sailed	Danube

BERLITZ'S RATINGS		
	Possible	Achieved
Hardware	100	67
Accommodation	100	58
Cuisine	100	61
Service	100	61
Miscellaneous	100	68
OVERALL SCORE 315 points out of 500		

A-Rosa Riva's colourful interior decor is bright and cheerful. The cabins are bright, quite spacious. Many of them have minimal facilities, lack storage space and have angular cabinetry. Many cabins have floor-to-ceiling slide-open French (open-air) balconies for fresh air. The modular bathrooms are plain, but practical. A fitness area includes a large (unisex) sauna. The cuisine is mostly self-service buffet-style, but with a decent variety; the wine glasses are small. The company organises good bicycle tours.

A-ROSA SILVA ★★★+

A TRENDY, WELL-RUN RIVERSHIP THAT IS AIMED AT THE YOUNG AND PHYSICALLY ACTIVE.

Operator .... A-ROSA River Cruises
Built 2012
Length (m) 135.0
Number of decks (excluding sun deck)................... 3
Passenger beds..186
Sit outside (real) balcony ....No
French (open-air) balcony ....Yes
Approximate cabin size (sq m) 14.5–29.0
Lift (elevator)..No
Rivers sailed............................. Rhine, Moselle, Main

BERLITZ'S RATINGS		
	Possible	Achieved
Hardware	100	69
Accommodation	100	63
Cuisine	100	61
Service	100	63
Miscellaneous	100	70
OVERALL SCORE 326 points out of 500		

The interior decor is colourful, bright, contemporary and cheerful. The cabins are modestly spacious, bright, trendy and practical – many have floor-to-ceiling slide-open French (open-air) balconies – with two slim beds that can be converted to a double. The bathrooms, however, are small and plain, but functional. The bistro-style restaurant is bright and cheerful, although chairs don't have armrests. The buffet-style cuisine is decent enough, but there's no 'wow' factor, and the wine glasses are small. Excursions include bicycle tours.

A-ROSA STELLA ★★★+

THIS CONTEMPORARY RIVERSHIP IS A GOOD OPTION FOR YOUNGER ACTIVE TYPES.

Operator .... A-ROSA River Cruises
Built 2005
Length (m) 125.8
Number of decks (excluding sun deck)................... 3
Passenger beds..174
Sit outside (real) balcony ....No
French (open-air) balcony ....Yes
Approximate cabin size (sq m) 14.5
Lift (elevator)..No
Rivers sailed..Rhône, Saône

BERLITZ'S RATINGS		
	Possible	Achieved
Hardware	100	65
Accommodation	100	61
Cuisine	100	61
Service	100	61
Miscellaneous	100	69
OVERALL SCORE 317 points out of 500		

The decor on this smart but high-density vessel is colourful and bright, with minimalist furnishings. The lobby spans two decks and is light and airy. The cabins, some of which have French (open-air) balconies, are unfussy but practical (although storage space is minimal), and have two slim beds that can be converted into a double. A wellness area includes a large (unisex) sauna and fitness equipment. The restaurant is bright and cheerful, and the buffet-style food is good but lacks 'wow' factor. A nice touch is the provision of bicycles. Overall, A-Rosa operates well-orchestrated cruises.

A-ROSA VIVA ★★★+
A WELL-RUN RIVERSHIP AIMED AT A YOUTHFUL, ACTIVE PASSENGERS.

Operator	A-ROSA River Cruises
Built	2010
Length (m)	135.0
Number of decks (excluding sun deck)	3
Passenger beds	202
Sit outside (real) balcony	No
French (open-air) balcony	Yes
Approximate cabin size (sq m)	14.5
Lift (elevator)	No
Rivers sailed	Seine

BERLITZ'S RATINGS		
	Possible	Achieved
Hardware	100	67
Accommodation	100	62
Cuisine	100	61
Service	100	62
Miscellaneous	100	71
OVERALL SCORE 323 points out of 500		

A-Rosa Viva's interior decor is bold and colourful. The brightly coloured cabins are trendy, practical and unpretentious, with two slim beds that can be converted to a double; some have floor-to-ceiling slide-open French (open-air) balconies. The bathrooms are modular, small and plain but functional. The food, while attractively presented, has little flair. Excursions, including good bicycle tours, are aimed at active types.

ASARA ★★★★+
THIS CONTEMPORARY, BUT HIGH-DENSITY VESSEL IS STYLISH AND COMFORTABLE.

Operator	Phoenix Cruises
Built	2017
Length (m)	135.0
Number of decks (excluding sun deck)	3
Passenger beds	191
Sit outside (real) balcony	No
French (open-air) balcony	Yes
Approximate cabin size (sq m)	12.0–17.0
Lift (elevator)	Yes
Rivers sailed	Rhine, Main, Danube

BERLITZ'S RATINGS		
	Possible	Achieved
Hardware	100	82
Accommodation	100	81
Cuisine	100	78
Service	100	81
Miscellaneous	100	81
OVERALL SCORE 403 points out of 500		

The interior decor is contemporary and tasteful, and the panoramic lounge is welcoming and comfortable. The cabins are well designed and have good storage space, with an attractive blond wood finish. Lighting and soundproofing are good. Two decks of cabins have floor-to-ceiling glass doors that open to a French (open-air) balcony. The bathrooms have large glazed shower enclosures, and space for toiletry items. The restaurant is very comfortable and has large windows. Highlights include some really good food, and service. A second (aft) restaurant makes for an alternative dining venue.

AURELIA ★★★+

AURELIA DELIVERS GOOD FOOD AND SERVICE IN A CONTEMPORARY SETTING.

Operator ....Phoenix Cruises
Built 2006
Length (m) 110.0
Number of decks (excluding sun deck)...................3
Passenger beds..154
Sit outside (real) balcony ....No
French (open-air) balcony ....Yes
Approximate cabin size (sq m) 10.0–14.0
Lift (elevator)..No
Rivers sailed............................. Rhine, Main, Danube

BERLITZ'S RATINGS		
	Possible	Achieved
Hardware	100	68
Accommodation	100	66
Cuisine	100	73
Service	100	68
Miscellaneous	100	71
OVERALL SCORE 346 points out of 500		

Aurelia is really comfortable and well proportioned, although it is a little dated and has rather bland decor. Cabins on the lowest deck have windows, but all others feature French (open-air) balconies with floor-to-ceiling slide-open doors. All are rather compact and have twin beds that are sofas by day. The bathrooms are small but practical and have glazed shower enclosures. The restaurant is quite pleasant, although chairs don't have armrests. The cuisine is good, with plenty of variety and creative presentation. Overall, *Aurelia* should provide you with a good cruise experience.

AVALON AFFINITY ★★★+

THIS FAIRLY MODERN RIVERSHIP PROVIDES A VERY DECENT CRUISE EXPERIENCE.

Operator ....Avalon Waterways
Built 2009
Length (m) 110.0
Number of decks (excluding sun deck)...................3
Passenger beds..138
Sit outside (real) balcony ....No
French (open-air) balcony ....Yes
Approximate cabin size (sq m) 16.0–24.0
Lift (elevator)..Yes
Rivers sailed..Rhone, Saone

BERLITZ'S RATINGS		
	Possible	Achieved
Hardware	100	69
Accommodation	100	68
Cuisine	100	63
Service	100	63
Miscellaneous	100	71
OVERALL SCORE 334 points out of 500		

Avalon Affinity is a little dated but it does have a fairly comfortable lounge. The lobby is clean and uncluttered. Four suites have river-facing beds and extra space, but other cabins are quite small, with limited drawer space. The bathrooms are decent, with glazed shower enclosures. The restaurant is quite attractive, but noisy and cramped. The menus are rather overstated, and the food really is quite bland, and there's little choice of cheese and fresh fruits. Overall there's a push for extra onboard revenue, particularly for 'premium' brand drinks, optional excursions and gratuities.

AVALON ARTISTRY II ★★★★
THIS RIVERSHIP HAS VERY GOOD FACILITIES, SMART DECOR AND REASONABLE CUISINE.

Operator	Avalon Waterways
Built	2013
Length (m)	110.0
Number of decks (excluding sun deck)	3
Passenger beds	138
Sit outside (real) balcony	No
French (open-air) balcony	Yes
Approximate cabin size (sq m)	16.0–28.0
Lift (elevator)	Yes
Rivers sailed	Rhine, Main, Danube

BERLITZ'S RATINGS		
	Possible	Achieved
Hardware	100	73
Accommodation	100	74
Cuisine	100	66
Service	100	65
Miscellaneous	100	73
OVERALL SCORE 351 points out of 500		

This comfortable, spacious rivership has a pleasant panoramic lounge and contemporary decor. The cabins are well designed and quite spacious. Most have French balconies, river-facing beds and good bathrooms with glazed shower enclosures and ample space for toiletries. Two delightful Royal Suites have extra-large bathrooms. The open-seating restaurant is attractive, but dinners are underwhelming. Breakfast and lunch buffets are quite good. Note that there is a constant push for extra revenue for things such as optional excursions, 'premium' drinks and gratuities.

AVALON CREATIVITY ★★★+
THIS COMFORTABLE, MODERN RIVERSHIP DELIVERS A MODERATELY GOOD CRUISE.

Operator	Avalon Waterways
Built	2009
Length (m)	110.0
Number of decks (excluding sun deck)	3
Passenger beds	140
Sit outside (real) balcony	No
French (open-air) balcony	Yes
Approximate cabin size (sq m)	16.0–24.0
Lift (elevator)	Yes
Rivers sailed	Seine

BERLITZ'S RATINGS		
	Possible	Achieved
Hardware	100	68
Accommodation	100	68
Cuisine	100	64
Service	100	64
Miscellaneous	100	70
OVERALL SCORE 334 points out of 500		

Avalon Creativity's interior decor is pleasant, but quite plain and uninspiring. The cabins are well designed, and have a decent amount of storage space and a minibar (items are at extra cost), but the decor is bland. The bathrooms are practical, but the shower enclosures are compact and space for toiletries is tight. The restaurant is quite attractive and fairly comfortable, but it is noisy. The cuisine is nothing special, and the menus are rather overstated. The choice of cheese and fresh fruit is quite limited. The push for extra onboard revenue is annoying, especially for 'premium' drink brands, and gratuities.

AVALON EXPRESSION ★★★★

THIS CONTEMPORARY RIVERSHIP PROVIDES THE SETTING FOR A GOOD RIVER CRUISE.

Operator ....Avalon Waterways
Built 2013
Length (m) 135.0
Number of decks (excluding sun deck)...................3
Passenger beds...166
Sit outside (real) balcony ....No
French (open-air) balcony ....Yes
Approximate cabin size (sq m) 16.0–28.0
Lift (elevator)..Yes
Rivers sailed.............................. Rhine, Main, Danube

BERLITZ'S RATINGS		
	Possible	Achieved
Hardware	100	73
Accommodation	100	74
Cuisine	100	67
Service	100	70
Miscellaneous	100	75
OVERALL SCORE 359 points out of 500		

Avalon Expression has a smart, country club-like decor. The accommodation with French (open-air) balconies is light and spacious (cabins on the lowest deck have standard windows), with queen-sized beds, and there's plenty of storage space. The bathrooms are large, with decent-sized glass-door shower enclosures. The menus are a little overstated, but the food itself is rather bland, accompanied by low-quality wines. Breakfast and lunch buffets are, however, quite good. The push for extra-cost items such as optional excursions, and 'premium' drink brands, and gratuities is irritating.

AVALON FELICITY ★★★+

THIS SMART, MODERN RIVERSHIP DELIVERS A VERY DECENT CRUISE.

Operator ....Avalon Waterways
Built 2010
Length (m) 110.0
Number of decks (excluding sun deck)...................3
Passenger beds...138
Sit outside (real) balcony ....No
French (open-air) balcony ....Yes
Approximate cabin size (sq m) 16.0–24.0
Lift (elevator)..Yes
Rivers sailed..Rhine

BERLITZ'S RATINGS		
	Possible	Achieved
Hardware	100	71
Accommodation	100	70
Cuisine	100	68
Service	100	62
Miscellaneous	100	72
OVERALL SCORE 343 points out of 500		

Although *Avalon Felicity*'s decor is rather plain and uninspiring, the cabins are quite well designed and practical, with good lighting and ample storage space for clothing items. Most have river-facing beds, and French balcony doors. The bathrooms have glazed shower enclosures and decent storage space for toiletries. The restaurant is moderately attractive, but it is very noisy, and has rather cramped seating. The cuisine is rather on the bland side, and there's not much choice. Overall, it's decent, but optional tours, 'premium' brand drinks and gratuities cost extra.

AVALON ILLUMINATION ★★★★
A SMART-LOOKING VESSEL TO PROVIDE YOU WITH A GOOD CRUISE EXPERIENCE.

Operator ....Avalon Waterways
Built 2014
Length (m) 135.0
Number of decks (excluding sun deck) 3
Passenger beds 166
Sit outside (real) balcony ....No
French (open-air) balcony ....Yes
Approximate cabin size (sq m) 16.0–28.0
Lift (elevator) ....Yes
Rivers sailed .... Rhine, Main, Danube

BERLITZ'S RATINGS		
	Possible	Achieved
Hardware	100	75
Accommodation	100	74
Cuisine	100	70
Service	100	72
Miscellaneous	100	75
OVERALL SCORE 366 points out of 500		

This well-proportioned rivership has very cheerful interior decor, good-quality fittings and a comfortable lounge. The cabins are pleasant, but the closet doors and drawers are noisy. The bathrooms are large, with decent-sized glass-door shower enclosures. The open-seating restaurant is attractive and comfortable, but despite grand-sounding menus, dinners are quite underwhelming and lack taste. Breakfast and lunch buffets are, however, decent enough. Note that optional tours plus gratuities and 'premium' brand drinks cost extra.

AVALON IMAGERY II ★★★★
THIS IS A SMART-LOOKING VESSEL WITH A HIGH COMFORT FACTOR.

Operator ....Avalon Waterways
Built 2016
Length (m) 110.0
Number of decks (excluding sun deck) 3
Passenger beds 128
Sit outside (real) balcony ....No
French (open-air) balcony ....Yes
Approximate cabin size (sq m) 16.0–28.0
Lift (elevator) ....Yes
Rivers sailed ....Rhine

BERLITZ'S RATINGS		
	Possible	Achieved
Hardware	100	79
Accommodation	100	76
Cuisine	100	71
Service	100	71
Miscellaneous	100	77
OVERALL SCORE 374 points out of 500		

This stylish, contemporary vessel has high-quality fittings and comfortable seating in its panorama lounge. The cabins are designed to be practical and have generous clothes-storage space; they have French balconies and most have river-facing beds. Lighting and soundproofing are good. The bathrooms have glazed shower enclosures. The open-seating restaurant is attractive and comfortable, but despite attractive menus, dinners are underwhelming. Breakfast and lunch buffets are quite good. Optional excursions plus gratuities and 'premium' brand drinks cost extra.

AVALON LUMINARY ★★★+

CHOOSE THIS SHIP FOR ITS ITINERARY, BUT DO BE WARY OF EXTRA-COST ITEMS.

Operator ....Avalon Waterways
Built 2010
Length (m) 110.0
Number of decks (excluding sun deck)................... 3
Passenger beds...138
Sit outside (real) balcony ....No
French (open-air) balcony ....Yes
Approximate cabin size (sq m) 16.0–24.0
Lift (elevator)...Yes
Rivers sailed............................. Rhine, Main, Danube

BERLITZ'S RATINGS		
	Possible	Achieved
Hardware	100	68
Accommodation	100	70
Cuisine	100	68
Service	100	61
Miscellaneous	100	68
OVERALL SCORE 335 points out of 500		

With the exception of four suites with river-facing beds, all cabins are the same size. While cabins on the lowest deck have windows, all others have French balconies with floor-to-ceiling slide-open doors. Clothes storage space is good, but the bathrooms are rather compact, although they do have glazed shower enclosures. The open-seating restaurant is attractive, but menus are overstated and the food is only moderately good and lacks finesse. Overall, *Avalon Luminary* will provide you with a decent cruise experience, but note that optional tours, gratuities and 'premium' drinks cost extra.

AVALON PANORAMA ★★★+

CHOOSE THIS CONTEMPORARY RIVERSHIP FOR THE ITINERARY RATHER THAN THE CUISINE.

Operator ....Avalon Waterways
Built 2011
Length (m) 135.0
Number of decks (excluding sun deck)................... 3
Passenger beds...166
Sit outside (real) balcony ....No
French (open-air) balcony ....Yes
Approximate cabin size (sq m) 16.0–28.0
Lift (elevator)...Yes
Rivers sailed............................. Rhine, Main, Danube

BERLITZ'S RATINGS		
	Possible	Achieved
Hardware	100	68
Accommodation	100	70
Cuisine	100	68
Service	100	64
Miscellaneous	100	72
OVERALL SCORE 342 points out of 500		

This is a well-proportioned rivership with cheerful decor and good fittings. Most of the practical, well-designed cabins (including two extra-spacious Royal Suites) have French (open-air) balconies with floor-to-ceiling slide-open doors, and other creature comforts. The restaurant is mildly attractive, and has decent open seating. Food-wise, the menus are nicely descriptive, but quite overstated. Dinners are generally disappointing and lack green vegetables, while self-service breakfast and lunch buffets are quite decent. Gratuities are not included, and drinks are at extra cost.

AVALON PASSION ★★★★

YOU'LL FIND A HIGH LEVEL OF COMFORT ABOARD THIS CONTEMPORARY RIVERSHIP.

Operator ....Avalon Waterways
Built 2016
Length (m) 135.0
Number of decks (excluding sun deck)....................3
Passenger beds...168
Sit outside (real) balcony ....No
French (open-air) balcony ....Yes
Approximate cabin size (sq m) 16.0–28.0
Lift (elevator)...Yes
Rivers sailed............................. Rhine, Main, Danube

BERLITZ'S RATINGS		
	Possible	Achieved
Hardware	100	79
Accommodation	100	75
Cuisine	100	72
Service	100	70
Miscellaneous	100	76
OVERALL SCORE 372 points out of 500		

The decor is contemporary and stylish, with good-quality fittings and furniture in the lounge. Most cabins are of a generous size and well laid out, with good lighting and storage space. Beds in all cabins, except those on the lowest deck, face French balconies with floor-to-ceiling slide-open doors; bathrooms have glazed shower enclosures. The open-seating restaurant is attractive and comfortable, but the dinners are underwhelming. Breakfast and lunch buffets are, however, quite good. Note that optional tours plus gratuities, and 'premium' quality drinks cost extra.

AVALON POETRY II ★★★★

THIS STYLISH AND COMFORTABLE RIVERSHIP DELIVERS A GOOD CRUISE EXPERIENCE.

Operator ....Avalon Waterways
Built 2014
Length (m) 110.0
Number of decks (excluding sun deck)....................3
Passenger beds...168
Sit outside (real) balcony ....No
French (open-air) balcony ....Yes
Approximate cabin size (sq m) 16.0–28.0
Lift (elevator)...Yes
Rivers sailed...Rhon, Saone

BERLITZ'S RATINGS		
	Possible	Achieved
Hardware	100	76
Accommodation	100	74
Cuisine	100	71
Service	100	70
Miscellaneous	100	74
OVERALL SCORE 365 points out of 500		

The stylish *Avalon Poetry II* has very comfortable main lounge seating. Most cabins are of a generous size and are well laid out. There is good clothes storage space, and beds in all cabins except those on the lowest deck face French balconies with floor-to-ceiling slide-open doors. Lighting and soundproofing are also good, and the bathrooms have glazed shower enclosures. The open-seating restaurant is comfortable and very pleasant. The food is decent enough, but bland, and has little flair, and the service lacks finesse. Gratuities, optional tours and 'premium' brand drinks cost extra.

AVALON TAPESTRY II ★★★★
THIS IS A GOOD CHOICE FOR A WELL-ORGANISED RIVER CRUISE EXPERIENCE.

Operator .... Avalon Waterways
Built 2015
Length (m) 135.0
Number of decks (excluding sun deck) 3
Passenger beds 140
Sit outside (real) balcony .... No
French (open-air) balcony .... Yes
Approximate cabin size (sq m) 16.0–28.0
Lift (elevator) .... Yes
Rivers sailed .... Seine

BERLITZ'S RATINGS		
	Possible	Achieved
Hardware	100	77
Accommodation	100	75
Cuisine	100	71
Service	100	70
Miscellaneous	100	75
OVERALL SCORE 368 points out of 500		

This comfortable vessel has pleasant decor in the observation lounge and lobby. The well-appointed cabins have good lighting with beds facing French open-air balconies (except for lowest deck cabins). The tiled bathrooms are attractive, although the shower enclosures are small; L'Occitane toiletries are provided. The open seating restaurant is attractive and comfortable, but chairs lack armrests; the food is decent enough, with good variety and large portions, but few green vegetables. Gratuities, optional tours and drinks (except for beer and wine for lunch and dinner) cost extra.

AVALON TRANQUILITY II ★★★★
THIS RIVERSHIP IS STYLISH AND HAS GOOD OVERALL CREATURE COMFORT FEATURES.

Operator .... Avalon Waterways
Built 2015
Length (m) 110.0
Number of decks (excluding sun deck) 3
Passenger beds 128
Sit outside (real) balcony .... No
French (open-air) balcony .... Yes
Approximate cabin size (sq m) 16.0–28.0
Lift (elevator) .... Yes
Rivers sailed .... Rhine

BERLITZ'S RATINGS		
	Possible	Achieved
Hardware	100	76
Accommodation	100	75
Cuisine	100	72
Service	100	71
Miscellaneous	100	76
OVERALL SCORE 370 points out of 500		

This comfortable, stylish vessel has lots of 'bling' in the interior decor of the observation lounge and lobby. Generously sized, well-appointed cabins – many with beds facing French balconies with floor-to-ceiling slide-open doors – have ample storage space, and decent soundproofing. The bathrooms are attractive and have decent-sized shower enclosures and L'Occitane toiletries. The open seating restaurant is attractive and comfortable. The food is decent enough, but menus are overstated, and there's no 'wow' factor. Note that optional tours, gratuities, and 'premium' brand drinks cost extra.

AVALON VISIONARY ★★★+
THIS RIVERSHIP DELIVERS A MODERATELY GOOD RIVER CRUISE EXPERIENCE.

Operator ....Avalon Waterways
Built 2012
Length (m) 135.0
Number of decks (excluding sun deck).................. 3
Passenger beds..138
Sit outside (real) balcony ....No
French (open-air) balcony ....Yes
Approximate cabin size (sq m) 16.0–28.0
Lift (elevator)..Yes
Rivers sailed.............................. Rhine, Main, Danube

BERLITZ'S RATINGS		
	Possible	Achieved
Hardware	100	73
Accommodation	100	72
Cuisine	100	63
Service	100	65
Miscellaneous	100	71
OVERALL SCORE 344 points out of 500		

Avalon Visionary is a stylish, smart-looking, contemporary vessel, with good-quality fittings and comfortable furniture. The cabins are light and spacious, with with French balconies, queen-sized beds (two suites have a king-size bed) and good storage space for clothes. Note that the small cabins on the lowest deck have non-opening windows only. The bathrooms are quite spacious and have glazed shower enclosures. The menus are overstated, and the food is rather nondescript and the wines are very young. Gratuities, optional tours and 'premium' brand drinks cost extra.

AVALON VISTA ★★★+
CHOOSE THIS CONTEMPORARY RIVERSHIP FOR THE ITINERARY RATHER THAN THE CUISINE.

Operator ....Avalon Waterways
Built 2012
Length (m) 135.0
Number of decks (excluding sun deck).................. 3
Passenger beds..166
Sit outside (real) balcony..No
French (open-air) balcony ....Yes
Approximate cabin size (sq m) 16.0–28.0
Lift (elevator)..Yes
Rivers sailed.............................. Rhine, Main, Danube

BERLITZ'S RATINGS		
	Possible	Achieved
Hardware	100	73
Accommodation	100	73
Cuisine	100	63
Service	100	66
Miscellaneous	100	71
OVERALL SCORE 346 points out of 500		

This well-proportioned rivership has very cheerful interior decor and good fittings. Most of the spacious cabins (including two extra-spacious Royal Suites) have French balconies with floor-to-ceiling slide-open doors, and abundant creature comforts. Food-wise, the menus are nicely descriptive, but quite overstated. Dinners are generally disappointing, but the self-serve breakfast and lunch buffets are really quite good. Gratuities, optional tours and 'premium' brand drinks cost extra.

AZOLLA ★★

A CHARMING VINTAGE RIVERSHIP FOR CHEAP AND CHEERFUL NO-FRILLS CRUISING.

Operator	Various tour operators
Built	1965
Length (m)	76.5
Number of decks (excluding sun deck)	2
Passenger beds	90
Sit outside (real) balcony	No
French (open-air) balcony	No
Approximate cabin size (sq m)	6.0–9.0
Lift (elevator)	No
Rivers sailed	Rhine

BERLITZ'S RATINGS		
	Possible	Achieved
Hardware	100	30
Accommodation	100	30
Cuisine	100	33
Service	100	34
Miscellaneous	100	35
OVERALL SCORE 162 points out of 500		

Many people go river cruising for the itinerary and destinations. If this is what you are looking for, try *Azolla*. This nicely refurbished vessel with olde-worlde English country club decor has dimensionally challenged (tiny) cabins and L-shaped single beds, tiny bathrooms and almost no storage space, but the windows do open and it may just be suitable. However, don't expect any hint of fine food or variety, because the galley is tiny and can only turn out the most basic meals, albeit to a nice tablecloth setting. The buffet breakfasts and lunches are – well, basic, and repetitive.

BEETHOVEN ★★★+

THIS FUSS-FREE FRENCH RIVERSHIP IS COMFORTABLE BUT NOW QUITE DATED.

Operator	CroisiEurope
Built	2004
Length (m)	110.0
Number of decks (excluding sun deck)	3
Passenger beds	180
Sit outside (real) balcony	No
French (open-air) balcony	No
Approximate cabin size (sq m)	13.0
Lift (elevator)	No
Rivers sailed	Rhine, Main, Danube

BERLITZ'S RATINGS		
	Possible	Achieved
Hardware	100	60
Accommodation	100	62
Cuisine	100	60
Service	100	60
Miscellaneous	100	62
OVERALL SCORE 304 points out of 500		

Beethoven has rather dated interior decor, and the small cabins lack (open-air) balconies. The beds are very slim (most of them cannot be moved together), and the tiny bathrooms have little space for toiletries. The low-ceilinged restaurant is cramped and noisy. However, if you like a casual French-style ambience and are happy with fairly decent food and wine, this unfussy vessel may be suitable for you. Go mainly for the itinerary and destinations. Note that the organized excursions and gratuities are at extra cost.

BELLEFLEUR ★★★
THIS COMFORTABLE OLDER RIVERSHIP OFFERS A LOW-COST CRUISE WITH FRENCH AMBIENCE.

Operator	APT
Built	2001
Length (m)	114.3
Number of decks (excluding sun deck)	3
Passenger beds	150
Sit outside (real) balcony	No
French (open-air) balcony	No
Approximate cabin size (sq m)	11.0–15.5
Lift (elevator)	No
Rivers sailed	Rhone, Saone

BERLITZ'S RATINGS		
	Possible	Achieved
Hardware	100	56
Accommodation	100	53
Cuisine	100	62
Service	100	60
Miscellaneous	100	64
OVERALL SCORE 295 points out of 500		

There are pleasant walk and view section outside the forward lounge, which has warm wood-accented decor, but several pillars obstruct sight lines, and the tub chairs are unfriendly for one's lower back. The cabins are nicely appointed – all have windows (no balconies); some have double beds, and others are twins that convert to sofas during the day. The constant music in hallways and on open decks is irritating. The open seating restaurant is pleasant enough, but it is quite cramped, and the food is acceptable, but unmemorable.

BELLEJOUR ★★★
THIS MODERN VESSEL HAS THE BASICS FOR A MODERATELY COMFORTABLE CRUISE.

Operator	Various tour operators
Built	2004
Length (m)	126.7
Number of decks (excluding sun deck)	3
Passenger beds	180
Sit outside (real) balcony	No
French (open-air) balcony	Yes
Approximate cabin size (sq m)	16.0
Lift (elevator)	No
Rivers sailed	Rhine, Main, Danube

BERLITZ'S RATINGS		
	Possible	Achieved
Hardware	100	61
Accommodation	100	60
Cuisine	100	57
Service	100	57
Miscellaneous	100	61
OVERALL SCORE 296 points out of 500		

This fairly smart-looking but high-density vessel has a lounge that is quite comfortable, but it's rather tired and the seating is quite cramped. Most of the cabins have French (open-air) balconies with floor-to-ceiling slide-open doors. Drawer and storage space is limited, and soundproofing could be better. The bathrooms are compact, and have very small shower enclosures. The restaurant is quite pleasant, but it is noisy. The cuisine is just so-so, with limited choice, little presentation flair and small glasses for wine.

BELLISSIMA ★★★
GOOD FOR SAILING AROUND THE VENETIAN LAGOON ON A LOW BUDGET.

Operator	Nicko Cruises
Built	2004
Length (m)	109.9
Number of decks (excluding sun deck)	2
Passenger beds	134
Sit outside (real) balcony	No
French (open-air) balcony	Yes
Approximate cabin size (sq m)	12.0–20.0
Lift (elevator)	No
Rivers sailed	Rhine, Main, Danube

BERLITZ'S RATINGS		
	Possible	Achieved
Hardware	100	60
Accommodation	100	60
Cuisine	100	57
Service	100	56
Miscellaneous	100	60
OVERALL SCORE 293 points out of 500		

Almost half of the cabins on the *Bellissima* have French (open-air) balconies. Except for one double-size cabin, all the others are quite small, with little storage space and compact bathrooms. The lounge is comfortable, although the decor is dated and the chairs are low-backed. The restaurant is plain and also has uncomfortable chairs. The food is uninspiring and the choice is limited, because the galley is very small.

BELLRIVA ★★+
AN ADEQUATE BUT HIGH-DENSITY AND DATED RIVERSHIP FOR A LOW-COST, NO-FRILLS CRUISE.

Operator	1A Vista Reisen
Built	1971
Length (m)	104.6
Number of decks (excluding sun deck)	2
Passenger beds	186
Sit outside (real) balcony	No
French (open-air) balcony	No
Approximate cabin size (sq m)	9.0–12.0
Lift (elevator)	No
Rivers sailed	Rhine

BERLITZ'S RATINGS		
	Possible	Achieved
Hardware	100	40
Accommodation	100	40
Cuisine	100	46
Service	100	48
Miscellaneous	100	48
OVERALL SCORE 222 points out of 500		

This older rivership feels rather cramped, but the decor of the lounge is quite pleasant, despite the uncomfortable low-backed chairs. The cabins (all of which have windows) are really quite small, with little storage space and poor reading lights. Bathrooms are compact and basic, with curtained-off showers and little space for toiletries. The restaurant has tight seating, with four people per table. The galley is small, as is the range and choice of meals. Go only for the itinerary.

BELVEDERE ★★★

CHOOSE THIS FAIRLY STYLISH RIVERSHIP FOR A GOOD-QUALITY RIVER CRUISE EXPERIENCE.

Operator ....Various tour operators
Built 2006
Length (m) 126.0
Number of decks (excluding sun deck)...................3
Passenger beds...176
Sit outside (real) balcony ....No
French (open-air) balcony ....Yes
Approximate cabin size (sq m) 16.0–22.0
Lift (elevator)..No
Rivers sailed..Danube

BERLITZ'S RATINGS		
	Possible	Achieved
Hardware	100	62
Accommodation	100	61
Cuisine	100	56
Service	100	56
Miscellaneous	100	62
OVERALL SCORE 297 points out of 500		

Belvedere is quite a modern-looking vessel, with attractive, unfussy interior decor. Many of the generously sized cabins have floor-to-ceiling slide-open French-style balconies, while others have windows. All except four suites are the same size and quite well appointed, with river-facing beds and fairly good bathroom facilities. A wellness area includes a small sauna. There's a decent restaurant, with a galley in the middle of the vessel (strangely, some cabins are aft of it), but the chairs don't have armrests. The food lacks variety, and the presentation is quite basic.

BIJOU DU RHÔNE ★★★

A FAIRLY WELL-APPOINTED RIVERSHIP FOR SOUTHERN FRENCH RIVER CRUISING.

Operator ....Nicko Cruises
Built 2000
Length (m) 114.3
Number of decks (excluding sun deck)...................3
Passenger beds...150
Sit outside (real) balcony ....No
French (open-air) balcony ....No
Approximate cabin size (sq m) 12.0–15.0
Lift (elevator)..No
Rivers sailed...Rhone

BERLITZ'S RATINGS		
	Possible	Achieved
Hardware	100	53
Accommodation	100	52
Cuisine	100	56
Service	100	55
Miscellaneous	100	60
OVERALL SCORE 276 points out of 500		

This is a nicely appointed rivership with an emphasis on blond wood and an interior decor that is minimalist and unfussy, but fairly comfortable. The cabins have good soundproofing; some have two beds, while others have one fixed and a fold-down bed (it's a daytime sofa to provide more space) and windows that open (upper deck cabins only). The restaurant is pleasant enough, but cramped. The food features some French or regional dishes, but there's no presentation flair and few green vegetables.

BIZET ★★★

CHOOSE THIS RIVERSHIP FOR THE ITINERARY AND DESTINATIONS, NOT THE FOOD.

Operator .... Grand Circle Cruise Line
Built 2002
Length (m) 110.0
Number of decks (excluding sun deck)................... 2
Passenger beds...120
Sit outside (real) balcony ....No
French (open-air) balcony ....Yes
Approximate cabin size (sq m) 12.0
Lift (elevator)..Yes
Rivers sailed.. Seine

BERLITZ'S RATINGS		
	Possible	Achieved
Hardware	100	53
Accommodation	100	52
Cuisine	100	54
Service	100	53
Miscellaneous	100	58
OVERALL SCORE 270 points out of 500		

This smart-looking, but now dated rivership, with its blue hull has little character in its interior decor. Some cabins have real sit-outside balconies and are hence lighter than others, which are small and plain, with slim beds that fold down from the wall to create the illusion of more daytime space. Bathrooms are compact and basic, with curtained-off showers and little space for toiletries. The French-style cuisine is underwhelming; green vegetables are lacking, and the wine glasses are small. Gratuities, drinks and tours cost extra.

BOLERO ★★★

THIS IS A QUITE CONSISTENT MIDDLE-OF-THE-ROAD RIVERSHIP THAT LACKS PANACHE.

Operator ....Nicko Cruises
Built 2003
Length (m) 126.7
Number of decks (excluding sun deck)................... 3
Passenger beds...180
Sit outside (real) balcony ....No
French (open-air) balcony ....Yes
Approximate cabin size (sq m) 15.0
Lift (elevator)..No
Rivers sailed..Danube

BERLITZ'S RATINGS		
	Possible	Achieved
Hardware	100	55
Accommodation	100	53
Cuisine	100	55
Service	100	55
Miscellaneous	100	57
OVERALL SCORE 275 points out of 500		

This is a high-density, but quite pleasant rivership. The lounge, while comfortable, is small, and has rather dated seating. Two full decks feature reasonably decent cabins with French (open-air) balconies (the cabins on the lowest deck have windows) and good storage space, but the beds are quite short. Bathrooms are practical but have poor amenities. The cuisine is so-so, and the service is rushed. Gratuities, drinks and tours cost extra.

BOTTICELLI ★★★

A CONSISTENT, STANDARD-QUALITY RIVER CRUISE FOR FRANCOPHILES ON A BUDGET.

Operator .... CroisiEurope
Built 2004
Length (m) 110.0
Number of decks (excluding sun deck)................... 2
Passenger beds...154
Sit outside (real) balcony ....No
French (open-air) balcony ....No
Approximate cabin size (sq m) 11.0
Lift (elevator)...No
Rivers sailed... Seine

BERLITZ'S RATINGS		
	Possible	Achieved
Hardware	100	56
Accommodation	100	58
Cuisine	100	58
Service	100	56
Miscellaneous	100	57
OVERALL SCORE 285 points out of 500		

Botticelli's interior decor is quite plain and non-descript; the lounge has low-backed seating. The cabins are rather dull, with short beds and tiny bathrooms with curtained showers, and little space for toiletries. The restaurant is pleasant enough, and the French food and wine is good. The French ambience is chic, and the itinerary is good – and the price is very modest. Note that excursions, gratuities and drinks are at extra cost.

BRABANT ★★★+

THIS ELEGANT RIVERSHIP PROVIDES A CRUISE EXPERIENCE OF A DECENT STANDARD.

Operator .... Fred. Olsen Cruise Lines
Built 2006
Length (m) 110.0
Number of decks (excluding sun deck)................... 3
Passenger beds...156
Sit outside (real) balcony ....No
French (open-air) balcony ....Yes
Approximate cabin size (sq m) 15.0–29.0
Lift (elevator)...Yes
Rivers sailed............................. Rhine, Main, Danube

BERLITZ'S RATINGS		
	Possible	Achieved
Hardware	100	62
Accommodation	100	63
Cuisine	100	62
Service	100	66
Miscellaneous	100	70
OVERALL SCORE 323 points out of 500		

Brabant (named after a former Fred. Olsen ocean-going ship) is a good-looking, very comfortable vessel, with understated decor and no bling in the lounge and reception lobby. Most of the well-designed cabins have French (open-air) balconies, and include mini-fridges. The bathrooms are also pleasant and feature large, practical shower enclosures (nine junior suites have bathtubs/showers). The restaurant is comfortable and has attractive decor. The cuisine is modest, and dinners are served with a full tablecloth setting.

CALYPSO ★★

THIS RIVERSHIP IS BEST CHOSEN FOR THE ITINERARY AND DESTINATIONS, NOT THE FOOD.

Operator ....Phoenix Cruises
Built 1978
Length (m) 75.6
Number of decks (excluding sun deck)...................2
Passenger beds...96
Sit outside (real) balcony ....No
French (open-air) balcony ....No
Approximate cabin size (sq m) 11.0–12.0
Lift (elevator)..No
Rivers sailed..Rhine

BERLITZ'S RATINGS		
	Possible	Achieved
Hardware	100	34
Accommodation	100	33
Cuisine	100	38
Service	100	40
Miscellaneous	100	40
OVERALL SCORE 185 points out of 500		

This short, high-density rivership can take you on a river cruise, but because it's a small, older vessel, the main lounge is always crowded. The cabins are dimensionally challenged (but the windows can be opened) and beds convert to seats during the day to give the impression of space. Soundproofing and lighting are both poor. Bathrooms are compact and basic, with curtained-off showers and little space for toiletries. The food from the tiny galley (and small wine glasses) is really uninspiring, so make the itinerary and low prices your reasons for booking. Overall, it's a basic, no-frills river cruise.

CAMARGUE ★★★

THIS SMART, UNFUSSY AND CASUAL RIVERSHIP IS NOW QUITE COMFORTABLE.

Operator ....CroisiEurope
Built 1995
Length (m) 110.0
Number of decks (excluding sun deck)...................2
Passenger beds...104
Sit outside (real) balcony ....No
French (open-air) balcony ....Yes
Approximate cabin size (sq m) 15.8
Lift (elevator)..No
Rivers sailed..Rhone, Saone

BERLITZ'S RATINGS		
	Possible	Achieved
Hardware	100	60
Accommodation	100	62
Cuisine	100	58
Service	100	55
Miscellaneous	100	62
OVERALL SCORE 297 points out of 500		

This fairly smart-looking older rivership now has updated, unfussy modern (orange, beige and brown) decor in the main lounge. Cabins have river-facing beds (although they are really short); there is minimal storage space, and soundproofing is poor. The bathrooms are small, as is the shower enclosure, and storage space for toiletries is minimal. The cuisine is quite decent, but quite straightforward, lacking flair and creativity, there is little choice, and breakfast buffets are repetitive. Note that drinks, excursions and gratuities are at extra cost.

CARISSIMA ★★★

THIS CHEAP AND CHEERFUL RIVERSHIP CATERS MAINLY TO NO-FRILLS BICYCLE TOURISTS.

Operator .... OAD
Built 2001
Length (m) 110.0
Number of decks (excluding sun deck) 2
Passenger beds 153
Sit outside (real) balcony .... No
French (open-air) balcony .... No
Approximate cabin size (sq m) 11.0–14.0
Lift (elevator) .... Yes
Rivers sailed .... Rhine, Main, Danube

BERLITZ'S RATINGS		
	Possible	Achieved
Hardware	100	52
Accommodation	100	51
Cuisine	100	51
Service	100	52
Miscellaneous	100	52
OVERALL SCORE 258 points out of 500		

The interior decor is somewhat dated and tired, but the lounge is reasonably comfortable – although cramped when full. The cabins are small, and all have sliding glass windows that open. However, there are no open-air balconies, there is little storage space for clothes, and lighting and soundproofing are both poor. The bathrooms are also small and functional, but with little storage space. The restaurant is moderately attractive, and many seats have armrests. The cuisine is decidedly of the low-budget variety, and repetitious. The wine glasses are very small.

CARMEN ★★★

THIS IS LOW-BUDGET, NO-FRILLS CRUISING FOR THOSE HAPPY WITH JUST THE BASICS.

Operator .... SijFa Cruises
Built 2001
Length (m) 114.0
Number of decks (excluding sun deck) 3
Passenger beds 136
Sit outside (real) balcony .... No
French (open-air) balcony .... No
Approximate cabin size (sq m) 11.0–14.0
Lift (elevator) .... Yes
Rivers sailed .... Various European rivers

BERLITZ'S RATINGS		
	Possible	Achieved
Hardware	100	54
Accommodation	100	52
Cuisine	100	51
Service	100	53
Miscellaneous	100	60
OVERALL SCORE 270 points out of 500		

This is a nicely appointed rivership with an emphasis on blond wood and an interior decor that is minimalist and unfussy, but fairly comfortable. The cabins have good soundproofing; some have two beds, while others have one fixed and one fold-down bed (it's a daytime sofa to provide more space) and Upper Deck cabins have windows that open. The restaurant is pleasant enough, but the seating is rather cramped. The food is, well, underwhelming, with poor presentation, and few green vegetables.

CASANOVA ★★★

THIS RIVERSHIP HAS ELEGANT DECOR AND DELIVERS A DECENT OVERALL EXPERIENCE.

Operator ....Nicko Cruises
Built 2001
Length (m) 103.0
Number of decks (excluding sun deck)....................2
Passenger beds...96
Sit outside (real) balcony......................................No
French (open-air) balcony ....Yes
Approximate cabin size (sq m) 12.0–16.0
Lift (elevator)..No
Rivers sailed........................ Various European rivers

BERLITZ'S RATINGS		
	Possible	Achieved
Hardware	100	58
Accommodation	100	57
Cuisine	100	55
Service	100	56
Miscellaneous	100	58
OVERALL SCORE 284 points out of 500		

Casanova features some fine original artwork. The cabins (particularly the bathrooms) have either a short double bed or two slim beds (one converts to a sofa by day to provide a sense of space), and they are bright and cheerful. Drawer and other storage space is really limited. The restaurant (you must reserve your table for the whole cruise) is cramped. The galley is small, so the choice of meals is disappointing. The breakfast buffets are repetitious. Gratuities, drinks and tours cost extra.

CHARLES DICKENS ★★★★

'OLIVER' WOULD APPROVE OF THE TRADITIONAL BRITISH STYLE AND AMBIENCE.

Operator .... Riviera Travel
Built 2015
Length (m) 110.0
Number of decks (excluding sun deck)....................3
Passenger beds...142
Sit outside (real) balcony.....................................Yes
French (open-air) balcony ....Yes
Approximate cabin size (sq m) 14.0–22.8
Lift (elevator)..Yes
Rivers sailed............................. Rhine, Main, Danube

BERLITZ'S RATINGS		
	Possible	Achieved
Hardware	100	77
Accommodation	100	76
Cuisine	100	68
Service	100	66
Miscellaneous	100	74
OVERALL SCORE 361 points out of 500		

This fine, spacious rivership has high-quality furnishings, restrained but warm interior decor, spacious and elegant two-deck high lobby, and overall there's an inviting ambience. The cabins are well designed and very practical, and the bathrooms have decent-sized glazed shower enclosures. The one-seating restaurant is quite comfortable. The cuisine is so-so, with repetitious breakfasts, and tailored to unfussy, less adventurous British tastes, although the variety is quite decent. The wine glasses are small.

CRYSTAL BACH ★★★★+
ULTRA-CHIC STYLING AND REFINEMENT PROVIDE AN ELEGANT, LUXE EXPERIENCE.

Operator ....Crystal River Cruises
Built 2017
Length (m) 135.0
Number of decks (excluding sun deck)................... 3
Passenger beds...106
Sit outside (real) balcony ....No
French (open-air) balcony ....Yes
Approximate cabin size (sq m) 17.5–82.0
Lift (elevator)..Yes
Rivers sailed.......................................Rhine, Moselle

BERLITZ'S RATINGS		
	Possible	Achieved
Hardware	100	89
Accommodation	100	84
Cuisine	100	82
Service	100	82
Miscellaneous	100	85
OVERALL SCORE 422 points out of 500		

With its tasteful contemporary decor and high ceilings, this is premium river cruising. The Palm Court lounge is restful, although four thick pillars impede sightlines. The well-appointed cabins have floor-to-ceiling electric windows, king-sized (or twin) beds, premium bed linen, Julius Meinl coffee machines, Etro bathrobes and toiletries (bathrooms have lightly heated floors), slippers, and 'butler' service. The main (bistro-style) restaurant has premium-quality china and glassware, while The Bistro is for casual bites and coffees. Overall, *Crystal Bach* provides an excellent cruise experience.

CRYSTAL DEBUSSY ★★★★+
FRESH, CONTEMPORARY STYLING AND GOOD DESIGN ELEMENTS AWAIT.

Operator ....Crystal River Cruises
Built 2018
Length (m) 135.0
Number of decks (excluding sun deck)................... 3
Passenger beds...106
Sit outside (real) balcony ....No
French (open-air) balcony ....Yes
Approximate cabin size (sq m) 17.5–82.0
Lift (elevator)..Yes
Rivers sailed...............................Rhine, Main, Danube

BERLITZ'S RATINGS		
	Possible	Achieved
Hardware	100	90
Accommodation	100	84
Cuisine	100	82
Service	100	82
Miscellaneous	100	86
OVERALL SCORE 424 points out of 500		

Really stylish and contemporary throughout, the interior decor is elegant and tasteful, with no 'bling'. The Palm Court lounge is lovely, although four thick pillars impede sightlines. The well-appointed cabins have floor-to-ceiling electric opening windows, excellent king-sized (or twin) beds, premium bed linen, Julius Meinl coffee machine, Etro bathrobes and toiletries (bathrooms have lightly heated floors), slippers, and 'butler' service. The bistro-style main restaurant features premium-quality china and glassware and is extremely comfortable. Dinner settings lack tablecloths.

CRYSTAL MAHLER ★★★★+
A STUNNING RIVERSHIP WITH ALL THE TRIMMINGS FOR A PREMIUM RIVER CRUISE.

Operator ....Crystal River Cruises
Built 2017
Length (m) 135.0
Number of decks (excluding sun deck)................... 3
Passenger beds..106
Sit outside (real) balcony.......................................No
French (open-air) balcony ....Yes
Approximate cabin size (sq m) 17.5–82.0
Lift (elevator)...Yes
Rivers sailed............................. Rhine, Main, Danube

BERLITZ'S RATINGS		
	Possible	Achieved
Hardware	100	89
Accommodation	100	84
Cuisine	100	82
Service	100	82
Miscellaneous	100	86
OVERALL SCORE 423 points out of 500		

This stylish rivership is all about premium, although it's too wide for some locks. The Palm Court observation lounge is delightful, although four thick pillars impede sightlines. The well-appointed cabins have floor-to-ceiling electric windows, king-sized (or twin) beds, premium bed linen, Julius Meinl coffee machines, Etro bathrobes and toiletries (bathrooms have lightly heated floors), slippers and 'butler' service. The main (bistro-style) restaurant has premium-quality china and glassware and is comfortable. Overall, *Crystal Mahler* provides an excellent cruise experience.

CRYSTAL MOZART ★★★★+
THIS OLDER DOUBLE-WIDE RIVERSHIP HAS OODLES OF SPACE AND CHARACTER.

Operator ....Crystal River Cruises
Built 1987
Length (m) 120.4
Number of decks (excluding sun deck)................... 3
Passenger beds..154
Sit outside (real) balcony.......................................No
French (open-air) balcony ....Yes
Approximate cabin size (sq m) 20.3–80.0
Lift (elevator)...Yes
Rivers sailed...Danube

BERLITZ'S RATINGS		
	Possible	Achieved
Hardware	100	90
Accommodation	100	78
Cuisine	100	74
Service	100	80
Miscellaneous	100	80
OVERALL SCORE 402 points out of 500		

This comfortable vessel has spacious public areas, a small indoor dip pool, sauna, steam room, hot tub and self-serve launderette, plus a promenade deck. 'Butler' service is for all. Many cabins have French (open-air) balconies, mood lighting and USB outlets. The bistro-style Waterside Restaurant is very attractive, with plenty of tables for two. The creative cuisine uses plenty of fresh, high-quality ingredients. Breakfast and lunch buffets are extensive, while dinner is a sit and be served meal. Blue (aft) serves comfort food and The Bistro is good for coffees, pastries and salads.

CRYSTAL RAVEL ★★★★+

THIS ULTRA-CONTEMPORARY RIVERSHIP EXUDES HIGH-QUALITY COMFORT FACTOR AND STYLE.

Operator	Crystal River Cruises
Built	2018
Length (m)	135.0
Number of decks (excluding sun deck)	3
Passenger beds	106
Sit outside (real) balcony	No
French (open-air) balcony	Yes
Approximate cabin size (sq m)	17.5–82.0
Lift (elevator)	Yes
Rivers sailed	Rhine, Main, Danube

BERLITZ'S RATINGS		
	Possible	Achieved
Hardware	100	90
Accommodation	100	84
Cuisine	100	82
Service	100	82
Miscellaneous	100	86
OVERALL SCORE 424 points out of 500		

With its high level of comfort, this stylish rivership delivers premium river cruising. The Palm Court observation lounge is delightful, and restful, although four thick pillars impede sightlines. The well-appointed cabins have floor-to-ceiling electric opening windows, excellent king-sized (or twin) beds, premium bed linen, Julius Meinl coffee machine, Etro bathrobes and toiletries (bathrooms have lightly heated floors), slippers, and 'butler' service. The (bistro-style, tablecloth-less) main restaurant features premium-quality china and glassware and is comfortable.

CYRANO DE BERGERAC ★★★+

THIS SMART-LOOKING RIVERSHIP HAS GOOD FEATURES AND A FRENCH AMBIENCE.

Operator	CroisiEurope
Built	2013
Length (m)	110.0
Number of decks (excluding sun deck)	3
Passenger beds	150
Sit outside (real) balcony	No
French (open-air) balcony	Yes
Approximate cabin size (sq m)	12.0
Lift (elevator)	No
Rivers sailed	Bordeaux region

BERLITZ'S RATINGS		
	Possible	Achieved
Hardware	100	74
Accommodation	100	71
Cuisine	100	63
Service	100	64
Miscellaneous	100	64
OVERALL SCORE 336 points out of 500		

This modern vessel has chic, quirky interior decor and some delightful artworks, but four thick pillars in the Palm Court lounge obstruct sightlines. The cabins – many have French balconies with floor-to-ceiling slide-open doors – are quite bland, but quite functional; twin beds can convert to doubles (but bedside reading lights are poor). The bathrooms have a good-sized circular glazed shower enclosure. The vessel has fairly decent, but not memorable, French cuisine (but good cheese selection), and young wines. Note that gratuities, drinks and tours cost extra.

DCS AMETHYST ★★★

A FAIRLY ATTRACTIVE RIVERSHIP OFFERING A MODERATE RIVER CRUISE EXPERIENCE.

Operator .... DCS
Built 2004
Length (m) 126.7
Number of decks (excluding sun deck).................... 3
Passenger beds...178
Sit outside (real) balcony ....No
French (open-air) balcony ....Yes
Approximate cabin size (sq m) 15.0–22.0
Lift (elevator)...No
Rivers sailed...Danube

BERLITZ'S RATINGS		
	Possible	Achieved
Hardware	100	57
Accommodation	100	57
Cuisine	100	56
Service	100	56
Miscellaneous	100	57
OVERALL SCORE 283 points out of 500		

DCS Amethyst is a fairly modern-looking but high-density vessel with attractive, unfussy interior decor. Many of the spacious cabins have French (open-air) balconies. All except the four suites are the same size and fairly well appointed, with river-facing beds and decent-sized bathrooms with glazed shower enclosures. A wellness area includes a hot tub and sauna. The restaurant is quite pleasant (the chairs lack armrests), but the food (except salad items) lacks choice, variety and any hint of flair.

DA VINCI ★★+

THIS SMART BUT OLDER RIVERSHIP IS DECENT ENOUGH FOR A LOW-BUDGET CRUISE.

Operator ....Shearings Holidays
Built 1995
Length (m) 104.5
Number of decks (excluding sun deck).................... 2
Passenger beds...110
Sit outside (real) balcony ....No
French (open-air) balcony ....No
Approximate cabin size (sq m) 11.0–12.0
Lift (elevator)...Yes
Rivers sailed......................... Various European rivers

BERLITZ'S RATINGS		
	Possible	Achieved
Hardware	100	43
Accommodation	100	44
Cuisine	100	45
Service	100	46
Miscellaneous	100	50
OVERALL SCORE 228 points out of 500		

Da Vinci is quite a pleasant vessel, but the interior furnishings are tired. The lounge has a nice wooden bar, but uncomfortable low-back chairs. The cabins are really small, with non-opening windows and two slim beds that fold up for use as sofas (to create the impression of space in the daytime), and tiny bathrooms. Facilities include a small sauna and fitness area. Although it's cramped, the restaurant is pleasant enough, but the food is underwhelming and lacks variety. The drink brands are basic; there's limited selection, and the wine glasses are small. Think: cheap and cheerful.

DANUBIA ★★

THIS OLDER-STYLE BUT CHARMING RIVERSHIP OFFERS MODESTLY PRICED CRUISES.

Operator .... Polster & Pohl
Built 1980
Length (m) 102.0
Number of decks (excluding sun deck)................... 2
Passenger beds...142
Sit outside (real) balcony....................................No
French (open-air) balcony ....No
Approximate cabin size (sq m) 10.0
Lift (elevator)..No
Rivers sailed..Danube

BERLITZ'S RATINGS		
	Possible	Achieved
Hardware	100	36
Accommodation	100	34
Cuisine	100	40
Service	100	43
Miscellaneous	100	44
OVERALL SCORE 197 points out of 500		

With its nostalgic interiors and rich wood panelling *Danubia* has a calm, restful character, although the lounge can feel rather cramped when full. The small cabins (all have the same design and layout) have windows (no balconies), two fixed, short beds and very little storage space. The bathrooms are really compact with a tiny shower area. The restaurant is quite homely, and moderately comfortable, while the food is quite basic yet somehow adequate – there's not much choice because the galley is so small.

DER KLEINE PRINZ ★★★+

THIS DATED, INTIMATE, BUDGET RIVERSHIP HAS SOMBRE DECOR BUT GOOD ARTWORK.

Operator ....Various tour operators
Built 1992
Length (m) 93.3
Number of decks (excluding sun deck)................... 2
Passenger beds.. 90
Sit outside (real) balcony....................................No
French (open-air) balcony ....No
Approximate cabin size (sq m) 16.0
Lift (elevator)...Yes
Rivers sailed..Danube

BERLITZ'S RATINGS		
	Possible	Achieved
Hardware	100	42
Accommodation	100	37
Cuisine	100	41
Service	100	44
Miscellaneous	100	47
OVERALL SCORE 211 points out of 500		

For anyone looking for a cruise at a low price, then *Der Kleine Prinz* may be suitable. It's an older vessel, lacking the bells and whistles of newer riverships, but it does manage to provide all the basics, and is quite comfortable. The cabins, all of which have windows, are quite spacious, but they are plain and dated with couple-unfriendly fixed beds that cannot be moved together. The bathrooms are small but adequate. The restaurant is moderately pleasant, but the food is decidedly underwhelming.

DIANA ★+

THIS VINTAGE RIVERSHIP PROVIDES NO-FRILLS CRUISES FOR BUDGET TRAVELLERS.

Operator .... Various tour operators
Built 1964
Length (m) 78.0
Number of decks (excluding sun deck) 2
Passenger beds 78
Sit outside (real) balcony .... No
French (open-air) balcony .... No
Approximate cabin size (sq m) 9.0
Lift (elevator) .... No
Rivers sailed .... Various European rivers

BERLITZ'S RATINGS		
	Possible	Achieved
Hardware	100	25
Accommodation	100	28
Cuisine	100	30
Service	100	32
Miscellaneous	100	32
OVERALL SCORE 147 points out of 500		

Short, with very limited interior space, and low ceilings, although this dated vessel does have mildly attractive decor in its public areas. The cabins have windows (those on the lower deck are miniscule), are very compact, with slim, short beds, dim lighting, poor soundproofing and tiny bathrooms (think: dancing with the shower curtain). The restaurant is pleasant enough, although the chairs lack armrests; it has a tiny galley, so don't expect much in terms of cuisine, which is basic. The wine glasses are also small. *Diana* is best chosen for its itinerary, low cost and cheerful atmosphere.

DOUCE FRANCE ★★+

THIS MIDDLE-OF-THE-ROAD RIVERSHIP IS DATED BUT REASONABLY COMFORTABLE.

Operator .... CroisiEurope
Built 1997
Length (m) 110.0
Number of decks (excluding sun deck) 2
Passenger beds 164
Sit outside (real) balcony .... No
French (open-air) balcony .... No
Approximate cabin size (sq m) 12.0
Lift (elevator) .... No
Rivers sailed .... Rhine, Main, Danube

BERLITZ'S RATINGS		
	Possible	Achieved
Hardware	100	43
Accommodation	100	44
Cuisine	100	53
Service	100	52
Miscellaneous	100	52
OVERALL SCORE 244 points out of 500		

Despite its small plain cabins with short beds, poor lighting and soundproofing, and bathrooms that have little storage space for personal items, this rivership may be acceptable for you if you are on a tight budget. The interior decor is fairly comfortable but uninspiring. It's one to choose mainly for its convivial ambience, the reasonably decent (although with little variety) French meals, wine and the itinerary. Excursions cost extra, but drinks and (young) wines are included.

DOURO CRUISER ★★★

THIS SMALL, HIGH-DENSITY RIVERSHIP MAY BE ADEQUATE FOR THE DOURO.

Operator ....Nicko Cruises
Built 2005
Length (m) 78.1
Number of decks (excluding sun deck) 3
Passenger beds.. 130
Sit outside (real) balcony ....No
French (open-air) balcony ....Yes
Approximate cabin size (sq m) 15.0
Lift (elevator)..No
Rivers sailed.. Douro

BERLITZ'S RATINGS		
	Possible	Achieved
Hardware	100	56
Accommodation	100	54
Cuisine	100	58
Service	100	57
Miscellaneous	100	58
OVERALL SCORE 283 points out of 500		

This vessel has a nicely decorated and furnished lounge. The cabins, however, are small and plain, but quite comfortable, although there's little storage space, the lighting and soundproofing are poor, and mirrors are positioned opposite the beds (bad feng shui). The bathrooms are really cramped and have very small showers. The restaurant is tight, and table seating is assigned. The food from the tiny galley is really uninspiring and the presentation lacks passion, plus the wine glasses are small, so make the itinerary and low prices your reasons for booking.

DOURO ELEGANCE ★★★★

SPECIALLY BUILT FOR DOURO RIVER CRUISES, IT HAS OODLES OF COMFORT TO OFFER.

Operator .... Riviera Travel
Built 2017
Length (m) 80.0
Number of decks (excluding sun deck) 3
Passenger beds.. 126
Sit outside (real) balcony ....No
French (open-air) balcony ....Yes
Approximate cabin size (sq m) 14.0–30.0
Lift (elevator)...Yes
Rivers sailed.. Douro

BERLITZ'S RATINGS		
	Possible	Achieved
Hardware	100	78
Accommodation	100	74
Cuisine	100	68
Service	100	70
Miscellaneous	100	73
OVERALL SCORE 363 points out of 500		

This smart-looking rivership is comfortable, and the decor is warm and inviting. Most cabins are fairly standard in terms of size and comfort, with decent storage space, and all have tea/coffee making facilities. Six suites and cabins other than those on the lowest deck have wall-to-wall push-button electric windows that provide a French (open-air) balcony. The restaurant is quite attractive and is quite comfortable, although the chairs don't have armrests. The food focuses on regional dishes, and the variety is not large, but it's quite tasty, but the wine glasses are small. Overall, this is a fine rivership.

DOURO PRINCESS ★★

THIS VERY DATED RIVERSHIP IS ADEQUATE FOR LOW BUDGET DOURO CRUISING.

Operator ....Various tour operators
Built 1963
Length (m) 68.0
Number of decks (excluding sun deck)....................2
Passenger beds...80
Sit outside (real) balcony ....No
French (open-air) balcony ....No
Approximate cabin size (sq m) 10.0–11.2
Lift (elevator)..No
Rivers sailed...................................... Douro

BERLITZ'S RATINGS		
	Possible	Achieved
Hardware	100	30
Accommodation	100	28
Cuisine	100	33
Service	100	34
Miscellaneous	100	38
OVERALL SCORE 163 points out of 500		

Douro Princess may be old, but it has lots of real wood panelling and cabinetry, and bags of character. The lounge is cramped but somehow pleasant enough, although many slim support pillars obstruct sight-lines. The cabins are extremely compact, with minimal storage space; the twin beds are short and slim (Upper Deck cabin beds can be pushed together). Some cabins have windows that open. The restaurant is cosy, and the food is regional and fairly basic (little choice), but it has taste.

DOURO QUEEN ★★★

THIS SMART-LOOKING RIVERSHIP HAS GOOD FEATURES FOR BUSY DOURO CRUISES.

Operator ....Various tour operators
Built 2005
Length (m) 77.4
Number of decks (excluding sun deck)....................2
Passenger beds...130
Sit outside (real) balcony ....No
French (open-air) balcony ....Yes
Approximate cabin size (sq m) 15.0
Lift (elevator)..No
Rivers sailed...................................... Douro

BERLITZ'S RATINGS		
	Possible	Achieved
Hardware	100	60
Accommodation	100	56
Cuisine	100	59
Service	100	60
Miscellaneous	100	62
OVERALL SCORE 297 points out of 500		

Douro Queen is a small, comfortable vessel with rich interior decor in the forward lounge. Cabins on the upper accommodation deck have French balconies (those on the lowest deck have windows), are more spacious and have decent soundproofing, but the decor is plain. The bathrooms are small but functional, although space for personal toiletries is minimal. The restaurant is on the lowest deck and is very cramped. The cuisine includes a mix of Portuguese and international dishes, which are attractively presented.

DOURO SERENITY ★★★★

THIS RIVERSHIP, BUILT SPECIFICALLY FOR DOURO RIVER CRUISING, IS CHIC.

Operator .... Riviera Travel
Built 2017
Length (m) 80.0
Number of decks (excluding sun deck)................... 2
Passenger beds...126
Sit outside (real) balcony.....................................No
French (open-air) balcony ....Yes
Approximate cabin size (sq m) 14.0–30.0
Lift (elevator)..Yes
Rivers sailed... Douro

BERLITZ'S RATINGS		
	Possible	Achieved
Hardware	100	78
Accommodation	100	75
Cuisine	100	68
Service	100	70
Miscellaneous	100	74
OVERALL SCORE 365 points out of 500		

This smart, contemporary rivership is very comfortable. Most cabins are standard in terms of size and comfort, with limited storage space, but all have tea-/coffee-making facilities. Six suites have large slide-open doors that provide a French (open-air) balcony; most other cabins have floor-to-ceiling windows that can be opened halfway for fresh air. The restaurant is quite attractive, although the chairs don't have armrests. The food focuses on regional dishes, and, while the variety is not exactly large, it is quite tasty and nicely presented. The wine glasses, however, are small.

DOURO SPIRIT ★★★

TRY THIS FAIRLY MODERN RIVERSHIP FOR A FAIRLY DECENT DOURO CRUISE.

Operator ....Various tour operators
Built 2011
Length (m) 79.5
Number of decks (excluding sun deck)................... 2
Passenger beds...130
Sit outside (real) balcony.....................................No
French (open-air) balcony ....Yes
Approximate cabin size (sq m) 15.0–22.2
Lift (elevator)..Yes
Rivers sailed... Douro

BERLITZ'S RATINGS		
	Possible	Achieved
Hardware	100	63
Accommodation	100	57
Cuisine	100	57
Service	100	58
Miscellaneous	100	61
OVERALL SCORE 296 points out of 500		

Douro Spirit is a rather high-density vessel. The cabins are comfortable, although not luxurious, and they have good soundproofing; the suites are more stylish. Most rooms have French balconies with floor-to-ceiling slide-open doors, and light colours abound. The bathrooms, however, are really plain and basic. The restaurant, which provides attractively presented Portuguese and international dishes, is pleasant, but don't expect any kind of finesse or flair.

EDELWEISS ★★★★

TRY THIS HIGH-QUALITY CONTEMPORARY RIVERSHIP FOR A FIRST-CLASS CRUISE.

Operator .... Thurgau Travel
Built 2013
Length (m) 110.0
Number of decks (excluding sun deck) 3
Passenger beds...180
Sit outside (real) balcony .... Yes
French (open-air) balcony .... Yes
Approximate cabin size (sq m) 14.0–22.0
Lift (elevator)... Yes
Rivers sailed............................. Rhine, Main, Danube

BERLITZ'S RATINGS		
	Possible	Achieved
Hardware	100	74
Accommodation	100	71
Cuisine	100	70
Service	100	66
Miscellaneous	100	72
OVERALL SCORE 353 points out of 500		

The interiors of the stylish, but high-density *Edelweiss* have high-quality fittings and furnishings, including hardwood panelling and fine carpeting. The cabins are well appointed and practical, and have ample storage space. The bathrooms have glazed shower enclosures and are really pleasant. Decent quality food is provided, and there's a good variety, but the wine glasses are small. Overall, this rivership provides the setting for a high-quality, high-value cruise.

ELBE PRINCESSE ★★★★

THIS CUSTOM-BUILT VESSEL FOR THE ELBE IS COMFORTABLE, INNOVATIVE AND CHIC.

Operator .... CroisiEurope
Built 2016
Length (m) 101.0
Number of decks (excluding sun deck) 2
Passenger beds... 80
Sit outside (real) balcony ....No
French (open-air) balcony .... Yes
Approximate cabin size (sq m) 11.0–14.5
Lift (elevator)..No
Rivers sailed.................................... Elbe, Havel, Oder

BERLITZ'S RATINGS		
	Possible	Achieved
Hardware	100	75
Accommodation	100	68
Cuisine	100	71
Service	100	68
Miscellaneous	100	74
OVERALL SCORE 356 points out of 500		

This rivership has an electrically driven mid-ship stern paddlewheel, a useful reinvention that helps in the river's shallow water. The lounge has clean, minimalist decor and cosy seating. The cabins are small, but include a hidden ceiling-mounted television and personal safe. Short-length beds face the river (most are twins or doubles while a few have fixed twin beds); some have sit-out balconies. The tiled bathrooms are small, but have glazed shower enclosures, and under-washbasin storage cupboards. The restaurant is quite pleasant and the food is good, but lacks flair.

ELBE PRINCESSE II NYR
THIS ELBE-SPECIFIC VESSEL IS INNOVATIVE, CHIC AND COMFORTABLE.

Operator .... CroisiEurope
Built 2018
Length (m) 101.0
Number of decks (excluding sun deck).................... 2
Passenger beds... 86
Sit outside (real) balcony ....No
French (open-air) balcony ....Yes
Approximate cabin size (sq m) 11.0–14.5
Lift (elevator)...No
Rivers sailed................................. Elbe, Havel, Oder

BERLITZ'S RATINGS		
	Possible	Achieved
Hardware	100	NYR
Accommodation	100	NYR
Cuisine	100	NYR
Service	100	NYR
Miscellaneous	100	NYR
OVERALL SCORE NYR points out of 500		

This rivership has an electrically driven mid-ship stern paddlewheel, a useful reinvention that helps in the river's shallow water. The lounge has clean, minimalist decor and cosy seating. The cabins are small, but include a hidden ceiling-mounted television and personal safe. They have short-length beds facing the river (most are twins or doubles while a few have fixed twin beds); some cabins have sit-out balconies. The small tiled bathrooms have glazed shower enclosures and under-washbasin storage cupboards. The restaurant is quite pleasant and the food is good but nothing special.

ELEGANT LADY ★★★
THIS SMART-LOOKING RIVERSHIP PROVIDES CRUISES THAT ARE GOOD VALUE.

Operator ....Plantours Cruises
Built 2002
Length (m) 110.0
Number of decks (excluding sun deck).................... 2
Passenger beds...128
Sit outside (real) balcony ....No
French (open-air) balcony ....No
Approximate cabin size (sq m) 14.0
Lift (elevator)...No
Rivers sailed.............................. Rhine, Main, Danube

BERLITZ'S RATINGS		
	Possible	Achieved
Hardware	100	54
Accommodation	100	52
Cuisine	100	50
Service	100	52
Miscellaneous	100	55
OVERALL SCORE 263 points out of 500		

Elegant Lady has nicely appointed interiors but limited public rooms (lounge and restaurant), which makes it feel cramped and overrun. The well-designed cabins are quite spacious (each has two slim beds), although the reading lights and soundproofing are poor and the bathrooms are small (but functional). The restaurant is pleasantly decorated. The food is hearty, but the choices are limited and both the quality and creativity are decidedly underwhelming.

EMERALD ★★★+

TRY THIS VESSEL FOR A REALLY COMFORTABLE, HIGH-QUALITY CRUISE EXPERIENCE.

Operator ....Tauck
Built 2006
Length (m) 110.0
Number of decks (excluding sun deck)................... 3
Passenger beds.. 98
Sit outside (real) balcony ....No
French (open-air) balcony ....Yes
Approximate cabin size (sq m) 14.0–28.0
Lift (elevator)..Yes
Rivers sailed..Rhone, Saone

BERLITZ'S RATINGS		
	Possible	Achieved
Hardware	100	67
Accommodation	100	62
Cuisine	100	65
Service	100	67
Miscellaneous	100	75
OVERALL SCORE 336 points out of 500		

Refitted in 2017, *Emerald* has warm and elegant interior decor in the lounge, lobby and hallways. The cabins are nicely appointed and decorated, and have ample storage space, good closets, effective lighting, high-quality mattresses and bed linen, and good soundproofing. The bathrooms have large glazed shower enclosures. There is also a small fitness room and sauna. The open-seating restaurant is very comfortable, and the food is unfussy and good, but not outstanding. An alternative, for lighter fare, is The Bistro, located aft.

EMERALD DAWN ★★★★

YOU'LL FIND EXCELLENT VALUE AND MODERN STYLE ABOARD THIS FINE VESSEL.

Operator ....Emerald Waterways
Built 2015
Length (m) 135.0
Number of decks (excluding sun deck)................... 3
Passenger beds..182
Sit outside (real) balcony ....No
French (open-air) balcony ....Yes
Approximate cabin size (sq m) 12.0–29.0
Lift (elevator)..Yes
Rivers sailed............................. Rhine, Main, Danube

BERLITZ'S RATINGS		
	Possible	Achieved
Hardware	100	80
Accommodation	100	76
Cuisine	100	75
Service	100	76
Miscellaneous	100	78
OVERALL SCORE 385 points out of 500		

One neat feature aboard this rivership is an aft indoor-outdoor pool that converts to a cinema by night. Cabins have large push-button, slide-down windows that provide the feel of a private balcony; deep drawers provide ample storage space, and there's a neat open-up vanity desk. The bathrooms are quite small but practical, and they have decent-sized tiled and glazed shower enclosures. The suites have more space, plus coffee machines and other perks. The open-seating restaurant is quite pleasant, but rather noisy; buffets are laid out well and the food is well labelled.

EMERALD DESTINY ★★★★

THIS SMART RIVERSHIP PROVIDES A HIGH-VALUE, WELL-ORGANIZED CRUISE.

Operator ....Emerald Waterways
Built 2017
Length (m) 135.0
Number of decks (excluding sun deck)................... 3
Passenger beds...186
Sit outside (real) balcony ....No
French (open-air) balcony ....Yes
Approximate cabin size (sq m) 12.0–29.0
Lift (elevator)..Yes
Rivers sailed............................. Rhine, Main, Danube

BERLITZ'S RATINGS		
	Possible	Achieved
Hardware	100	78
Accommodation	100	77
Cuisine	100	75
Service	100	75
Miscellaneous	100	80
OVERALL SCORE 385 points out of 500		

The contemporary style is evident throughout; it's cheerful and bright, and there's no 'bling,' but it's also a fairly high-density rivership. The cabins are well designed and quite spacious; all except those on the lowest deck have electrically operated wall-to-wall slide-down windows ('sun balconies'). The bathrooms are very good. A nice feature is a small aft (heated) pool with retractable roof that can convert into a cinema by night. The open-seating restaurant is quite comfortable and attractive, but noisy; buffets are laid out well and the food is labelled well.

EMERALD LIBERTÉ ★★★★

THIS WELL-RUN RIVERSHIP OFFERS VERY COMFORTABLE CRUISING AND DECENT FOOD.

Operator ....Emerald Waterways
Built 2017
Length (m) 110.0
Number of decks (excluding sun deck)................... 3
Passenger beds...138
Sit outside (real) balcony ....No
French (open-air) balcony ....Yes
Approximate cabin size (sq m) 12.0–29.0
Lift (elevator)..Yes
Rivers sailed...Rhone, Saone

BERLITZ'S RATINGS		
	Possible	Achieved
Hardware	100	77
Accommodation	100	76
Cuisine	100	75
Service	100	75
Miscellaneous	100	80
OVERALL SCORE 383 points out of 500		

Emerald Liberté was built specifically for the rivers of France. It has bags of contemporary style and is well appointed. It has very comfortable, extra-large cabins, most of which have French balconies with floor-to-ceiling slide-down windows, good beds (some with direct river views) and mini-fridges. The bathrooms have large shower enclosures. Aft is a small (heated) pool with retractable roof that can convert into a cinema by night. The open seating restaurant is nicely appointed and the varied cuisine is well above average. An alternative eatery, aft (The Bistro), is for lighter fare.

EMERALD RADIANCE ★★★★

TRY THIS SMART RIVERSHIP FOR A WELL-ORGANIZED DOURO CRUISE EXPERIENCE.

Operator ....Emerald Waterways
Built 2017
Length (m) 110.0
Number of decks (excluding sun deck)....................3
Passenger beds...112
Sit outside (real) balcony ....No
French (open-air) balcony ....Yes
Approximate cabin size (sq m) 16.0–29.0
Lift (elevator)...Yes
Rivers sailed.. Douro

BERLITZ'S RATINGS		
	Possible	Achieved
Hardware	100	77
Accommodation	100	75
Cuisine	100	72
Service	100	74
Miscellaneous	100	80
OVERALL SCORE 378 points out of 500		

Contemporary and stylish decor abounds in the public areas. Accommodation hallways are plain and unfussy. The cabins are well designed and practical, but cabinetry is angular. Most cabins have floor-to-ceiling open-air French balconies (the lowest deck cabins have windows). Bathrooms are stylish, and practical. The open-seating restaurant is pleasant enough, but the low-back chairs are uncomfortable. The Portuguese-themed cuisine is good, but buffets lack flair and are rather limited. However, friendly Portuguese service prevails.

EMERALD SKY ★★★★

THIS SMART RIVERSHIP HAS STATE-OF-THE-ART FEATURES AND STYLISH CABINS.

Operator ....Emerald Waterways
Built 2014
Length (m) 135.0
Number of decks (excluding sun deck)....................3
Passenger beds...182
Sit outside (real) balcony ....No
French (open-air) balcony ....Yes
Approximate cabin size (sq m) 16.0–29.0
Lift (elevator)...Yes
Rivers sailed.............................. Rhine, Main, Danube

BERLITZ'S RATINGS		
	Possible	Achieved
Hardware	100	76
Accommodation	100	76
Cuisine	100	75
Service	100	75
Miscellaneous	100	79
OVERALL SCORE 381 points out of 500		

Emerald Sky is a really stylish but fairly high-density rivership with a nicely appointed interior; aft is a small pool that can be covered and turned into a cinema by night. The cabins are well designed and quite spacious; all except those on the lowest deck have electrically operated wall-to-wall slide-down windows ('sun balconies'). The contemporary bathrooms have large glazed shower enclosures and small washbasins. The restaurant is a little cramped (it's also noisy), but has attractive decor.

EMERALD STAR ★★★★

THIS SMART, CONTEMPORARY RIVERSHIP IS DESIGNED FOR THE YOUTHFUL TRAVELLER.

Operator ....Emerald Waterways
Built 2014
Length (m) 135.0
Number of decks (excluding sun deck)....................3
Passenger beds..182
Sit outside (real) balcony ....No
French (open-air) balcony ....Yes
Approximate cabin size (sq m) 16.0–29.0
Lift (elevator)..Yes
Rivers sailed.............................. Rhine, Main, Danube

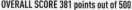

BERLITZ'S RATINGS		
	Possible	Achieved
Hardware	100	76
Accommodation	100	76
Cuisine	100	75
Service	100	75
Miscellaneous	100	79
OVERALL SCORE 381 points out of 500		

The high-density *Emerald Star* has a well-appointed interior (check out the petrified 'Polo Mint' artworks in the atrium). The cabins have ample deep-drawer storage space, and bathrooms have large glazed shower enclosures. All cabins except those on the lowest deck have push-button electric opening windows ('sun balconies'). Aft is a small (heated) pool with retractable roof that can convert into a cinema by night. The restaurant is quite comfortable, but can be rather noisy.

EMERALD SUN ★★★★

THIS SMART RIVERSHIP DELIVERS A HIGH-QUALITY, HIGH-VALUE CRUISE EXPERIENCE.

Operator ....Emerald Waterways
Built 2015
Length (m) 135.0
Number of decks (excluding sun deck)....................3
Passenger beds..182
Sit outside (real) balcony ....No
French (open-air) balcony ....Yes
Approximate cabin size (sq m) 12.0–29.0
Lift (elevator)..Yes
Rivers sailed.............................. Rhine, Main, Danube

BERLITZ'S RATINGS		
	Possible	Achieved
Hardware	100	77
Accommodation	100	76
Cuisine	100	75
Service	100	76
Miscellaneous	100	80
OVERALL SCORE 384 points out of 500		

Cabins have a nice vanity desk and push-button slide-down windows to give the impression of having a balcony. Deep (soft-close) drawers provide ample storage. Suites have more space, coffee machines and other perks. Bathrooms are small but practical and have good, tiled, glazed shower enclosures. The delightful aft indoor-outdoor pool converts to a cinema by night. The restaurant has a good buffet layout to reduce congestion.

EMILY BRONTÉ ★★★★

THIS RIVERSHIP WOULD BE AN EXCELLENT CHOICE FOR A QUALITY CRUISE EXPERIENCE.

Operator .... Riviera Travel
Built 2017
Length (m) 135.0
Number of decks (excluding sun deck) 3
Passenger beds..167
Sit outside (real) balcony ....No
French (open-air) balcony ....Yes
Approximate cabin size (sq m) 17.0–25.0
Lift (elevator)..Yes
Rivers sailed ....Rhine

BERLITZ'S RATINGS		
	Possible	Achieved
Hardware	100	78
Accommodation	100	75
Cuisine	100	68
Service	100	70
Miscellaneous	100	75
OVERALL SCORE 366 points out of 500		

This delightful vessel has restrained but contemporary decor and furniture, and a spacious, traditional, two-deck high lobby. The cabins have warm wood accents and high-quality furniture and fabrics. The cabins are comfortable (although those designated as 'suites' are not large), with a good amount of storage space, and twin beds that can become doubles. The tiled bathrooms, meanwhile, have decent-sized glazed shower enclosures and good lighting. The restaurant is pleasant, but the cuisine is underwhelming – breakfasts are repetitious, and the wine glasses are small.

ESMERALDA ★★+

THIS OLDER VESSEL PROVIDES ALL THE BASICS FOR LOW BUDGET, NO-FRILLS CRUISING.

Operator ....Various tour operators
Built 1979
Length (m) 90.0
Number of decks (excluding sun deck) 2
Passenger beds..126
Sit outside (real) balcony ....No
French (open-air) balcony ....No
Approximate cabin size (sq m) 11.0
Lift (elevator)..Yes
Rivers sailed ....Rhine

BERLITZ'S RATINGS		
	Possible	Achieved
Hardware	100	48
Accommodation	100	44
Cuisine	100	44
Service	100	46
Miscellaneous	100	50
OVERALL SCORE 232 points out of 500		

This pleasant, older rivership has very limited facilities, but the lounge/bar is comfortable enough. The cabins are very tight on space and have two pull-down beds (to provide more daytime space), but lighting and sound-proofing are poor, and storage space is very limited. The bathrooms (and shower area) are tiny. The restaurant is vaguely pleasant – it has cramped, but manageable, seating. The food isn't great either: it lacks both taste and variety, and the breakfast buffets are rather poor and repetitious. Think: cheap and cheerful and go mainly for the itinerary and destinations.

ESPRIT ★★★+

CHOOSE THIS VESSEL FOR A REALLY COMFORTABLE, HIGH-QUALITY CRUISE EXPERIENCE.

Operator ....Tauck
Built 2010
Length (m) 110.0
Number of decks (excluding sun deck)...................3
Passenger beds...98
Sit outside (real) balcony ....No
French (open-air) balcony ....Yes
Approximate cabin size (sq m) 14.0–28.0
Lift (elevator)..Yes
Rivers sailed............................. Rhine, Main, Danube

BERLITZ'S RATINGS		
	Possible	Achieved
Hardware	100	71
Accommodation	100	72
Cuisine	100	64
Service	100	67
Miscellaneous	100	73
OVERALL SCORE 347 points out of 500		

This rivership, refitted in 2017 for few passengers, has warm, elegant interior decor in the lounge, lobby and hallways. The cabins are nicely appointed and decorated and have ample storage space, good closets, decent lighting, high-quality mattresses and bed linen, and good soundproofing. The bathrooms have large glazed shower enclosures. Facilities include a fitness room and sauna. The open-seating restaurant is very comfortable, and the food is unfussy and good, but not outstanding. An alternative, for lighter fare, is The Bistro, located aft.

EXCELLENCE ALLEGRA ★★★+

THIS HIGH-DENSITY RIVERSHIP HAS SOME GOOD FEATURES AND SWISS STYLE.

Operator ....Excellence River Cruise
Built 2011
Length (m) 135.0
Number of decks (excluding sun deck)...................3
Passenger beds...178
Sit outside (real) balcony ....No
French (open-air) balcony ....Yes
Approximate cabin size (sq m) 12.0–15.0
Lift (elevator)..No
Rivers sailed................................. Rhine, Main, Mosel

BERLITZ'S RATINGS		
	Possible	Achieved
Hardware	100	68
Accommodation	100	67
Cuisine	100	64
Service	100	65
Miscellaneous	100	67
OVERALL SCORE 331 points out of 500		

With a two-deck high lobby and contemporary, but restrained decor, *Excellence Allegra* is very comfortable. The cabins – many of which have French balconies with floor-to-ceiling slide-open doors (those on the lowest deck have small windows) – are quiet and well designed, with a decent amount of storage space. Each bathroom has a glazed shower enclosure. Facilities include a nice indoor sauna/hot tub area. The comfortable restaurant serves unfussy cuisine, with few green vegetables and repetitious breakfasts. The wines are young, and the wine glasses are small.

EXCELLENCE CORAL ★★★

THIS CHARMING, COMPACT RIVERSHIP PROVIDES A FAIRLY DECENT CRUISE EXPERIENCE.

Operator	Excellence River Cruises
Built	1998
Length (m)	135.0
Number of decks (excluding sun deck)	2
Passenger beds	87
Sit outside (real) balcony	No
French (open-air) balcony	No
Approximate cabin size (sq m)	10.0–13.0
Lift (elevator)	No
Rivers sailed	Elbe, Havel, Oder

BERLITZ'S RATINGS

	Possible	Achieved
Hardware	100	56
Accommodation	100	50
Cuisine	100	60
Service	100	55
Miscellaneous	100	58

OVERALL SCORE 279 points out of 500

Excellence Coral, while small, has pleasant interior decor with warm wood and brass accenting. A lounge and restaurant are the only two public rooms, so it feels rather small inside. Although the cabins are small (as are the bathrooms), they are attractively decorated and have windows (no balconies). The restaurant is quite attractive, but the chairs don't have armrests. The cuisine is, for the most part, decent, but there's little flair, and breakfast buffets are repetitive.

EXCELLENCE MELODIA ★★★+

THIS IS A CONTEMPORARY, STYLISH-LOOKING GLASS-FRONTED RIVERSHIP.

Operator	Excellence River Cruise
Built	2011
Length (m)	135.0
Number of decks (excluding sun deck)	3
Passenger beds	178
Sit outside (real) balcony	No
French (open-air) balcony	Yes
Approximate cabin size (sq m)	12.0–15.0
Lift (elevator)	No
Rivers sailed	Rhine, Main, Danube

BERLITZ'S RATINGS

	Possible	Achieved
Hardware	100	69
Accommodation	100	65
Cuisine	100	64
Service	100	65
Miscellaneous	100	70

OVERALL SCORE 333 points out of 500

With propulsion machinery separated from the passenger accommodation, all this twin cruiser's stylish cabins – many of them have French (open-air) balconies – are quiet, although they don't have good ceiling soundproofing. The cabins are small (as are the bathrooms), and the beds are fixed (one converts to a sofa by day, for more space). Large glass windows provide great views from the lounge and restaurant, which are nicely appointed. The food is good, with a decent enough variety but not much flair.

EXCELLENCE PEARL ★★★

THIS MODERNISED AND REFITTED RIVERSHIP IS REASONABLY COMFORTABLE.

Operator ....Excellence River Cruise
Built 2003
Length (m) 82.0
Number of decks (excluding sun deck)................... 2
Passenger beds... 82
Sit outside (real) balcony ....No
French (open-air) balcony ....Yes
Approximate cabin size (sq m) 16.0
Lift (elevator)...No
Rivers sailed.............................. Rhine, Main, Danube

BERLITZ'S RATINGS		
	Possible	Achieved
Hardware	100	58
Accommodation	100	56
Cuisine	100	60
Service	100	60
Miscellaneous	100	61
OVERALL SCORE 295 points out of 500		

In general the interior decor is a little bland and lacking in character, especially the lobby. The cabins are well appointed and include a minibar, and have twin beds that are convertible to a double bed. Some cabins have French balconies with floor-to-ceiling slide-open doors. The restaurant has large windows, but the banquette seating makes serving difficult. Overall, the cuisine is decent, but there's not much variety; the buffet breakfasts are repetitious, and the wine gasses are small.

EXCELLENCE PRINCESS ★★★★

A SMART-LOOKING RIVERSHIP THAT EXUDES SWISS STYLE, AMBIENCE AND COMFORT.

Operator ....Excellence River Cruises
Built 2014
Length (m) 135.0
Number of decks (excluding sun deck)................... 3
Passenger beds...186
Sit outside (real) balcony ....No
French (open-air) balcony ....Yes
Approximate cabin size (sq m) 13.0–20.0
Lift (elevator)...Yes
Rivers sailed.............................. Rhine, Main, Danube

BERLITZ'S RATINGS		
	Possible	Achieved
Hardware	100	74
Accommodation	100	73
Cuisine	100	67
Service	100	67
Miscellaneous	100	72
OVERALL SCORE 353 points out of 500		

This fine vessel has a two-deck high lobby with traditional decor. The cabins are quite comfortable, with twin beds that convert to doubles, and there is a decent amount of storage space. The bathrooms have decent-sized shower enclosures and lighting. The restaurant is pleasant, and most chairs have armrests, but the general cuisine is underwhelming, with repetitious breakfasts. However, some 'foodie' cruises feature visiting Michelin-starred chefs with their signature dishes and wine-paired menus. An extra-cost grill restaurant is aft. Excursions cost extra.

EXCELLENCE QUEEN ★★★+

THIS CONTEMPORARY, ELEGANT RIVERSHIP PROVIDES A GOOD-QUALITY CRUISE EXPERIENCE.

Operator ....Excellence River Cruises
Built 2010
Length (m) 110.0
Number of decks (excluding sun deck)....................3
Passenger beds...142
Sit outside (real) balcony ....No
French (open-air) balcony ....Yes
Approximate cabin size (sq m) 13.0–30.0
Lift (elevator)..Yes
Rivers sailed............................ Rhine, Main, Danube

BERLITZ'S RATINGS		
	Possible	Achieved
Hardware	100	68
Accommodation	100	64
Cuisine	100	67
Service	100	66
Miscellaneous	100	67
OVERALL SCORE 332 points out of 500		

The high-density *Excellence Queen* features dark-wood interiors that are elegant and stylish, with intricate wrought-iron railings on stairways and no bling. The cabins (those on the upper and middle deck have floor-to-ceiling sliding glass doors that open to a French balcony) are nicely appointed and comfortable and each has a double bed; bathrooms have shower enclosures with glazed doors. There's a nice restaurant where the cuisine is good but it doesn't really stand out (more variety and flair are needed).

EXCELLENCE RHÔNE ★★★+

THIS MODERN RIVERSHIP IS QUITE RELIABLE FOR A WELL-ROUNDED CRUISE.

Operator ....Excellence River Cruises
Built 2006
Length (m) 110.0
Number of decks (excluding sun deck)....................3
Passenger beds...142
Sit outside (real) balcony ....No
French (open-air) balcony ....Yes
Approximate cabin size (sq m) 12.0–18.0
Lift (elevator)..Yes
Rivers sailed..Rhone, Saone

BERLITZ'S RATINGS		
	Possible	Achieved
Hardware	100	65
Accommodation	100	63
Cuisine	100	64
Service	100	64
Miscellaneous	100	68
OVERALL SCORE 324 points out of 500		

This smaller, stylish vessel has very pleasant interior decor that is modern without being glitzy. There is a wide variety of cabin types. Two accommodation decks have cabins with floor-to-ceiling, slide-open glass doors opening to French balconies for fresh air; lower deck cabins have non-opening windows. All cabins are pleasantly decorated and have either a double bed or two single beds, plus decent bathrooms. The Bellini Restaurant is comfortable, with warm decor. The food is very decent and includes many French regional dishes.

EXCELLENCE ROYAL ★★★+

THIS SMART-LOOKING RIVERSHIP DELIVERS A GOOD-QUALITY CRUISE EXPERIENCE.

Operator ....Excellence River Cruises
Built 2010
Length (m) 110.0
Number of decks (excluding sun deck).................... 3
Passenger beds..144
Sit outside (real) balcony ....No
French (open-air) balcony ....Yes
Approximate cabin size (sq m) 13.0–17.0
Lift (elevator)..Yes
Rivers sailed.. Seine

BERLITZ'S RATINGS		
	Possible	Achieved
Hardware	100	68
Accommodation	100	64
Cuisine	100	65
Service	100	65
Miscellaneous	100	67
OVERALL SCORE 329 points out of 500		

Excellence Royal has elegant and stylish dark-wood interiors, with intricate wrought-iron railings and accents in the lobby. The cabins are well appointed and quite comfortable, with double beds. Two cabin decks feature slide-open glass doors for fresh air, while the lower deck cabins have non-opening windows. The bathrooms have plain walls and small glass shower enclosures. The cuisine is good, although nothing really stands out, and more variety is needed.

FERNAO DE MAGALHAES ★★★

AN OLDER DOURO RIVERSHIP THAT DELIVERS AN ADEQUATE RIVER DOURO CRUISE.

Operator ....Various tour operators
Built 2003
Length (m) 75.0
Number of decks (excluding sun deck).................... 3
Passenger beds..142
Sit outside (real) balcony ....No
French (open-air) balcony ....No
Approximate cabin size (sq m) 12.0–13.0
Lift (elevator)..No
Rivers sailed.. Douro

BERLITZ'S RATINGS		
	Possible	Achieved
Hardware	100	56
Accommodation	100	50
Cuisine	100	55
Service	100	56
Miscellaneous	100	57
OVERALL SCORE 274 points out of 500		

This rivership is pleasant enough, but the interior decor is really dated. The main lounge is very cramped and has seating that is not really comfortable. The cabins are very small and have slim beds that generally can't be moved together (none of the cabins has a balcony). The bathrooms are tiny too, with little storage space for toiletries. The restaurant is quite pleasant, but cramped, with seating at large round tables. The cuisine focuses on local Portuguese dishes and is adequate, but nothing more, and the wine glasses are small.

FILIA RHENI II ★★★
THIS SMART-LOOKING RIVERSHIP DELIVERS DECENT FOOD AND A GOOD QUALITY CRUISE.

Operator	Saga Travel
Built	2000
Length (m)	110.0
Number of decks (excluding sun deck)	3
Passenger beds	150
Sit outside (real) balcony	No
French (open-air) balcony	No
Approximate cabin size (sq m)	14.0
Lift (elevator)	No
Rivers sailed	Danube

BERLITZ'S RATINGS		
	Possible	Achieved
Hardware	100	55
Accommodation	100	54
Cuisine	100	63
Service	100	62
Miscellaneous	100	64
OVERALL SCORE 298 points out of 500		

Filia Rheni II is nicely appointed and has a large lounge featuring Scandinavian decor and panoramic windows. The cabins are small and lacking in storage space, but they are practical and comfortable. The bathrooms are also compact. The food is creative, with oodles of variety and taste, and it's well presented, with tablecloths and crisp napkins, for dinner. This is a well-organised Saga Travel product.

FRANCE ★★★
THIS UNPRETENTIOUS RIVERSHIP PROVIDES A STANDARD, DECENT-VALUE RIVER CRUISE.

Operator	CroisiEurope
Built	2001
Length (m)	110.0
Number of decks (excluding sun deck)	2
Passenger beds	160
Sit outside (real) balcony	No
French (open-air) balcony	No
Approximate cabin size (sq m)	12.0
Lift (elevator)	No
Rivers sailed	Seine

BERLITZ'S RATINGS		
	Possible	Achieved
Hardware	100	56
Accommodation	100	56
Cuisine	100	57
Service	100	56
Miscellaneous	100	57
OVERALL SCORE 282 points out of 500		

Many people choose a river cruise simply for the itinerary and destination experiences. If you fall into this category, then *France*, with its high-density and very small cabins (with inferior sound insulation and a lack of storage space), tiny bathrooms and limited storage space may be suitable. The general decor is, however, quite bland. The restaurant is pleasant enough, cramped and serves average food and wines, of limited variety, although it has a decent selection of cheese. Choose it for the itinerary and rather French ambience.

FREDERIC CHOPIN ★★★

A SMALL BUT SMART-LOOKING RIVERSHIP THAT IS ADEQUATE FOR A NO-FRILLS CRUISE.

Operator ....Nicko Cruises
Built 2002
Length (m) 83.0
Number of decks (excluding sun deck)...................... 2
Passenger beds.. 79
Sit outside (real) balcony.......................................No
French (open-air) balcony ....No
Approximate cabin size (sq m) 9.0–13.0
Lift (elevator)...No
Rivers sailed....................................Elbe, Havel, Oder

BERLITZ'S RATINGS		
	Possible	Achieved
Hardware	100	55
Accommodation	100	55
Cuisine	100	56
Service	100	56
Miscellaneous	100	58
OVERALL SCORE 280 points out of 500		

Frederic Chopin has small, rather cramped interiors, and the facilities are limited. The cabins are dimensionally challenged, although they do have mini-fridges (Upper Deck cabins have floor-to-ceiling slide-open windows; lower deck cabins have fixed windows); and most have either a double bed or two lower beds. The bathrooms are really tiny. The cuisine is reasonably decent, as are the wines. Gratuities, drinks and tours cost extra.

GÉRARD SCHMITTER ★★★+

THIS SMART-LOOKING RIVERSHIP HAS GOOD FEATURES AND A DECIDEDLY FRENCH AMBIENCE.

Operator ....CroisiEurope
Built 2012
Length (m) 110.0
Number of decks (excluding sun deck).................... 3
Passenger beds..176
Sit outside (real) balcony.......................................No
French (open-air) balcony ....Yes
Approximate cabin size (sq m) 12.0
Lift (elevator)...No
Rivers sailed...........................Rhine, Main, Danube

BERLITZ'S RATINGS		
	Possible	Achieved
Hardware	100	73
Accommodation	100	67
Cuisine	100	60
Service	100	65
Miscellaneous	100	65
OVERALL SCORE 330 points out of 500		

This modern rivership has chic, rather quaint decor with nice artworks throughout. The cabins are fairly plain but practical, with twin beds that convert to a double bed, and French balconies with floor-to-ceiling slide-open doors. Downsides include the lack of storage space. Bathrooms have outdated curtained showers. There's decent, rich cuisine (especially the cheese selection), but the wines are young. Note that organized excursions, drinks and gratuities cost extra.

GIL EANES ★★★+

DELIVERS AN ADEQUATE CRUISE EXPERIENCE, BUT THERE'S REALLY NO FINESSE.

Operator .... CroisiEurope
Built 2015
Length (m) 80.0
Number of decks (excluding sun deck)...................2
Passenger beds..132
Sit outside (real) balcony ....No
French (open-air) balcony ....Yes
Approximate cabin size (sq m) 14.0
Lift (elevator)...Yes
Rivers sailed... Douro

BERLITZ'S RATINGS	Possible	Achieved
Hardware	100	74
Accommodation	100	68
Cuisine	100	62
Service	100	65
Miscellaneous	100	67
OVERALL SCORE 336 points out of 500		

This rivership cruises exclusively on the Douro. The interior decor is uncluttered and unfussy, but there are many obstructive pillars in public areas, including in the lounge where they impede sightlines. Two aft 'suites' have a balcony; other cabins have windows; all have river-facing beds. Bathrooms are small and tight, but have glazed shower enclosures. The restaurant has assigned tables, but the chairs don't have armrests. The cuisine is decent enough, but uninspiring, with set menus for lunch and little choice for dinner. Gratuities, drinks and tours cost extra.

GRACE ★★★★

THIS WOULD BE A VERY GOOD CHOICE FOR A SPACIOUS AND STYLISH RIVER CRUISE.

Operator ....Tauck
Built 2016
Length (m) 135.0
Number of decks (excluding sun deck)...................3
Passenger beds..130
Sit outside (real) balcony ....No
French (open-air) balcony ....Yes
Approximate cabin size (sq m) 14.0–28.0
Lift (elevator)...Yes
Rivers sailed..Rhine

BERLITZ'S RATINGS	Possible	Achieved
Hardware	100	80
Accommodation	100	78
Cuisine	100	70
Service	100	70
Miscellaneous	100	77
OVERALL SCORE 375 points out of 500		

This rivership's lounge is really comfortable, with fine furnishings, comfortable seating and no bling. The cabins are nicely appointed (most have floor-to-ceiling doors that open to a French balcony) and very comfortable, with good storage space, high-quality bed linen and good lighting and soundproofing. The bathrooms have good-sized glazed shower enclosures, and large washbasins. The pleasant one-seating restaurant is comfortable and provides decent menu choice, but the cuisine lacks flair and creativity. An aft venue (Arthur's) is an alternative bistro-style venue for lighter fare.

HORIZON ★+

THIS VINTAGE RIVERSHIP IS BEST CONSIDERED FOR CHEAP AND CHEERFUL CRUISING.

Operator ....Various tour operators
Built 1956
Length (m) 79.9
Number of decks (excluding sun deck)...................2
Passenger beds..98
Sit outside (real) balcony.......................................No
French (open-air) balcony ....No
Approximate cabin size (sq m) 9.5
Lift (elevator)...No
Rivers sailed...................................... Rhine, Moselle

BERLITZ'S RATINGS		
	Possible	Achieved
Hardware	100	27
Accommodation	100	28
Cuisine	100	30
Service	100	30
Miscellaneous	100	30
OVERALL SCORE 145 points out of 500		

Although this vessel is really old, having been converted and rebuilt, its interior decor is actually quite warm and inviting – rather like an intimate low-ceilinged English pub. The twin-bedded cabins are dimensionally challenged (one bed converts into a sofa to provide more daytime space), and there's little storage space for clothing, but at least the windows can be opened. Both the lighting and soundproofing are poor. The bathrooms have a shower, washbasin and toilet. The single seating restaurant is compact, but has pleasant decor, but the food choices are limited and basic due to the tiny galley and storage space.

INFANTE DON HENRIQUE ★★★

EXPECT A COMFORTABLE, STANDARD CRUISE ON THIS SMALL DOURO RIVERSHIP.

Operator .... CroisiEurope
Built 2003
Length (m) 75.0
Number of decks (excluding sun deck)...................2
Passenger beds..142
Sit outside (real) balcony.......................................No
French (open-air) balcony ....No
Approximate cabin size (sq m) 12.5
Lift (elevator)..Yes
Rivers sailed... Douro

BERLITZ'S RATINGS		
	Possible	Achieved
Hardware	100	55
Accommodation	100	55
Cuisine	100	57
Service	100	58
Miscellaneous	100	60
OVERALL SCORE 285 points out of 500		

This rivership has a compact, nicely decorated lounge and restaurant, but otherwise, it's small and the facilities are limited. Most cabins have large windows and two short beds (some can be converted to make a double, while some are fixed); the reading lights and soundproofing are both poor, and the bathrooms are very small. Although limited, the cuisine includes several Portuguese and some international dishes, but the wine glasses are small.

INSPIRE ★★★★
THIS SMART RIVERSHIP WILL PROVIDE YOU WITH A HIGH-QUALITY CRUISE EXPERIENCE.

Operator	Tauck
Built	2014
Length (m)	135.0
Number of decks (excluding sun deck)	3
Passenger beds	142
Sit outside (real) balcony	No
French (open-air) balcony	Yes
Approximate cabin size (sq m)	14.0–28.0
Lift (elevator)	Yes
Rivers sailed	Rhine

BERLITZ'S RATINGS		
	Possible	Achieved
Hardware	100	77
Accommodation	100	77
Cuisine	100	70
Service	100	70
Miscellaneous	100	74
OVERALL SCORE 368 points out of 500		

Inspire is a fine vessel, with warm, restrained interior decor and a very pleasant ambience. The cabins and bathrooms are nicely appointed and most have French balconies with floor-to-ceiling slide-open doors; they are practically designed and have good closet and drawer space. All bathrooms have glazed shower enclosures. Small 'spa' facilities include a sauna, steam room, and fitness room. The comfortable, open-seating restaurant has attractive decor; an aft venue (Arthur's) is an alternative for light fare.

JANE AUSTEN ★★★★
BLING IS ABSENT IN THIS VERY COMFORTABLE ENGLISH-STYLE RIVERSHIP.

Operator	Riviera Travel
Built	2014
Length (m)	135.0
Number of decks (excluding sun deck)	3
Passenger beds	140
Sit outside (real) balcony	No
French (open-air) balcony	Yes
Approximate cabin size (sq m)	15.0–22.5
Lift (elevator)	Yes
Rivers sailed	Rhine, Main, Danube

BERLITZ'S RATINGS		
	Possible	Achieved
Hardware	100	76
Accommodation	100	75
Cuisine	100	70
Service	100	70
Miscellaneous	100	73
OVERALL SCORE 364 points out of 500		

This delightful vessel has restrained interior decor and furniture, and a spacious, but traditional two-deck-high lobby. The cabins have one-piece ceilings, warm wood accents and high-quality furniture. They are comfortable (although the 'suites' are not large at all), have decent storage space, and twin beds that convert to doubles. Tiled bathrooms have decent-sized glazed shower enclosures and lighting. Pleasant restaurant, but the cuisine is underwhelming, breakfasts are repetitious, and wine glasses are small.

JOHANNES BRAHMS ★★★
THIS IS A SHALLOW DRAUGHT VESSEL FOR LOW-BUDGET RIVER CRUISES.

Operator	Various tour operators
Built	1998
Length (m)	81.9
Number of decks (excluding sun deck)	2
Passenger beds	80
Sit outside (real) balcony	No
French (open-air) balcony	No
Approximate cabin size (sq m)	11.0
Lift (elevator)	No
Rivers sailed	Oder

BERLITZ'S RATINGS		
	Possible	Achieved
Hardware	100	50
Accommodation	100	48
Cuisine	100	52
Service	100	53
Miscellaneous	100	55
OVERALL SCORE 258 points out of 500		

Johannes Brahms is a modestly comfortable vessel, but with limited facilities due to its small size. The interior decor is dated, but comfortable. The small, cramped cabins have windows (no balconies) and short beds, but they are fairly practical, although there is little storage space for clothing items. The cabin lighting is limited and soundproofing is poor. The bathrooms, too, are dimensionally challenged. There's a pleasant dining room, but uninspiring food and limited choice. One for the destinations or tight budgets.

JOY ★★★★
THIS WOULD BE A GOOD CHOICE FOR A STYLISH, FIRST-RATE, WELL ORGANISED CRUISE.

Operator	Tauck
Built	2016
Length (m)	135.0
Number of decks (excluding sun deck)	3
Passenger beds	142
Sit outside (real) balcony	No
French (open-air) balcony	Yes
Approximate cabin size (sq m)	14.0–28.0
Lift (elevator)	Yes
Rivers sailed	Danube

BERLITZ'S RATINGS		
	Possible	Achieved
Hardware	100	81
Accommodation	100	79
Cuisine	100	75
Service	100	75
Miscellaneous	100	77
OVERALL SCORE 387 points out of 500		

The main lounge of this smart-looking rivership has decor that is both warm and restrained, with no bling. User-friendly cabins are well designed, practical, have good storage space and closets, decoration, lighting and soundproofing. The bathrooms are very comfortable and have glazed shower enclosures and space for personal toiletry items. The restaurant has comfortable seating and refined decor, with food that is good, but lacks wow factor. An aft venue (Arthur's) is an alternative for light fare.

KATHARINA VON BORA ★★★

THIS SMALL, SMART-LOOKING RIVERSHIP IS ADEQUATE FOR A BASIC CRUISE.

Operator ....Nicko Cruises
Built 2000
Length (m) 83.0
Number of decks (excluding sun deck)..................... 2
Passenger beds... 80
Sit outside (real) balcony ....No
French (open-air) balcony ....No
Approximate cabin size (sq m) 12.0–13.0
Lift (elevator)...No
Rivers sailed........................ Various European rivers

BERLITZ'S RATINGS		
	Possible	Achieved
Hardware	100	52
Accommodation	100	55
Cuisine	100	55
Service	100	55
Miscellaneous	100	57
OVERALL SCORE 274 points out of 500		

Katharina von Bora, with its red hull, has small and quite cramped interior spaces, and facilities are limited, but the interior decor is quite pleasant, with ample wood accents. The cabins are adequate although dimensionally challenged with tiny bathrooms; most have either double beds or two lower beds, as well as a mini-fridge. The galley is tiny, so the cuisine is pretty basic, as are the wines, but the restaurant itself is both attractive and comfortable.

KOENIGSTEIN ★★+

THIS SMALL, STANDARD-QUALITY RIVERSHIP IS OUTDATED BUT FULL OF CHARACTER.

Operator .... Konigstein River Cruises
Built 1992
Length (m) 68.0
Number of decks (excluding sun deck)..................... 2
Passenger beds... 60
Sit outside (real) balcony ....No
French (open-air) balcony ....No
Approximate cabin size (sq m) 11.0
Lift (elevator)...No
Rivers sailed................... Elbe, Havel, Moldau, Vltava

BERLITZ'S RATINGS		
	Possible	Achieved
Hardware	100	40
Accommodation	100	40
Cuisine	100	43
Service	100	43
Miscellaneous	100	44
OVERALL SCORE 210 points out of 500		

Koenigstein's interior decor is rather dark, but there are some interesting artwork and the vessel is surprisingly cosy. The cabins have slim, short beds, and the bathrooms are very small; storage space is very tight, lighting for reading is awful, and so is the soundproofing. The restaurant is pleasant, but the seating is rather cramped. The galley is small, so the variety of food is really limited. It might be adequate for a no-frills experience and some decent itineraries, but that's about all.

L'EUROPE ★★★

THIS MODEST VESSEL OFFERS A DECENT CRUISE AND INCLUDES A LITTLE FRENCH CHIC.

Operator	CroisiEurope
Built	2006
Length (m)	110.0
Number of decks (excluding sun deck)	3
Passenger beds	178
Sit outside (real) balcony	No
French (open-air) balcony	No
Approximate cabin size (sq m)	12.0
Lift (elevator)	No
Rivers sailed	Rhine, Main, Danube

BERLITZ'S RATINGS	Possible	Achieved
Hardware	100	60
Accommodation	100	54
Cuisine	100	55
Service	100	54
Miscellaneous	100	56
OVERALL SCORE 279 points out of 500		

This interior decor is quite warm and the lounge itself is pleasant. The cabins are practical but extremely small, and storage space is tight; the reading lights are extremely poor, as is the soundproofing. The bathrooms are extremely tight and utilitarian, but at least L'Occitane toiletries are provided. The restaurant is pleasant enough, but the meals are nothing special, although the cheese selection is good. Choose it for the destination over the rivership itself.

LA BELLE DE CADIX ★★★

THIS HIGH-DENSITY RIVERSHIP PROVIDES A DECENT BUT HECTIC CRUISE EXPERIENCE.

Operator	CroisiEurope
Built	2005
Length (m)	110.0
Number of decks (excluding sun deck)	3
Passenger beds	176
Sit outside (real) balcony	No
French (open-air) balcony	No
Approximate cabin size (sq m)	9.0-12.0
Lift (elevator)	No
Rivers sailed	Guadalquiver

BERLITZ'S RATINGS	Possible	Achieved
Hardware	100	60
Accommodation	100	55
Cuisine	100	57
Service	100	55
Miscellaneous	100	60
OVERALL SCORE 287 points out of 500		

Modern, with warm interior decor, this rivership has very small cabins, some with double beds, and some have twins that convert to a double (but the bedside reading lights are poor). The bathrooms are also dinky. There are too few crew members. On the plus side, there's a compact but pleasantly decorated restaurant. The French cuisine is average, but the selection of cheese is good. Gratuities, drinks and tours cost extra.

LA BOHEME ★★★
THIS OLDER RIVERSHIP DELIVERS A STANDARD-QUALITY CRUISE EXPERIENCE.

Operator .... CroisiEurope
Built 1995
Length (m) 110.0
Number of decks (excluding sun deck) 2
Passenger beds 164
Sit outside (real) balcony .... No
French (open-air) balcony .... No
Approximate cabin size (sq m) 12.0
Lift (elevator) .... No
Rivers sailed .... Rhine, Main, Danube

BERLITZ'S RATINGS		
	Possible	Achieved
Hardware	100	52
Accommodation	100	51
Cuisine	100	57
Service	100	55
Miscellaneous	100	57
OVERALL SCORE 272 points out of 500		

La Boheme's cabins (none with French open-air balcony) have either a double bed or a two-bed configuration or even a third bed. The bathrooms are functional, but very small, and there's little storage space for personal toiletries. Go because of its relaxed French ambience, unfussy food (but a decent cheese selection) and light wines, and for the itinerary. Note that excursions cost extra. Gratuities, drinks and tours cost extra.

LADY ANNE ★★
THIS TIRED GRANNY OF A RIVERSHIP IS ADEQUATE FOR BUDGET, NO-FRILLS CRUISING.

Operator .... Feenstra Rhine Line
Built 1963
Length (m) 70.0
Number of decks (excluding sun deck) 2
Passenger beds 106
Sit outside (real) balcony .... No
French (open-air) balcony .... No
Approximate cabin size (sq m) 6.0
Lift (elevator) .... No
Rivers sailed .... Rhine

BERLITZ'S RATINGS		
	Possible	Achieved
Hardware	100	31
Accommodation	100	31
Cuisine	100	46
Service	100	41
Miscellaneous	100	40
OVERALL SCORE 189 points out of 500		

Everything about the *Lady Anne* is really pretty basic, but it somehow manages to have some character. The crew is amiable, and the ambience is intimate. The cabins have either fixed beds or one bed and a folding sofa bed or one upper/lower berth; the lighting for reading is poor, however, and the bathrooms really are tiny (some cabins have only a washbasin). It's best described as a vintage water taxi with food that passengers view as between barely adequate and decent, although there is little choice or variety. Go for the itinerary, the friendliness and the low price.

LAFAYETTE ★★★+

THIS SMALL VESSEL PROVIDES THE BASICS FOR A MODERATELY COMFORTABLE CRUISE.

Operator .... CroisiEurope
Built 2014
Length (m) 90.0
Number of decks (excluding sun deck) 2
Passenger beds 84
Sit outside (real) balcony .... No
French (open-air) balcony .... No
Approximate cabin size (sq m) 16.0
Lift (elevator) .... No
Rivers sailed .... Rhine, Main, Danube

BERLITZ'S RATINGS		
	Possible	Achieved
Hardware	100	72
Accommodation	100	66
Cuisine	100	64
Service	100	62
Miscellaneous	100	66
OVERALL SCORE 330 points out of 500		

The public areas have clean, contemporary, unfussy interior decor. The cabins are dimensionally challenged, but many have floor-to-ceiling windows; there's little storage space, and soundproofing could be improved. White modular bathrooms are crisp and basic, but functional. There is assigned seating in the restaurant, but the chairs lack armrests. The cuisine exudes value consciousness, but is acceptable if you don't have high expectations. Gratuities, drinks and tours cost extra.

LEONARDO DA VINCI ★★★

THIS FRENCH-STYLE RIVERSHIP DELIVERS A GOOD-VALUE, COMFORTABLE CRUISE.

Operator .... CroisiEurope
Built 2003
Length (m) 105.0
Number of decks (excluding sun deck) 2
Passenger beds 144
Sit outside (real) balcony .... No
French (open-air) balcony .... No
Approximate cabin size (sq m) 10.0–12.0
Lift (elevator) .... No
Rivers sailed .... Rhine, Main, Danube

BERLITZ'S RATINGS		
	Possible	Achieved
Hardware	100	57
Accommodation	100	54
Cuisine	100	57
Service	100	55
Miscellaneous	100	56
OVERALL SCORE 279 points out of 500		

If you like straightforward French food and wine and are happy with a comfortable but small (no balcony) cabin, slim beds and tiny bathroom with limited storage space, then *Leonardo da Vinci* may be suitable for you. Choose it for its laid-back French ambience, itinerary and destinations. The seating in the restaurant is tight. The food is decent enough, but there's no passion, and the presentation is just so-so. Note that excursions and drinks are at extra cost.

LEONORA ★★★+

THIS COMFORTABLE VESSEL WILL PROVIDE YOU WITH A DECENT ALL-ROUND CRUISE.

Operator	Various tour operators
Built	2008
Length (m)	110.0
Number of decks (excluding sun deck)	3
Passenger beds	138
Sit outside (real) balcony	Yes
French (open-air) balcony	No
Approximate cabin size (sq m)	16.0–24.0
Lift (elevator)	Yes
Rivers sailed	Rhine, Main, Danube

BERLITZ'S RATINGS

	Possible	Achieved
Hardware	100	65
Accommodation	100	60
Cuisine	100	60
Service	100	60
Miscellaneous	100	67

OVERALL SCORE 312 points out of 500

This nicely outfitted and quite comfortable vessel features warm woods that are characteristic of the restful interior decor. The cabins are of a generous size and well appointed. Many have French (open-air) balconies and good storage space. The bathrooms are attractive and have decent-sized shower enclosures. The restaurant, however, is rather cramped and noisy; the cuisine is not unadventurous, but menus are rather overstated and the food overall is underwhelming.

LOIRE PRINCESSE ★★★+

THIS CUSTOM-BUILT VESSEL IS DESIGNED SPECIFICALLY FOR THE SHALLOW RIVER LOIRE.

Operator	CroisiEurope
Built	2015
Length (m)	90.0
Number of decks (excluding sun deck)	2
Passenger beds	96
Sit outside (real) balcony	Yes
French (open-air) balcony	No
Approximate cabin size (sq m)	15.0
Lift (elevator)	No
Rivers sailed	Loire

BERLITZ'S RATINGS

	Possible	Achieved
Hardware	100	74
Accommodation	100	68
Cuisine	100	65
Service	100	63
Miscellaneous	100	71

OVERALL SCORE 341 points out of 500

This rivership has electrically driven mid-ship side paddlewheels (a fine reinvention) help in the shallow water. The lounge has clean, minimalist decor (with 'fireplace') and cosy seating. Cabins are really small, but include a hidden ceiling-mount television and personal safe. Short-length beds face the river (some are inseparable, but most are twins or doubles); some have sit-out balconies. Small tiled bathrooms have glazed shower enclosures and under-washbasin storage cupboards. The cuisine is value-conscious and lacking in choice. Gratuities, drinks and tours cost extra.

LORD BYRON ★★★★

A HIGH-QUALITY CONTEMPORARY RIVERSHIP FOR A FIRST-CLASS CRUISE EXPERIENCE.

Operator ....Riviera Travel
Built 2012
Length (m) 110.0
Number of decks (excluding sun deck).................... 3
Passenger beds...140
Sit outside (real) balcony.....................................No
French (open-air) balcony ....Yes
Approximate cabin size (sq m) 14.0–22.0
Lift (elevator)...No
Rivers sailed.............................. Rhine, Main, Danube

BERLITZ'S RATINGS		
	Possible	Achieved
Hardware	100	73
Accommodation	100	74
Cuisine	100	71
Service	100	74
Miscellaneous	100	74
OVERALL SCORE 366 points out of 500		

The interiors of the stylish *Lord Byron* are all about high-quality fittings and furnishings, such as hardwood panelling and plush carpeting. The atrium lobby features Edwardian-era decor and is delightful. The well-appointed, practical cabins have ample storage space, and the bathrooms, with fully glazed shower enclosures, are a pleasure to use. In addition, the cuisine is of a decent (although not high) quality, and quite varied. What you'll experience is a good overall cruise in really comfortable surroundings.

MAXIMA 1 ★★★+

THIS MODERN RIVERSHIP PROVIDES DECENT CREATURE COMFORTS.

Operator ....Nicko Cruises
Built 2003
Length (m) 126.7
Number of decks (excluding sun deck).................... 3
Passenger beds...136
Sit outside (real) balcony.....................................No
French (open-air) balcony ....Yes
Approximate cabin size (sq m) 16.0
Lift (elevator)...No
Rivers sailed.............................. Rhine, Main, Danube

BERLITZ'S RATINGS		
	Possible	Achieved
Hardware	100	62
Accommodation	100	63
Cuisine	100	56
Service	100	57
Miscellaneous	100	64
OVERALL SCORE 302 points out of 500		

The vessel has fairly good facilities, although the interior decor lacks any hint of warmth. The lounge is pleasant, but quite cramped. The cabins – many of which have French (open-air) balconies – have double beds or twin singles, mini-fridges and personal safes. While the bathrooms are small, they are quite practical. The restaurant is reasonably comfortable, but seating is cramped. The cuisine, however, is underwhelming, and breakfast buffets are repetitive.

MICHAELANGELO ★★★

CHOOSE THIS FRENCH RIVERSHIP FOR A STANDARD BUT CONSISTENT EXPERIENCE.

Operator	CroisiEurope
Built	2000
Length (m)	110.0
Number of decks (excluding sun deck)	2
Passenger beds	158
Sit outside (real) balcony	No
French (open-air) balcony	No
Approximate cabin size (sq m)	10.0–12.0
Lift (elevator)	No
Rivers sailed	Venetian Lagoon

BERLITZ'S RATINGS		
	Possible	Achieved
Hardware	100	56
Accommodation	100	51
Cuisine	100	58
Service	100	56
Miscellaneous	100	59
OVERALL SCORE 280 points out of 500		

Michaelangelo's interior decor is plain and uninspiring. The cabins are practical, although diminutive (the beds are small and short), and insulation is poor. Bathrooms have basic amenities but there's little shelf space for toiletries. The low-budget cuisine is just so-so, and there is little variety. Choose it for its mainly French ambience and for the itinerary and because it's Venice. Gratuities, drinks and tours cost extra.

MIGUEL TORGA ★★★+

THIS DOURO-SPECIFIC RIVERSHIP INCLUDES SOME FRENCH STYLE TOUCHES.

Operator	CroisiEurope
Built	2017
Length (m)	80.0
Number of decks (excluding sun deck)	2
Passenger beds	132
Sit outside (real) balcony	No
French (open-air) balcony	Yes
Approximate cabin size (sq m)	12.0–19.0
Lift (elevator)	No
Rivers sailed	Douro

BERLITZ'S RATINGS		
	Possible	Achieved
Hardware	100	74
Accommodation	100	65
Cuisine	100	66
Service	100	70
Miscellaneous	100	70
OVERALL SCORE 345 points out of 500		

This small vessel has a pleasant lounge with good-quality furnishings. The cabins have river-facing beds, but there's very little storage space, and the bathrooms have very small shower enclosures. A dip pool is located on the open deck. The dining room is quite attractive and caters to all passengers in one seating, although several thick support pillars disturb the sightlines, and the food is basically Portuguese, plus some French (comfort food) favorites. The breakfast buffets are somewhat repetitive, but the sweet pastries are good. Note that gratuities, drinks and tours cost extra.

MISTRAL ★★★

THIS IS A RATHER DATED RIVERSHIP THAT HAS A MODICUM OF FRENCH CHIC.

Operator ....CroisiEurope
Built 1999
Length (m) 110.0
Number of decks (excluding sun deck)................... 2
Passenger beds..158
Sit outside (real) balcony ....No
French (open-air) balcony ....No
Approximate cabin size (sq m) 12.0
Lift (elevator)..No
Rivers sailed...Rhone, Saone

BERLITZ'S RATINGS		
	Possible	Achieved
Hardware	100	51
Accommodation	100	48
Cuisine	100	58
Service	100	55
Miscellaneous	100	60
OVERALL SCORE 272 points out of 500		

This older vessel has a comfortable albeit dated lounge, but the interior decor lacks any sense of character. The cabins are basically practical, although diminutive (the beds are small and short and the lighting is poor), and sound insulation is poor. The food includes some French favourites, and, although not great, at least the cheese selection is good. Drinks, excursions and gratuities are at extra cost. Choose it for its mainly French ambience and for the itinerary.

MODIGLIANI ★★★

A CONSISTENT, STANDARD-QUALITY VENETIAN LAGOON CRUISE WITH FRENCH FOOD.

Operator ....CroisiEurope
Built 2001
Length (m) 110.0
Number of decks (excluding sun deck)................... 2
Passenger beds..160
Sit outside (real) balcony ....No
French (open-air) balcony ....No
Approximate cabin size (sq m) 12.0
Lift (elevator)..No
Rivers sailed............................. Rhine, Main, Danube

BERLITZ'S RATINGS		
	Possible	Achieved
Hardware	100	56
Accommodation	100	50
Cuisine	100	60
Service	100	55
Miscellaneous	100	60
OVERALL SCORE 281 points out of 500		

This rivership offers basic comforts and unpretentious interior decor that lacks any hint of character. The (no-balcony) cabins have rather short beds and poor lighting and soundproofing, and small bathrooms that are low on storage space. It does, however, provide decent but unfussy French (rather than Italian) food and wine, although the breakfasts are repetitive. Choose it mainly for its friendly ambience, itinerary and destinations. Note that excursions cost extra.

MONA LISA ★★★

THIS RIVERSHIP HAS SMALL, PLAIN CABINS, BUT CHIC FRENCH AMBIENCE AND FOOD.

Operator	CroisiEurope
Built	2000
Length (m)	82.5
Number of decks (excluding sun deck)	2
Passenger beds	100
Sit outside (real) balcony	No
French (open-air) balcony	No
Approximate cabin size (sq m)	12.0
Lift (elevator)	No
Rivers sailed	Rhine, Main, Danube

BERLITZ'S RATINGS		
	Possible	Achieved
Hardware	100	57
Accommodation	100	52
Cuisine	100	58
Service	100	56
Miscellaneous	100	58
OVERALL SCORE 281 points out of 500		

The lounge is pleasant, but the seating needs updating, and there's not enough of it. If you like unpretentious French food and wine and are happy with a very small (no-balcony) cabin that lacks any hint of character (it has poor lighting), with very slim beds and tiny bathroom with limited storage space, then *Mona Lisa* may be suitable. It's best to consider it mainly for its French ambience, itinerary and destinations. Note that excursions, drinks and gratuities are at extra cost.

MONARCH BARONESS ★★★+

THIS SPACIOUS, STYLISH RIVERSHIP HAS ALL YOU NEED FOR A GOOD CRUISE EXPERIENCE.

Operator	Gate 1 Travel
Built	2007
Length (m)	110.0
Number of decks (excluding sun deck)	3
Passenger beds	146
Sit outside (real) balcony	No
French (open-air) balcony	Yes
Approximate cabin size (sq m)	15.5–23.5
Lift (elevator)	Yes
Rivers sailed	Rhine, Main, Danube

BERLITZ'S RATINGS		
	Possible	Achieved
Hardware	100	69
Accommodation	100	75
Cuisine	100	63
Service	100	65
Miscellaneous	100	71
OVERALL SCORE 343 points out of 500		

This rivership (formerly *AmaLegro*) is nicely appointed to suit North American tastes, and has warm interior decor. Many cabins have French (open-air) balconies accessed by floor-to-ceiling sliding glass doors. They have reasonably good soundproofing, and good storage space, and are very comfortable. The bathrooms are large and have glazed shower enclosures. Note that the stairway to the lower deck cabins has very small steps. The restaurant is pleasantly attired. However, while the cuisine is decent, it lacks flair, finesse and variety.

MONARCH EMPRESS ★★★★

THIS SMART RIVERSHIP DELIVERS A HIGH-VALUE WELL-ORGANIZED CRUISE EXPERIENCE.

Operator .... Gate 1 Travel
Built 2016
Length (m) 110.0
Number of decks (excluding sun deck) 3
Passenger beds 144
Sit outside (real) balcony .... No
French (open-air) balcony .... Yes
Approximate cabin size (sq m) 13.0–19.5
Lift (elevator) .... No
Rivers sailed .... Rhine, Main, Danube

BERLITZ'S RATINGS		
	Possible	Achieved
Hardware	100	74
Accommodation	100	74
Cuisine	100	68
Service	100	68
Miscellaneous	100	73
OVERALL SCORE 357 points out of 500		

Designed specifically to suit North American tastes, the interior decor is clean and contemporary. The lounge is pleasant, but some chairs are low and uncomfortable. There's also a quiet aft lounge with minimal decor, while the ultra-white reception area is really attractive. The cabins, most of which have French (open-air) balconies and floor-to-ceiling sliding glass doors, are really quite comfortable, as are the bathrooms, although the glazed shower enclosure is very small. The restaurant is comfortable and while the cuisine is decent enough, it is tailored to a price and lacks flair and finesse.

MONARCH QUEEN ★★★+

THIS WOULD BE A DECENT CHOICE FOR A GOOD RIVER CRUISE EXPERIENCE.

Operator .... Gate 1 Travel
Built 2006
Length (m) 110.0
Number of decks (excluding sun deck) 3
Passenger beds 144
Sit outside (real) balcony .... No
French (open-air) balcony .... Yes
Approximate cabin size (sq m) 15.5–23.5
Lift (elevator) .... No
Rivers sailed .... Rhine, Main, Danube

BERLITZ'S RATINGS		
	Possible	Achieved
Hardware	100	68
Accommodation	100	74
Cuisine	100	63
Service	100	65
Miscellaneous	100	71
OVERALL SCORE 341 points out of 500		

This rivership (formerly *AmaDagio*) is nicely appointed and has tasteful interior decor to suit North American tastes. The lounge is very comfortable. The cabins, most of which have French (open-air) balconies and floor-to-ceiling sliding glass doors, have reasonably good soundproofing, good storage space and are very comfortable. The bathrooms are generously sized, with glazed shower enclosures. Note that the stairway to the lower deck cabins has very small steps. The restaurant is pleasantly attired, while the cuisine is decent, but lacks flair and finesse.

MONET ★★★

THIS COMFORTABLE, BUT NOW DATED, RIVERSHIP HAS A MODICUM OF FRENCH FLAIR.

Operator .... CroisiEurope
Built 1999
Length (m) 110.0
Number of decks (excluding sun deck).................... 2
Passenger beds...160
Sit outside (real) balcony ....No
French (open-air) balcony ....No
Approximate cabin size (sq m) 12.0
Lift (elevator)..No
Rivers sailed............................. Rhine, Main, Danube

BERLITZ'S RATINGS		
	Possible	Achieved
Hardware	100	53
Accommodation	100	48
Cuisine	100	56
Service	100	56
Miscellaneous	100	56
OVERALL SCORE 269 points out of 500		

Monet has dated interior decor, small (no-balcony) cabins with slim beds (most can't be moved together) and tiny bathrooms with little space for toiletries. But if you like an unpretentious, casual ambience, moderately decent food and wine (limited choice), it may be suitable for you. Travel for the itinerary. The restaurant is aft; the colours are nice, but several pillars obstruct the flow. Note that tours, drinks and gratuities are at extra cost.

MY STORY ★★

GO ONLY FOR THE ITINERARY AND DESTINATIONS, NOT FOR THE COMFORT OR THE FOOD.

Operator .... Select Voyages
Built 1971
Length (m) 105.0
Number of decks (excluding sun deck).................... 2
Passenger beds...200
Sit outside (real) balcony ....No
French (open-air) balcony ....No
Approximate cabin size (sq m) 9.0–12.0
Lift (elevator)..Yes
Rivers sailed............................. Rhine, Main, Danube

BERLITZ'S RATINGS		
	Possible	Achieved
Hardware	100	34
Accommodation	100	34
Cuisine	100	34
Service	100	37
Miscellaneous	100	40
OVERALL SCORE 179 points out of 500		

This reasonably smart-looking but dated rivership has had many name changes, but is nonetheless fairly comfortable. Often used for bicycle-tour participants, it has decent public areas, but the cabins are really dimensionally challenged (as are the bathrooms) and have no balconies, little storage space and poor soundproofing and lighting. The low-quality rustic food exudes value consciousness, but may be acceptable if you don't have high expectations (the galley is very small).

NESTROY ★★★+

THIS MODERN-LOOKING RIVERSHIP DELIVERS A STANDARD, INEXPENSIVE CRUISE EXPERIENCE.

Operator ....Various tour operators
Built 2007
Length (m) 124.8
Number of decks (excluding sun deck)....................3
Passenger beds...226
Sit outside (real) balcony.......................................No
French (open-air) balcony ....Yes
Approximate cabin size (sq m) 12.0–17.0
Lift (elevator)..Yes
Rivers sailed..Danube

BERLITZ'S RATINGS		
	Possible	Achieved
Hardware	100	67
Accommodation	100	62
Cuisine	100	58
Service	100	57
Miscellaneous	100	62
OVERALL SCORE 306 points out of 500		

Nestroy is quite a smart-looking vessel, with an attractive, comfortable lounge, which can become crowded. While suites have queen-sized beds, all other cabins are extremely compact, with slim pull-down beds that can't be pushed together (these act as sofas during the day), and little storage space. The bathrooms are functional, just. The restaurant is old-world, but the chairs do have armrests. The cuisine is uninspiring and average, with little variety, and breakfasts are repetitious.

NICKOVISION NYR

EXPECT GOOD VALUE FOR MONEY FROM THIS MODERN, HIGH-DENSITY RIVERSHIP.

Operator ....Nicko Cruises
Built 2018
Length (m) 135.0
Number of decks (excluding sun deck)....................3
Passenger beds...220
Sit outside (real) balcony.......................................No
French (open-air) balcony ....Yes
Approximate cabin size (sq m) 14.0
Lift (elevator)..Yes
Rivers sailed............................ Rhine, Main, Danube

BERLITZ'S RATINGS		
	Possible	Achieved
Hardware	100	NYR
Accommodation	100	NYR
Cuisine	100	NYR
Service	100	NYR
Miscellaneous	100	NYR
OVERALL SCORE NYR points out of 500		

This new, exceptionally smart-looking vessel has a contemporary, light and airy interior, without any bling. Facilities include a small pool and sauna, but this is an ultra-high-density vessel so it *will* feel crowded in public areas. The cabins are small by today's standards, but the layout is quite practical, and all but lower deck cabins have a floor-to-ceiling sliding glass door and open-air balcony. The restaurant has attractive nautical colours, but the chairs lack armrests. This would be a good choice for a lively new rivership at a very reasonable price.

NORMANDIE ★★★+

CHOOSE THIS DATED FRENCH RIVERSHIP FOR A FAIRLY BASIC CRUISE EXPERIENCE.

Operator ....Various tour operators
Built 1989
Length (m) 91.2
Number of decks (excluding sun deck)...................2
Passenger beds..100
Sit outside (real) balcony...No
French (open-air) balcony ....No
Approximate cabin size (sq m) 7.0–11.0
Lift (elevator)...No
Rivers sailed..Danube

BERLITZ'S RATINGS		
	Possible	Achieved
Hardware	100	46
Accommodation	100	45
Cuisine	100	48
Service	100	50
Miscellaneous	100	52
OVERALL SCORE 241 points out of 500		

If you like unpretentious value-conscious French cuisine and wine and can accept an extremely small, plain cabin, with slim beds that turn into sofas by day, and a tiny bathroom with almost no space for toiletries then *Normandie* may be a possibility. The restaurant is pleasant enough, but pretty cramped, and the chairs lack armrests. Go mainly for its comfortable ambience and for the itinerary and destinations. Note that excursions cost extra, as do drinks and gratuities.

OLYMPIA ★★★+

THIS SMALL, OLDER-STYLE, NICELY FURNISHED RIVERSHIP HAS A WARM ATMOSPHERE.

Operator .... Newmarket Holidays
Built 1984
Length (m) 88.5
Number of decks (excluding sun deck)...................2
Passenger beds..102
Sit outside (real) balcony...No
French (open-air) balcony ....No
Approximate cabin size (sq m) 10.0–12.0
Lift (elevator)...No
Rivers sailed...Rhine

BERLITZ'S RATINGS		
	Possible	Achieved
Hardware	100	43
Accommodation	100	43
Cuisine	100	48
Service	100	50
Miscellaneous	100	51
OVERALL SCORE 235 points out of 500		

Olympia is a fairly comfortable, older and therefore basic rivership that is for low-budget cruising. The cabins are compact and basic, although they do have large windows and reasonable storage space for clothing items. Most have two (fixed, rather short) slim beds, but three have double beds. The bathrooms are tiny but functional. Downsides include dim lighting in the accommodation hallway. Average-quality (uninspiring) food is tailored to British passengers' tastes but lacks flair, and the breakfasts are repetitious.

OSCAR WILDE ★★★★

CHOOSE THIS MODERN RIVERSHIP FOR A HIGH-QUALITY RIVER CRUISE EXPERIENCE.

Operator .... Riviera Travel
Built 2017
Length (m) 135.0
Number of decks (excluding sun deck) 3
Passenger beds 169
Sit outside (real) balcony .... No
French (open-air) balcony .... Yes
Approximate cabin size (sq m) 17.0–25.5
Lift (elevator) .... Yes
Rivers sailed .... Rhine, Moselle

BERLITZ'S RATINGS		
	Possible	Achieved
Hardware	100	77
Accommodation	100	77
Cuisine	100	68
Service	100	73
Miscellaneous	100	76
OVERALL SCORE 371 points out of 500		

This rivership exudes British style combined with both contemporary and traditional features. It has high-quality furnishings, extremely comfortable interior decor and no bling. The two-deck-high reception lobby is spacious. The cabins are well designed and quite practical; bathrooms have decent-sized glazed shower enclosures, and the soundproofing is quite good. The one-seating restaurant is quite comfortable. The cuisine is of really high-quality and specifically tailored to British tastes (breakfasts are somewhat repetitive).

POSEIDON ★★

A SMALL, OLDER RIVERSHIP WITH DATED FACILITIES FOR CHEAP AND CHEERFUL CRUISING.

Operator .... Various tour operators
Built 1980
Length (m) 78.0
Number of decks (excluding sun deck) 2
Passenger beds 96
Sit outside (real) balcony .... No
French (open-air) balcony .... No
Approximate cabin size (sq m) 8.0–10.0
Lift (elevator) .... No
Rivers sailed .... Various European rivers

BERLITZ'S RATINGS		
	Possible	Achieved
Hardware	100	39
Accommodation	100	36
Cuisine	100	37
Service	100	40
Miscellaneous	100	41
OVERALL SCORE 193 points out of 500		

The delightful bird's-eye-maple interior, old-world style and comfortable chairs help make this a rivership with character, despite its rather tired, well-worn look. The small cabins have one pull-down bed (creating space when pushed up in the daytime) and one sofa bed, and the lighting is poor (forget reading in bed). The bathrooms are tiny and cramped. The food from the tiny galley is uninspiring (the wine glasses are small too), so it's best to make the itinerary and low prices your reasons for booking. Overall, it's a basic, no-frills river cruise.

PRIMADONNA ★★★

THIS EXTRA-WIDE RIVERSHIP HAS AMPLE SPACE TO PROVIDE A VERY COMFORTABLE CRUISE.

Operator ....Donau Touristik
Built 1998
Length (m) 113.4
Number of decks (excluding sun deck).....................3
Passenger beds...152
Sit outside (real) balcony ....Yes
French (open-air) balcony ....Yes
Approximate cabin size (sq m) 11.0–16.0
Lift (elevator)...Yes
Rivers sailed...Danube

BERLITZ'S RATINGS		
	Possible	Achieved
Hardware	100	63
Accommodation	100	57
Cuisine	100	58
Service	100	58
Miscellaneous	100	62
OVERALL SCORE 298 points out of 500		

Built on two hulls specifically for operating only on the Danube, *Primadonna* has a spacious two-deck-high interior lobby (highly unusual aboard any rivership), dip pools and a wood sauna. The interior decor is modern, and there's no glitz. Some 40 cabins have small wedge-shaped French (open-air) balconies. Many cabins and bathrooms, though, are small, and storage space is tight. The food is quite varied and of good quality, although the breakfasts are repetitious. Overall, it provides a very comfortable setting for a river cruise experience.

PRINCESS ★★

THIS SMALL, DUMPY-LOOKING RIVERSHIP IS FOR CHEAP, NO-FRILLS RIVER CRUISING.

Operator ....Various tour operators
Built 1980
Length (m) 80.0
Number of decks (excluding sun deck)...................2
Passenger beds...102
Sit outside (real) balcony ....No
French (open-air) balcony ....No
Approximate cabin size (sq m) 10.0
Lift (elevator)...No
Rivers sailed................................. Elbe, Havel, Oder

BERLITZ'S RATINGS		
	Possible	Achieved
Hardware	100	39
Accommodation	100	36
Cuisine	100	40
Service	100	38
Miscellaneous	100	40
OVERALL SCORE 193 points out of 500		

The exterior won't win any contest for handsome looks, but the interior decor is nicely restrained and quite warm. The cabins, however, are very dimensionally challenged and simple, with fold-away beds to create the impression of space during the daytime, and the lighting and soundproofing are both poor. As for the bathrooms – you need to dance with the (outdated) shower curtain. Choose it for the itinerary and for its cheap-and-cheerful, no-frills price, but not for the food, which is utterly basic, because the galley and storage spaces are tiny.

PRINCESSE D'AQUITAINE ★★★

THIS SMART FRENCH RIVERSHIP DELIVERS A STANDARD BUT GOOD-VALUE CRUISE.

Operator	CroisiEurope
Built	2001
Length (m)	110.0
Number of decks (excluding sun deck)	2
Passenger beds	138
Sit outside (real) balcony	No
French (open-air) balcony	No
Approximate cabin size (sq m)	12.0–13.0
Lift (elevator)	No
Rivers sailed	Bordeaux region

BERLITZ'S RATINGS		
	Possible	Achieved
Hardware	100	58
Accommodation	100	57
Cuisine	100	60
Service	100	57
Miscellaneous	100	61
OVERALL SCORE 293 points out of 500		

This attractive-looking rivership has fairly bland interior decor, but if you are happy with rustic French-style cuisine and wine and a comfortable but small (no-balcony) cabin, thin beds (and mattresses) and a small bathroom with little storage space, then this rivership may be suitable. It's best to go for its pleasant ambience, decent itinerary and the destinations. Note that excursions cost extra.

PRINCESSE DE PROVENCE ★★★

THIS IS AN ELEGANTLY DECORATED RIVERSHIP OFFERING DECENT HOSPITALITY.

Operator	Konigstein River Cruises
Built	1992
Length (m)	110.7
Number of decks (excluding sun deck)	2
Passenger beds	148
Sit outside (real) balcony	No
French (open-air) balcony	No
Approximate cabin size (sq m)	11.0
Lift (elevator)	No
Rivers sailed	Rhone, Saone

BERLITZ'S RATINGS		
	Possible	Achieved
Hardware	100	47
Accommodation	100	46
Cuisine	100	51
Service	100	55
Miscellaneous	100	58
OVERALL SCORE 257 points out of 500		

This vessel's lovely, old-world interior decor includes an abundance of rich woods and brass fittings, especially in the Panorama Salon. The cabins are very small and include two fixed beds (one folds into the wall by day) and tiny but functional bathrooms. The restaurant has cramped seating and poor lighting. The food is adequate, but the variety is limited by the tiny galley.

PRINSES CHRISTINA ★★

THIS OLDER RIVERSHIP PROVIDES A NO-FRILLS CRUISE FOR THOSE ON A TIGHT BUDGET.

Operator ....Various tour operators
Built 1969
Length (m) 71.0
Number of decks (excluding sun deck)................... 3
Passenger beds...107
Sit outside (real) balcony ....No
French (open-air) balcony ....No
Approximate cabin size (sq m) 9.0
Lift (elevator)...No
Rivers sailed......................... Various European rivers

BERLITZ'S RATINGS		
	Possible	Achieved
Hardware	100	30
Accommodation	100	31
Cuisine	100	33
Service	100	35
Miscellaneous	100	37
OVERALL SCORE 166 points out of 500		

If you can accept extremely small cabins with slim (fixed) beds, and you don't expect the food to be anything other than basic, *Prinses Christina* may be adequate. The interior decor does, however, have character, and includes nicely polished wood. The lighting in the interior passageways is rather dark (restful), and the ceilings are low. The restaurant is pleasant, but the chairs do not have armrests (there's no room). The food is uninspiring and minimalist, and breakfasts are repetitious. Go for the itinerary/destinations, and not the comfort.

PRINSES JULIANA ★★

THIS OUTDATED, UNHANDSOME RIVERSHIP MAY BE ADEQUATE FOR LOW-COST CRUISES.

Operator ....Various tour operators
Built 1960
Length (m) 95.0
Number of decks (excluding sun deck)................... 1
Passenger beds...138
Sit outside (real) balcony ....No
French (open-air) balcony ....No
Approximate cabin size (sq m) 9.0
Lift (elevator)...No
Rivers sailed... Mosel, Rhine

BERLITZ'S RATINGS		
	Possible	Achieved
Hardware	100	28
Accommodation	100	30
Cuisine	100	32
Service	100	34
Miscellaneous	100	34
OVERALL SCORE 158 points out of 500		

This dated, very high-density vessel has a square front and few crew members. Nice observation lounge with old world-style seating. The ultra-compact cabins have fixed twin beds that fold up during the day for more space. There's almost no storage space, and both the lighting and soundproofing are poor. The bathrooms are tiny and really (caravan) basic. The restaurant (aft of the lounge in the vessel's centre) is moderately attractive, but cramped, and the buffet display is tiny; there's little choice, and breakfasts are simply repetitious.

PRINZESSIN ISABELLA ★★★

THIS WOULD BE A GOOD CHOICE FOR A GENERAL WELL-ROUNDED RIVER CRUISE EXPERIENCE.

Operator	Various tour operators
Built	2002
Length (m)	125.5
Number of decks (excluding sun deck)	3
Passenger beds	172
Sit outside (real) balcony	No
French (open-air) balcony	Yes
Approximate cabin size (sq m)	14.0–21.0
Lift (elevator)	Yes
Rivers sailed	Danube

BERLITZ'S RATINGS		
	Possible	Achieved
Hardware	100	60
Accommodation	100	55
Cuisine	100	61
Service	100	60
Miscellaneous	100	62
OVERALL SCORE 298 points out of 500		

The cabins are fairly spacious and comfortable, with the costliest grades featuring floor-to-ceiling glass doors and French-style open-air balconies and twin beds that can be converted to doubles. Other cabins have large (non-opening) windows, with fold-down beds that act as sofas by day to provide the impression of more space. The bathrooms are small but quite practical, and they have glazed shower enclosures. The restaurant is located aft; the food is reasonably decent, but there is little variety or presentation finesse.

PRINZESSIN KATHARINA ★★+

THIS DELIGHTFUL, GRAND HOTEL-STYLE RIVERSHIP DELIVERS CHARM AND GOOD CUISINE.

Operator	Various tour operators
Built	1991
Length (m)	110.0
Number of decks (excluding sun deck)	2
Passenger beds	152
Sit outside (real) balcony	No
French (open-air) balcony	Yes
Approximate cabin size (sq m)	11.0
Lift (elevator)	No
Rivers sailed	Douro

BERLITZ'S RATINGS		
	Possible	Achieved
Hardware	100	47
Accommodation	100	44
Cuisine	100	48
Service	100	50
Miscellaneous	100	52
OVERALL SCORE 241 points out of 500		

Named after a (now-deceased) Greek princess, this small, older, fairly decent, high-density rivership has a beautiful lounge/bar and glamorous traditional interior decor. 'Upper Deck' cabins have French (open-air) balconies, with one fixed bed and one pull-down 'Pullman' bed (providing more daytime space). 'Main Deck' cabins have non-opening windows and fixed beds in an 'L'-shape. The aft, grand hotel-style dining room is compact; the food is quite decent, but the choice is quite limited (the galley is small), and the self-serve buffets are repetitive.

PRINZESSIN SISI ★★★

A DECENT-LOOKING RIVERSHIP THAT OFFERS CRUISES FOR LOW-BUDGET TRAVELLERS.

Operator ....Various tour operators
Built 2000
Length (m) 111.2
Number of decks (excluding sun deck)....................2
Passenger beds...156
Sit outside (real) balcony ....No
French (open-air) balcony ....No
Approximate cabin size (sq m) 12.0–15.0
Lift (elevator)..Yes
Rivers sailed.............................. Rhine, Main, Danube

BERLITZ'S RATINGS		
	Possible	Achieved
Hardware	100	54
Accommodation	100	56
Cuisine	100	60
Service	100	58
Miscellaneous	100	58
OVERALL SCORE 286 points out of 500		

This high-density vessel has large windows that provide an abundance of light in the lounge and lobby area. The decor is rather bland and lacks any hint of character, but at least there's no bling. The cabins are quite practical, though small, and have little drawer space for clothing items; the lighting and soundproofing could be better. The restaurant is quite attractive and comfortable, while the food is fairly standard fare, and the choice is quite limited (the galley is small).

PROVENCE ★★+

THIS LITTLE BARGE-LIKE VESSEL HAS THE BASICS FOR A MODERATELY COMFORTABLE CRUISE.

Operator .... Grand Circle Cruise Line
Built 2000
Length (m) 89.0
Number of decks (excluding sun deck)....................2
Passenger beds... 46
Sit outside (real) balcony ....Yes
French (open-air) balcony ....Yes
Approximate cabin size (sq m) 19.0–19.5
Lift (elevator)..No
Rivers sailed...Rhone, Saone

BERLITZ'S RATINGS		
	Possible	Achieved
Hardware	100	50
Accommodation	100	47
Cuisine	100	46
Service	100	48
Miscellaneous	100	55
OVERALL SCORE 246 points out of 500		

The interior decor of this French-built vessel is not particularly inspiring, but it does have some character. The cabins (eight of which have little sit-out balconies) are adequate, but sparsely furnished. The lighting and soundproofing are poor, and there is little drawer space. The bathrooms are really cramped, and have really basic showers. The restaurant is quite comfortable, but the cuisine is only marginally above basic, with very limited choice due to the small galley and preparation area. Gratuities, drinks and tours cost extra.

QUEEN ISABEL ★★★+

THIS SMART-LOOKING RIVERSHIP PROVIDES A GOOD DOURO CRUISE EXPERIENCE.

Operator ....Uniworld Grand River Cruises
Built 2013
Length (m) 79.0
Number of decks (excluding sun deck)....................3
Passenger beds...116
Sit outside (real) balcony ....Yes
French (open-air) balcony ....Yes
Approximate cabin size (sq m) 15.0–30.0
Lift (elevator)...Yes
Rivers sailed... Douro

BERLITZ'S RATINGS		
	Possible	Achieved
Hardware	100	70
Accommodation	100	68
Cuisine	100	68
Service	100	66
Miscellaneous	100	72
OVERALL SCORE 344 points out of 500		

Queen Isabel features some beautiful Portuguese furniture and fittings and has a small pool and mini-spa. The cabins, most of which have full or French (open-air) balconies, are nicely appointed and have decent-sized bathrooms with L'Occitane toiletries. The cuisine is good and features many Portuguese specialities, although breakfasts are repetitive. This is a rather nice way to travel on the River Douro.

REGINA RHENI ★★★+

CHOOSE THIS SMART-LOOKING VESSEL FOR A HIGH-QUALITY CRUISE WITH GOOD FOOD.

Operator ....Rijfers River Cruises
Built 2000
Length (m) 110.0
Number of decks (excluding sun deck)....................3
Passenger beds...160
Sit outside (real) balcony ....No
French (open-air) balcony ....No
Approximate cabin size (sq m) 11.0–14.0
Lift (elevator)..No
Rivers sailed........................... Rhine, Main, Danube

BERLITZ'S RATINGS		
	Possible	Achieved
Hardware	100	57
Accommodation	100	56
Cuisine	100	64
Service	100	64
Miscellaneous	100	63
OVERALL SCORE 304 points out of 500		

A nicely appointed rivership, *Regina Rheni* has a large, fairly comfortable lounge with panoramic windows. The interior decor is Scandinavian minimalist in terms of furnishings, but it is, nonetheless very comfortable. Despite being small, the galley turns out a wide variety of food that is really good, with plenty of taste and attractive presentation. The wine glasses are rather small, however. Overall, this is a well-organized cruise.

REMBRANDT VON RIJN ★★★+
THIS OLDER-STYLE RIVERSHIP MAY BE ADEQUATE BASIC, NO-FRILLS CRUISING.

Operator ....Various tour operators
Built 1985
Length (m) 110.0
Number of decks (excluding sun deck)....................2
Passenger beds...106
Sit outside (real) balcony ....No
French (open-air) balcony ....No
Approximate cabin size (sq m) ....N/A
Lift (elevator)..Yes
Rivers sailed............................. Rhine, Main, Danube

BERLITZ'S RATINGS		
	Possible	Achieved
Hardware	100	40
Accommodation	100	41
Cuisine	100	42
Service	100	44
Miscellaneous	100	45
OVERALL SCORE 212 points out of 500		

This rivership is dated, but comfortable, with warm old-style interiors including a delightful lounge accented by lots of polished wood. The cabins are small, with short twin (fold-away) beds, limited storage space, poor reading lighting and poor sound-proofing; the bathrooms are diminutive, too. The food includes a very limited choice, due to the small galley; breakfasts are repetitive. This is cheap and cheerful, so go for the itinerary. Gratuities, drinks and tours cost extra.

RENOIR ★★★
THIS LITTLE VESSEL OFFERS A STANDARD CRUISING EXPERIENCE THAT LACKS PANACHE.

Operator .... CroisiEurope
Built 1999
Length (m) 110.0
Number of decks (excluding sun deck)....................2
Passenger beds...158
Sit outside (real) balcony ....No
French (open-air) balcony ....No
Approximate cabin size (sq m) 12.0
Lift (elevator)..No
Rivers sailed.. Seine

BERLITZ'S RATINGS		
	Possible	Achieved
Hardware	100	48
Accommodation	100	48
Cuisine	100	57
Service	100	56
Miscellaneous	100	60
OVERALL SCORE 269 points out of 500		

The *Renoir* will provide you with a well-organised, middle-of-the road cruise experience, although the cabins are quite small (with a wide choice of bed configurations), as are the bathrooms, plus storage space is limited, the lighting and soundproofing are poor, and there are no balcony cabins. The restaurant is cramped and chairs lack armrests. The cuisine lacks creativity and variety (the galley is very small), although there's the cheese selection is quite good, the breakfasts are repetitious, and the wine glasses are small. Gratuities, drinks and tours cost extra.

REX RHENI ★★+
THIS SMALL, HIGH-DENSITY RIVERSHIP DELIVERS AN AVERAGE BASIC CRUISE EXPERIENCE.

Operator .... Saga Travel
Built 1979
Length (m) 90.5
Number of decks (excluding sun deck).................. 3
Passenger beds...150
Sit outside (real) balcony ....No
French (open-air) balcony ....No
Approximate cabin size (sq m) 11.25
Lift (elevator)..No
Rivers sailed.. Mosel, Rhine

BERLITZ'S RATINGS		
	Possible	Achieved
Hardware	100	43
Accommodation	100	44
Cuisine	100	50
Service	100	45
Miscellaneous	100	52
OVERALL SCORE 234 points out of 500		

Rex Rheni is an older type of rivership with just a small lounge/bar and restaurant, plus an open sundeck, so it feels cramped. Note that the stairways between decks have steep, short steps. The cabins are really small and utilitarian, with bathrooms that have curtained-off showers only, and there's little storage space for toiletry items. The restaurant is a little cramped, but fairly pleasant. The food, however, is uninspiring, and there's little choice.

RHINE MELODY ★★★
THIS SMART LOOKING RIVERSHIP DELIVERS GOOD-VALUE CRUISES OVERALL.

Operator ....Nicko Cruises
Built 2005
Length (m) 133.0
Number of decks (excluding sun deck).................. 3
Passenger beds...198
Sit outside (real) balcony ....No
French (open-air) balcony ....No
Approximate cabin size (sq m) 12.0–15.0
Lift (elevator)..No
Rivers sailed...Rhine

BERLITZ'S RATINGS		
	Possible	Achieved
Hardware	100	60
Accommodation	100	58
Cuisine	100	56
Service	100	56
Miscellaneous	100	57
OVERALL SCORE 287 points out of 500		

This well-designed but high-density rivership has good natural light in its interiors. The lounge is pleasant enough, although slim pillars obstruct sightlines from many seats. The cabins are nicely appointed, and upper deck cabin have French (open-air) balconies, while all others have windows. Some cabins have double beds, and others are twins that convert to sofas during the day. The restaurant is pleasant enough, but it is quite cramped, and the food is quite decent, but unmemorable and the choices are limited.

RHINE PRINCESS ★★

THIS OLDER RIVERSHIP IS ONLY ADEQUATE FOR THOSE ON A REALLY TIGHT BUDGET.

Operator ....Kras Reizen
Built 1960
Length (m) 83.2
Number of decks (excluding sun deck)....................3
Passenger beds..120
Sit outside (real) balcony ....No
French (open-air) balcony ....No
Approximate cabin size (sq m) 15.0
Lift (elevator)...Yes
Rivers sailed... Mosel, Rhine

BERLITZ'S RATINGS		
	Possible	Achieved
Hardware	100	30
Accommodation	100	32
Cuisine	100	34
Service	100	35
Miscellaneous	100	34
OVERALL SCORE 165 points out of 500		

This is an old, much-rebuilt and unhandsome vessel, although the interior decor is actually quite pleasant. The cabins, however, are small and dimensionally challenged, with slim, short (fold-up) beds (to pro-vide the illusion of more daytime space); the lighting and soundproofing are poor, and the bathrooms are really basic and tight on space. The galley is tiny and can only turn out the most basic meals, so expect only the basics. Best advice: it might be better to look for something else, unless you really can't stretch your budget.

RHINEPRINZESSIN ★★★

THIS REBUILT, HIGH-DENSITY VESSEL IS FOR INEXPENSIVE NO-FRILLS CRUISING.

Operator ....Phoenix Cruises
Built 1999
Length (m) 110.0
Number of decks (excluding sun deck)....................3
Passenger beds..140
Sit outside (real) balcony ....No
French (open-air) balcony ....Yes
Approximate cabin size (sq m) 15.0
Lift (elevator)...Yes
Rivers sailed..Rhine

BERLITZ'S RATINGS		
	Possible	Achieved
Hardware	100	52
Accommodation	100	50
Cuisine	100	60
Service	100	58
Miscellaneous	100	60
OVERALL SCORE 280 points out of 500		

The low-ceilinged lounge has several pillars, and is cramped. The cabins are small, there is mini-mal storage space, the beds are very slim (many fold down from the wall), and the soundproofing is poor. The bathrooms are really dimensionally chal-lenged. This is low-price, low-quality cruising. The restaurant is moderately comfortable, and the low-cost food is surprisingly decent; note that the wine glasses are small.

RIGOLETTO ★★★+
THIS OUTDATED RIVERSHIP PROVIDES A VERY BASIC CRUISE EXPERIENCE.

Operator	SijFa Cruises
Built	1987
Length (m)	105.0
Number of decks (excluding sun deck)	2
Passenger beds	120
Sit outside (real) balcony	No
French (open-air) balcony	No
Approximate cabin size (sq m)	12.0
Lift (elevator)	No
Rivers sailed	Danube

BERLITZ'S RATINGS		
	Possible	Achieved
Hardware	100	43
Accommodation	100	45
Cuisine	100	46
Service	100	48
Miscellaneous	100	51
OVERALL SCORE 233 points out of 500		

Rigoletto is reasonably comfortable and typical of 1980s-built vessels without (open-air) balcony cabins. However, the interior decor is what could almost be called elegant, with lots of wood and brass accenting. The cabins are small with very little storage space. Most cabins have single beds that fold down from opposite walls. The bathrooms (including the shower enclosure) are tiny. The restaurant is pleasant enough, but the galley is small and simply cannot produce much in terms of variety. Breakfasts are repetitious. Consider *Rigoletto* for no-frills river cruising.

RIVER ADAGIO ★★★
A COMFORTABLE RIVERSHIP THAT DELIVERS A STANDARD CRUISE EXPERIENCE.

Operator	Grand Circle Cruise Line
Built	2003
Length (m)	125.0
Number of decks (excluding sun deck)	2
Passenger beds	164
Sit outside (real) balcony	Yes
French (open-air) balcony	Yes
Approximate cabin size (sq m)	12.0–15.0
Lift (elevator)	Yes
Rivers sailed	Rhine, Main, Danube

BERLITZ'S RATINGS		
	Possible	Achieved
Hardware	100	54
Accommodation	100	51
Cuisine	100	51
Service	100	51
Miscellaneous	100	55
OVERALL SCORE 262 points out of 500		

River Adagio is comfortable, with brass fittings featuring heavily in its design scheme, but it's now dated. All the cabins are the same size; some have French (open-air) balconies, but the lighting and soundproofing are poor. The twin beds are fixed, with one converting to a sofa by day to give the impression of space. The bathrooms are pleasant enough, but the toilets are noisy. The restaurant is modestly comfortable. The cuisine, however, is quite unmemorable, and the choice is extremely limited, because the galley is very small.

RIVER ALLEGRO ★★+

CHOOSE THIS RIVERSHIP MOSTLY FOR THE ITINERARY AND DESTINATIONS, NOT THE FOOD.

Operator	Grand Circle Cruise Line
Built	1991
Length (m)	97.5
Number of decks (excluding sun deck)	2
Passenger beds	90
Sit outside (real) balcony	No
French (open-air) balcony	No
Approximate cabin size (sq m)	11.0
Lift (elevator)	No
Rivers sailed	Elbe, Havel, Moldau, Vltava

BERLITZ'S RATINGS		
	Possible	Achieved
Hardware	100	44
Accommodation	100	41
Cuisine	100	50
Service	100	50
Miscellaneous	100	51
OVERALL SCORE 236 points out of 500		

This small, dated vessel navigates Europe's smaller waterways. The interior decor includes lots of brass and dark wood, but the lounge is small and cramped. The cabins have non-opening windows; they are really dimensionally challenged and basic (slim beds convert to daytime seating to provide the illusion of space), lack storage space, have poor soundproofing and lighting, and tiny bathrooms with glazed shower enclosures. The restaurant is compact and has little character. The food is just so-so, and, because the galley is small, the choice is limited.

RIVER ARIA ★★★

THIS RIVERSHIP SHOULD PROVIDE YOU WITH A DECENT CRUISE EXPERIENCE.

Operator	Grand Circle Cruise Line
Built	2001
Length (m)	125.0
Number of decks (excluding sun deck)	3
Passenger beds	164
Sit outside (real) balcony	No
French (open-air) balcony	Yes
Approximate cabin size (sq m)	12.0–15.0
Lift (elevator)	Yes
Rivers sailed	Rhine, Main, Danube

BERLITZ'S RATINGS		
	Possible	Achieved
Hardware	100	52
Accommodation	100	56
Cuisine	100	53
Service	100	56
Miscellaneous	100	57
OVERALL SCORE 274 points out of 500		

River Aria is a fairly comfortable vessel, with brass fittings featuring heavily in its design scheme, which is now rather dated. All the cabins are the same size; some have floor-to-ceiling slide-open open-air balconies, with twin beds that are fixed, with one converting to a sofa by day to give the impression of more space. The bathrooms are pleasant enough, but the toilets are noisy. The restaurant is quite attractive, but the cuisine is unmemorable.

RIVER ART ★★★
THIS SMALL, COMFORTABLE RIVERSHIP IS BEST CHOSEN FOR ITS IN-DEPTH ITINERARIES.

Operator ....Nicko Cruises
Built 2005
Length (m) 109.9
Number of decks (excluding sun deck)....................2
Passenger beds..128
Sit outside (real) balcony ....No
French (open-air) balcony ....Yes
Approximate cabin size (sq m) 13.0–20.0
Lift (elevator)..No
Rivers sailed...Rhine

BERLITZ'S RATINGS		
	Possible	Achieved
Hardware	100	56
Accommodation	100	57
Cuisine	100	56
Service	100	56
Miscellaneous	100	60
OVERALL SCORE 285 points out of 500		

River Art has comfortable, pleasant interior decor without any bling, but the lounge seating is rather cramped. The cabins are all nicely appointed – those on the upper deck cabins have French (open-air) balconies – and are actually quite spacious, as are the bathrooms. Two slim, short beds fold away during the day, and only one cabin has a double bed. The restaurant is quite attractive. The cuisine is, however, quite standard, with no flair and little choice, because the galley is very small. The wine glasses are small too.

RIVER CONCERTO ★★★
THIS OLDER, NOW DATED RIVERSHIP DELIVERS A MODERATE CRUISE EXPERIENCE.

Operator ....Grand Circle Cruise Line
Built 2000
Length (m) 110.0
Number of decks (excluding sun deck)....................3
Passenger beds..143
Sit outside (real) balcony ....No
French (open-air) balcony ....No
Approximate cabin size (sq m) 12.0–15.0
Lift (elevator)..Yes
Rivers sailed............................Rhine, Main, Danube

BERLITZ'S RATINGS		
	Possible	Achieved
Hardware	100	52
Accommodation	100	53
Cuisine	100	54
Service	100	55
Miscellaneous	100	58
OVERALL SCORE 272 points out of 500		

The interior decor is rather dated and lacks character; also, the lounge chairs are not comfortable. Some upper deck cabins have floor-to-ceiling slide-open doors and small sit-outside balcony, and twin beds that convert to doubles. Others have two pull-down (couple-unfriendly) fixed slim beds that convert to daytime sofas to provide more space. The reading lights and sound insulation are poor, and bathroom space is really tight. The restaurant is cramped and serves average food with little choice and poor presentation, but the service is friendly.

RIVER COUNTESS ★★★

CHOOSE THIS RIVERSHIP FOR ITS GOOD-QUALITY FURNISHINGS AND ITINERARY.

Operator ....Uniworld Grand River Cruises
Built 2003
Length (m) 110.0
Number of decks (excluding sun deck) 3
Passenger beds 130
Sit outside (real) balcony ....No
French (open-air) balcony ....No
Approximate cabin size (sq m) 14.0–21.0
Lift (elevator) ....Yes
Rivers sailed ....Venetian Lagoon

BERLITZ'S RATINGS		
	Possible	Achieved
Hardware	100	57
Accommodation	100	56
Cuisine	100	60
Service	100	58
Miscellaneous	100	60
OVERALL SCORE 291 points out of 500		

The *River Countess* is a dated, but nicely appointed, vessel, with interior decor that is quite tasteful, though rather dated. Cabins are small, with limited storage – the 'Rhine Deck' suites and cabins have French (open-air) balconies, while all others have windows only. The bathrooms are also small. The open-seating aft restaurant is quite attractive and comfortable. The cuisine is decent and includes a healthy choice menu. Amenities include a small fitness area.

RIVER DISCOVERY II ★★★+

GOOD FACILITIES AND DECENT FOOD MAKE THIS RIVERSHIP A SOUND CHOICE.

Operator .... Vantage River Cruises
Built 2013
Length (m) 135.0
Number of decks (excluding sun deck) 3
Passenger beds 176
Sit outside (real) balcony ....No
French (open-air) balcony ....Yes
Approximate cabin size (sq m) 11.5–33.0
Lift (elevator) ....Yes
Rivers sailed ....Rhone, Saone

BERLITZ'S RATINGS		
	Possible	Achieved
Hardware	100	73
Accommodation	100	70
Cuisine	100	58
Service	100	60
Miscellaneous	100	64
OVERALL SCORE 325 points out of 500		

This rivership has been designed to suit American tastes, with an interior decor that is quite classy. This contemporary vessel has a good range of cabins, most of which have French balconies with floor-to-ceiling slide-open doors and twin beds that convert to doubles. However, the cabin insulation is poor. The open-seating restaurant is fairly comfortable, if rather tight on space. The cuisine is reasonably good – it includes a healthy choice menu – but it simply lacks flair and presentation finesse. Complimentary bicycles are carried.

RIVER DUCHESS ★★★
THIS IS AN ELEGANT RIVERSHIP WITH ATTRACTIVE FEATURES FOR A DECENT CRUISE.

Operator .... Uniworld Boutique River Cruises
Built 2003
Length (m) 110.0
Number of decks (excluding sun deck).................... 3
Passenger beds..130
Sit outside (real) balcony ....No
French (open-air) balcony ....Yes
Approximate cabin size (sq m) 14.0–21.0
Lift (elevator)...Yes
Rivers sailed............................. Rhine, Main, Danube

BERLITZ'S RATINGS		
	Possible	Achieved
Hardware	100	57
Accommodation	100	58
Cuisine	100	60
Service	100	58
Miscellaneous	100	60
OVERALL SCORE 293 points out of 500		

The *River Duchess* is a nicely appointed vessel. However, the cabins are small, with limited storage– the 'Rhine Deck' suites and cabins have French balconies with floor-to-ceiling slide-open doors, while all others have windows only. The bathrooms are also small. The open-seating aft restaurant is comfortable. The cuisine is reasonably good and includes a healthy choice menu, although lacking in finesse and unmemorable. Amenities include a fitness area.

RIVER EMPRESS ★★★
THIS COMPACT RIVERSHIP IS A GOOD CHOICE FOR A WELL-ROUNDED CRUISE.

Operator .... Uniworld Boutique River Cruises
Built 2002
Length (m) 110.0
Number of decks (excluding sun deck).................... 3
Passenger beds..130
Sit outside (real) balcony ....No
French (open-air) balcony ....Yes
Approximate cabin size (sq m) 14.0–21.0
Lift (elevator)...Yes
Rivers sailed............................. Rhine, Main, Danube

BERLITZ'S RATINGS		
	Possible	Achieved
Hardware	100	56
Accommodation	100	58
Cuisine	100	60
Service	100	58
Miscellaneous	100	60
OVERALL SCORE 292 points out of 500		

River Empress is a nicely appointed vessel. Cabins are small, with limited storage – the 'Rhine Deck' suites and cabins have French (open-air) balconies, while all others have windows only. The bathrooms are also small. The open-seating aft restaurant is comfortable. The cuisine is reasonably good and includes a healthy choice menu, although it is overall lacking in finesse. Amenities include a fitness area.

RIVER HARMONY ★★★

THIS SMALL RIVERSHIP IS DATED BUT HAS DECENT PRACTICAL FEATURES.

Operator .... Grand Circle Cruise Line
Built 1999
Length (m) 110.0
Number of decks (excluding sun deck) 3
Passenger beds 143
Sit outside (real) balcony ....No
French (open-air) balcony ....Yes
Approximate cabin size (sq m) 12.0–15.0
Lift (elevator) ....Yes
Rivers sailed .... Rhine, Main, Danube

BERLITZ'S RATINGS		
	Possible	Achieved
Hardware	100	53
Accommodation	100	50
Cuisine	100	52
Service	100	53
Miscellaneous	100	57
OVERALL SCORE 265 points out of 500		

River Harmony is now rather dated, with plain interior decor. Some 15 upper deck cabins have floor-to-ceiling slide-open doors and a small sit outside balcony, with twin beds that convert to doubles. Other cabins have two pull-down (couple-unfriendly) fixed slim beds that convert to daytime sofas to provide more space. Reading lights and sound insulation are both inferior, and bathroom space is very tight, but there is a glazed shower enclosure, which is a plus. The restaurant is cramped and serves average food with little choice and poor presentation, but the service is friendly.

RIVER MELODY ★★★

THIS DATED RIVERSHIP STILL PROVIDES A DECENT BACKDROP FOR A RIVER CRUISE.

Operator .... Grand Circle Cruise Line
Built 1999
Length (m) 110.0
Number of decks (excluding sun deck) 3
Passenger beds 143
Sit outside (real) balcony ....No
French (open-air) balcony ....Yes
Approximate cabin size (sq m) 12.0–15.0
Lift (elevator) ....Yes
Rivers sailed .... Rhine, Main, Danube

BERLITZ'S RATINGS		
	Possible	Achieved
Hardware	100	52
Accommodation	100	50
Cuisine	100	52
Service	100	54
Miscellaneous	100	56
OVERALL SCORE 264 points out of 500		

This small rivership with plain decor is comfortable, if dated. Some 15 upper deck cabins have floor-to-ceiling slide-open doors and a small sit-outside balcony, with twin beds that convert to doubles. Other cabins have two pull-down (couple-unfriendly) fixed slim beds that convert to daytime sofas to provide more space. Reading lights and sound insulation are both inferior, and bathroom space is very tight, but there is a glazed shower enclosure. The restaurant is cramped and serves average food with little choice and poor presentation, but the service is friendly. The wine glasses are small, too.

RIVER PRINCESS ★★★+

THIS MODERN RIVERSHIP MIGHT BE A GOOD CHOICE FOR A WELL-ROUNDED CRUISE.

Operator .... Uniworld Boutique River Cruises
Built 2001
Length (m) 110.0
Number of decks (excluding sun deck).................. 3
Passenger beds..128
Sit outside (real) balcony ....No
French (open-air) balcony ....Yes
Approximate cabin size (sq m) 14.0–21.0
Lift (elevator)..Yes
Rivers sailed.............................. Rhine, Main, Danube

BERLITZ'S RATINGS		
	Possible	Achieved
Hardware	100	61
Accommodation	100	57
Cuisine	100	60
Service	100	64
Miscellaneous	100	62
OVERALL SCORE 304 points out of 500		

River Princess is a nicely appointed vessel. Cabins are small, with limited storage – the 'Rhine Deck' suites and cabins have French (open-air) balconies, while all others have windows only. The bathrooms are also small, but practical and well appointed. The open-seating aft restaurant is comfortable. The cuisine is reasonably good and includes a healthy choice menu, although it lacks finesse and presentation. Amenities include a fitness area.

RIVER QUEEN ★★★

A RETRO-LOOK BOUTIQUE RIVERSHIP WITH TASTEFUL FEATURES AND BAGS OF STYLE.

Operator .... Uniworld Boutique River Cruises
Built 1999
Length (m) 110.0
Number of decks (excluding sun deck).................. 3
Passenger beds..128
Sit outside (real) balcony ....No
French (open-air) balcony ....No
Approximate cabin size (sq m) 13.0–20.0
Lift (elevator)..Yes
Rivers sailed.............................. Rhine, Main, Danube

BERLITZ'S RATINGS		
	Possible	Achieved
Hardware	100	55
Accommodation	100	55
Cuisine	100	60
Service	100	60
Miscellaneous	100	61
OVERALL SCORE 291 points out of 500		

The interior of the *River Queen* is in the elegant Art Deco style. The spacious cabins are well equipped and comfortable, but their windows don't open. The open-seating restaurant is delightful, although cramped. The disappointing food, however, lacks variety (breakfast buffets are repetitive). Amenities include a wellness area with sauna, a launderette and complimentary bicycles.

RIVER RHAPSODY ★★★

ALTHOUGH DATED, THIS RIVERSHIP HAS DECENT BASIC FEATURES AND IS GOOD VALUE.

Operator .... Grand Circle Cruise Line
Built 1999
Length (m) 110.0
Number of decks (excluding sun deck)................... 3
Passenger beds...143
Sit outside (real) balcony ....No
French (open-air) balcony .... Yes
Approximate cabin size (sq m) 12.0–15.0
Lift (elevator)...Yes
Rivers sailed.............................. Rhine, Main, Danube

BERLITZ'S RATINGS		
	Possible	Achieved
Hardware	100	51
Accommodation	100	51
Cuisine	100	52
Service	100	55
Miscellaneous	100	57
OVERALL SCORE 266 points out of 500		

This small rivership with plain decor is comfortable, if dated, although the lounge is quite attractive. Some upper deck cabins have floor-to-ceiling slide-open doors and a small sit-outside balcony, plus twin beds that convert to doubles. Other cabins have two pull-down fixed slim beds that convert to sofas to provide more daytime space. Reading lights and sound insulation are poor, and bathroom space is very tight, but there is a glazed shower enclosure. The food is just average, with little choice or flair, and there are few green vegetables, and the wine glasses are small.

RIVER ROYALE ★★★

FOR BORDEAUX CRUISES, THIS RIVERSHIP SHOULD PROVE TO BE A SOUND CHOICE.

Operator .... Uniworld Boutique River Cruises
Built 2006
Length (m) 110.0
Number of decks (excluding sun deck)................... 3
Passenger beds...128
Sit outside (real) balcony ....No
French (open-air) balcony .... Yes
Approximate cabin size (sq m) 13.0–20.0
Lift (elevator)...Yes
Rivers sailed.................................... Bordeaux region

BERLITZ'S RATINGS		
	Possible	Achieved
Hardware	100	58
Accommodation	100	56
Cuisine	100	60
Service	100	60
Miscellaneous	100	60
OVERALL SCORE 294 points out of 500		

Designed to suit American tastes, with an interior decor that includes many French touches, this is a classy rivership. The cabins, though not large, are practical, although there is limited drawer space for clothing. Most cabins have French open-air balconies with floor-to-ceiling slide-open doors, and twin beds that convert to doubles. However, the cabin insulation is not good. The open-seating restaurant is fairly comfortable, if rather tight on space, but the chairs lack armrests. The cuisine is reasonably sound, but it lacks flair and presentation finesse. The wine glasses are of a good size.

RIVER SPLENDOR ★★★+

WITH FINE FACILITIES AND FEATURES, THIS CONTEMPORARY RIVERSHIP IS A GOOD CHOICE.

Operator .... Vantage River Cruises
Built 2013
Length (m) 135.0
Number of decks (excluding sun deck)................... 3
Passenger beds...176
Sit outside (real) balcony.......................................No
French (open-air) balcony ....Yes
Approximate cabin size (sq m) 14.0–28.0
Lift (elevator)..Yes
Rivers sailed............................. Rhine, Main, Danube

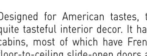

BERLITZ'S RATINGS		
	Possible	Achieved
Hardware	100	73
Accommodation	100	71
Cuisine	100	60
Service	100	58
Miscellaneous	100	64
OVERALL SCORE 326 points out of 500		

Designed for American tastes, this rivership has quite tasteful interior decor. It has a good range of cabins, most of which have French balconies with floor-to-ceiling slide-open doors and twin beds that convert to doubles. The bathrooms are decent, but there's little space for toiletries. The open-seating restaurant is comfortable, but noisy. The cuisine is reasonably good – it includes a healthy choice menu – but it lacks flair, and is adapted for American tastes. Complimentary bicycles are carried.

RIVER VENTURE ★★★+

THIS CONTEMPORARY RIVERSHIP HAS GOOD FACILITIES AND SHOULD BE A DECENT CHOICE.

Operator .... Vantage River Cruises
Built 2013
Length (m) 110.0
Number of decks (excluding sun deck)................... 3
Passenger beds...136
Sit outside (real) balcony.......................................No
French (open-air) balcony ....Yes
Approximate cabin size (sq m) 11.5–23.0
Lift (elevator)..No
Rivers sailed...Seine

BERLITZ'S RATINGS		
	Possible	Achieved
Hardware	100	73
Accommodation	100	73
Cuisine	100	60
Service	100	58
Miscellaneous	100	64
OVERALL SCORE 328 points out of 500		

Designed for American tastes, this vessel has a good range of cabins, most of which have French (open-air) balconies and twin beds that convert to doubles; the lighting and soundproofing are good. Bathrooms are quite spacious and have glazed showers. Owner's suite occupants get more perks, and space. The open-seating restaurant is quite comfortable (tables are for four or six). The cuisine is reasonably decent – it includes a healthy choice menu, but it is uninspiring and lacks flair. Complimentary bicycles are carried on board. Some tours are included, but gratuities are not.

RIVER VOYAGER ★★★★

SMART RIVERSHIP PROVIDES A HIGH-QUALITY, GOOD-VALUE RIVER CRUISE EXPERIENCE.

Operator .... Vantage River Cruises
Built 2016
Length (m) 135.0
Number of decks (excluding sun deck).................... 3
Passenger beds....................................176
Sit outside (real) balcony.......................................No
French (open-air) balcony ....Yes
Approximate cabin size (sq m) 11.5–33.0
Lift (elevator)..Yes
Rivers sailed.............................. Rhine, Main, Danube

BERLITZ'S RATINGS		
	Possible	Achieved
Hardware	100	76
Accommodation	100	75
Cuisine	100	62
Service	100	68
Miscellaneous	100	72
OVERALL SCORE 353 points out of 500		

With its decidedly American jazz-themed decor, this rivership has an appealingly cool feel. The cabins are well designed (the lighting is excellent) and the info-tainment system is good, although storage space is limited. Bathrooms have large glazed shower enclosures, space for toiletries and anti-mist bathroom mirrors. Owner's suite occupants get more perks, and space. Facilities include a small fitness room. The restaurant has comfortable seating, but the cuisine, while good, lacks presentation and flair. Some tours are included, but gratuities are not. Bicycles are provided.

ROBERT BURNS NYR

THIS CONTEMPORARY RIVERSHIP IS DESIGNED JUST FOR BRITISH TASTES.

Operator .... Riviera Travel
Built 2018
Length (m) 135.0
Number of decks (excluding sun deck).................... 3
Passenger beds....................................167
Sit outside (real) balcony.......................................No
French (open-air) balcony ....Yes
Approximate cabin size (sq m) 17.0–25.5
Lift (elevator)..Yes
Rivers sailed.............................. Rhine, Main, Danube

BERLITZ'S RATINGS		
	Possible	Achieved
Hardware	100	NYR
Accommodation	100	NYR
Cuisine	100	NYR
Service	100	NYR
Miscellaneous	100	NYR
OVERALL SCORE NYR points out of 500		

NEW RIVERSHIP

This is a well-designed rivership with high-quality furnishings, restrained but warm interior decor, a spacious and elegant two-deck-high lobby, and overall inviting atmosphere. The cabins are well designed and practical, with decent storage space. The bathrooms have decent-sized glazed shower enclosures. The one-seating restaurant is attractive and quite comfortable. The cuisine is so-so and tailored to unadventurous British tastes (breakfasts are repetitious, and the wine glasses are small).

ROTTERDAM ★★

THIS SMALL, OLDER RIVERSHIP IS PASSABLE FOR A NO-FRILLS CRUISE EXPERIENCE.

Operator ....Shearings Holidays
Built 1969
Length (m) 75.7
Number of decks (excluding sun deck)....................2
Passenger beds...120
Sit outside (real) balcony ....No
French (open-air) balcony ....No
Approximate cabin size (sq m) 11.0–14.0
Lift (elevator)..No
Rivers sailed............................ Rhine, Main, Danube

BERLITZ'S RATINGS		
	Possible	Achieved
Hardware	100	32
Accommodation	100	31
Cuisine	100	34
Service	100	36
Miscellaneous	100	40
OVERALL SCORE 173 points out of 500		

Rotterdam is a much-rebuilt high-density vessel, with limited facilities – basically just a lounge/bar, whose interior decor is warm and welcoming. The cabins are bland, but cosy and adequate, although lighting and soundproofing are both poor. The cabins have windows only, some of which can be opened. There are three solo-occupancy cabins. Unusually (and confusingly), there are cabins between the galley (kitchen) and the restaurant. The restaurant is quite attractive, but the chairs lack armrests, and the wine glasses are very small.

ROUSSE ★★

THIS HIGH-DENSITY VESSEL IS ONLY FOR A BASIC LOW-BUDGET, NO-FRILLS CRUISE.

Operator ....Various tour operators
Built 1984
Length (m) 113.5
Number of decks (excluding sun deck)....................2
Passenger beds...190
Sit outside (real) balcony ....No
French (open-air) balcony ....No
Approximate cabin size (sq m) 9.0–17.0
Lift (elevator)..Yes
Rivers sailed..Danube

BERLITZ'S RATINGS		
	Possible	Achieved
Hardware	100	40
Accommodation	100	40
Cuisine	100	40
Service	100	40
Miscellaneous	100	40
OVERALL SCORE 200 points out of 500		

This old-style vessel has fairly decent interior decor, but the observation lounge is really cramped when full. The cabins are utterly compact. Most have two slim beds, one of which folds away during the day to provide more space; some cabins have a third berth. Cabin lighting is minimal, as is the soundproofing, and the bathroom is really basic with little space for toiletry items. The restaurant is quite pleasant, although the chairs are uncomfortable. The food is passable – just – and the wine glasses are small

ROUSSE PRESTIGE ★★★
FOR A LOW-BUDGET BUT GOOD-VALUE CRUISE ABOARD A COMPACT RIVERSHIP.

Operator	Various tour operators
Built	2004
Length (m)	110.0
Number of decks (excluding sun deck)	3
Passenger beds	156
Sit outside (real) balcony	No
French (open-air) balcony	No
Approximate cabin size (sq m)	11.0–17.0
Lift (elevator)	No
Rivers sailed	Danube

BERLITZ'S RATINGS

	Possible	Achieved
Hardware	100	61
Accommodation	100	60
Cuisine	100	55
Service	100	55
Miscellaneous	100	60

OVERALL SCORE 291 points out of 500

Rousse Prestige is well proportioned, although it is a little dated, and the decor is totally bland. Cabins on the lowest deck have windows, but all others feature French (open-air) balconies with floor-to-ceiling slide-open doors. All are rather compact and have twin beds that become day sofas. The bathrooms are very small, but practical facilities include a small wellness area and laundry service. The restaurant is aft and has comfortable seating, although the chairs don't have armrests. The food is just so-so (carbohydrate-rich) and lacks variety; breakfasts are repetitive, and there is much use of tinned fruit.

ROYAL CROWN ★★★
THIS SMALL, GRAND HOTEL-STYLE RIVERSHIP EVOKES THE PAST WITH ABUNDANT FLAIR.

Operator	Various tour operators
Built	1994
Length (m)	110.0
Number of decks (excluding sun deck)	2
Passenger beds	90
Sit outside (real) balcony	No
French (open-air) balcony	No
Approximate cabin size (sq m)	19.0
Lift (elevator)	No
Rivers sailed	Rhine, Main, Danube

BERLITZ'S RATINGS

	Possible	Achieved
Hardware	100	61
Accommodation	100	57
Cuisine	100	50
Service	100	58
Miscellaneous	100	60

OVERALL SCORE 286 points out of 500

This vessel's lovely grand-hotel-style interior decor recreates the 1930s, with its wood-rich, elegant public rooms, chic marble finishes and high-quality soft furnishings. The cabins are of a decent size, although perhaps a little small by today's standards, but they are ornately decorated. Six suites have king-size beds, while all others have either queen-sized beds or twin beds. The restaurant has attractive decor, comfortable seating and, despite the small galley, meals that are quite pleasant, but lack variety and presentation finesse.

SALVINIA ★+

THIS VINTAGE, HIGH-DENSITY RIVERSHIP IS ADEQUATE FOR A BASIC, NO-FRILLS CRUISE.

Operator ....Various tour operators
Built 1939
Length (m) 91.5
Number of decks (excluding sun deck)................... 2
Passenger beds..130
Sit outside (real) balcony ....No
French (open-air) balcony ....No
Approximate cabin size (sq m) 9.0
Lift (elevator)..Yes
Rivers sailed...Rhine

BERLITZ'S RATINGS		
	Possible	Achieved
Hardware	100	20
Accommodation	100	20
Cuisine	100	28
Service	100	30
Miscellaneous	100	30
OVERALL SCORE 128 points out of 500		

Salvinia is an old (much-rebuilt) lady, but she still has plenty of character and decor to match. The dimensionally challenged cabins have poor lighting and soundproofing, and non-opening windows. Almost all cabins have one fixed and one slim fold-down bed (to provide more daytime space). The bathrooms have curtained-off showers and little space. The cuisine in the cramped restaurant is barely passable. This is cheap and cheerful no-frills river cruising, so it's best to consider it only for the destinations.

SANS SOUCI ★★★

SPECIALLY DESIGNED FOR ELBE CRUISES, THIS RIVERSHIP IS A DECENT CHOICE.

Operator ....Various tour operators
Built 2000
Length (m) 82.0
Number of decks (excluding sun deck)................... 2
Passenger beds.. 81
Sit outside (real) balcony ....No
French (open-air) balcony ....Yes
Approximate cabin size (sq m) 11.0
Lift (elevator)..Yes
Rivers sailed.......................... Elbe-Saal, Havel, Oder

BERLITZ'S RATINGS		
	Possible	Achieved
Hardware	100	55
Accommodation	100	56
Cuisine	100	57
Service	100	55
Miscellaneous	100	58
OVERALL SCORE 281 points out of 500		

Sans Souci is a smart, very compact vessel, with a deep blue hull. It has cabins that are quite well designed, and all of them have windows – some of which slide open for fresh air. However, the slim fold-away beds are short, and the bathrooms are really small and basic. The restaurant is very charming and warm; the food is quite tasty, but the choices are minimal, and the self-serve buffet breakfasts are repetitive. Dinners come with (very young) regional wines.

SAPPHIRE ★★★+

THIS WINNER FROM TAUCK DELIVERS AN EXCELLENT ALL-ROUND UPMARKET CRUISE.

Operator	Tauck
Built	2008
Length (m)	110.0
Number of decks (excluding sun deck)	3
Passenger beds	98
Sit outside (real) balcony	No
French (open-air) balcony	Yes
Approximate cabin size (sq m)	14.0–28.0
Lift (elevator)	Yes
Rivers sailed	Seine

BERLITZ'S RATINGS

	Possible	Achieved
Hardware	100	70
Accommodation	100	68
Cuisine	100	65
Service	100	66
Miscellaneous	100	74
OVERALL SCORE 343 points out of 500		

This well-designed contemporary rivership has a very pleasant lounge and a warm, elegant interior. It has spacious cabins, with mini-fridges; most have French balconies with floor-to-ceiling slide-open doors, and very comfortable beds. Fourteen of the cabins can sleep three people. The bathrooms are well outfitted, with large glazed shower enclosures and L'Occitane toiletries. The open-seating restaurant chairs lack armrests. The cuisine is unpretentious but tasty, and there's ample choice. An alternative, for lighter fare, is The Bistro, located aft.

SAVOR ★★★★

THIS RIVERSHIP HAS FINE STATE-OF-THE-ART FEATURES AND SPACIOUS CABINS.

Operator	Tauck
Built	2014
Length (m)	135.0
Number of decks (excluding sun deck)	3
Passenger beds	142
Sit outside (real) balcony	No
French (open-air) balcony	Yes
Approximate cabin size (sq m)	14.0–27.0
Lift (elevator)	Yes
Rivers sailed	Rhine, Main, Danube

BERLITZ'S RATINGS

	Possible	Achieved
Hardware	100	76
Accommodation	100	76
Cuisine	100	74
Service	100	75
Miscellaneous	100	75
OVERALL SCORE 376 points out of 500		

Savor has decor that is quite elegant, and the lounge seating is very comfortable. The spacious cabins and 22 double-size suites (which offer room service breakfasts) have French balconies with floor-to-ceiling slide-open doors (cabins on the lowest deck have small windows), coffee machine, excellent bed linen and Molton Brown toiletries; the bathrooms have heated floors. Beverages are unlimited. The main restaurant is forward, while an alternative venue (Arthur's), for lighter fare, is located aft.

SAXONIA ★★★

THIS SMALL RIVERSHIP HAS ELEGANT DECOR AND PROVIDES A DECENT CRUISE.

Operator ....Phoenix Cruises
Built 2001
Length (m) 82.0
Number of decks (excluding sun deck)....................2
Passenger beds..87
Sit outside (real) balcony ....No
French (open-air) balcony ....No
Approximate cabin size (sq m) 11.0–12.0
Lift (elevator)...No
Rivers sailed........................... Elbe-Saal, Havel, Oder

BERLITZ'S RATINGS		
	Possible	Achieved
Hardware	100	54
Accommodation	100	54
Cuisine	100	54
Service	100	55
Miscellaneous	100	56
OVERALL SCORE 273 points out of 500		

This older style rivership will provide you with a decent middle-of-the road cruise experience. The lounge is pleasant, but dated, and seating is tight. Although the cabins are quite small, as are the bathrooms (with little storage space), they are quite comfortable (including a mini-fridge) and have fine wood cabinetry. The food variety and choice are both rather limited (because the galley is small), and wines are of the basic variety. Overall, this is no-frills river cruising, so it's best to consider it only for the destinations or the price.

SCENIC AMBER ★★★★

THIS EXCELLENT VESSEL PROVIDES A WELL-PROGRAMMED CRUISE EXPERIENCE.

Operator ....Scenic
Built 2017
Length (m) 135.0
Number of decks (excluding sun deck)....................3
Passenger beds...169
Sit outside (real) balcony ....No
French (open-air) balcony ....Yes
Approximate cabin size (sq m) 19.0–44.0
Lift (elevator)..Yes
Rivers sailed............................. Rhine, Main, Danube

BERLITZ'S RATINGS		
	Possible	Achieved
Hardware	100	76
Accommodation	100	73
Cuisine	100	73
Service	100	74
Miscellaneous	100	76
OVERALL SCORE 372 points out of 500		

This is an elegantly decorated, drinks-inclusive rivership (although 'premium' brand drinks do cost extra). The lounge is very comfortable, and has high-quality seating and colourful soft furnishings. Most cabins have French balconies with floor-to-ceiling slide-open doors, are spacious and there is plenty of storage space and good lighting. The bathrooms are well designed, and have large glazed shower enclosures. The very pleasant restaurant has comfortable seating, and the cuisine is quite good (although breakfasts are repetitious). Bicycles are available for the active.

SCENIC AZURE ★★★★

CHOOSE THIS VERY COMFORTABLE VESSEL FOR A VERY STYLISH DOURO CRUISE.

Operator ....Scenic
Built 2016
Length (m) 80.0
Number of decks (excluding sun deck)................... 3
Passenger beds... 96
Sit outside (real) balcony ....No
French (open-air) balcony ....Yes
Approximate cabin size (sq m) 16.0–39.0
Lift (elevator)..Yes
Rivers sailed... Douro

BERLITZ'S RATINGS		
	Possible	Achieved
Hardware	100	77
Accommodation	100	78
Cuisine	100	78
Service	100	78
Miscellaneous	100	81
OVERALL SCORE 392 points out of 500		

This very smart-looking vessel has tasteful, contemporary interior decor. The cabins are quite spacious for this size of vessel, many of which have French balconies with floor-to-ceiling slide-open doors (but awful metal tables). They are practical and have decent closet and storage space – just watch out for the nail-catching sliding door on the closet. Bathrooms, too, are of a good size, with a glazed shower enclosure. The open-seating restaurant has a good ceiling height, and comfortable seating. The cuisine is very good and features many Portuguese dishes.

SCENIC CRYSTAL ★★★★

THIS RIVERSHIP IS JUST THE TICKET FOR A FINE OVERALL CRUISE EXPERIENCE.

Operator ....Scenic
Built 2012
Length (m) 135.0
Number of decks (excluding sun deck)................... 3
Passenger beds...171
Sit outside (real) balcony ....No
French (open-air) balcony ....Yes
Approximate cabin size (sq m) 19.0–30.0
Lift (elevator)..Yes
Rivers sailed............................. Rhine, Main, Danube

BERLITZ'S RATINGS		
	Possible	Achieved
Hardware	100	77
Accommodation	100	77
Cuisine	100	78
Service	100	76
Miscellaneous	100	80
OVERALL SCORE 388 points out of 500		

Scenic Crystal is a lovely vessel with delightful decor. Most cabins have French balconies with floor-to-ceiling and are spacious, with high-quality linens. The well-designed bathrooms feature L'Occitane toiletries. The restaurant is quite cramped, but offers multiple table configurations. The cuisine is very good. Amenities include good, although small, wellness facilities. An 'all-inclusive' product, but 'premium' drinks cost extra.

SCENIC DIAMOND ★★★★

THIS RIVERSHIP IS A GOOD CHOICE FOR A WELL-PROGRAMMED CRUISE EXPERIENCE.

Operator	Scenic
Built	2009
Length (m)	135.0
Number of decks (excluding sun deck)	3
Passenger beds	155
Sit outside (real) balcony	No
French (open-air) balcony	Yes
Approximate cabin size (sq m)	15.0–47.0
Lift (elevator)	Yes
Rivers sailed	Bordeaux region

BERLITZ'S RATINGS		
	Possible	Achieved
Hardware	100	72
Accommodation	100	76
Cuisine	100	78
Service	100	73
Miscellaneous	100	76
OVERALL SCORE 375 points out of 500		

Scenic Diamond is a good vessel with elegant decor and a small but decent wellness area. Most cabins have French balconies with floor-to-ceiling slide-open doors, are spacious and feature high-quality linens. The well-designed bathrooms feature L'Occitane products. The restaurant is quite cramped but has multiple table configurations. The cuisine is good, but not that good. An 'all-inclusive' product, but 'premium' drinks cost extra.

SCENIC GEM ★★★★+

THIS WOULD BE A GOOD CHOICE FOR A STYLISH, WELL-ORGANIZED RIVER CRUISE.

Operator	Scenic
Built	2014
Length (m)	110.0
Number of decks (excluding sun deck)	3
Passenger beds	128
Sit outside (real) balcony	No
French (open-air) balcony	Yes
Approximate cabin size (sq m)	15.0–42.0
Lift (elevator)	Yes
Rivers sailed	Seine

BERLITZ'S RATINGS		
	Possible	Achieved
Hardware	100	80
Accommodation	100	80
Cuisine	100	82
Service	100	78
Miscellaneous	100	82
OVERALL SCORE 402 points out of 500		

This rivership has all the latest contemporary features, including a very comfortable, fairly spacious lounge with an in-built healthy eats display. The contemporary cabins are practical, well-designed units. Most have convertible beds, large bathrooms, decent storage space, and 'sun' balconies with wood-look floor. The restaurant is bright and pleasant, with food that tries hard, but is nothing special. It's marketed as an 'all-inclusive' product, but 'premium' drinks cost extra.

SCENIC JADE ★★★★+

THIS EXCELLENT RIVERSHIP DELIVERS A FIRST-RATE CRUISE WITH STYLE.

Operator ....Scenic
Built 2014
Length (m) 135.0
Number of decks (excluding sun deck)................... 3
Passenger beds...171
Sit outside (real) balcony ....No
French (open-air) balcony ....Yes
Approximate cabin size (sq m) 19.0–30.0
Lift (elevator)..Yes
Rivers sailed............................ Rhine, Main, Danube

BERLITZ'S RATINGS		
	Possible	Achieved
Hardware	100	80
Accommodation	100	81
Cuisine	100	82
Service	100	78
Miscellaneous	100	83
OVERALL SCORE 404 points out of 500		

This fine contemporary vessel has smart interior lounge decor. Most cabins are roomy and have electric windows and high-quality bed linen. Well-designed bathrooms have L'Occitane amenities, and very good showers. An exercise room and separate massage room are provided. The restaurant is a little cramped but it has multiple seating configurations. Bicycles are available for the active. The cuisine is not outstanding, but it is very good. It's 'all-inclusive', but 'premium' wines cost extra.

SCENIC JASPER ★★★★+

THIS FINE RIVERSHIP PROVIDES A REALLY HIGH-QUALITY INCLUSIVE EXPERIENCE.

Operator ....Scenic
Built 2015
Length (m) 135.0
Number of decks (excluding sun deck)................... 3
Passenger beds...171
Sit outside (real) balcony ....No
French (open-air) balcony ....Yes
Approximate cabin size (sq m) 15.0–44.0
Lift (elevator)..Yes
Rivers sailed............................ Rhine, Main, Danube

BERLITZ'S RATINGS		
	Possible	Achieved
Hardware	100	82
Accommodation	100	82
Cuisine	100	82
Service	100	81
Miscellaneous	100	84
OVERALL SCORE 411 points out of 500		

This extremely comfortable contemporary vessel has chocolate and grey interior decor, and fine furniture. Cabins have soft-close doors and drawers, an excellent infotainment and GPS-based self-guide system, and high-quality bedding and bed linen. The bathrooms are spacious and have a large glazed shower enclosure; the upper accommodation deck suites feature colour-light showers. Bicycles are available for the active. There's a good variety of food and regional wines are included, but the 'wow' factor just isn't there.

SCENIC JEWEL ★★★★+

THIS RIVERSHIP IS JUST THE TICKET FOR A REALLY FINE CRUISE EXPERIENCE.

Operator	Scenic
Built	2013
Length (m)	135.0
Number of decks (excluding sun deck)	3
Passenger beds	171
Sit outside (real) balcony	No
French (open-air) balcony	Yes
Approximate cabin size (sq m)	15.0–30.0
Lift (elevator)	Yes
Rivers sailed	Rhine, Main, Danube

BERLITZ'S RATINGS		
	Possible	Achieved
Hardware	100	80
Accommodation	100	80
Cuisine	100	82
Service	100	80
Miscellaneous	100	81
OVERALL SCORE 403 points out of 500		

Scenic Jewel is a fine vessel with very pleasing lounge decor. Most of the cabins have 'sun' balconies (with very large opening windows), are spacious and feature high-quality linens. The well-designed bathrooms have L'Occitane products. Facilities include a small fitness area. The restaurant is rather tight on space, but offers multiple table configurations. The cuisine is good but not outstanding. It's an 'all inclusive' product, although 'premium' drinks cost extra.

SCENIC OPAL ★★★★+

THIS WELL-DESIGNED RIVERSHIP PROVIDES AN INCLUSIVE CRUISE EXPERIENCE.

Operator	Scenic
Built	2015
Length (m)	135.0
Number of decks (excluding sun deck)	3
Passenger beds	171
Sit outside (real) balcony	No
French (open-air) balcony	Yes
Approximate cabin size (sq m)	15.0–44.0
Lift (elevator)	Yes
Rivers sailed	Rhine

BERLITZ'S RATINGS		
	Possible	Achieved
Hardware	100	83
Accommodation	100	82
Cuisine	100	83
Service	100	81
Miscellaneous	100	82
OVERALL SCORE 411 points out of 500		

This is an extremely comfortable, contemporary vessel, with chocolate and grey decor, and fine furnishings. The nicely proportioned cabins have soft-close doors and drawers, and an excellent infotainment and self-guide system. Another bonus is the decent sized glass shower enclosure – suites on the upper accommodation deck feature colour-light showers. The comfortable but noisy restaurant delivers generally sound cuisine.

SCENIC PEARL ★★★★

THIS IS A VERY STYLISH RIVERSHIP THAT DELIVERS A WELL-PROGRAMMED CRUISE.

Operator ....Scenic
Built 2011
Length (m) 135.0
Number of decks (excluding sun deck)................... 2
Passenger beds...............................171
Sit outside (real) balcony ....No
French (open-air) balcony ....Yes
Approximate cabin size (sq m) 15.0–30.0
Lift (elevator)...Yes
Rivers sailed............................. Rhine, Main, Danube

BERLITZ'S RATINGS		
	Possible	Achieved
Hardware	100	76
Accommodation	100	76
Cuisine	100	78
Service	100	74
Miscellaneous	100	80
OVERALL SCORE 384 points out of 500		

Scenic Pearl is an elegantly decorated vessel , whose panorama lounge has contemporary decor and comfortable seating. Most cabins have 'Sun Lounge' French balconies with floor-to-ceiling slide-open doors, are spacious and feature high-quality linens. The well-designed bathrooms feature L'Occitane products. The restaurant is a little cramped, but it does offer multiple table configurations. The cuisine is very good overall. Facilities include a small, decent wellness area. It's 'all inclusive', but 'premium' drinks cost extra.

SCENIC RUBY ★★★★

CHOOSE THIS STYLISH RIVERSHIP FOR A GOOD-QUALITY RIVER CRUISE EXPERIENCE.

Operator ....Scenic
Built 2009
Length (m) 134.9
Number of decks (excluding sun deck)................... 3
Passenger beds...............................171
Sit outside (real) balcony ....No
French (open-air) balcony ....Yes
Approximate cabin size (sq m) 15.0–30.0
Lift (elevator)...Yes
Rivers sailed............................. Rhine, Main, Danube

BERLITZ'S RATINGS		
	Possible	Achieved
Hardware	100	71
Accommodation	100	74
Cuisine	100	77
Service	100	73
Miscellaneous	100	75
OVERALL SCORE 370 points out of 500		

This tastefully decorated, contemporary vessel has warm colors. Most cabins have 'Sun Lounge' (open-air) balconies and are quite spacious with ample storage space. The well-designed bathrooms feature large glazed shower enclosures, and L'Occitane products are provided. The restaurant, however, is quite cramped, but it has multiple table configurations. The cuisine is very good but lacks finesse. It's 'all inclusive', although 'premium' drinks cost extra.

SCENIC SAPPHIRE ★★★★

THIS WELL-DESIGNED RIVERSHIP PROVIDES A VERY INCLUSIVE CRUISE EXPERIENCE.

Operator ....Scenic
Built 2008
Length (m) 135.0
Number of decks (excluding sun deck)...................3
Passenger beds..155
Sit outside (real) balcony ....No
French (open-air) balcony ....Yes
Approximate cabin size (sq m) 15.0–47.0
Lift (elevator)...Yes
Rivers sailed...Rhone, Saone

BERLITZ'S RATINGS		
	Possible	Achieved
Hardware	100	71
Accommodation	100	74
Cuisine	100	77
Service	100	74
Miscellaneous	100	76
OVERALL SCORE 372 points out of 500		

Scenic Sapphire is an elegantly decorated, contemporary vessel that is very comfortable. Most cabins have both 'Sun Lounge' balconies, are spacious and feature high-quality linens. The well-designed bathrooms, with good shower enclosure, feature L'Occitane products. Restaurant seating is a little tight, but offers flexible table configurations. The cuisine is pretty good, and quite varied. Facilities include a small, decent wellness area. It's 'all inclusive', although 'premium' drinks do cost extra.

SEINE COMTESSE ★★★

THIS HIGH-DENSITY RIVERSHIP HAS FAIRLY MODERN STYLE AND THERE'S NO 'BLING.'

Operator ....Nicko Cruises
Built 2001
Length (m) 114.3
Number of decks (excluding sun deck)...................3
Passenger beds..150
Sit outside (real) balcony ....No
French (open-air) balcony ....No
Approximate cabin size (sq m) 12.0–15.0
Lift (elevator)...No
Rivers sailed...Seine

BERLITZ'S RATINGS		
	Possible	Achieved
Hardware	100	57
Accommodation	100	56
Cuisine	100	55
Service	100	55
Miscellaneous	100	58
OVERALL SCORE 281 points out of 500		

The interior decor of this red-hulled vessel displays minimalist colours using light woods and is quite restful. The lounge is narrow, but it has a walk-around deck outside, with wooden seating. The cabins are of a decent size but quite plain (those on the lowest deck have non-opening windows), and many have fixed twin beds that turn into sofas to provide more daytime space. The restaurant is pleasant, with floor-to-ceiling windows. The cuisine is standardized and unfussy and lacks presentation and finesse; green vegetables, fish and fresh fruit choices are minimal.

SEINE PRINCESS ★★★+

THIS OLDER VESSEL PROVIDES UNFUSSY LOW-COST FRENCH STYLE AND SEMI-CHIC.

Operator .... CroisiEurope
Built 2002
Length (m) 110.0
Number of decks (excluding sun deck)................... 2
Passenger beds...138
Sit outside (real) balcony..................................No
French (open-air) balcony ....No
Approximate cabin size (sq m) 13.0
Lift (elevator)...No
Rivers sailed... Seine

BERLITZ'S RATINGS		
	Possible	Achieved
Hardware	100	61
Accommodation	100	61
Cuisine	100	63
Service	100	60
Miscellaneous	100	61
OVERALL SCORE 306 points out of 500		

The interior decor of warm woods and burnt orange is pleasant, but pillars inhabit both the lounge and the restaurant, interrupting sightlines and making the rooms feel cramped. The cabins are small, with short twin beds, poor soundproofing and bedside reading lights; the bathrooms are diminutive, too, with limited storage space. Overall, it's a middle-of-the road experience, so go for the itinerary, not the food – due to the small galley (wine glasses are small, too). Note that excursions, drinks and gratuities cost extra.

SELECT EXPLORER ★★★

THIS SMART-LOOKING VESSEL HAS GOOD FEATURES, BUT VERY SMALL CABINS.

Operator ....Various tour operators
Built 2001
Length (m) 125.5
Number of decks (excluding sun deck)................... 3
Passenger beds...170
Sit outside (real) balcony..................................No
French (open-air) balcony ....Yes
Approximate cabin size (sq m) 14.0–21.0
Lift (elevator)...No
Rivers sailed............................. Rhine, Main, Danube

BERLITZ'S RATINGS		
	Possible	Achieved
Hardware	100	57
Accommodation	100	56
Cuisine	100	56
Service	100	56
Miscellaneous	100	58
OVERALL SCORE 283 points out of 500		

This high-density vessel has a wine-coloured hull, restful interior decor and a decent library/reading area and a wood-panelled, single-height lobby. Some cabins have French (open-air) balconies; others have windows (some open, some don't). Smaller cabins have two pull-down sofa beds that can't be pushed together. The bathrooms and shower enclosures are very small, and there's little space for toiletries. The restaurant (aft) has floor-to-ceiling windows and is comfortable, but the cuisine is underwhelming, and the wine glasses are small.

SERENADE I ★★★+

THIS COMPACT VESSEL PROVIDES THE SETTING FOR A DECENT CRUISE EXPERIENCE.

Operator ....Titan travel
Built 2005
Length (m) 110.0
Number of decks (excluding sun deck).................. 3
Passenger beds..136
Sit outside (real) balcony.....................................No
French (open-air) balcony ....Yes
Approximate cabin size (sq m) 16.0–22.0
Lift (elevator)..Yes
Rivers sailed.............................. Rhine, Main, Danube

BERLITZ'S RATINGS		
	Possible	Achieved
Hardware	100	63
Accommodation	100	61
Cuisine	100	58
Service	100	58
Miscellaneous	100	63
OVERALL SCORE 303 points out of 500		

This modern vessel has a restful decor and spacious cabins. Many have floor-to-ceiling doors to a French open-air balcony, a fridge and tea- and coffee-making facilities, but limited drawer space. Bathrooms have both a bathtub and separate shower. Facilities include a small infra-red sauna, and two exercise bikes. The restaurant is attractive but value-conscious food means limited choice – particularly for dinner (breakfast and lunch are self-serve buffets). The fruit and cheese selection is poor, and the wine glasses are small. Gratuities, drinks and most excursions cost extra.

SERENADE 2 ★★★+

THIS IS A VERY COMFORTABLE COMPACT RIVERSHIP AIMED AT BRITISH TRAVELLERS.

Operator ....Shearings Holidays
Built 2007
Length (m) 110.0
Number of decks (excluding sun deck).................. 3
Passenger beds..137
Sit outside (real) balcony.....................................No
French (open-air) balcony ....Yes
Approximate cabin size (sq m) 16.0
Lift (elevator)..Yes
Rivers sailed.............................. Rhine, Main, Danube

BERLITZ'S RATINGS		
	Possible	Achieved
Hardware	100	65
Accommodation	100	62
Cuisine	100	56
Service	100	56
Miscellaneous	100	62
OVERALL SCORE 301 points out of 500		

The vessel has a very pleasant observation lounge with contemporary interior decor. The single-deck-high lobby is rather cramped. The cabins are of a good size and have twin beds, although storage space could be better; all cabins have tea-/coffee-making facilities. The bathrooms have a full bathtub and a separate shower enclosure. The restaurant is pleasant enough, but the seating is quite cramped. Some tours are included, and some cost extra.

SERENITY ★★★

THIS HIGH-DENSITY FAIRLY MODERN RIVERSHIP IS NOTABLE FOR ITS BOLD EXTERIOR.

Operator ....Various tour operators
Built 2006
Length (m) 110.0
Number of decks (excluding sun deck).................... 2
Passenger beds...180
Sit outside (real) balcony ....No
French (open-air) balcony ....Yes
Approximate cabin size (sq m) 12.0–12.5
Lift (elevator)...Yes
Rivers sailed............................. Rhine, Main, Danube

BERLITZ'S RATINGS		
	Possible	Achieved
Hardware	100	61
Accommodation	100	60
Cuisine	100	56
Service	100	57
Miscellaneous	100	61
OVERALL SCORE 295 points out of 500		

Serenity has a wine-coloured exterior and restful interior decoration. The lounge is pleasant, but the many slim pillars are irritating and interrupt sightlines. 'Panorama Deck' cabins have French (open-air) balconies; all others have windows (some open, some don't). The cabins are small, with twin beds (these cannot be pushed together), and these fold down to become daytime seats. The lighting is very poor for reading. The bathrooms are pretty cramped, but acceptable. The cuisine is basically sound, but there's very little variety, the breakfast buffets are repetitious, and the wine glasses are small.

SOFIA ★★+

THIS IS A HIGH-DENSITY OLDER VESSEL FOR A NO-FRILLS LOW-PRICE RIVER CRUISE.

Operator ....Various tour operators
Built 1984
Length (m) 113.5
Number of decks (excluding sun deck).................... 3
Passenger beds...190
Sit outside (real) balcony ....No
French (open-air) balcony ....No
Approximate cabin size (sq m) 10.0–11.0
Lift (elevator)...No
Rivers sailed..Danube

BERLITZ'S RATINGS		
	Possible	Achieved
Hardware	100	40
Accommodation	100	38
Cuisine	100	39
Service	100	46
Miscellaneous	100	46
OVERALL SCORE 209 points out of 500		

Sofia packs its travellers into really small cabins with only the most basic facilities (main deck cabin windows can be opened), but these do include a wash basin. In the bathrooms, it's a case of breathing in because there's very little space, and there's limited room, too, for personal toiletry items. The vessel does, however, have a small wellness area with a sauna, and a medical doctor is on board. The midship restaurant is moderately attractive, but the seating is very cramped. The cuisine is basic, and lacks variety and creativity in presentation.

SONATA ★★★+

THIS HIGH-DENSITY RIVERSHIP SHOULD DELIVER A FAIRLY COMFORTABLE CRUISE.

Operator .... Werner Tours
Built 2010
Length (m) 135.0
Number of decks (excluding sun deck)................... 3
Passenger beds...188
Sit outside (real) balcony ....No
French (open-air) balcony ....Yes
Approximate cabin size (sq m) 12.0–15.0
Lift (elevator)...No
Rivers sailed.............................. Rhine, Main, Danube

BERLITZ'S RATINGS		
	Possible	Achieved
Hardware	100	66
Accommodation	100	63
Cuisine	100	60
Service	100	63
Miscellaneous	100	65
OVERALL SCORE 317 points out of 500		

The two-deck lobby has modern decor, although the lounge has uncomfortable low-back chairs. The cabins – many of which have French (open-air) balconies – are quiet, although they are small and have fixed beds (one converts to a sofa by day for more space). The bathrooms are compact, with little space for toiletries. Large glass windows provide river views from both the lounge and restaurant. The food is just about adequate, but uninspiring, and is lacking in variety and green vegetables. The wine glasses are small.

SPIRIT OF CHARTWELL ★★★

CHOOSE THIS REGAL-STYLE RIVERSHIP FOR A FINE DOURO CRUISE EXPERIENCE.

Operator ....Various tour operators
Built 1997
Length (m) 53.8
Number of decks (excluding sun deck)................... 2
Passenger beds.. 30
Sit outside (real) balcony ....No
French (open-air) balcony ....No
Approximate cabin size (sq m) .... N/A
Lift (elevator)...No
Rivers sailed... Douro

BERLITZ'S RATINGS		
	Possible	Achieved
Hardware	100	57
Accommodation	100	56
Cuisine	100	57
Service	100	60
Miscellaneous	100	61
OVERALL SCORE 291 points out of 500		

Famed for being chartered in 2012 as the 'royal barge' for Queen Elizabeth II's Diamond Jubilee celebrations, *Spirit of Chartwell* is all about British country-house style. The wood-rich cabins have two fixed beds and bedside reading lamps from the ocean liners S.S. *France* and *Olympia*. The restaurant has mostly banquette-style seating. The food is unfussy, but tasty, Portuguese fare, but there's little variety, and the breakfast buffets are repetitive.

S.S. ANTOINETTE ★★★★
THIS UPPER-RANGE VESSEL IS WELL DESIGNED AND HAS GRAND HOTEL-STYLE FEATURES.

Operator	Uniworld Boutique River Cruises
Built	2011
Length (m)	135.0
Number of decks (excluding sun deck)	3
Passenger beds	154
Sit outside (real) balcony	Yes
French (open-air) balcony	Yes
Approximate cabin size (sq m)	15.0–36.0
Lift (elevator)	Yes
Rivers sailed	Rhine, Main, Danube

BERLITZ'S RATINGS

	Possible	Achieved
Hardware	100	76
Accommodation	100	77
Cuisine	100	74
Service	100	71
Miscellaneous	100	74

OVERALL SCORE 372 points out of 500

Its name pays homage to its elegant namesake (Marie Antoinette) and is imbued with ornate, 18th-century Versailles-style decor and a lobby with a nice *trompe l'oeil* ceiling and a superb chandelier. Each finely decorated, spacious cabin has a Nespresso machine, ample storage space, floor-to-ceiling French (open-air) balcony doors, a bathroom with large shower enclosure, heated towel rails and L'Occitane products. The vessel also has a small heated indoor pool and neat Leopard Bar. The cuisine is underwhelming and includes repetitious breakfasts, and the wine glasses are small.

S.S. BEATRICE ★★★
THIS RIVERSHIP HAS OODLES OF PANACHE AND PROVIDES AN 'INCLUSIVE' CRUISE.

Operator	Uniworld Boutique River Cruises
Built	2007
Length (m)	125.0
Number of decks (excluding sun deck)	3
Passenger beds	166
Sit outside (real) balcony	No
French (open-air) balcony	Yes
Approximate cabin size (sq m)	14.0–28.0
Lift (elevator)	Yes
Rivers sailed	Danube

BERLITZ'S RATINGS

	Possible	Achieved
Hardware	100	62
Accommodation	100	58
Cuisine	100	61
Service	100	56
Miscellaneous	100	61

OVERALL SCORE 298 points out of 500

This attractive rivership (refitted and refurbished in 2018) has elegant interior decor throughout. The cabins are fairly spacious, and most have twin beds convertible to a queen-sized one. Many cabins feature floor-to-ceiling sliding glass doors and French (open-air) balcony, good storage space and welcoming bathrooms. The open-seating restaurant is both attractive and comfortable. The cuisine is decent, but predictable, and lacks finesse. The included wines are young, but acceptable. Facilities include a complimentary passenger laundry.

S.S. CATHERINE ★★★★

CHOOSE THIS STYLISH RIVERSHIP FOR A HIGH-QUALITY RIVER CRUISE EXPERIENCE.

Operator .... Uniworld Boutique River Cruises
Built 2014
Length (m) 135.0
Number of decks (excluding sun deck) 3
Passenger beds 159
Sit outside (real) balcony .... Yes
French (open-air) balcony .... Yes
Approximate cabin size (sq m) 11.0–38.0
Lift (elevator) .... Yes
Rivers sailed .... Rhone, Saone

BERLITZ'S RATINGS		
	Possible	Achieved
Hardware	100	80
Accommodation	100	80
Cuisine	100	74
Service	100	73
Miscellaneous	100	74
OVERALL SCORE 381 points out of 500		

The emerald green and white decor is the personal choice of owner's wife Beatrice Tollman. Mirrors and bling are everywhere. The two-deck-high lobby is ornate and opulent, although rather cluttered. The Baroque decor in cabins (each has a coffee machine) is stylish, but quite busy; the beds are excellent. Bathrooms have heated floors and good shower enclosures. Features include a heated indoor pool and a passenger laundry. The cuisine, while decent enough, is generally underwhelming. Ghoulish green exterior lighting makes it look like a fairground at night.

S.S. JOIE DE VIVRE ★★★★

OPULENT PARISIAN DECOR IS EVIDENT IN THIS RATHER DELIGHTFUL RIVERSHIP.

Operator .... Uniworld Boutique River Cruises
Built 2017
Length (m) 125.0
Number of decks (excluding sun deck) 3
Passenger beds 128
Sit outside (real) balcony .... Yes
French (open-air) balcony .... Yes
Approximate cabin size (sq m) 15.0–38.0
Lift (elevator) .... Yes
Rivers sailed .... Seine

BERLITZ'S RATINGS		
	Possible	Achieved
Hardware	100	82
Accommodation	100	81
Cuisine	100	74
Service	100	75
Miscellaneous	100	76
OVERALL SCORE 388 points out of 500		

The interior decor is in the grand hotel tradition, with delightful flamboyant belle époque images everywhere. The cabins have plush bed linen and classy fittings, as well as large, push-button windows (and mosquito blinds), and an excellent amount of storage space. The marble-clad bathrooms have heated floors. A small, aft indoor pool has a hydraulic floor allowing it to become a pop-up supper club (with movies). The restaurant is comfortable and of decent quality, with plenty of variety; it is based on French cuisine and international favorites. Wi-Fi and gratuities are included.

S.S. MARIA THERESA ★★★★

IT HAS REALLY OPULENT DECOR BUT UNDERWHELMING FOOD AND SERVICE.

Operator .... Uniworld Boutique River Cruises
Built 2015
Length (m) 135.0
Number of decks (excluding sun deck).................... 3
Passenger beds..150
Sit outside (real) balcony ....Yes
French (open-air) balcony ....Yes
Approximate cabin size (sq m) 15.0–38.0
Lift (elevator)..Yes
Rivers sailed.............................. Rhine, Main, Danube

BERLITZ'S RATINGS		
	Possible	Achieved
Hardware	100	81
Accommodation	100	81
Cuisine	100	74
Service	100	74
Miscellaneous	100	75
OVERALL SCORE 385 points out of 500		

This rivership has an extremely ornate Austrian Habsburg Empire period-style interior decor, and mirrors are everywhere. The lobby has a *trompe l'oeil* ceiling. The cabins have plush bed linen and large, push-button opening windows (and mosquito blinds) that are good but noisy. Facilities include a small heated glass-enclosed indoor pool, which converts to a supper club or a cinema venue for movie nights, a bar and a passenger laundry. The restaurant is very comfortable and attractive, but the cuisine, while good, lacks flair and finesse.

STATENDAM ★★

THIS IS NO-FRILLS, VERY HIGH-DENSITY CRUISING FOR THE BUDGET-MINDED.

Operator ....Various tour operators
Built 1966
Length (m) 104.3
Number of decks (excluding sun deck).................... 3
Passenger beds..186
Sit outside (real) balcony ....No
French (open-air) balcony ....No
Approximate cabin size (sq m) 9.5
Lift (elevator)..No
Rivers sailed.............................. Rhine, Moselle

BERLITZ'S RATINGS		
	Possible	Achieved
Hardware	100	37
Accommodation	100	35
Cuisine	100	40
Service	100	40
Miscellaneous	100	40
OVERALL SCORE 192 points out of 500		

The interior decor of this dated vessel is a throwback to yesteryear – it's rather akin to the inside of an English pub. The forward lounge has uncomfortable tub chairs and is crowded. The cabins are, well, ultra-compact, with little storage space for clothes, but at least the pull-down beds provide daytime space to sit during the day; the lighting and soundproofing are poor. The restaurant is quite attractive and has large windows. The food from the tiny galley is uninspiring – as are the small wine glasses – so it's best to make the itinerary and low prices your reasons for booking.

SWISS CORONA ★★★+

THIS VERY COMFORTABLE VESSEL OFFERS A GOOD-QUALITY CRUISE EXPERIENCE.

Operator .... Riviera Travel
Built 2004
Length (m) 110.0
Number of decks (excluding sun deck) 3
Passenger beds 154
Sit outside (real) balcony .... No
French (open-air) balcony .... Yes
Approximate cabin size (sq m) 15.0–18.0
Lift (elevator) .... Yes
Rivers sailed .... Rhone

BERLITZ'S RATINGS		
	Possible	Achieved
Hardware	100	62
Accommodation	100	57
Cuisine	100	60
Service	100	63
Miscellaneous	100	66
OVERALL SCORE 308 points out of 500		

Swiss Corona is an attractive vessel, with a mix of classic and modern interior decor. There are six suites with beds that face the river, so you have nice views when you wake up). Some cabins have floor-to-ceiling slide-open French (open-air) balconies, but many only have windows. All are nicely appointed. The restaurant is cosy but has dark decor and small windows. The cuisine is good and quite varied, but not outstanding.

SWISS CROWN ★★★

THIS MODERN STYLE RIVERSHIP WILL PROVIDE YOU WITH A WELL-ROUNDED CRUISE.

Operator .... Scylla
Built 2000
Length (m) 110.0
Number of decks (excluding sun deck) 3
Passenger beds 156
Sit outside (real) balcony .... No
French (open-air) balcony .... Yes
Approximate cabin size (sq m) 13.0–16.0
Lift (elevator) .... Yes
Rivers sailed .... Rhine, Main, Danube

BERLITZ'S RATINGS		
	Possible	Achieved
Hardware	100	56
Accommodation	100	54
Cuisine	100	60
Service	100	64
Miscellaneous	100	64
OVERALL SCORE 298 points out of 500		

The nicely appointed *Swiss Crown* is a very comfortable rivership with unfussy interior decor. The cabins are quite plain but quite comfortable; some have twin beds that can be converted to doubles, while others have one or two slim beds that convert to sofas by day. The bathrooms are compact, but practical. The restaurant is attractive, while the cuisine is adequate but the variety is limited and slightly underwhelming.

SWISS CRYSTAL ★★★

THIS RIVERSHIP IS A GOOD CHOICE FOR A WELL-ROUNDED CRUISE EXPERIENCE.

Operator ....Scylla
Built 1995
Length (m) 101.3
Number of decks (excluding sun deck)....................2
Passenger beds..125
Sit outside (real) balcony ....No
French (open-air) balcony ....No
Approximate cabin size (sq m) ....N/A
Lift (elevator)..No
Rivers sailed.............................. Rhine, Main, Danube

BERLITZ'S RATINGS		
	Possible	Achieved
Hardware	100	50
Accommodation	100	54
Cuisine	100	60
Service	100	62
Miscellaneous	100	64
OVERALL SCORE 290 points out of 500		

This smaller-than-average rivership has fuss-free interior decor that is actually quite elegant. The cabin decor, however, is rather bland; some have televisions in an awkward viewing position. All have windows, mini-fridges and twin beds, one of which converts to a daytime sofa. Bathrooms are compact. The food is decent but nothing special. An open-deck hot tub is a bonus.

SWISS DIAMOND ★★★

A SIMPLY DESIGNED RIVERSHIP OFFERING A WELL-ROUNDED RIVER CRUISE.

Operator ....Various tour operators
Built 1996
Length (m) 101.3
Number of decks (excluding sun deck)...................2
Passenger beds..123
Sit outside (real) balcony ....No
French (open-air) balcony ....No
Approximate cabin size (sq m) 12.0
Lift (elevator)..No
Rivers sailed.............................. Rhine, Main, Danube

BERLITZ'S RATINGS		
	Possible	Achieved
Hardware	100	51
Accommodation	100	54
Cuisine	100	60
Service	100	62
Miscellaneous	100	65
OVERALL SCORE 292 points out of 500		

This smaller-than-average rivership has fuss-free interior decoration that is almost elegant. The cabins are quite plainly decorated, but they are comfortable, although some have televisions in an awkward viewing position. All cabins have windows, mini-fridges and twin beds, one of which converts to a sofa (to provide more space during the day). The bathrooms are compact, with little space for toiletry items. The restaurant is quite attracting, and comfortable, but noisy, while the food is unfussy and decent, but nothing special.

SWISS GLORIA ★★★+

THIS COMFORTABLE VESSEL WILL PROVIDE YOU WITH A WELL-ROUNDED CRUISE.

Operator ....Phoenix Cruises
Built 2005
Length (m) 110.0
Number of decks (excluding sun deck)...................3
Passenger beds..153
Sit outside (real) balcony ....No
French (open-air) balcony ....Yes
Approximate cabin size (sq m) 14.0–17.0
Lift (elevator)..Yes
Rivers sailed.............................. Rhine, Main, Danube

BERLITZ'S RATINGS		
	Possible	Achieved
Hardware	100	63
Accommodation	100	57
Cuisine	100	62
Service	100	64
Miscellaneous	100	71
OVERALL SCORE 317 points out of 500		

Swiss Gloria is a well-appointed vessel featuring a wellness area with a sauna and hot tub. The interior decor is traditional and welcoming. The cabins are quite spacious and practically designed, with good sized beds; many have floor-to-ceiling slide-open French (open-air) balconies. The restaurant is very comfortable, with rich polished wood accents. The cuisine is good, and there's decent choice, particularly for self-serve buffet breakfasts.

SWISS JEWEL ★★★+

CHOOSE THIS STYLISH RIVERSHIP FOR AN EXCELLENT, WELL-ORGANISED RIVER CRUISE.

Operator ....Various tour operators
Built 2009
Length (m) 110.0
Number of decks (excluding sun deck)...................3
Passenger beds..124
Sit outside (real) balcony ....No
French (open-air) balcony ....Yes
Approximate cabin size (sq m) 15.0–30.0
Lift (elevator)..Yes
Rivers sailed.............................. Rhine, Main, Danube

BERLITZ'S RATINGS		
	Possible	Achieved
Hardware	100	65
Accommodation	100	57
Cuisine	100	65
Service	100	66
Miscellaneous	100	71
OVERALL SCORE 324 points out of 500		

This vessel features lovely interior decor reminiscent of Victorian-era grand hotels. The cabins feel spacious – some have French (open-air) balconies, some have floor-to-ceiling windows – and all have good soundproofing and decent bathrooms, the largest with mini-bathtubs. The cuisine is good, offering ample choice and quality ingredients. Facilities include a hot tub on the sun deck (pleasant during spring and fall cool days); bicycles are also available.

SWISS PEARL ★★★

THIS OLDER RIVERSHIP CAN STILL DELIVER A GOOD-VALUE CRUISE EXPERIENCE.

Operator	Various tour operators
Built	1993
Length (m)	110.0
Number of decks (excluding sun deck)	2
Passenger beds	123
Sit outside (real) balcony	No
French (open-air) balcony	No
Approximate cabin size (sq m)	N/A
Lift (elevator)	No
Rivers sailed	Rhone, Saone

BERLITZ'S RATINGS		
	Possible	Achieved
Hardware	100	50
Accommodation	100	53
Cuisine	100	60
Service	100	63
Miscellaneous	100	60
OVERALL SCORE 286 points out of 500		

Despite being rather dated, *Swiss Pearl* has moderately comfortable interiors and features include a fitness room with hot tub. The cabins are of a reasonable size – all have mini-fridges, safes, good wardrobe space and windows. The largest cabins have generous-sized bathrooms with bathtubs. The galley is very small, so the meal choices and variety are rather limited.

SWISS RUBY ★★★+

CHOOSE THIS SMALL RIVERSHIP FOR A DECENT-QUALITY RIVER CRUISE EXPERIENCE.

Operator	Rivage River Cruises
Built	2002
Length (m)	85.0
Number of decks (excluding sun deck)	2
Passenger beds	88
Sit outside (real) balcony	No
French (open-air) balcony	Yes
Approximate cabin size (sq m)	11.0
Lift (elevator)	No
Rivers sailed	French rivers

BERLITZ'S RATINGS		
	Possible	Achieved
Hardware	100	61
Accommodation	100	56
Cuisine	100	64
Service	100	66
Miscellaneous	100	70
OVERALL SCORE 317 points out of 500		

Short and specially designed for cruising on shallow rivers such as the Elbe, *Swiss Ruby* has traditional facilities, with very tasteful decor. The cabins are small with short twin or double beds (those on the lower deck have couple-unfriendly fixed twin beds). Upper deck cabins have floor-to-ceiling (open-air) balconies. Cabin lighting and soundproofing are not so good. The bathrooms are compact, but quite practical. The restaurant is quite pleasant (the chairs don't have armrests, and wine glasses are small), but the meal choices are limited due to the small galley. Go mainly for the itinerary.

SWISS TIARA ★★★+
THIS MODERN BUT COMPACT VESSEL IS A GOOD CHOICE FOR A DECENT-QUALITY CRUISE.

Operator	Riviera Travel
Built	2006
Length (m)	110.0
Number of decks (excluding sun deck)	3
Passenger beds	153
Sit outside (real) balcony	No
French (open-air) balcony	Yes
Approximate cabin size (sq m)	14.0–18.0
Lift (elevator)	Yes
Rivers sailed	Rhine, Main, Danube

BERLITZ'S RATINGS	Possible	Achieved
Hardware	100	65
Accommodation	100	65
Cuisine	100	66
Service	100	66
Miscellaneous	100	70
OVERALL SCORE 332 points out of 500		

This well-built, highly comfortable rivership has unstuffy, understated interior decor and high-quality furnishings. The cabins – many of which have French (open-air) balconies – are, however, quite small, although they do include mini-fridges, very comfortable beds and fine linens. The bathrooms have glazed shower enclosures and are very practical. The food is decent and unfussy, but there's little variety; the wine glasses are also small.

SWITZERLAND ★★★
THIS MODESTLY COMFORTABLE VESSEL HAS SOME DECENT STYLE AND FOOD OVERALL.

Operator	Phoenix Reisen
Built	1988
Length (m)	100.0
Number of decks (excluding sun deck)	2
Passenger beds	120
Sit outside (real) balcony	No
French (open-air) balcony	No
Approximate cabin size (sq m)	11.0–18.0
Lift (elevator)	No
Rivers sailed	Rhine, Main, Danube

BERLITZ'S RATINGS	Possible	Achieved
Hardware	100	52
Accommodation	100	51
Cuisine	100	58
Service	100	58
Miscellaneous	100	58
OVERALL SCORE 277 points out of 500		

This short, dated rivership has tasteful interior decor and includes oodles of wood and brass finishes, but few facilities. The cabins are really compact (most have fixed twin beds), but they do have windows that open. However, the bathrooms are very small and have minimal storage space. The restaurant has grand hotel-style decor (the chairs, though comfortable, lack armrests). Despite the small galley, the food is actually good (vegetarian dishes are also available), has taste and is well presented, considering the value-for-money inclusive cruise pricing.

SWITZERLAND II ★★★

THIS RATHER DATED BUT FAIRLY COMFORTABLE VESSEL HAS CHARACTER.

Operator ....Various tour operators
Built 1991
Length (m) 99.6
Number of decks (excluding sun deck)...................2
Passenger beds..108
Sit outside (real) balcony ....No
French (open-air) balcony ....No
Approximate cabin size (sq m) 10.5–25.0
Lift (elevator)...No
Rivers sailed.............................. Rhine, Main, Danube

BERLITZ'S RATINGS		
	Possible	Achieved
Hardware	100	54
Accommodation	100	51
Cuisine	100	55
Service	100	58
Miscellaneous	100	58
OVERALL SCORE 276 points out of 500		

This small vessel has interior decor that is quite handsome, with lots of rich woods and brass, in the style of a grand hotel. The cabins have two beds (many are in an 'L' shape) and wooden writing desk, but little drawer and storage space (two suites have bathtubs). The bathrooms are extremely compact, and there's little room for toiletries. The restaurant has warm decor and furnishings and is comfortable (but chairs don't have armrests), and the cuisine is surprisingly good, although the wine glasses are small. A few bicycles are carried for passenger use.

SYMPHONIE II ★★★

THIS IS A COMPACT FRENCH RIVERSHIP THAT DELIVERS A STRAIGHTFORWARD CRUISE.

Operator .... CroisiEurope
Built 1997
Length (m) 110.0
Number of decks (excluding sun deck)...................2
Passenger beds..110
Sit outside (real) balcony ....No
French (open-air) balcony ....Yes
Approximate cabin size (sq m) 12.0
Lift (elevator)...No
Rivers sailed.............................. Rhine, Main, Danube

BERLITZ'S RATINGS		
	Possible	Achieved
Hardware	100	58
Accommodation	100	53
Cuisine	100	57
Service	100	57
Miscellaneous	100	60
OVERALL SCORE 285 points out of 500		

Following an extensive refit in 2017, the lounge is now smart and contemporary. The upper deck cabins have French balconies with floor-to-ceiling slide-open doors, river-facing beds and bathrooms of a fairly decent size. The restaurant is comfortable, as is the seating. If you don't mind unpretentious French cuisine and wine and are happy with an older, but updated vessel, then *Symphonie II* may be suitable. Choose it mainly for its chic ambience and for the itinerary. Note that drinks, excursions and gratuities cost extra.

THE A ★★★

THIS BLACK RIVERSHIP HAS MINIMALIST DECOR AND MOJO FOR ITS MILLENNIAL CLIENTELE.

Operator ....U by Uniworld
Built 1993
Length (m) 110.0
Number of decks (excluding sun deck)................... 2
Passenger beds...120
Sit outside (real) balcony ....No
French (open-air) balcony ....Yes
Approximate cabin size (sq m) 12.0–24.0
Lift (elevator)..No
Rivers sailed............................. Rhine, Main, Danube

BERLITZ'S RATINGS		
	Possible	Achieved
Hardware	100	48
Accommodation	100	50
Cuisine	100	61
Service	100	56
Miscellaneous	100	60
OVERALL SCORE 275 points out of 500		

The A has a black Darth Vader hull and urban warehouse decor. The cabins are adequate, with twin beds convertible to queen-size ones, and many have floor-to-ceiling glass doors, just enough space for backpacks, but poor soundproofing. Lower deck Studio cabins have slim windows. The bathrooms are adequate, but tight. The open-seating American Diner-style eatery provides two meals, with rather predictable rustic and small-bite food, and small wine glasses. Facilities include spa/fitness rooms and complimentary passenger laundry. Drinks, tours and port charges cost extra.

THE B ★★★

A COMPACT RIVERSHIP WITH CONTEMPORARY DECOR FOR YOUTHFUL, URBAN CRUISERS.

Operator ....U by Uniworld
Built 1995
Length (m) 110.0
Number of decks (excluding sun deck)................... 2
Passenger beds...120
Sit outside (real) balcony ....No
French (open-air) balcony ....Yes
Approximate cabin size (sq m) 12.0–24.0
Lift (elevator)..No
Rivers sailed... Seine

BERLITZ'S RATINGS		
	Possible	Achieved
Hardware	100	49
Accommodation	100	50
Cuisine	100	61
Service	100	56
Miscellaneous	100	60
OVERALL SCORE 276 points out of 500		

The B has a Darth Vader black hull and an urban warehouse interior decor with mojo. The colourful hostel-style cabins are adequate, with twin beds convertible to queen-size; many have floor-to-ceiling glass doors just enough space for backpacks, but poor soundproofing. The bathrooms are adequate, but tight. The open-seating bistro-style American Diner provides only two meals, with rather predictable rustic and small-bite food and small wine glasses. Facilities include spa/fitness rooms and complimentary passenger laundry. Drinks, tours and port charges cost extra.

THOMAS HARDY ★★★★
THIS VERY COMFORTABLE RIVERSHIP IS DESIGNED TO TOTALLY SUIT BRITISH TASTES.

Operator .... Riviera Travel
Built 2017
Length (m) 135.0
Number of decks (excluding sun deck) 3
Passenger beds 167
Sit outside (real) balcony .... No
French (open-air) balcony .... Yes
Approximate cabin size (sq m) 17.0–25.5
Lift (elevator) .... Yes
Rivers sailed .... Danube

BERLITZ'S RATINGS		
	Possible	Achieved
Hardware	100	78
Accommodation	100	77
Cuisine	100	68
Service	100	72
Miscellaneous	100	78
OVERALL SCORE 373 points out of 500		

This delightful vessel has restrained, but contemporary decor and a spacious two-deck-high lobby. The cabins have one-piece ceilings, warm wood accents and high-quality furniture and fabrics. The cabins are comfortable (although those designated as 'suites' are not large) and have a good amount of storage space, and come with twin beds that can be converted to doubles. The tiled bathrooms have decent-sized glazed shower enclosures and good lighting. The restaurant is pleasant, but the cuisine is underwhelming – breakfasts are repetitive, and the wine glasses are small.

THURGAU SILENCE ★★★+
A STYLISH GLASS-FRONTED RIVERSHIP THAT CAN DELIVER A GOOD CRUISE EXPERIENCE.

Operator .... Thurgau Travel
Built 2006
Length (m) 135.0
Number of decks (excluding sun deck) 3
Passenger beds 201
Sit outside (real) balcony .... No
French (open-air) balcony .... Yes
Approximate cabin size (sq m) 13.0
Lift (elevator) .... No
Rivers sailed .... Rhine, Main, Danube

BERLITZ'S RATINGS		
	Possible	Achieved
Hardware	100	65
Accommodation	100	61
Cuisine	100	58
Service	100	58
Miscellaneous	100	66
OVERALL SCORE 308 points out of 500		

Large glass windows provide excellent views in the lounge and restaurant. With the propulsion machinery separated from the passenger accommodation, the cabins – many with floor-to-ceiling slide-open French balconies – are quiet, although they are rather small with little storage space and compact bathrooms. In some cabins, the beds are fixed – one converts to a sofa by day to create more space. The dining room is attractive, although the chairs don't have armrests. The food is so-so and lacks variety and flair.

THURGAU ULTRA ★★★+

CHOOSE THIS RIVERSHIP FOR ITS ABUNDANCE OF NATURAL LIGHT AND STYLISH DECOR.

Operator ....Thurgau Travel
Built 2007
Length (m) 135.0
Number of decks (excluding sun deck)....................3
Passenger beds..104
Sit outside (real) balcony.......................................Yes
French (open-air) balcony ....Yes
Approximate cabin size (sq m) 18.0–30.0
Lift (elevator)...Yes
Rivers sailed............................. Rhine, Main, Danube

BERLITZ'S RATINGS

	Possible	Achieved
Hardware	100	68
Accommodation	100	65
Cuisine	100	64
Service	100	64
Miscellaneous	100	69

OVERALL SCORE 330 points out of 500

The rich and elegant decor includes an abundance of polished wood panelling and cabinetry, and is outfitted to a very high standard. It also has quiet cabins because the propulsion unit is separate from the accommodation area (some suites have a bathtub, but most of the others have shower enclosures). A cigar-smoking lounge is cosy and tastefully decorated. The restaurant seats all passengers in an open-seating arrangement, and has comfortable chairs and nice table settings. The cuisine is good, although there's no 'wow' factor. Drinks (including soft drinks) and optional tours cost extra.

TRAVELMARVEL DIAMOND ★★★+

THIS RIVERSHIP HAS GOOD FACILITIES AND DELIVERS DECENT OVERALL CRUISE VALUE.

Operator .... Travelmarvel (APT)
Built 2007
Length (m) 135.0
Number of decks (excluding sun deck)....................3
Passenger beds..170
Sit outside (real) balcony..No
French (open-air) balcony ....Yes
Approximate cabin size (sq m) 16.0–24.0
Lift (elevator)..No
Rivers sailed...Danube

BERLITZ'S RATINGS

	Possible	Achieved
Hardware	100	65
Accommodation	100	60
Cuisine	100	67
Service	100	65
Miscellaneous	100	64

OVERALL SCORE 321 points out of 500

The public rooms have large glass windows, which provide a feeling of space. This 'twin cruiser' offers quiet cabins, because the propulsion unit is separate from the accommodation. Many cabins have French balconies with floor-to-ceiling slide-open doors and are stylish but small, although storage space is good. Large glass windows afford great views in the lounge and restaurant. Bicycles are available for the active. Cruises are less expensive than the riverships of parent company APT, but with cuisine that is of a lower quality.

TRAVELMARVEL JEWEL ★★★+

THIS GLASS-FRONTED, MODERN VESSEL DELIVERS A GOOD CRUISE EXPERIENCE.

Operator .... Travelmarvel (APT)
Built 2007
Length (m) 135.0
Number of decks (excluding sun deck).................. 3
Passenger beds..170
Sit outside (real) balcony.......................................No
French (open-air) balcony ....Yes
Approximate cabin size (sq m) 16.0–24.0
Lift (elevator)..No
Rivers sailed..Danube

BERLITZ'S RATINGS		
	Possible	Achieved
Hardware	100	65
Accommodation	100	60
Cuisine	100	67
Service	100	65
Miscellaneous	100	64
OVERALL SCORE 321 points out of 500		

With the propulsion machinery separated from the passenger accommodation, the cabins – many of them with French balconies with floor-to-ceiling slide-open doors – are quiet, in addition to being stylish, although rather small. The beds, however, are fixed (one converts to a sofa by day). The bathrooms are really compact, with little storage space for toiletries. Large floor-to-ceiling glass windows afford fine views in the lounge and restaurant. The cuisine is nothing special, but it is fit for purpose, and price.

TRAVELMARVEL SAPPHIRE ★★★+

MODERATELY PRICED, THIS RIVERSHIP IS GOOD FOR YOUTHFUL, ACTIVE TYPES.

Operator .... Travelmarvel (APT)
Built 2006
Length (m) 135.0
Number of decks (excluding sun deck).................. 3
Passenger beds..164
Sit outside (real) balcony.......................................No
French (open-air) balcony ....Yes
Approximate cabin size (sq m) 15.0–22.0
Lift (elevator)..No
Rivers sailed..Danube

BERLITZ'S RATINGS		
	Possible	Achieved
Hardware	100	66
Accommodation	100	60
Cuisine	100	67
Service	100	67
Miscellaneous	100	66
OVERALL SCORE 326 points out of 500		

A 'twin-cruiser' with its propulsion unit aft translates to cabins that are quiet. The forward observation lounge is good, with large windows. Bicycles are available for the active. The cabins are practically laid-out. Many cabins have French balconies with floor-to-ceiling slide-open doors, a double bed or twin single beds, mini-fridges and personal safes are small. Bathrooms have small shower enclosures and little storage space for toiletry items. The restaurant is cramped and noisy, but the cuisine is actually quite decent and has flair.

TREASURES ★★★★

THIS COMFORTABLE MODERN RIVERSHIP DELIVERS A WELL-ROUNDED RIVER CRUISE.

Operator	Tauck
Built	2011
Length (m)	110.0
Number of decks (excluding sun deck)	3
Passenger beds	98
Sit outside (real) balcony	No
French (open-air) balcony	Yes
Approximate cabin size (sq m)	14.0–28.0
Lift (elevator)	Yes
Rivers sailed	Rhine, Main, Danube

BERLITZ'S RATINGS		
	Possible	Achieved
Hardware	100	76
Accommodation	100	76
Cuisine	100	68
Service	100	68
Miscellaneous	100	72
OVERALL SCORE 360 points out of 500		

Nicely appointed, with plenty of character, *Treasures* is a very comfortable rivership, with unfussy interior decor that is quite elegant. The seven suites are delightful spaces. Other cabins are well designed and practically laid out, as are the bathrooms, which have L'Occitane toiletries. The cuisine in the open-seating restaurant is good, with quality ingredients used and ample choice. Aft is The Bistro, for lighter fare. Amenities include a hot tub on the sun deck, and bicycles are available.

VAN GOGH ★★★

THIS STANDARD OLDER-STYLE VESSEL HAS SIMPLE FRENCH AMBIENCE AND DATED CHIC.

Operator	CroisiEurope
Built	1999
Length (m)	110.0
Number of decks (excluding sun deck)	2
Passenger beds	160
Sit outside (real) balcony	No
French (open-air) balcony	No
Approximate cabin size (sq m)	12.0
Lift (elevator)	No
Rivers sailed	Rhone, Saone

BERLITZ'S RATINGS		
	Possible	Achieved
Hardware	100	53
Accommodation	100	54
Cuisine	100	56
Service	100	55
Miscellaneous	100	57
OVERALL SCORE 275 points out of 500		

If you like unpretentious French cuisine and wine and are happy with a comfortable but small cabin with slim beds, no balcony and a tiny bathroom with a limited storage space (and noisy closet doors), then *Van Gogh* may appeal to you. Go for the comfortable ambience and for the itinerary and destinations. The restaurant is rather cramped, and the food is just so-so, nothing more, and there's little choice, although the selection of French cheese is quite good. Note that excursions and gratuities are at extra cost.

VASCO DA GAMA ★★★

THIS VERY COMPACT RIVERSHIP PROVIDES TRANSPORTATION, BUT LITTLE ELSE.

Operator .... CroisiEurope
Built 2002
Length (m) 75.0
Number of decks (excluding sun deck)................... 2
Passenger beds..142
Sit outside (real) balcony ....No
French (open-air) balcony ....No
Approximate cabin size (sq m) 10.0–12.0
Lift (elevator)..Yes
Rivers sailed.. Douro

BERLITZ'S RATINGS		
	Possible	Achieved
Hardware	100	56
Accommodation	100	49
Cuisine	100	55
Service	100	56
Miscellaneous	100	58
OVERALL SCORE 274 points out of 500		

The average-looking, high-density *Vasco da Gama* provides a standard middle-of-the road cruise experience, although the cabins are small and have very little drawer space, dim lighting and poor soundproofing. The bathrooms are also dimensionally challenged, and storage space for toiletry items is limited. The French food is simple and unfussy (with few green vegetables) but it lacks variety and creativity due to the vessel's small galley; the wine glasses are small, too. Note that excursions and gratuities are at extra cost.

VERDI ★★+

GO FOR THE LOW PRICE AND ITINERARY RATHER THAN COMFORT ABOARD THIS RIVERSHIP.

Operator .... SijFa Cruises
Built 2001
Length (m) 114.0
Number of decks (excluding sun deck)................... 3
Passenger beds..136
Sit outside (real) balcony ....No
French (open-air) balcony ....No
Approximate cabin size (sq m) 14.0
Lift (elevator)..Yes
Rivers sailed...Rhine

BERLITZ'S RATINGS		
	Possible	Achieved
Hardware	100	52
Accommodation	100	50
Cuisine	100	45
Service	100	46
Miscellaneous	100	51
OVERALL SCORE 244 points out of 500		

The interior decor of this dated vessel is quite attractive, with some nice wood and brass accents. The lounge has several pillars that obstruct views and are irritating. The cabins are rather small, with little storage space, poor bedside reading lights and soundproofing. The bathrooms are cramped, with a shower but little storage space. The restaurant, although fairly pleasant, has a low ceiling and is noisy, and the chairs lack armrests. Value-conscious food equals very limited choice and quality, and the wine glasses are small.

VICTOR HUGO ★★★

THIS RIVERSHIP PROVIDES A STANDARD RIVER CRUISE THAT IS NOTHING SPECIAL.

Operator .... CroisiEurope
Built 2000
Length (m) 82.5
Number of decks (excluding sun deck)................... 2
Passenger beds...100
Sit outside (real) balcony ....No
French (open-air) balcony ....No
Approximate cabin size (sq m) 10.0–12.0
Lift (elevator)...No
Rivers sailed..Rhine

BERLITZ'S RATINGS		
	Possible	Achieved
Hardware	100	51
Accommodation	100	50
Cuisine	100	54
Service	100	56
Miscellaneous	100	56
OVERALL SCORE 267 points out of 500		

Victor Hugo has a bright, unfussy interior decor, although the lounge furniture looks dated. The cabins are very small, and have windows (no balconies), slim, short beds (most of which can't be moved together) and little drawer space for clothing items. The bathrooms are tiny, as is the space for personal toiletry items. If you like unpretentious French food, wine and ambience (the restaurant could be called attractive), Victor Hugo may suit. Choose it mainly for the itinerary and destinations (note: excursions and gratuities cost extra).

VIKING AEGIR ★★★★

CHOOSE THIS RIVERSHIP FOR A WELL-ORGANISED, HIGH-QUALITY CRUISE EXPERIENCE.

Operator .... Viking River Cruises
Built 2012
Length (m) 135.0
Number of decks (excluding sun deck)................... 3
Passenger beds...190
Sit outside (real) balcony ....Yes
French (open-air) balcony ....Yes
Approximate cabin size (sq m) 12.5–41.0
Lift (elevator)..Yes
Rivers sailed............................. Rhine, Main, Danube

BERLITZ'S RATINGS		
	Possible	Achieved
Hardware	100	81
Accommodation	100	84
Cuisine	100	75
Service	100	75
Miscellaneous	100	76
OVERALL SCORE 391 points out of 500		

The well-designed *Viking Aegir* has a functional rather than luxurious decor, but there's ample natural light. The innovative, practical layout of the cabins includes floor-to-ceiling French (open-air) balconies, good living and storage space, and bathrooms with large, glazed shower enclosures. The restaurant is attractive and comfortable, and has a good ceiling height and huge river view windows. The cuisine is tasty and unpretentious; there is a good variety and choice, and it is nicely presented. The Aquavit Terrace, located forward, has bistro-style food for breakfast and lunch.

VIKING ALRUNA ★★★★

THIS WELL-DESIGNED, CONTEMPORARY SHIP WILL PROVIDE A GOOD CRUISE EXPERIENCE.

Operator .... Viking River Cruises
Built 2016
Length (m) 135.0
Number of decks (excluding sun deck) 3
Passenger beds...190
Sit outside (real) balcony ....Yes
French (open-air) balcony ....Yes
Approximate cabin size (sq m) 12.5–41.0
Lift (elevator)..Yes
Rivers sailed..Rhine

BERLITZ'S RATINGS		
	Possible	Achieved
Hardware	100	83
Accommodation	100	84
Cuisine	100	75
Service	100	75
Miscellaneous	100	77
OVERALL SCORE 394 points out of 500		

Viking Alruna has a light Scandinavian blond-wood decor with an abundance of natural light. Well-designed, nicely appointed suites and cabins all have French (open-air) balconies; they are both comfortable and practical, and bathrooms have large, glazed shower enclosures. Two suites located aft are particularly spacious; each has a separate bedroom and wrap-around balcony. The restaurant is attractive, comfortable, has a good ceiling height, large windows, and unfussy food that is presented well. The Aquavit Terrace (for breakfast and lunch) offers good light bites.

VIKING ALSVIN ★★★★

THIS STYLISH, SPACIOUS VESSEL WILL PROVIDE YOU WITH A WELL-ORGANISED CRUISE.

Operator .... Viking River Cruises
Built 2014
Length (m) 135.0
Number of decks (excluding sun deck) 3
Passenger beds...190
Sit outside (real) balcony ....Yes
French (open-air) balcony ....Yes
Approximate cabin size (sq m) 12.5–41.0
Lift (elevator)..Yes
Rivers sailed............................. Rhine, Main, Danube

BERLITZ'S RATINGS		
	Possible	Achieved
Hardware	100	82
Accommodation	100	84
Cuisine	100	75
Service	100	76
Miscellaneous	100	76
OVERALL SCORE 393 points out of 500		

Viking Alsvin has warm Scandinavian-style minimalist blond-wood decor and abundant natural light due to numerous floor-to-ceiling glass windows. All cabins have full or French (open-air) balconies (some have both), with quality bedding, ample storage space and good bathrooms with large glazed shower enclosures. The suites (each has a separate bedroom and wrap-around balcony) are very spacious. The restaurant is attractive, comfortable, has a good ceiling height and large windows. The cuisine is unpretentious, but tasty and well presented; there is also a decent variet

VIKING ASTRILD ★★★★

AN EXCELLENT CHOICE FOR A FIRST-RATE, WELL-ORCHESTRATED RIVER CRUISE IN STYLE.

Operator .... Viking River Cruises
Built 2015
Length (m) 110.0
Number of decks (excluding sun deck).................. 2
Passenger beds.. 98
Sit outside (real) balcony ....Yes
French (open-air) balcony ....Yes
Approximate cabin size (sq m) 13.0–23.0
Lift (elevator)...No
Rivers sailed.. Elbe

BERLITZ'S RATINGS		
	Possible	Achieved
Hardware	100	83
Accommodation	100	84
Cuisine	100	78
Service	100	75
Miscellaneous	100	76
OVERALL SCORE 396 points out of 500		

Specially designed for the River Elbe, this rivership has a clean uncluttered design, and has abundant natural light, due to floor-to-ceiling glass walls in the cabins, restaurant, and observation lounge. The cabins have ample (soft-close) drawer and other storage space, premium mattresses, a vanity desk, bedside tables, good reading lights embedded in the headboard and a lighting dimmer. The restaurant is attractive and very comfortable, while the food is tasty and there's plenty of variety.

VIKING ATLA ★★★★

THIS STYLISH RIVERSHIP WILL LAUNCH YOU ON A WELL-ORGANISED CRUISE.

Operator .... Viking River Cruises
Built 2013
Length (m) 135.0
Number of decks (excluding sun deck).................. 3
Passenger beds...190
Sit outside (real) balcony ....Yes
French (open-air) balcony ....Yes
Approximate cabin size (sq m) 12.5–41.0
Lift (elevator)...Yes
Rivers sailed.. Rhine

BERLITZ'S RATINGS		
	Possible	Achieved
Hardware	100	81
Accommodation	100	83
Cuisine	100	78
Service	100	75
Miscellaneous	100	76
OVERALL SCORE 393 points out of 500		

With a Scandinavian minimalist interior decor, characterised by light colours, *Viking Atla* is a very comfortable rivership, with an abundance of natural light from floor-to-ceiling glass windows. All cabins have full or French (open-air) balconies (some have both), a practical layout and good bathrooms with large glazed shower enclosures. The restaurant is attractive, has a good ceiling height, and huge river view windows. The cuisine is tasty and unpretentious; with good variety and choice, and nicely presented. The Aquavit Terrace, forward, has bistro-style food for breakfast and lunch.

VIKING BALDUR ★★★★

A GOOD CHOICE FOR A WELL-PROGRAMMED, STYLISH, FIRST-RATE RIVER CRUISE.

Operator .... Viking River Cruises
Built 2014
Length (m) 135.0
Number of decks (excluding sun deck) 3
Passenger beds 190
Sit outside (real) balcony ....Yes
French (open-air) balcony ....Yes
Approximate cabin size (sq m) 12.5–41.0
Lift (elevator) ....Yes
Rivers sailed .... Rhine, Main, Danube

BERLITZ'S RATINGS		
	Possible	Achieved
Hardware	100	82
Accommodation	100	84
Cuisine	100	78
Service	100	76
Miscellaneous	100	76
OVERALL SCORE 396 points out of 500		

Viking Baldur has tasteful and warm Scandinavian-style minimalist decor, and abundant natural light from floor-to-ceiling windows. All cabins have full or French (open-air) balconies (some have both) and are very practical, with quality bedding, ample storage space and good bathrooms with large glazed shower enclosures. The suites (each has a separate bedroom and wrap-around balcony) are very spacious. The restaurant is attractive and comfortable, and has a good ceiling height and large windows. The unpretentious cuisine is tasty, there is ample variety and choice.

VIKING BESTLA ★★★★

THIS HIGH-TECH VESSEL IS SET TO BE GREAT FOR A WELL-ORGANISED CRUISE.

Operator .... Viking River Cruises
Built 2014
Length (m) 135.0
Number of decks (excluding sun deck) 3
Passenger beds 190
Sit outside (real) balcony ....Yes
French (open-air) balcony ....Yes
Approximate cabin size (sq m) 12.5–41.0
Lift (elevator) ....Yes
Rivers sailed .... Rhine, Main, Danube

BERLITZ'S RATINGS		
	Possible	Achieved
Hardware	100	82
Accommodation	100	84
Cuisine	100	78
Service	100	76
Miscellaneous	100	76
OVERALL SCORE 396 points out of 500		

With a light Scandinavian-style interior, *Viking Bestla* has a spacious, light and airy feel. The well-designed, functional double-sized suites (with separate bedroom) and roomy cabins have French (open-air) balconies, extremely comfortable, generously sized beds and premium mattresses. Two suites each feature a separate bedroom, wet room, lounge and wrap-around balcony. The restaurant is attractive and has tasteful decor, and there is an alternative Aquavit Terrace for breakfast and lunch, offering good, unfussy food that is both tasty and well presented.

VIKING BEYLA ★★★★

CHOOSE THIS COMPACT RIVERSHIP FOR A FIRST-RATE RIVER CRUISE IN GOOD STYLE.

Operator .... Viking River Cruises
Built 2015
Length (m) 110.0
Number of decks (excluding sun deck)................... 2
Passenger beds.. 98
Sit outside (real) balcony ....Yes
French (open-air) balcony ....Yes
Approximate cabin size (sq m) 13.0–23.0
Lift (elevator)..No
Rivers sailed...Elbe

BERLITZ'S RATINGS		
	Possible	Achieved
Hardware	100	83
Accommodation	100	84
Cuisine	100	78
Service	100	76
Miscellaneous	100	76
OVERALL SCORE 397 points out of 500		

Specially designed for the River Elbe, this rivership has a clean uncluttered design. There are lots of glass walls in cabins, restaurant and lounge. Cabins have ample (soft-close) drawer and other storage space, vanity desk, bedside tables and good reading lights embedded in the headboard, and a lighting dimmer. The restaurant is attractive and has tasteful decor. The food has plenty of taste, and there is ample variety.

VIKING BRAGI ★★★★

A STYLISH CHOICE FOR A WELL-PROGRAMMED, FIRST-RATE RIVER CRUISE.

Operator .... Viking River Cruises
Built 2012
Length (m) 135.0
Number of decks (excluding sun deck)................... 3
Passenger beds...190
Sit outside (real) balcony ....Yes
French (open-air) balcony ....Yes
Approximate cabin size (sq m) 12.5–41.0
Lift (elevator)..Yes
Rivers sailed............................. Rhine, Main, Danube

BERLITZ'S RATINGS		
	Possible	Achieved
Hardware	100	81
Accommodation	100	84
Cuisine	100	78
Service	100	76
Miscellaneous	100	74
OVERALL SCORE 393 points out of 500		

Viking Bragi has extremely comfortable Scandinavian blond-wood interior decor with an abundance of natural light. Well-designed, nicely appointed suites and cabins all have French (open-air) balconies, and bathrooms have large, glazed shower enclosures. Two suites located aft are particularly spacious; each has a separate bedroom and wrap-around balcony. The restaurant is attractive, comfortable, has a good ceiling height, and large river-view windows, and unfussy food that is presented well. An alternative Aquavit Terrace (for breakfast and lunch) offers good light bites.

VIKING BURI ★★★★

CHOOSE THIS STYLISH VESSEL FOR A WELL-ORGANISED OVERALL CRUISE.

Operator .... Viking River Cruises
Built 2014
Length (m) 135.0
Number of decks (excluding sun deck)................... 3
Passenger beds...190
Sit outside (real) balcony.....................................No
French (open-air) balcony ....Yes
Approximate cabin size (sq m) 12.5–41.0
Lift (elevator)..Yes
Rivers sailed...Rhone, Saone

BERLITZ'S RATINGS		
	Possible	Achieved
Hardware	100	82
Accommodation	100	84
Cuisine	100	78
Service	100	76
Miscellaneous	100	76
OVERALL SCORE 396 points out of 500		

With a light Scandinavian interior, *Viking Buri* feels quite spacious, with lots of natural light from its numerous floor-to-ceiling windows. The well-designed and appointed cabins have full or French (open-air) balconies (some have both), generously sized beds with quality bedding, ample storage space, good soundproofing, and the nice bathrooms have large glazed shower enclosures. The tastefully decorated restaurant and the alternative Aquavit Terrace (the latter for breakfast and lunch only) offers good fuss-free food.

VIKING DELLING ★★★★

THIS WOULD BE A GOOD CHOICE FOR A FIRST-RATE CRUISE ON A STYLISH VESSEL.

Operator .... Viking River Cruises
Built 2014
Length (m) 135.0
Number of decks (excluding sun deck)................... 3
Passenger beds...190
Sit outside (real) balcony.....................................Yes
French (open-air) balcony ....Yes
Approximate cabin size (sq m) 12.5–41.0
Lift (elevator)..Yes
Rivers sailed...Rhone, Saone

BERLITZ'S RATINGS		
	Possible	Achieved
Hardware	100	82
Accommodation	100	84
Cuisine	100	78
Service	100	77
Miscellaneous	100	76
OVERALL SCORE 397 points out of 500		

Viking Delling has minimalist, but tasteful and warm, Scandinavian-style decor and abundant natural light from floor-to-ceiling glass windows. The cabins have full or French (open-air) balconies (some have both) and they are very practical, with quality bedding, ample storage space and good bathrooms with large glazed shower enclosures. The suites (each has a separate bedroom and wrap-around balcony) are very spacious. The restaurant is attractive and comfortable, and has a good ceiling height and large windows. The unpretentious cuisine is tasty, there is ample variety and choice.

VIKING EGIL ★★★★

THIS RIVERSHIP HAS VERY GOOD FACILITIES, SMART DECOR AND DECENT FOOD.

Operator .... Viking River Cruises
Built 2016
Length (m) 135.0
Number of decks (excluding sun deck)................... 3
Passenger beds 190
Sit outside (real) balcony....................................Yes
French (open-air) balcony ....Yes
Approximate cabin size (sq m) 12.5–41.0
Lift (elevator)..Yes
Rivers sailed............................ Rhine, Main, Danube

BERLITZ'S RATINGS		
	Possible	Achieved
Hardware	100	83
Accommodation	100	84
Cuisine	100	78
Service	100	76
Miscellaneous	100	77
OVERALL SCORE 398 points out of 500		

Viking Egil features warm, minimalist Scandinavian-style decor, and abundant natural light from floor-to-ceiling glass windows. The cabins have full or French (open-air) balconies (some have both) and are very practical, with quality bedding, ample storage space and good bathrooms with large glazed shower enclosures. The suites (each has a separate bedroom and wrap-around balcony) are very spacious. The restaurant is attractive and comfortable, and has a good ceiling height and large windows. The unpretentious cuisine is tasty, there is ample variety and choice.

VIKING EIR ★★★★

THIS WELL-DESIGNED, CONTEMPORARY SHIP WILL PROVIDE A GOOD CRUISE EXPERIENCE.

Operator .... Viking River Cruises
Built 2015
Length (m) 135.0
Number of decks (excluding sun deck)................... 3
Passenger beds 190
Sit outside (real) balcony....................................Yes
French (open-air) balcony ....Yes
Approximate cabin size (sq m) 12.5–41.0
Lift (elevator)..Yes
Rivers sailed...Rhine

BERLITZ'S RATINGS		
	Possible	Achieved
Hardware	100	83
Accommodation	100	84
Cuisine	100	78
Service	100	76
Miscellaneous	100	77
OVERALL SCORE 398 points out of 500		

With a Scandinavian-style interior, *Viking Var* has a spacious, airy feeling and tasteful light interior decor, plus an abundance of natural light from its numerous floor-to-ceiling glass windows. The double-sized suites and spacious cabins have good reading lights and soundproofing, are well designed and functional, and have full (sit outside) or French open-air balconies. The large beds are really comfortable. The nicely decorated restaurant and Aquavit Terrace (the latter for breakfast and lunch) provide good, unfussy food that is nicely presented, although it lacks 'wow' factor.

VIKING EISTLA ★★★★

THIS IS A STYLISH, CONTEMPORARY RIVERSHIP FOR A REALLY WELL-ORGANISED CRUISE.

Operator .... Viking River Cruises
Built 2014
Length (m) 135.0
Number of decks (excluding sun deck)................... 3
Passenger beds...190
Sit outside (real) balcony ....Yes
French (open-air) balcony ....Yes
Approximate cabin size (sq m) 12.5–41.0
Lift (elevator)..Yes
Rivers sailed............................. Rhine, Main, Danube

BERLITZ'S RATINGS		
	Possible	Achieved
Hardware	100	82
Accommodation	100	84
Cuisine	100	78
Service	100	76
Miscellaneous	100	77
OVERALL SCORE 397 points out of 500		

Viking Eistla has extremely comfortable Scandinavian blond-wood interiors, and a two-deck-high lobby flooded with natural light. Well-designed and appointed suites and cabins, all with full or French (open-air) balconies are both comfortable and practical, with bathrooms that have large, glazed shower enclosures. The tastefully decorated restaurant and alternative Aquavit Terrace (the latter for breakfast and lunch) provide good, unfussy, simple food rather than fancy cuisine.

VIKING EMBLA ★★★★

THIS STYLISH VESSEL SHOULD PROVE TO BE A GOOD CHOICE FOR A WELL-ORGANISED CRUISE.

Operator .... Viking River Cruises
Built 2012
Length (m) 135.0
Number of decks (excluding sun deck)................... 3
Passenger beds...190
Sit outside (real) balcony ....Yes
French (open-air) balcony ....Yes
Approximate cabin size (sq m) 12.5–41.0
Lift (elevator)..Yes
Rivers sailed............................. Rhine, Main, Danube

BERLITZ'S RATINGS		
	Possible	Achieved
Hardware	100	81
Accommodation	100	84
Cuisine	100	78
Service	100	75
Miscellaneous	100	77
OVERALL SCORE 395 points out of 500		

Viking Embla has tasteful, warm Scandinavian-style minimalist decor, and abundant natural light from floor-to-ceiling windows. The well-designed and appointed cabins have full or French (open-air) balconies (some have both), quality bedding, ample storage space, good bathrooms with large glazed shower enclosures, and good soundproofing. The suites (each has a separate bedroom and wrap-around balcony) are very spacious. The restaurant is attractive and comfortable, with large river-view windows. The unpretentious cuisine is tasty, there is ample variety and choice.

VIKING FORSETI ★★★★

THIS RIVERSHIP HAS STATE-OF-THE-ART FEATURES AND GOOD FOOD AND SERVICE.

Operator	Viking River Cruises
Built	2013
Length (m)	135.0
Number of decks (excluding sun deck)	3
Passenger beds	190
Sit outside (real) balcony	Yes
French (open-air) balcony	Yes
Approximate cabin size (sq m)	12.5–41.0
Lift (elevator)	Yes
Rivers sailed	Gironde

BERLITZ'S RATINGS		
	Possible	Achieved
Hardware	100	81
Accommodation	100	84
Cuisine	100	78
Service	100	74
Miscellaneous	100	76
OVERALL SCORE 393 points out of 500		

Viking Forseti features minimalist, but tasteful, Scandinavian-style interior decor, and abundant natural light through its numerous floor-to-ceiling glass windows. The well-designed, nicely appointed suites and cabins – with full or French (open-air) balconies are comfortable and practical, and have good lighting and soundproofing. The bathrooms have large, glazed shower enclosures. The restaurant is attractive and comfortable. Both it and an alternative Aquavit Terrace (the latter for breakfast and lunch) both provide good, unfussy food.

VIKING FREYA ★★★★

THIS HIGH-TECH, STYLISH VESSEL DELIVERS A WELL-ORGANISED CRUISE.

Operator	Viking River Cruises
Built	2012
Length (m)	135.0
Number of decks (excluding sun deck)	3
Passenger beds	190
Sit outside (real) balcony	Yes
French (open-air) balcony	Yes
Approximate cabin size (sq m)	12.5–41.0
Lift (elevator)	Yes
Rivers sailed	Danube

BERLITZ'S RATINGS		
	Possible	Achieved
Hardware	100	81
Accommodation	100	81
Cuisine	100	78
Service	100	76
Miscellaneous	100	77
OVERALL SCORE 393 points out of 500		

The well-designed *Viking Freya* features minimalist Scandinavian decor. A practical, innovative layout has created reasonably spacious cabins with French (open-air) balconies and good storage space, plus bathrooms with heated floors and high-tech shower walls that convert from clear to frosted. Two suites each have a separate bedroom, lounge, wet room and wrap-around balcony. The restaurant (plus the Aquavit Terrace for breakfast and lunch) delivers good, unfussy food that is nicely presented. Overall, this is a good-quality product.

VIKING GEFJON ★★★★

THIS WELL-DESIGNED, CONTEMPORARY SHIP PROVIDES A GOOD CRUISE EXPERIENCE.

Operator .... Viking River Cruises
Built 2015
Length (m) 135.0
Number of decks (excluding sun deck).................... 3
Passenger beds..190
Sit outside (real) balcony .... Yes
French (open-air) balcony .... Yes
Approximate cabin size (sq m) 12.5–41.0
Lift (elevator)... Yes
Rivers sailed............................. Rhine, Main, Danube

BERLITZ'S RATINGS		
	Possible	Achieved
Hardware	100	83
Accommodation	100	84
Cuisine	100	78
Service	100	76
Miscellaneous	100	76
OVERALL SCORE 397 points out of 500		

Viking Gefjon features minimalist, but tasteful, Scandinavian-style interior decor, with natural light through numerous floor-to-ceiling glass windows. Cabins have full or French (open-air) balconies (some have both) and are practical, with quality bedding, good storage space and bathrooms with large glazed shower enclosures. The suites (each with separate bedroom and wraparound balcony) are very spacious. The restaurant is attractive, and has a good ceiling height and large riverview windows. The unpretentious cuisine is tasty; there is ample variety and choice, and it is presented well.

VIKING GULLVEIG ★★★★

CHOOSE THIS STYLISH CONTEMPORARY RIVERSHIP FOR A WELL-ORGANISED CRUISE.

Operator .... Viking River Cruises
Built 2014
Length (m) 135.0
Number of decks (excluding sun deck).................... 3
Passenger beds..190
Sit outside (real) balcony .... Yes
French (open-air) balcony .... Yes
Approximate cabin size (sq m) 12.5–41.0
Lift (elevator)... Yes
Rivers sailed...Rhine

BERLITZ'S RATINGS		
	Possible	Achieved
Hardware	100	82
Accommodation	100	84
Cuisine	100	78
Service	100	76
Miscellaneous	100	76
OVERALL SCORE 396 points out of 500		

Viking Gullveig has a Scandinavian blond-wood decor with an abundance of natural light. Well-designed, nicely appointed suites and cabins all have French (open-air) balconies, and bathrooms have large, glazed shower enclosures. Two suites located aft are particularly spacious; each has a separate bedroom and wrap-around balcony. The restaurant is attractive and comfortable, and has a good ceiling height and large river-view windows; it offers unfussy food that is presented well. The alternative Aquavit Terrace (for breakfast and lunch) offers good light bites.

VIKING HEIMDAL ★★★★

THIS AIRY, SPACIOUS VESSEL OFFERS A STYLISH, WELL-ORGANISED CRUISE EXPERIENCE.

Operator .... Viking River Cruises
Built 2014
Length (m) 135.0
Number of decks (excluding sun deck)................... 3
Passenger beds...190
Sit outside (real) balcony...................................Yes
French (open-air) balcony ....Yes
Approximate cabin size (sq m) 12.5–41.0
Lift (elevator)..Yes
Rivers sailed..Rhone, Saone

BERLITZ'S RATINGS		
	Possible	Achieved
Hardware	100	82
Accommodation	100	84
Cuisine	100	78
Service	100	76
Miscellaneous	100	77
OVERALL SCORE 397 points out of 500		

The minimalist Scandinavian decor is complemented by an abundance of natural light from floor-to-ceiling windows. The well-designed and appointed cabins have full or French (open-air) balconies (some have both), quality bedding, ample storage space, good bathrooms with large glazed shower enclosures. The suites (each has a separate bedroom and wrap-around balcony) are very spacious. The restaurant is attractive and comfortable, and has a lovely high ceiling and large river-view windows. The unpretentious cuisine is tasty, there is ample variety and choice.

VIKING HEMMING ★★★★

A STYLISH, CONTEMPORARY RIVERSHIP FOR A REALLY WELL-ORGANISED CRUISE.

Operator .... Viking River Cruises
Built 2014
Length (m) 80.0
Number of decks (excluding sun deck)................... 3
Passenger beds...106
Sit outside (real) balcony....................................No
French (open-air) balcony ....Yes
Approximate cabin size (sq m) 14.0–28.0
Lift (elevator)..Yes
Rivers sailed .... Douro

BERLITZ'S RATINGS		
	Possible	Achieved
Hardware	100	76
Accommodation	100	76
Cuisine	100	75
Service	100	73
Miscellaneous	100	74
OVERALL SCORE 374 points out of 500		

Viking Hemming has tasteful and warm Scandinavian-style minimalist decor, and abundant natural light from floor-to-ceiling glass windows. All cabins have full or French (open-air) balconies (some have both) and are really practical, with quality bedding, ample storage space and good bathrooms with large glazed shower enclosures. The suites (each has a separate bedroom and wrap-around balcony) are very spacious. The restaurant is attractive and comfortable, and has a good ceiling height and large windows. The unpretentious cuisine is tasty, there is ample variety and choice.

VIKING HERJA ★★★★

THIS SPACIOUS VESSEL PROVIDES A WELL-ORGANISED CRUISE AND SCANDINAVIAN HYGGE.

Operator .... Viking River Cruises
Built 2017
Length (m) 135.0
Number of decks (excluding sun deck).................... 3
Passenger beds...190
Sit outside (real) balcony......................................Yes
French (open-air) balcony ....Yes
Approximate cabin size (sq m) 12.5–41.0
Lift (elevator)..Yes
Rivers sailed............................. Rhine, Main, Danube

BERLITZ'S RATINGS		
	Possible	Achieved
Hardware	100	84
Accommodation	100	84
Cuisine	100	78
Service	100	76
Miscellaneous	100	77
OVERALL SCORE 399 points out of 500		

Viking Herja has minimalist, but warm, Scandinavian-style decor, and abundant natural light from floor-to-ceiling glass windows. The cabins have full or French (open-air) balconies (some have both) and are really practical, with quality bedding, ample storage space and good bathrooms with large glazed shower enclosures. The suites (each has a separate bedroom and wrap-around balcony) are very spacious. The restaurant is attractive and comfortable, and has a good ceiling height and large windows. The unpretentious cuisine is tasty, there is ample variety and choice.

VIKING HERMOD ★★★★

CHOOSE THIS STYLISH, CONTEMPORARY RIVERSHIP FOR A REALLY WELL-ORGANISED CRUISE.

Operator .... Viking River Cruises
Built 2014
Length (m) 135.0
Number of decks (excluding sun deck).................... 3
Passenger beds...190
Sit outside (real) balcony......................................Yes
French (open-air) balcony ....Yes
Approximate cabin size (sq m) 12.5–41.0
Lift (elevator)..Yes
Rivers sailed...Rhone

BERLITZ'S RATINGS		
	Possible	Achieved
Hardware	100	84
Accommodation	100	84
Cuisine	100	78
Service	100	76
Miscellaneous	100	77
OVERALL SCORE 399 points out of 500		

With its Scandinavian interior, *Viking Hermod* has a spacious, light-filled feel. The double-sized suites and roomy cabins have good soundproofing, are well designed and functional, and all have full or French (open-air) balconies. The large beds are extremely comfortable. The tastefully decorated restaurant and the additional Aquavit Terrace (the latter for breakfast and lunch) offer good, unfussy food and good presentation.

VIKING HILD ★★★★

THIS LIGHT, AIRY AND SPACIOUS VESSEL PROVIDES HIGH-QUALITY CREATURE COMFORTS.

Operator .... Viking River Cruises
Built 2017
Length (m) 135.0
Number of decks (excluding sun deck).................... 3
Passenger beds...190
Sit outside (real) balcony ....Yes
French (open-air) balcony ....Yes
Approximate cabin size (sq m) 12.5–41.0
Lift (elevator)...Yes
Rivers sailed.............................. Rhine, Main, Danube

BERLITZ'S RATINGS		
	Possible	Achieved
Hardware	100	84
Accommodation	100	84
Cuisine	100	78
Service	100	76
Miscellaneous	100	77
OVERALL SCORE 399 points out of 500		

The Scandinavian interior decor is light and airy, with blond woods and very tasteful minimalist design. The main lounge is small but comfortable. The cabins have full and/or 'French (open-air) balconies due to ingenious design, with good soundproofing, and ample storage space. Two suites located aft are particularly spacious and each has a separate bedroom and wrap-around balcony. The restaurant is attractive and comfortable, and has a good ceiling height and large river-view windows. The Aquavit Terrace (for breakfast and lunch) features unfussy food, but with ample choice.

VIKING HLIN ★★★★

THIS WELL-DESIGNED, CONTEMPORARY VESSEL WILL PROVIDE A GOOD CRUISE EXPERIENCE.

Operator .... Viking River Cruises
Built 2014
Length (m) 135.0
Number of decks (excluding sun deck).................... 3
Passenger beds...190
Sit outside (real) balcony ....Yes
French (open-air) balcony ....Yes
Approximate cabin size (sq m) 12.5–41.0
Lift (elevator)...Yes
Rivers sailed.............................. Rhine, Main, Danube

BERLITZ'S RATINGS		
	Possible	Achieved
Hardware	100	82
Accommodation	100	84
Cuisine	100	78
Service	100	76
Miscellaneous	100	77
OVERALL SCORE 397 points out of 500		

Viking Hlin has minimalist, but warm Scandinavian-style interior decor, and abundant natural light from floor-to-ceiling glass windows. The cabins have full or French (open-air) balconies (some have both) and they are really practical, with quality bedding, ample storage space and good bathrooms with large glazed shower enclosures. The suites (each has a separate bedroom and wrap-around balcony) are very spacious. The restaurant is attractive and comfortable, and has a good ceiling height and large river-view windows. The unpretentious cuisine is tasty, there is ample variety and choice.

VIKING IDI ★★★★

CHOOSE THIS VERY CONTEMPORARY RIVERSHIP FOR A WELL-ROUNDED CRUISE EXPERIENCE.

Operator .... Viking River Cruises
Built 2014
Length (m) 135.0
Number of decks (excluding sun deck)................... 3
Passenger beds...190
Sit outside (real) balcony ....Yes
French (open-air) balcony ....Yes
Approximate cabin size (sq m) 12.5–41.0
Lift (elevator)...Yes
Rivers sailed............................ Rhine, Main, Danube

BERLITZ'S RATINGS		
	Possible	Achieved
Hardware	100	82
Accommodation	100	84
Cuisine	100	78
Service	100	75
Miscellaneous	100	77
OVERALL SCORE 396 points out of 500		

Viking Idi has light, airy and tasteful interior decor, with a minimalist blond-wood look and a two-deck-high atrium lobby. The practical, well-designed cabins, all with full or French (open-air) balconies, are very comfortable, with ample storage space for clothing items (the suites are especially spacious). Bathrooms have large glazed showers. The restaurant (plus the Aquavit Terrace for breakfast and lunch) offers good, unfussy food, and is nicely presented.

VIKING IDUN ★★★★

THIS STYLISH VESSEL WOULD BE A GOOD CHOICE FOR A WELL-ORGANISED CRUISE.

Operator .... Viking River Cruises
Built 2012
Length (m) 135.0
Number of decks (excluding sun deck)................... 3
Passenger beds...190
Sit outside (real) balcony ....Yes
French (open-air) balcony ....Yes
Approximate cabin size (sq m) 12.5–41.0
Lift (elevator)...Yes
Rivers sailed...Danube

BERLITZ'S RATINGS		
	Possible	Achieved
Hardware	100	81
Accommodation	100	81
Cuisine	100	78
Service	100	76
Miscellaneous	100	76
OVERALL SCORE 392 points out of 500		

The minimalist Scandinavian decor is complemented by an abundance of natural light from numerous floor-to-ceiling windows. All cabins have full or French (open-air) balconies (some have both) and are really practical, with quality bedding, ample storage space and good bathrooms with large glazed shower enclosures. The suites (each has a separate bedroom and wrap-around balcony) are very spacious. The restaurant is attractive and comfortable, and has a good ceiling height and large river-view windows. The unpretentious cuisine is tasty, there is ample variety and choice.

VIKING INGVI ★★★★
THIS STYLISH RIVERSHIP WILL LAUNCH YOU ON A WELL-ORGANISED CRUISE.

Operator .... Viking River Cruises
Built 2014
Length (m) 135.0
Number of decks (excluding sun deck).................... 3
Passenger beds...190
Sit outside (real) balcony....................................Yes
French (open-air) balcony ....Yes
Approximate cabin size (sq m) 12.5–41.0
Lift (elevator)..Yes
Rivers sailed...Rhine

BERLITZ'S RATINGS		
	Possible	Achieved
Hardware	100	83
Accommodation	100	84
Cuisine	100	78
Service	100	75
Miscellaneous	100	77
OVERALL SCORE 397 points out of 500		

Viking Ingvi has a minimalist yet comfortable Scandinavian interior, flooded with natural light. The well-designed, nicely appointed suites and cabins (all with French (open-air) balconies) are both comfortable and practical, with bathrooms that have large, glazed shower enclosures. Two suites located aft are particularly spacious and each has a separate bedroom and wrap-around balcony. The tastefully decorated restaurant and alternative Aquavit Terrace (the latter for breakfast and lunch) offer good, unfussy food.

VIKING JARL ★★★★
A GOOD CHOICE FOR A WELL-PROGRAMMED, FIRST-RATE RIVER CRUISE ON A STYLISH VESSEL.

Operator .... Viking River Cruises
Built 2013
Length (m) 135.0
Number of decks (excluding sun deck).................... 3
Passenger beds...190
Sit outside (real) balcony....................................Yes
French (open-air) balcony ....Yes
Approximate cabin size (sq m) 12.5–41.0
Lift (elevator)..Yes
Rivers sailed............................. Rhine, Main, Danube

BERLITZ'S RATINGS		
	Possible	Achieved
Hardware	100	81
Accommodation	100	84
Cuisine	100	78
Service	100	76
Miscellaneous	100	76
OVERALL SCORE 395 points out of 500		

Viking Jarl has a minimalist yet warm Scandinavian-style interior with blond wood accents and abundant natural light from floor-to-ceiling glass windows. All cabins have full or French (open-air) balconies (some have both), with quality bedding, ample storage space and good bathrooms with large glazed shower enclosures. The suites (each has a separate bedroom and wrap-around balcony) are very spacious. The restaurant is attractive and comfortable, and has a good ceiling height and large river-view windows. The unpretentious cuisine is tasty, there is ample variety and choice.

VIKING KADLIN ★★★★

THIS RIVERSHIP HAS VERY GOOD FACILITIES, SMART DECOR AND DECENT FOOD.

Operator .... Viking River Cruises
Built 2016
Length (m) 135.0
Number of decks (excluding sun deck)................... 3
Passenger beds.......................................190
Sit outside (real) balcony ....Yes
French (open-air) balcony ....Yes
Approximate cabin size (sq m) 12.5–41.0
Lift (elevator)...Yes
Rivers sailed... Seine

BERLITZ'S RATINGS		
	Possible	Achieved
Hardware	100	83
Accommodation	100	84
Cuisine	100	78
Service	100	76
Miscellaneous	100	77
OVERALL SCORE 398 points out of 500		

Viking Kadlin has minimalist but tasteful and warm Scandinavian-style interior decor, and abundant natural light due to the numerous floor-to-ceiling glass windows. All cabins have full or French (open-air) balconies (some have both) and are really designed well, have quality bedding, ample storage space and good bathrooms with large glazed shower enclosures. The suites (each has a separate bedroom and wrap-around balcony) are extremely spacious. The unpretentious cuisine is tasty; there is ample variety and choice, and it is nicely presented.

VIKING KARA ★★★★

THIS WELL-DESIGNED, CONTEMPORARY VESSEL DELIVERS A GOOD CRUISE EXPERIENCE.

Operator .... Viking River Cruises
Built 2016
Length (m) 135.0
Number of decks (excluding sun deck)................... 3
Passenger beds.......................................190
Sit outside (real) balcony ....Yes
French (open-air) balcony ....Yes
Approximate cabin size (sq m) 12.5–41.0
Lift (elevator)...Yes
Rivers sailed............................. Rhine, Main, Danube

BERLITZ'S RATINGS		
	Possible	Achieved
Hardware	100	83
Accommodation	100	84
Cuisine	100	78
Service	100	76
Miscellaneous	100	77
OVERALL SCORE 398 points out of 500		

Viking Kara has Scandinavian-style minimalist decor and abundant natural light from floor-to-ceiling glass windows. All cabins have full or French (open-air) balconies (some have both) and they are really practical, with quality bedding, ample storage space and good bathrooms with large glazed shower enclosures. The suites (each has a separate bedroom and wrap-around balcony) are very spacious. The restaurant is attractive and comfortable, and has a good ceiling height and large river-view windows. The unpretentious cuisine is tasty, there is ample variety and choice.

VIKING KVASIR ★★★★

THIS WELL-DESIGNED, CONTEMPORARY RIVERSHIP WILL DELIVER A GOOD CRUISE EXPERIENCE.

Operator .... Viking River Cruises
Built 2014
Length (m) 135.0
Number of decks (excluding sun deck)................... 3
Passenger beds..190
Sit outside (real) balcony ....Yes
French (open-air) balcony ....Yes
Approximate cabin size (sq m) 12.5–41.0
Lift (elevator)..Yes
Rivers sailed............................ Rhine, Main, Danube

BERLITZ'S RATINGS		
	Possible	Achieved
Hardware	100	83
Accommodation	100	83
Cuisine	100	78
Service	100	76
Miscellaneous	100	76
OVERALL SCORE 396 points out of 500		

Viking Kvasir is well designed, with an attractive Scandinavian interior. An innovative, practical layout includes decent storage space, French (open-air) balconies and bathrooms with heated flooring and high-tech shower walls that change from clear to frosted. Two suites located aft are particularly spacious and each has a separate bedroom and wrap-around balcony. The restaurant is attractive and comfortable, with large river-view windows. The cuisine is nicely varied, with decent ingredients, but the small-portion main dinner courses are likely to be slightly underwhelming.

VIKING LIF ★★★★

CHOOSE THIS STYLISH CONTEMPORARY RIVERSHIP FOR A WELL-ORGANISED CRUISE.

Operator .... Viking River Cruises
Built 2013
Length (m) 135.0
Number of decks (excluding sun deck)................... 3
Passenger beds..190
Sit outside (real) balcony ....Yes
French (open-air) balcony ....Yes
Approximate cabin size (sq m) 12.5–41.0
Lift (elevator)..Yes
Rivers sailed............................ Rhine, Main, Danube

BERLITZ'S RATINGS		
	Possible	Achieved
Hardware	100	82
Accommodation	100	83
Cuisine	100	78
Service	100	76
Miscellaneous	100	76
OVERALL SCORE 395 points out of 500		

With its blond wood-rich Scandinavian interior, *Viking Lif* has a spacious, light-filled, spacious feeling. A practical, innovative design incorporates French (open-air) balconies, decent storage space, extremely comfortable beds and bathrooms that feature comparatively large shower enclosures. Two suites each have a separate bedroom, lounge, wet room, and wrap-around balcony. The nicely decorated restaurant, and the alternative Aquavit Terrace (the latter for breakfast and lunch) provide good, unfussy, but nicely presented food.

VIKING LOFN ★★★★
THIS SPACIOUS VESSEL DELIVERS A WELL-ORGANISED CRUISE WITH SCANDINAVIAN HYGGE.

Operator .... Viking River Cruises
Built 2015
Length (m) 135.0
Number of decks (excluding sun deck)................... 3
Passenger beds...190
Sit outside (real) balcony ....Yes
French (open-air) balcony ....Yes
Approximate cabin size (sq m) 12.5–41.0
Lift (elevator)..Yes
Rivers sailed.............................. Rhine, Main, Danube

BERLITZ'S RATINGS		
	Possible	Achieved
Hardware	100	83
Accommodation	100	84
Cuisine	100	78
Service	100	76
Miscellaneous	100	76
OVERALL SCORE 397 points out of 500		

Viking Lofn has minimalist, but tasteful and warm, Scandinavian-style decor and abundant natural light due to numerous floor-to-ceiling glass windows. The cabins have full or French (open-air) balconies (some have both) and are really practical, with quality bedding, ample storage space and good bathrooms with large glazed shower enclosures. The suites (each has a separate bedroom and wrap-around balcony) are very spacious. The restaurant is attractive and comfortable, with large river-view windows. The unpretentious cuisine is tasty; there is ample variety and choice.

VIKING MAGNI ★★★★
THIS WOULD MAKE A VERY GOOD CHOICE FOR A STYLISH, CONTEMPORARY CRUISE.

Operator .... Viking River Cruises
Built 2013
Length (m) 135.0
Number of decks (excluding sun deck)................... 3
Passenger beds...190
Sit outside (real) balcony ....Yes
French (open-air) balcony ....Yes
Approximate cabin size (sq m) 12.5–41.0
Lift (elevator)..Yes
Rivers sailed.............................. Rhine, Main, Danube

BERLITZ'S RATINGS		
	Possible	Achieved
Hardware	100	82
Accommodation	100	83
Cuisine	100	78
Service	100	76
Miscellaneous	100	75
OVERALL SCORE 394 points out of 500		

With its Scandinavian interior, characterised by pale colours and blond wood, this fine rivership is light and airy with plenty of natural light. All cabins have full or French (open-air) balconies (some have both) and attractive bathrooms with large glazed showers. Two suites located aft are particularly spacious and each has a separate bedroom and wrap-around balcony. The restaurant is attractive and comfortable, and has large windows. The cuisine is tasty and unpretentious; there is a good variety and choice. The Aquavit Terrace, located forward, has bistro-style breakfasts and lunches.

VIKING MANI ★★★★

CHOOSE THIS STYLISH CONTEMPORARY RIVERSHIP FOR A WELL-ORGANISED CRUISE.

Operator .... Viking River Cruises
Built 2015
Length (m) 135.0
Number of decks (excluding sun deck).................. 3
Passenger beds...190
Sit outside (real) balcony ....Yes
French (open-air) balcony ....Yes
Approximate cabin size (sq m) 12.5–41.0
Lift (elevator)..Yes
Rivers sailed.......................................Rhine

BERLITZ'S RATINGS

	Possible	Achieved
Hardware	100	83
Accommodation	100	84
Cuisine	100	78
Service	100	76
Miscellaneous	100	76
OVERALL SCORE 397 points out of 500		

Viking Mani has minimalist, Scandinavian-style decor, and abundant natural light from floor-to-ceiling windows. The cabins are well designed, with full or French (open-air) balconies (some have both) and are really practical, with quality bedding, ample storage space and good bathrooms with large glazed shower enclosures. The suites (each has a separate bedroom and wrap-around balcony) are very spacious. The restaurant is attractive and comfortable, with large river-view windows. The unpretentious cuisine is tasty, there is ample variety and choice, and it is nicely presented.

VIKING MIMIR ★★★★

THIS RIVERSHIP HAS VERY GOOD FACILITIES, SMART DECOR AND DECENT FOOD.

Operator .... Viking River Cruises
Built 2015
Length (m) 135.0
Number of decks (excluding sun deck).................. 3
Passenger beds...190
Sit outside (real) balcony ....Yes
French (open-air) balcony ....Yes
Approximate cabin size (sq m) 12.5–41.0
Lift (elevator)..Yes
Rivers sailed............................. Rhine, Main, Danube

BERLITZ'S RATINGS

	Possible	Achieved
Hardware	100	83
Accommodation	100	84
Cuisine	100	78
Service	100	76
Miscellaneous	100	77
OVERALL SCORE 398 points out of 500		

Viking Mimir has tasteful Scandinavian-style minimalist interior decor, and natural light through numerous floor-to-ceiling glass windows. All cabins have full or French (open-air) balconies (some have both) and are really practical, with quality bedding, ample storage space and good bathrooms (large glazed shower enclosures). The suites (each has a separate bedroom and wrap-around balcony) are excellent. The restaurant is attractive, and has a good ceiling height and large river-view windows. The unpretentious cuisine is tasty, there is ample variety and choice, and it is nicely presented.

VIKING MODI ★★★★

CHOOSE THIS CONTEMPORARY RIVERSHIP FOR A WELL-PROGRAMMED CRUISE.

Operator .... Viking River Cruises
Built 2015
Length (m) 135.0
Number of decks (excluding sun deck) 3
Passenger beds 190
Sit outside (real) balcony ....Yes
French (open-air) balcony ....Yes
Approximate cabin size (sq m) 12.5–41.0
Lift (elevator) ....Yes
Rivers sailed .... Rhine, Main, Danube

BERLITZ'S RATINGS		
	Possible	Achieved
Hardware	100	83
Accommodation	100	84
Cuisine	100	78
Service	100	76
Miscellaneous	100	77
OVERALL SCORE 398 points out of 500		

The Scandinavian minimalist decor, characterised by pale colours and blond woods, is light and airy with lots of natural light from floor-to-ceiling glass windows. All cabins have full or French (open-air) balconies (some have both) and attractive bathrooms with large glazed showers. Two suites located aft are particularly spacious and each has a separate bedroom, lounge, wet room, and wrap-around balcony. The tastefully decorated restaurant and alternative Aquavit Terrace (the latter for breakfast and lunch) provide good, unfussy, simple food rather than fancy cuisine.

VIKING NERTHUS ★★★★

THIS STYLISH RIVERSHIP WILL LAUNCH YOU ON A WELL-ORGANISED CRUISE.

Operator .... Viking River Cruises
Built 2015
Length (m) 135.0
Number of decks (excluding sun deck) 3
Passenger beds 190
Sit outside (real) balcony ....Yes
French (open-air) balcony ....Yes
Approximate cabin size (sq m) 12.5–41.0
Lift (elevator) ....Yes
Rivers sailed .... Various European rivers

BERLITZ'S RATINGS		
	Possible	Achieved
Hardware	100	83
Accommodation	100	84
Cuisine	100	78
Service	100	76
Miscellaneous	100	77
OVERALL SCORE 398 points out of 500		

This contemporary rivership features Scandinavian-style decor and abundant natural light from floor-to-ceiling windows. The cabins have full or French (open-air) balconies (some have both) and are really practical, with quality bedding, ample storage space and good bathrooms with large glazed shower enclosures. Two aft suites (each has a separate bedroom and wrap-around balcony) are very spacious. The restaurant is attractive and comfortable, and has a good ceiling height and large river-view windows. The unpretentious cuisine is tasty; there is ample variety.

VIKING NJORD ★★★★

CHOOSE THIS COMFORTABLE VESSEL FOR A WELL-ORGANISED, STYLISH CRUISE.

Operator	Viking River Cruises
Built	2012
Length (m)	135.0
Number of decks (excluding sun deck)	3
Passenger beds	208
Sit outside (real) balcony	Yes
French (open-air) balcony	Yes
Approximate cabin size (sq m)	12.5–41.0
Lift (elevator)	Yes
Rivers sailed	Danube

BERLITZ'S RATINGS	Possible	Achieved
Hardware	100	81
Accommodation	100	81
Cuisine	100	78
Service	100	76
Miscellaneous	100	75
OVERALL SCORE 391 points out of 500		

Viking Njord is well designed, with Scandinavian-style decor. An innovative, practical layout has created fairly spacious, well-appointed cabins with French (open-air) balconies, decent storage space and bathrooms with heated flooring and high-tech shower walls that change from clear to frosted. The restaurant is attractive and comfortable, and has a good ceiling height and large river-view windows. The cuisine is tasty and unpretentious; there is a good variety and choice, and it is nicely presented. The Aquavit Terrace, located forward, has bistro-style food for breakfast and lunch.

VIKING ODIN ★★★★

A STYLISH CHOICE FOR A WELL-PROGRAMMED, FIRST-RATE CRUISE WITH HYGGE.

Operator	Viking River Cruises
Built	2012
Length (m)	135.0
Number of decks (excluding sun deck)	3
Passenger beds	208
Sit outside (real) balcony	Yes
French (open-air) balcony	Yes
Approximate cabin size (sq m)	12.5–41.0
Lift (elevator)	Yes
Rivers sailed	Danube, Main, Moselle, Rhine

BERLITZ'S RATINGS	Possible	Achieved
Hardware	100	81
Accommodation	100	81
Cuisine	100	78
Service	100	75
Miscellaneous	100	77
OVERALL SCORE 392 points out of 500		

With its Scandinavian minimalist interior decor, characterised by light colours, *Viking Odin* is light, airy and very comfortable. All cabins have full or French (open-air) balconies (some have both) and are really practical, with attractive bathrooms with large glazed showers. The double-sized suites are extremely spacious. The restaurant is comfortable, and quite spacious. The unfussy cuisine has plenty of taste, and there is a good variety. The alternative Aquavit Terrace (the latter for breakfast and lunch only) offer good, unfussy but nicely presented food to match.

VIKING OSFRID ★★★★

THIS WELL-DESIGNED, CONTEMPORARY SHIP WITH SCANDINAVIAN DECOR.

Operator .... Viking River Cruises
Built 2016
Length (m) 80.0
Number of decks (excluding sun deck) 3
Passenger beds..106
Sit outside (real) balcony ....Yes
French (open-air) balcony ....Yes
Approximate cabin size (sq m) 14.0–28.0
Lift (elevator)..Yes
Rivers sailed... Douro

BERLITZ'S RATINGS		
	Possible	Achieved
Hardware	100	83
Accommodation	100	83
Cuisine	100	77
Service	100	75
Miscellaneous	100	78
OVERALL SCORE 396 points out of 500		

Viking Osfrid has Scandinavian-style blond wood-accented decor, and abundant natural light from floor-to-ceiling windows. All cabins have full or French (open-air) balconies (some have both), quality bedding, ample storage space and good bathrooms with large glazed shower enclosures. The suites (each has a separate bedroom and wrap-around balcony) are very spacious. The restaurant is attractive and comfortable, and has a good ceiling height and large river-view windows. The unpretentious cuisine is tasty, there is ample variety and choice, and it is nicely presented.

VIKING RINDA ★★★★

CHOOSE THIS CONTEMPORARY RIVERSHIP FOR A WELL-PROGRAMMED CRUISE EXPERIENCE.

Operator .... Viking River Cruises
Built 2013
Length (m) 135.0
Number of decks (excluding sun deck) 3
Passenger beds..190
Sit outside (real) balcony ....Yes
French (open-air) balcony ....Yes
Approximate cabin size (sq m) 12.5–41.0
Lift (elevator)..Yes
Rivers sailed... Seine

BERLITZ'S RATINGS		
	Possible	Achieved
Hardware	100	83
Accommodation	100	84
Cuisine	100	78
Service	100	75
Miscellaneous	100	75
OVERALL SCORE 395 points out of 500		

Viking Rinda has Scandinavian-style decor, and abundant natural light from floor-to-ceiling windows. The well-designed and appointed cabins have full or French (open-air) balconies (some have both), generously sized beds with quality bedding, ample storage space, good soundproofing, and bathrooms have large glazed shower enclosures. The suites (each has a separate bedroom, lounge, wet room and wrap-around balcony) are extremely comfortable. The restaurant is comfortable and attractive, and its cuisine is unpretentious but tasty; there is ample variety and choice.

VIKING ROLF ★★★★

THIS LIGHT, AIRY AND SPACIOUS VESSEL PROVIDES HIGH-QUALITY CREATURE COMFORTS.

Operator .... Viking River Cruises
Built 2016
Length (m) 135.0
Number of decks (excluding sun deck)................... 3
Passenger beds...190
Sit outside (real) balcony ....Yes
French (open-air) balcony ....Yes
Approximate cabin size (sq m) 12.5–41.0
Lift (elevator)..Yes
Rivers sailed .... Seine

BERLITZ'S RATINGS		
	Possible	Achieved
Hardware	100	84
Accommodation	100	84
Cuisine	100	78
Service	100	76
Miscellaneous	100	77
OVERALL SCORE 399 points out of 500		

With its tasteful, minimalist Scandinavian-style interior, *Viking Rolf* has a spacious, airy feeling, and plenty of natural light through floor-to-ceiling glass windows. The double-sized suites and spacious cabins have good reading lights and soundproofing, are well designed and functional, and have full (sit outside) or French open-air balconies. The large beds are really comfortable. The tastefully decorated restaurant and the Aquavit Terrace (the latter for breakfast and lunch) provide good, unfussy food that is tasty and nicely presented.

VIKING SKADI ★★★★

THIS STYLISH VESSEL PROVIDES A COMFORTABLE, WELL-ORGANISED CRUISE.

Operator .... Viking River Cruises
Built 2013
Length (m) 135.0
Number of decks (excluding sun deck)................... 3
Passenger beds...190
Sit outside (real) balcony ....Yes
French (open-air) balcony ....Yes
Approximate cabin size (sq m) 12.5–41.0
Lift (elevator)..Yes
Rivers sailed............................. Rhine, Main, Danube

BERLITZ'S RATINGS		
	Possible	Achieved
Hardware	100	83
Accommodation	100	84
Cuisine	100	78
Service	100	75
Miscellaneous	100	77
OVERALL SCORE 397 points out of 500		

With its tasteful Scandinavian decor, characterised by light colours plus an abundance of glass which lets in the natural light, *Viking Skadi* is airy and very comfortable. All cabins have full or French (open-air) balconies (some have both) and are really practical, with attractive bathrooms with large glazed showers. The suites (each has a separate bedroom and wrap-around balcony) are very spacious. The restaurant is attractive and comfortable, and has a good ceiling height and large river-view windows. The unfussy cuisine is tasty and well presented, and there's a good variety of dishes.

VIKING SKIRMIR ★★★★

THIS WELL-DESIGNED, CONTEMPORARY SHIP WILL PROVIDE A GOOD CRUISE EXPERIENCE.

Operator .... Viking River Cruises
Built 2015
Length (m) 135.0
Number of decks (excluding sun deck)................... 3
Passenger beds..190
Sit outside (real) balcony.....................................Yes
French (open-air) balcony ....Yes
Approximate cabin size (sq m) 12.5–41.0
Lift (elevator)..Yes
Rivers sailed........................... Rhine, Main, Danube

BERLITZ'S RATINGS		
	Possible	Achieved
Hardware	100	83
Accommodation	100	84
Cuisine	100	78
Service	100	76
Miscellaneous	100	77
OVERALL SCORE 398 points out of 500		

Viking Skirmir is well designed, with functional Scandinavian-style decor, and abundant natural light from floor-to-ceiling windows. All cabins feature full or French (open-air) balconies (some have both), quality bedding, ample storage space; bathrooms have large glazed shower enclosures. The suites (each has a separate bedroom and wrap-around balcony) are very spacious. The restaurant is attractive and comfortable, and has a good ceiling height and large river-view windows. The cuisine is unpretentious but tasty, there is ample variety and choice, and it is nicely presented.

VIKING TIALFI ★★★★

TRY THIS VERY COMFORTABLE VESSEL FOR A WELL-ORGANISED CRUISE EXPERIENCE.

Operator .... Viking River Cruises
Built 2016
Length (m) 135.0
Number of decks (excluding sun deck)................... 3
Passenger beds..190
Sit outside (real) balcony.....................................Yes
French (open-air) balcony ....Yes
Approximate cabin size (sq m) 12.5–41.0
Lift (elevator)..Yes
Rivers sailed..Rhine

BERLITZ'S RATINGS		
	Possible	Achieved
Hardware	100	83
Accommodation	100	84
Cuisine	100	78
Service	100	76
Miscellaneous	100	77
OVERALL SCORE 398 points out of 500		

With its minimalist, wood-accented Scandinavian-style decor, *Viking Tialfi* has a spacious feeling, and there's an abundance of floor-to-ceiling windows. The double-sized suites, and spacious cabins have good reading lights and soundproofing, are well designed and functional, and have either full (sit outside) or French open-air balconies (the two suites have a wrap-around balcony). The large beds are very comfortable. The nicely accented restaurant is comfortable, and, with the Aquavit Terrace (the latter for breakfast and lunch) provide good, unfussy food that is nicely presented.

VIKING TOR ★★★★

A SUPERBLY DESIGNED, VERY COMFORTABLE CONTEMPORARY SHIP FOR GREAT CRUISING.

Operator .... Viking River Cruises
Built 2013
Length (m) 135.0
Number of decks (excluding sun deck)................... 3
Passenger beds...190
Sit outside (real) balcony....................................Yes
French (open-air) balcony ....Yes
Approximate cabin size (sq m) 12.5–41.0
Lift (elevator)..Yes
Rivers sailed............................ Rhine, Main, Danube

BERLITZ'S RATINGS		
	Possible	Achieved
Hardware	100	83
Accommodation	100	84
Cuisine	100	78
Service	100	75
Miscellaneous	100	77
OVERALL SCORE 397 points out of 500		

Viking Tor features Scandinavian-style decor, and abundant natural light from floor-to-ceiling windows. The cabins are well designed and appointed and have full or French (open-air) balconies (some have both), generously sized beds with quality bedding, ample storage space, good soundproofing; bathrooms have large glazed shower enclosures. The suites (each has a separate bedroom and wrap-around balcony) are very spacious. The restaurant is attractive and comfortable, with large river-view windows. The unpretentious cuisine is tasty, there is ample variety and choice.

VIKING TORGIL ★★★★

THIS STYLISH RIVERSHIP WILL LAUNCH YOU ON A WELL-ROUNDED CRUISE.

Operator .... Viking River Cruises
Built 2014
Length (m) 80.0
Number of decks (excluding sun deck)................... 3
Passenger beds...106
Sit outside (real) balcony....................................Yes
French (open-air) balcony ....Yes
Approximate cabin size (sq m) 14.0–28.0
Lift (elevator)..Yes
Rivers sailed.. Douro

BERLITZ'S RATINGS		
	Possible	Achieved
Hardware	100	76
Accommodation	100	76
Cuisine	100	75
Service	100	73
Miscellaneous	100	74
OVERALL SCORE 374 points out of 500		

The minimalist Scandinavian interior decor is complemented by an abundance of natural light from numerous floor-to-ceiling windows. The well-designed, nicely appointed suites and cabins all have full or French (open-air) balconies, are both comfortable and practical, and have good storage space and practical bathrooms with large glazed shower enclosures. The cheerfully decorated restaurant provides decent, tasty food that is nicely presented, although it just lacks the elusive 'wow' factor.

VIKING VAR ★★★★

THIS STYLISH VESSEL IS A GOOD CHOICE FOR A WELL-ORGANISED CRUISE.

Operator .... Viking River Cruises
Built 2013
Length (m) 135.0
Number of decks (excluding sun deck).................... 3
Passenger beds..190
Sit outside (real) balcony ....Yes
French (open-air) balcony ....Yes
Approximate cabin size (sq m) 12.5–41.0
Lift (elevator)..Yes
Rivers sailed.............................. Rhine, Main, Danube

BERLITZ'S RATINGS		
	Possible	Achieved
Hardware	100	83
Accommodation	100	84
Cuisine	100	78
Service	100	75
Miscellaneous	100	77
OVERALL SCORE 397 points out of 500		

With its Scandinavian-style interior decor, *Viking Var* has a spacious, airy feeling, aided by the abundance of floor-to-ceiling glass windows. The double-sized suites and spacious cabins have good reading lights and soundproofing, are well designed and functional, and have full (sit outside) or French open-air balconies (the two suites have a wrap-around balcony), and high-quality beds that are really comfortable. The restaurant has high ceilings, and, together with the Aquavit Terrace (the latter for breakfast and lunch) provides good, unfussy food that is nicely presented.

VIKING VE ★★★★

THIS RIVERSHIP SHOULD DELIVER A VERY ENJOYABLE RIVER CRUISE EXPERIENCE.

Operator .... Viking River Cruises
Built 2015
Length (m) 135.0
Number of decks (excluding sun deck).................... 3
Passenger beds..190
Sit outside (real) balcony ....Yes
French (open-air) balcony ....Yes
Approximate cabin size (sq m) 12.5–41.0
Lift (elevator)..Yes
Rivers sailed.............................. Rhine, Main, Danube

BERLITZ'S RATINGS		
	Possible	Achieved
Hardware	100	83
Accommodation	100	84
Cuisine	100	78
Service	100	75
Miscellaneous	100	77
OVERALL SCORE 397 points out of 500		

Viking Ve features Scandinavian-style decor, and abundant natural light from floor-to-ceiling windows. The cabins have full or French (open-air) balconies (some have both), quality bedding, ample storage space and bathrooms with large glazed shower enclosures. Two suites (each has a separate bedroom and wrap-around balcony) are very spacious. The restaurant is attractive and comfortable, with large river-view windows. The cuisine is tasty and unpretentious, and there is a good variety and choice. The Aquavit Terrace, located forward, has bistro-style food for breakfast and lunch.

VIKING VIDAR ★★★★

THIS WELL-DESIGNED, CONTEMPORARY SHIP WILL PROVIDE A GOOD CRUISE EXPERIENCE.

Operator .... Viking River Cruises
Built 2015
Length (m) 135.0
Number of decks (excluding sun deck).................. 3
Passenger beds..190
Sit outside (real) balcony ....Yes
French (open-air) balcony ....Yes
Approximate cabin size (sq m) 12.5–41.0
Lift (elevator)..Yes
Rivers sailed.............................. Rhine, Main, Danube

BERLITZ'S RATINGS		
	Possible	Achieved
Hardware	100	83
Accommodation	100	84
Cuisine	100	78
Service	100	76
Miscellaneous	100	77
OVERALL SCORE 398 points out of 500		

With its Scandinavian-style interior, *Viking Vidar* has a spacious, airy feeling and very tasteful light decor, and an abundance of glass windows throughout. The cabins are well designed and appointed and have full or French (open-air) balconies (some have both), generously sized beds with quality bedding, ample storage space, good soundproofing, and the nice bathrooms have large glazed shower enclosures. The restaurant is attractive, with large river-view windows, while the Aquavit Terrace (for breakfast and lunch) provides good, unfussy food that is nicely presented.

VIKING VILHJALM ★★★★

THIS STYLISH VESSEL PROVIDES A COMFORTABLE, WELL-ORGANISED CRUISE.

Operator .... Viking River Cruises
Built 2016
Length (m) 135.0
Number of decks (excluding sun deck).................. 3
Passenger beds..190
Sit outside (real) balcony ....Yes
French (open-air) balcony ....Yes
Approximate cabin size (sq m) 12.5–41.0
Lift (elevator)..Yes
Rivers sailed.............................. Rhine, Main, Danube

BERLITZ'S RATINGS		
	Possible	Achieved
Hardware	100	83
Accommodation	100	84
Cuisine	100	78
Service	100	76
Miscellaneous	100	77
OVERALL SCORE 398 points out of 500		

With its wood-accented Scandinavian-style decor and floor-to-ceiling windows , *Viking Vilhjalm* has a spacious feel. The double-sized suites and spacious cabins have good reading lights and soundproofing, are well designed, and have either full (sit outside) or French open-air balconies (the two suites have a wrap-around balcony). The large beds are very comfortable. The nicely accented restaurant is comfortable and provides good, unfussy food that is nicely presented; it is complemented by the similar offering from the Aquavit Terrace (the latter for breakfast and lunch).

VIKING VILI ★★★★

THIS RIVERSHIP HAS VERY GOOD FACILITIES, SMART DECOR AND GOOD CUISINE.

Operator .... Viking River Cruises
Built 2015
Length (m) 135.0
Number of decks (excluding sun deck).................. 3
Passenger beds...190
Sit outside (real) balcony.......................................Yes
French (open-air) balcony ....Yes
Approximate cabin size (sq m) 12.5–41.0
Lift (elevator)..Yes
Rivers sailed.............................. Rhine, Main, Danube

BERLITZ'S RATINGS		
	Possible	Achieved
Hardware	100	82
Accommodation	100	84
Cuisine	100	78
Service	100	76
Miscellaneous	100	77
OVERALL SCORE 397 points out of 500		

This is another example of a rivership with Scandinavian-style decor, and abundant natural light from floor-to-ceiling windows. The cabins have full or French (open-air) balconies (some have both) and are really practical, with quality bedding, ample storage space and good bathrooms with large glazed shower enclosures. The suites (each has a separate bedroom and wrap-around balcony) are very spacious. The restaurant is attractive and comfortable, with large river-view windows. The unpretentious cuisine is tasty, there is ample variety and choice, and it is nicely presented.

VIKTORIA ★★★

THIS IS A WELL-DESIGNED VESSEL WITH MODEST, BUT ATTRACTIVE FEATURES.

Operator ....Nicko Cruises
Built 2004
Length (m) 126.7
Number of decks (excluding sun deck).................. 3
Passenger beds...180
Sit outside (real) balcony...No
French (open-air) balcony ....Yes
Approximate cabin size (sq m) 16.0
Lift (elevator)..No
Rivers sailed.............................. Rhine, Main, Danube

BERLITZ'S RATINGS		
	Possible	Achieved
Hardware	100	62
Accommodation	100	61
Cuisine	100	56
Service	100	56
Miscellaneous	100	60
OVERALL SCORE 295 points out of 500		

Viktoria is a rivership with tasteful interior decor, and there's a pleasant wellness area with sauna. The nicely decorated cabins, many with French (open-air) balconies, are relatively spacious, with twin side-by-side beds that can be separated if required. The restaurant has attractive warm wood interior decor, and the cuisine is reasonably sound, although the variety is limited for dinner (it is quite good at breakfast).

VIRGINIA ★★
THIS VERY SMALL VINTAGE VESSEL PROVIDES SIMPLY A VERY BASIC, INEXPENSIVE CRUISE.

Operator ....Shearings Holidays
Built 1965
Length (m) 67.5
Number of decks (excluding sun deck)................... 3
Passenger beds...107
Sit outside (real) balcony..No
French (open-air) balcony ....No
Approximate cabin size (sq m) 9.0
Lift (elevator)..No
Rivers sailed................................ Rhine, Moselle

BERLITZ'S RATINGS		
	Possible	Achieved
Hardware	100	32
Accommodation	100	33
Cuisine	100	36
Service	100	40
Miscellaneous	100	41
OVERALL SCORE 182 points out of 500		

Virginia has two public rooms: a lounge/bar and a restaurant, both set low in the vessel. The cabins have been refurbished and have modern furnishings, but they are very cramped, with little closet and drawer space, so take only minimal clothing items. The bathrooms are tiny, and there's simply no space for personal toiletry items. The restaurant is mildly attractive, but comfortable it isn't. As for food, there's little choice because the galley is very small, and so the self-service buffets are really quite poor and basic. This is really no-frills river cruising.

VISTA FLAMENCO ★★★
THIS SMART, COMFORTABLE RIVERSHIP PROVIDES GOOD-VALUE, LOW-BUDGET CRUISES.

Operator .... 1AVista Reisen
Built 2005
Length (m) 135.0
Number of decks (excluding sun deck)................... 3
Passenger beds...200
Sit outside (real) balcony..No
French (open-air) balcony ....Yes
Approximate cabin size (sq m) 13.0
Lift (elevator)..No
Rivers sailed..Danube

BERLITZ'S RATINGS		
	Possible	Achieved
Hardware	100	65
Accommodation	100	60
Cuisine	100	55
Service	100	53
Miscellaneous	100	60
OVERALL SCORE 293 points out of 500		

Forerunner of the 'twin cruiser' concept, *Vista Flamenco* has fairly bright, but unfussy interior decor in the lounge and public areas. The rivership has small, modern, fairly quiet cabins, and many of them have floor-to-ceiling slide-open doors and (French) open-air balconies. The beds are fixed, however, and one converts to a sofa by day for more space to move around in. Large glass windows allow good views from the lounge and from the restaurant, which serves food that is best described as adequate, and nothing more.

VIVALDI ★★★
THIS FRENCH-STYLE RIVERSHIP PROVIDES A FAIRLY DECENT OVERALL CRUISE.

Operator	CroisiEurope
Built	2009
Length (m)	110.0
Number of decks (excluding sun deck)	3
Passenger beds	176
Sit outside (real) balcony	No
French (open-air) balcony	No
Approximate cabin size (sq m)	12.0
Lift (elevator)	Yes
Rivers sailed	Rhine, Main, Danube

BERLITZ'S RATINGS		
	Possible	Achieved
Hardware	100	63
Accommodation	100	54
Cuisine	100	56
Service	100	57
Miscellaneous	100	58
OVERALL SCORE 288 points out of 500		

The lounge and overall interior decor are pleasant enough, and there's no glitz. Cabins (no balconies) have slim beds (or double bed), noisy closet doors, poor lighting for reading and little storage space (take minimum clothing); bathrooms are cramped, with a tiny circular shower enclosure. Beware: the stairway to the lower deck cabins has short steps. The restaurant (aft) is pleasant enough, but the chairs don't have armrests. The cuisine is standard and unfussy, like the wines. Go for the French ambience, the itinerary and destinations, and the price point. Excursions cost extra.

WILLIAM SHAKESPEARE ★★★★
EXUDES BRITISH STYLE AND MIXES CONTEMPORARY AND TRADITIONAL FEATURES.

Operator	Riviera Travel
Built	2014
Length (m)	110.0
Number of decks (excluding sun deck)	3
Passenger beds	142
Sit outside (real) balcony	Yes
French (open-air) balcony	Yes
Approximate cabin size (sq m)	14.0–22.0
Lift (elevator)	Yes
Rivers sailed	Rhine, Main, Danube

BERLITZ'S RATINGS		
	Possible	Achieved
Hardware	100	75
Accommodation	100	72
Cuisine	100	65
Service	100	69
Miscellaneous	100	73
OVERALL SCORE 354 points out of 500		

This fine, well-designed rivership, with high-quality furnishings and an inviting ambience, has restrained, tasteful interior decor without any bling. The two-deck-high reception lobby is open and spacious. The cabins are quite practical and provide ample clothing storage space, and the lighting and soundproofing are both good. The bathrooms have fairly large glazed shower enclosures. The one-seating restaurant is quite comfortable. The cuisine is of a decent quality, although it's not memorable; it's specifically tailored to British tastes, and the breakfasts are repetitious.

American Empress in The Dalles, Oregon

River Cruising in the USA

A river cruise aboard a stern paddlewheel steamboat offers an experience found nowhere else, from the deep south's famed hospitality to the dramatic scenery of the Pacific Northwest.

River cruising in the USA is quite different to river cruising in Europe, and this book is hence divided into two separate parts.

In Europe, riverships are built within the hull, while traditional steamboats/riverboats in the USA have always been built on platforms. Another difference is in their propulsion. In Europe, riverships are driven by diesel engines; in the USA, they have traditionally been driven by steam engines, although replica 'steamboats' are now driven by diesel engines, and propelled by huge red wooden paddlewheels aft.

There are also distinct differences in the cuisine, service standards, and excursions (most of which evolve around American history, 'Americana' and that loveable river wordsmith, Mark Twain).

A few key differences between European and American riverships to be aware of:

Compared with ocean-going cruise ships, steamboat/riverboat cruises are expensive, and food and service standards are lower. Drink prices are also high – the same as on land in the USA

Gangway to the *American Queen*.

(there are no duty-free prices). Also, port charges and Federal Passenger Vessel Fees will be added to the cruise fare.

There are always two captains aboard US steamboats/riverboats: one acts as the pilot, whereas the other is the captain. Both, however, are actually licensed captains (they take turns).

River distances are given in land miles, and not nautical miles, as aboard oceangoing cruise ships.

How it all began...

In the early 1800s, Robert Fulton, a New Jersey landowner, obtained a patent granting exclusive monopoly for all steamboat operations on the great rivers, and it was the successful 1811 voyage of the steamboat New Orleans that started it all when Nicholas J. Roosevelt (the great-grandfather of 'Teddy' Roosevelt) sailed his wood-fired steam craft down the Mississippi, from Pittsburgh all the way to New Orleans. The age of the steamboat was born.

The USA's South began its development around the Mississippi River (declared to be the western boundary of the United States when the river passed into Spanish hands in 1769). In the early 1800s steamboats along the waterway offered transport possibilities; as a result, trade grew between neighbouring states, which hastened the further development of the steamboat not only for transporting freight, but also as recreational travel for passengers. The development of the steamboat was rapid, and stern paddle-wheelers grew in size because of the demand. They had a shallow draft, and, being wide, could operate in a variety of conditions and remain stable.

From 1811 until approximately 1830, steamboat numbers grew dramatically, and companies enjoyed soaring profits. The best sailing time occurred during high water, when vessels carried cotton, flour, livestock, tobacco, whiskey – and passengers – along the Mississippi, Tennessee, and Cumberland rivers. A typical steamboat had three decks, the uppermost one being called a 'hurricane deck', although this was simply an observation and lounging area. Steamboat social life developed with cabins (tiny, but larger than a stagecoach interior) introduced along a vessel's length, and affluent passengers sought to travel in greater comfort, while deck passengers travelled with the cargo, and often slept on bales of cotton or grain.

The rise in the use of iron and steel meant that the steamboat's hull could be built with iron instead of wood. This allowed them to carry more weight, and so the decks above the hull's platform could be built up, adding a larger number of cabins, public rooms and entertainment spaces to cater to the growth in passenger demand. An iron hull also helped to balance the huge weight of the paddlewheels, which weighed several tons on the larger vessels.

Designers added increasingly decorative elements, mainly to attract and please the ladies. Filigree decoration was added, and smoke-stacks (funnels) became taller, attracting attention as the steamboats moved along the river, while keeping – or attempting to keep – any soot and hot cinders away from open passenger decks.

One setback occurred when the 'Panic of 1837' happened in the financial markets, and the recession that followed saw profits decrease, companies go bankrupt, and unemployment go up.

In the mid-1840s the acquisition of Oregon (and California) opened up the West Coast to steamboat traffic, and stern paddle-wheelers became instrumental in the development of the region known as the Pacific Northwest. Eventually, however, they too were generally supplanted by the expansion of railroads and roads, and the last passenger steamboat was withdrawn in 1917.

America's Civil War (1861–5), also known as the 'War Between the States' (think: Vivien Leigh and Clark Gable in Gone With the Wind), was also a setback to steamboat travel, since a major objective was fought to control the country's key rivers, especially the Mississippi and the Tennessee. Civilian paddle-wheelers were commandeered for military use. Trade on the river was suspended for two years because the Confederates blockaded the Mississippi before the Union victory at Vicksburg reopened the river on 4 July 1863.

A gradual decline of the steamboats came about due to the development of the railroad, from around 1832. By 1840 over 2,800 miles (4,506km) of track had been built in the states east of the Mississippi River. These – the rise of the railroads and the Civil War – closed most western river commercial traffic and marked a turning point for the Steamboat Age. The 'iron road' (railroad) was faster for hauling freight (and passengers), and the steamboats simply couldn't compete.

Thankfully, the steamboats didn't disappear entirely, although they did lose their competitive edge and continued to serve urban centres and the hundreds of smaller ports and landings. They were useful in delivering farm equipment and consumer goods to towns upriver, and returned carrying lumber, livestock, farm produce – and passengers.

Meanwhile, by the late 1860s, the remaining paddle-wheel steamboats on the Mississippi had become increasingly fanciful with more entertainment on board. Now carrying several hundred passengers, these vessels became floating music halls, or show

STEAMBOAT ERA LANGUAGE

Some of America's most colourful figures of speech, still in use today, particularly in the Deep South, were coined more than 100 years ago, when the fancy steamboats dominated the nation's rivers. Here's how some of them came about:

'Letting off steam' came directly from the steamboats, when the huge side and stern paddle-wheelers were powered by steam. From time to time, the pressure from the boilers became too high, and it had to be relieved through special check valves. So, relieving that pressure, letting off steam, became a description for humans whose emotions had run too high.

'Outlandish' came about as a result of people who lived west of the Mississippi river: they were called 'outlanders'. Early pioneers who travelled there were often rowdy and wore loud clothing, and were thus referred to as 'outlandish'.

'High on the hog' comes from live hogs sometimes being carried aboard steamboats for slaughtering and cooking, as well as for transportation. They were washed thoroughly before they were sent aboard – after all, no one wanted their steamboat smelling dirty! The water used to wash them was thrown out, and 'hog wash' came to mean anything useless.

Passengers ate 'high on the hog', and the captain and his officers were handsomely paid for moving thousands of bales of cotton and hay on a single voyage, which also led to another phrase: 'bringing home the bacon'.

Some of the poorer folk who sought land on which to settle floated down the river on rafts. The oars they used to help them steer were knows as 'riffs'. These folk became known as 'riffraff', which later became a term used to describe disreputable people. Likewise, in the early 1800s, many boys of English or German origin had names such as William, Wilbur or Willy. They travelled by steamboat on the Ohio River to the hills of West Virginia, Kentucky and Tennessee. They then became known as 'hillbillies'.

Some people would carry fiddles (violins) with them and they would play along the riverbanks and wharves for pennies. So, if you didn't work, you would be accused of 'fiddlin' around'.

People who were rich enough to ravel on the steamboats in the best accommodation (the higher up the steamboat the better) became known as 'high falutin' folks' because their accommodation was nearer the chimneys, or flutes. Again, the steamboats with the tallest chimneys, or stacks, were thought to be 'well stacked'.

On an open deck of *American Empress.*

palaces, and gambling parlours became common-place. Passenger cabins became larger and were furnished with fine, polished inlaid woods, sofas, oil paintings and electric lamps. The toilet facilities were poor, however (unlike those on today's steam-boats, which have private bathrooms with showers, washbasin and toilet), and little heat was provided, except from pot-bellied stoves.

In the dining salon (usually located in a steam-boat's centre, with ladies' cabins aft and men's cab-ins forward) the cuisine was extravagant (particularly compared to what was available on shore), with the best steamboats providing the finest cutlery, table linens, meat, game, fruit and nuts.

New Era

Fortunately, a resurgence of the steamboats was brought about in the 1970s with the return of rec-reational steam paddle-wheelers to the Mississippi, Cumberland and Tennessee rivers by the Delta Queen Steamboat Company (the company's roots date back to 1890). The *Delta Queen* (entered service in 1927; refurbished in 2015) the *American Queen* (launched in 1995) and the *Mississippi Queen* (launched in 1976) – all three were designated as official US postal sta-tions – fire their boilers with diesel oil, not wood or coal, as in the Steamboat Age.

Of the three, only the *American Queen* is in opera-tion today, reintroduced with the same name by the American Queen Steamboat Company in 2012. The *Mississippi Queen* was scrapped in 2010. Smallest of the three, the *Delta Queen* was built in Scotland, and designated a U.S. National Historic Landmark in June 1989. No longer able to sail with overnight passengers because its Safety of Life at Sea certi-fication exemption expired in 2009 (its upper struc-ture was built almost entirely of wood), it presently resides in Chattanooga, Tennessee and operates as a floating hotel.

In 2000, the Delta Queen Steamboat Company re-introduced (replica) steamboat-style cruising in the Pacific Northwest, with *Columbia Queen* (presently named *Louisiane* and operated by French America Line). Following the tragic events of 11 September 2001, the 111-year-old company filed for bankruptcy protection. Its assets, including the steamboats, were sold by the US Maritime Administration (MARAD) to various entities, but the vessels stopped operations completely in 2008.

Yesteryear Cruising Today

Taking a river cruise in the USA aboard a stern pad-dle-wheeler is now popular again. This is because, although it is expensive when compared to river cruising in Europe, in the fast-paced contemporary world, increasing numbers of people are fascinated by the lifestyle and traditions of the serene, almost timeless, bygone era, and want to understand and experience what life and travel was like in the days of the Great Steamboat Era, when Mark Twain said: 'When man can go 700 miles an hour, he will want to go seven again.'

To sum up, river cruising in the USA is very different to river cruising on Europe's waterways, where stern paddle-wheelers and showboats, or steam engines, or calliopes – those musical oddities – simply don't exist. The romance of antebellum houses or the whalebone-hooped bustle dresses of yesteryear add to the appeal.

MARK TWAIN: A POTTED HISTORY

Mark Twain (real name Samuel Langhorne Clemens) was born in Florida, Missouri, on 30 November 1835. He grew up in the nearby Mississippi River town of Hannibal, Missouri, and fell in love with the river at an early age, although his father was a lawyer. The river, 'the majestic, magnificent Mississippi, rolling its mile-wide tide along, shining in the sun' made him envious of the steamboat men, and it became his boyhood dream and ambition to become one of them, a steamboat captain.

In 1857, at the age of 21, he took a trip on the Mississippi from St Louis aboard a steamboat called *Paul Jones* and apprenticed himself to become a steamboat captain. He trained under Captain Horace Bixby, a 'lightening pilot', and spent three years navigating the constantly changing river aboard various paddlewheel steamboats.

Due to the American Civil War (1861–5), traffic on the river was closed in the spring of 1861, and Clemens served briefly as a volunteer in the Confederate States Army, after which he worked in the mining, prospecting and timber industries. In 1862 he was hired as a writer for the Virginia City *Territorial Enterprise* and soon began to sign his work 'Mark Twain'. But this was not just a name – meaning 'mark number two', it was the river term for two fathoms or 3.6m (12ft) deep, which was the point at which the water was safe for steamboat navigation.

It was the Mississippi River that inspired not only his pen name, but also some of his most popular literary works. Both his novel *The Adventures of Tom Sawyer* (1876) and its sequel *Adventures of Huckleberry Finn* (1884) were drawn from his boyhood escapades beside the river. *Life on the Mississippi* (1883) chronicled his experiences as a steamboat traveller and pilot, all the way from St Paul to New Orleans. His piloting days were over by the time the book was published, although he always longed to return to the river he loved so much and knew so well. Mark Twain died on 21 April 1910, at the age of 74.

In *Life on the Mississippi (1883)* Twain wrote, 'Mississippi steamboating was born about 1812; at the end of thirty year it had grown to mighty proportions; and in less than thirty year more it was dead! Of course it is not absolutely dead; but contrasted with what it was in its prime vigor,

Mississippi steamboating may be called dead.

How marvellous that steamboating still exists today, more than 100 years after this rather ominous prediction.

Quotes from Mark Twain's *Life on the Mississippi* (1883)

The river

The face of the water, in time, became a wonderful book...and it was not a book to be read once and thrown aside, for it had a new story to tell every day. One cannot see too many summer sunrises on the Mississippi... First, there is the eloquence of silence...the water is glass-smooth, then a bird pipes up, another follows, and soon the pipings develop into a jubilant riot of music.

I still kept in mind a certain wonderful sunset which I witnessed when steamboating was new to me. A broad expanse of the river was turned to blood; in the middle distance the red hue brightened into gold... the dissolving lights drifted steadily, enriching it every passing moment with new marvels of colouring. The great Mississippi, the majestic, the magnificent Mississippi, rolling its mile-wide tide along, shining in the sun.

Four years at West Point, and plenty of books and schooling, will learn a man a great deal, I reckon, but it won't learn him the river.

League after league, it still pours its chocolate tide along, between its solid forest walls...and so the day goes, the night comes, and again the day – and still the same – majestic, unchanging sameness of serenity, repose, tranquility...

Steamboats

She is long and sharp and trim and pretty; she has two tall fancy-topped chimneys, with a gilded device of some kind swung between them; a fanciful pilot-house, all glass and 'gingerbread'.

She was as clean and dainty as a drawing-room; when I looked down her long, gilded saloon, it was like gazing through a splendid tunnel; she had an oil-picture...on every stateroom door; she glittered with no end of prism-fringed chandeliers, the clerk's office was elegant, the bar was marvelous, and the barkeeper had been barbered and upholstered at incredible cost.

The steamboats were finer than anything on shore. Compared with superior dwelling houses and first-class hotels in the valley, they were indubitably magnificent, they were 'palaces'.

Steamboats

This section details the introduction and development of the 19th-century steamboat as a method of transportation for civilian, military and recreational purposes.

Steamboats are all about stepping back in time, to the days that Mark Twain loved. 'She is long and sharp and trim and pretty,' he wrote to describe one.

Looking much like multi-layered wedding cakes, and as iconically American as apple pie or Dixieland jazz, stern-paddlewheel steamboats became popular in the late 1880s, when they provided a key transport route into America's heartlands from the Deep South. Travelling aboard one of the stern-paddlewheel steamboats is like stepping back into the world of American folklore. There is a certain charm and old-world graciousness about them, with all their polished woods, impressive brass and flowing staircases.

Travelling on the river is a great way of taking a vacation. Onboard activities include daily 'riverlorian' talks about the culture, history and folklore of the river, calliope concerts, sing-alongs, engine room visits, Cajun cooking, craft lessons, and line-dancing lessons. The food on board is best described

as 'Down Home American' fare, which translates to hearty steaks, shrimp, Creole sauces, fried food and just a hint of fresh vegetables.

All about steamboats

Widely used on rivers in the 19th century, steamboats are shallow-draft vessels with propulsion derived from a huge stern-mounted steam-driven paddlewheel. The earliest use of steam power in a boat was recorded in 1786, when the American inventor John Fitch (1743–98) propelled a small craft on the Delaware River. Although the patents for steam-driven vessels lie with the British inventor James Watt (in 1791), it was Robert Fulton, an American, who used the design and patents for the steam engine. He built and tested a steamboat that ran four times along the River Seine in Paris, on 9 August 1803. He used a low-pressure engine with a vertical cylinder from which steam was sent to a condenser, while a jet of cold water and steam created a partial vacuum. Fulton returned to the US in December 1806, and, with his partner and financial backer Robert Livingston, set about developing a successful steamboat. Named the *Clermont*, it measured about 160 tons, was 40.5m (133ft) long, with a beam of 5.4m (18ft) and a draft of 2.1m (7ft). *Clermont* (or *The North River Steamboat of Clermont*, to give it its full name) was powered by a Boulton & Watt low-pressure steam engine located in the hold, and open to view.

The boiler, aft of the engine, was covered by a crude cabin for the officers. The two side wheels had 12 paddles that were uncovered, so that the water splashed onto the deck with each revolution. The rudder was similar to that of a sailing vessel, and moved by a tiller. It had a funnel rising 9m (30ft) – almost as high as the two masts that could be equipped with sails should the engine fail. Although it didn't look like a real ship (it looked more like a tea kettle), it was nonetheless a bold experiment of imagination and creativity.

A notice in the *American Citizen*, on 17 August 1807, announced the eventful day: 'Mr Fulton's ingenious steamboat, invented with a view to the navigation of the Mississippi from New Orleans upward, sails to-day from the North River, near State's Prison, to Albany. The velocity is calculated at four miles an hour. It is said it will a progress of two against the current of the Mississippi and if so it will certainly be a valuable acquisition to the commerce of western states.'

The crowd assembled on the dock at Greenwich (Connecticut), where the *Clermont* lay, cheered

Fitch operating his steamboat on the Delaware.

Riverboat S.S. *Brown* in Memphis, early 1900s.

as it pulled out into the current at one o'clock and churned proudly upstream. It was a proud day indeed for American transportation. The *Clermont* reached Albany in 32 hours (the return trip was made in 30 hours), and the power of propelling boats by steam was proven.

The *Clermont* that plied between New York and Albany in 1807, after which the pair built several vessels. But it was not until 1811 that a vessel was built specifically to traverse the lower Mississippi River, when Fulton obtained a patent granting exclusive monopoly for all steamboat operations on the great rivers, which gave Fulton and his partner an edge over any competition.

The vessel, a side-wheel packet steamer, using two low-pressure steam engines, was named the *New Orleans*, and built at Pittsburgh. It cost $38,000 and measured between 300 and 400 tons, with a single deck. The bow carried freight, the engine and boiler stood exposed in the centre, and the aft consisted of a salon divided into two parts: the forward, larger, section for gentlemen (it doubled as the dining room), while the aft section was for ladies. Nicholas Roosevelt was the captain, and his wife, Lydia Latrobe Roosevelt, sailed with him (she was heavily pregnant and gave birth during the trip). A large crowd gathered at Pittsburgh to witness its departure on Sunday 20 October 1811. It took four months to reach New Orleans on 10 January 1812, stopping along the way to demonstrate how the steamboat could sail against the current.

This type of packet steamer dominated the river transportation scene for the next 40 years, providing the quickest passenger transportation throughout mid-America. The *New Orleans* operated for a further two years, until it became snagged on 14 July 1814, two miles upstream from Baton Rouge. Her boiler and part of her machinery were salvaged and placed in the second vessel of the same name.

Steamboat development

The steamboat was an important American technological advance in the early 19th century. Later, it was found that a large paddlewheel located at the *stern* of a steamboat could provide the best form of propulsion, and thus reduced the need for a deep draft hull. After 1830, this became the standard for all future steamboats. As these vessels became larger, with more facilities to attract wealthy passengers, those built in the late 19th century had enclosed upper deck cabins, with lounges decorated in ornate hotel style. The tall funnels provided good draft for the apprentices who fired the boilers. Pilothouses (the steamboat's answer to the navigation bridge) stood above 'Texas' decks to provide a longer river view. Keels disappeared, which helped to reduce the weight, while buoyancy and stability were improved with longer, narrower hulls and straight sides. Landings without docks were made possible by giving the stem (bow) a long, gradual 'rake', or angle of entry into the water. They could then ride up onto a sloping shore and lower the gangways. No

Playing the calliope on deck in the winter.

The boilers were traditionally placed lengthwise, side-by-side across the main deck forepart, counterbalanced by the weight of the engines and the wheels aft. A water pipe connected them underneath to maintain a common level in each boiler, while the tops of the boilers were joined by a steam line that led to the engines. The funnels were a standard height of 15.2m (50ft) in 1840, but later reached as much as 30.5m (100ft) aboard such steamboats as the *Grand Republic* of 1867.

Side-wheel steamboats became popular, due to their greater manoeuvrability compared to the stern paddle-wheelers, with one engine driving one side-wheel. The best examples of these were the *JM White*, *Natchez*, *Robert E. Lee*, and *Grand Republic*. However, when towboats emerged after the Civil War, it was found that stern-wheel boats were more effective, and their pushing power made them ideal for propelling fleets of barges. The aft paddlewheel also protected it from debris and obstructions. More design modifications resulted in cranks being placed at right angles at each end of the wheel shaft, resulting in a smoother power flow from the engines.

further mooring was needed, because slow revolutions of the stern-wheel paddles kept the vessel in place against the current.

The improved design meant faster boats that were easier to handle in shallow water and in the swift current of the rapids. Main decks were built higher, and 'guards', the main deck extensions beyond the hull over the sides, were made wider and longer. A steamboat's beauty was judged by the grace of her hull lines, but, since the guards obscured the hull, decoration was added to the superstructure; gingerbread architecture and 'Steamboat Gothic' became the norm. The vessels gained feathered funnel tops, and elaborately carved cabin decorations became commonplace.

In 1825, the contest between low- and high-pressure designs was largely resolved in favour of the latter because it was better suited to the shallow navigation conditions of the waterways. It also had more reserve power, was lighter in weight, occupied less space and was less expensive to build. Misuse and excessive pressures, often required for more speed, resulted in numerous boiler explosions, thus in 1852 the Steamboat Inspection Service Act was introduced.

The long, slow stroke of the high-pressure engine resulted in about 22 revolutions per minute, best suited to the operation of the large paddle wheels. After about 1840, two engines rather than one were incorporated into the latest designs, for more power, and due to the popularity of side-wheelers. Engines were moved to the sides rather than occupying prime central space (for cargo).

CALLIOPES

A calliope is a steam-whistle organ with a very shrill and extremely loud sound that can be heard for miles – hence its use aboard steamboats of the period to announce their imminent arrival and departure. Its sound has been likened to screeching, out of tune pan-pipes.

The instrument consists of a boiler that forces steam through a set of whistle pipes (the calliope aboard *American Queen*, for example, has 37 brass whistle pipes. Typically, it is 'played' either by a keyboard, or a pinned cylinder (like the old player piano or barrel organ), by directing the steam into the correct pipes. The calliope typically has a single manual keyboard that resembles one of those small, simple electric organs popular in homes in the 1960s. The steam whistle aboard *American Queen* has a 37-note keyboard, while most calliopes had 24 notes.

The calliope was invented in the US by a farmer, Joshua C. Stoddard, in about 1850. He introduced it on 4 July 1855 and patented it soon after. It was often used to attract attention at circuses and fairs. It was successful, although its name, ka-li-o-pe, from the Greek word meaning sweet- or magnificent-voiced, belies its slightly out-of-tune characteristics. Stoddard organised the American Steam Company, but lost the business five years later to Arthur S. Denny, who later claimed to have invented the calliope himself. Within a year, almost every steamboat had one.

The steamboat further developed from an all-wood construction to one of iron and steel. Wood was cheap – and could easily be modified and re-worked – so there was a resistance among owners to change. Wood was used for the paddle wheels, and the connecting rod or pitman (to some degree wood absorbed the shocks due to sudden wheel stoppages on striking obstructions. Engines were, however, constructed almost entirely of wrought and cast iron (except for a few of the earliest examples of low-pressure engines).

Western steamboats (those made for rivers west of the Appalachians) were mainly constructed in Cincinnati, Louisville and Pittsburgh. While they had engines made either in the eastern United States or were imported from England (examples include *Columbus* and *United States*, both of 1819), in the main they were built in the west. The lighter, high-pressure engine became standard within a few years, developed jointly by Oliver Evans in the United States and Richard Trevithick in England. Evans took out a patent based on the high-pressure engine in 1804. With its power reserve, by 1840, the high-pressure engine had become standardized. More power was obtained mainly by using larger cylinders and by increasing the size and number of boilers.

In the early days, there were two classes of passenger: cabin passenger or deck passenger. Cabin passengers had a cabin. Males and females were segregated to avoid illicit sexual relations, and un-married couples travelling together ran the risk of being put ashore if discovered. Deck passengers got a piece of the deck – the one they sat on with whatever freight was being carried. The price of deck passage was generally one-fifth or one-sixth of that of a cabin passenger – a wide variation indeed.

In early steamboat cabins, candles and whale-oil lamps provided illumination, but these were replaced by gas lighting from about 1840; electric lighting was introduced around 1870, although this was in fact slow to catch on.

The voice of a steamboat is its whistle. The first steam whistle was introduced aboard the *Revenue* in 1844. One blast means to pass on the starboard (right) side. Two blasts means to pass on the port (left) side. Three bells are sounded to signal departures.

The golden age of the steamboat is defined as the decade preceding the Civil War (ie 1850–1860). The principal factor in the decline of the steamboat was, of course, the railroad, developed to provide improved transportation connections for internal commerce, which became increasingly regional.

Steamboat travel today

Today's excursions in destinations tend to revolve around city tours and visits to battlefields, historical sites and gracious antebellum homes. Depending on the itinerary you choose, and which part of the river you cruise on, additional interest tours might include Elvis Presley's Graceland (Lower Mississippi).

Hop-On Hop-Off Shore Excursions, *American Duchess*.

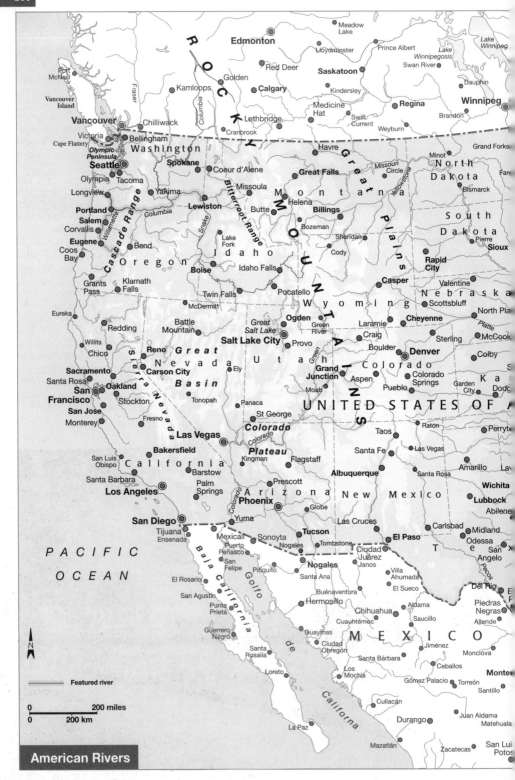

American Rivers

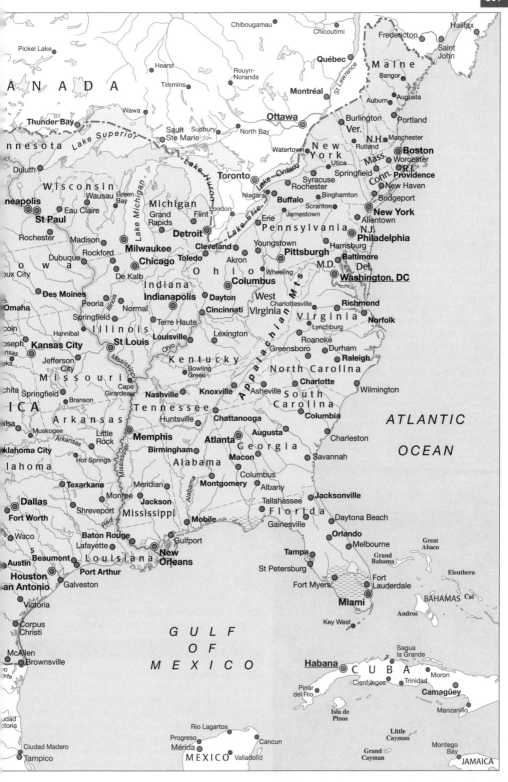

The Mississippi Region

The Mississippi River is the country's most important economic highway. In the 19th century, steamboats provided large-scale transportation of passengers and freight along this mighty river.

Cruising along 'Ol' Man River' at less than 10 knots without a care in the world is quite special – pure Americana. Think: antebellum (Neoclassical-style) houses, practised Southern belle charm, hoop skirts and cool mint juleps. You get the feeling that country plantation life hasn't quite disappeared. The slow pace of life is an antidote to the pressures of today's life on land, and there are no immigration or customs procedures in America's heartland to go through.

Author and poet Mark Twain (1835–1910), an enthusiastic fan of river cruising and a former Mississippi steamboat pilot, once said: 'When man can go 700 miles an hour, he'll want to go seven again.' That is ever more poignant today, as the pace of life on either side of the river becomes ever faster, and the need to slow down becomes ever greater.

If Europe's Danube is the 'Mother of all rivers', then the USA's mighty Mississippi River should be called the 'Granddaddy of all rivers'. Perhaps that's why the famous Jerome Kern song from the Broadway musical 'Showboat' begins: 'Ol' Man River.'

The Mississippi at Upper Mississippi River NWR.

The Mississippi River – whose name is derived from the Native American Algonquin Indian name *Misi sipi*, or 'big river' – is the USA's principal waterway, and drains the country's central basin. It is one also one of the country's longest rivers, at 3,782km (2,350 miles), although on the world scale many other rivers are longer.

Its main tributaries drain an area equivalent to one-eighth of the entire continent, and it is entirely within the continental United States. By adding the Missouri-Jefferson (Red Rock) river system, downstream of the Mississippi confluence, it actually becomes the fourth longest river in the world. The total navigable length adds up to a whopping 25,750km (16,000 miles).

Show me the Muddy – the 'Big Muddy'

It was during the Ice Age that the Mississippi Valley assumed its present shape. Its source lies in a clear stream from the Lake Itasca area of northwest Minnesota; it then flows on a southerly course to empty finally into the muddy deltas of the Gulf of Mexico, over which time it drains most of the central plains, between the Rocky Mountains and the Appalachians. There are about 170 bridges along the river's navigable length.

Two of the largest tributaries – the Missouri River and the Ohio River – contribute to the Mississippi River, which acts as the boundary for Minnesota, Wisconsin, Iowa, Illinois, Missouri, Kentucky, Tennessee, Arkansas, Mississippi and Louisiana, but it actually only runs through Minnesota and Louisiana. It goes from calm trickle to raging torrent, but when it reaches the Gulf of Mexico, it becomes slow, marshy and muddy, and deposits immense quantities of silt into its constantly expanding delta.

For river cruises, there are two principal (but arbitrary) geographical sections to the Mississippi: the Lower Mississippi and the Upper Mississippi.

UPPER MISSISSIPPI

Along the northernmost region, from Ashport, Tennessee, to St Louis, Missouri, and then to St Paul, the lumber industry in particular brought rapid growth to the grass prairies of Iowa, Illinois, Minnesota and Wisconsin. It is where, in 1673, the French missionary, Jacques Marquette, and explorer, Louis Joliet, traded furs with indigenous American peoples.

The head of river navigation is in Minneapolis, where the Mississippi drops 20m (65.6ft) over the

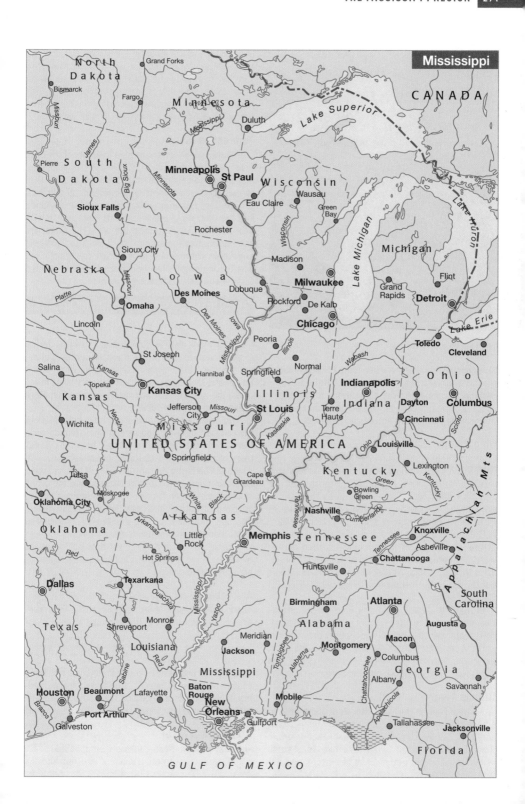

Mississippi

North Dakota
Grand Forks
Bismarck
Fargo
Missouri
Minnesota
Mississippi
Duluth
Lake Superior
CANADA
Lake Huron

South Dakota
Pierre
James
Big Sioux
Sioux Falls
Minneapolis
St Paul
Minnesota
Wisconsin
Wausau
Eau Claire
Green Bay
Wisconsin
Lake Michigan
Michigan
Flint
Grand Rapids
Detroit

Rochester
Madison
Milwaukee

Nebraska
Missouri
Platte
Iowa
Sioux City
Des Moines
Omaha
Lincoln
Dubuque
Rockford
De Kalb
Chicago
Des Moines
Iowa
Mississippi

St Joseph
Peoria
Normal
Springfield
Illinois
Wabash
Ohio
Toledo
Cleveland

Salina
Kansas
Topeka
Kansas City
Hannibal
Indianapolis
Indiana
Dayton
Columbus

Kansas
Jefferson City
Missouri
St Louis
Terre Haute
Cincinnati
Scioto
Wichita
Neosho
Missouri
Kaskaskia

UNITED STATES OF AMERICA
Springfield
Louisville
Ohio
Lexington
Green
Kentucky

Tulsa
Cape Girardeau
Kentucky
Bowling Green
Muskogee
White
Black
Oklahoma City
Arkansas
Arkansas
Little Rock
Nashville
Tennessee
Cumberland
Knoxville
Asheville
Appalachian Mts

Oklahoma
Memphis
Tennessee
Chattanooga
Red
Hot Springs
Mississippi
Huntsville
Tennessee

Dallas
Texarkana
Birmingham
Atlanta
South Carolina
Ouachita
Monroe
Augusta

Texas
Shreveport
Alabama
Macon
Red
Meridian
Montgomery
Columbus
Georgia
Louisiana
Jackson
Tombigbee
Albany
Savannah
Sabine
Mississippi
Chattahoochee

Houston
Beaumont
Lafayette
Baton Rouge
New Orleans
Mobile
Alabama
Apalachicola
Tallahassee
Jacksonville
Brazos
Port Arthur
Galveston
Gulfport
Florida

GULF OF MEXICO

The Mississippi River north of Memphis.

St Anthony Falls. When we talk about the Mississippi, we must include the Arkansas, Atchafalaya, Cumberland, Illinois, Kanawha, Ouachita and Tennessee rivers. During the early spring, some sections of the river can be frozen over and closed to traffic.

Ohio River

George Washington, who, when speaking of the Ohio River, said: 'I know of no other country where I should rather fix my habitation.' Often called 'the beautiful river', the Ohio is formed by the confluence of the Allegheny and Monongahela rivers in Pittsburgh, Pennsylvania, and, at almost 1,600km (1,000 miles) long, is the principal eastern tributary of the Mississippi. It flows westward then southward; its banks form boundaries for the states of West Virginia, Ohio, Kentucky, Indiana and Illinois before its waters enter the Mississippi River at Cairo, Illinois.

In the 19th century, industry flourished along its riverbanks, with textiles, clothing, furniture, foundries, soaps, candles, cotton and tobacco the principal endeavours. Since the Mississippi flooded regularly, extensive river-control works including locks and dams were also introduced at that time.

Illinois River

The Illinois River is the most important upper Mississippi tributary, formed in northeastern Illinois by the confluence of the Des Plains and Kankakee rivers. It flows for approximately 439km (273 miles) past some of the best scenery in the 'Land of Lincoln' and enters the Mississippi at Grafton.

Kanawha River

Formed in Fayette County, it crosses through the Metro Valley of West Virginia, and flows northwest to join the Ohio River at Point Pleasant. The Kanawha River valley has extensive deposits of salt brines (chlorine, bromine, iodine, calcium, magnesium, and potash) and also has natural-gas and oil wells.

Tennessee River

The Tennessee River, the largest tributary of the Ohio River, is approximately 1,049km (652 miles) long, and is navigable throughout its entire course. It is formed by the confluence of the Holston and French Broad rivers near Knoxville, Tennessee, and empties into the Ohio River below Paducah, Kentucky, falling about 610m (2,000ft) along the way. The Cherokee nation occupied the area north of Decatur, Alabama and Lookout Mountain, which they could see, and was the inspiration for their wigwam village, called Chattanooga, or 'rock rising to a point'.

LOWER MISSISSIPPI (MEMPHIS TO NEW ORLEANS)

South of Memphis, the warm, humid climate and rich soil make this region among the most fertile in the United States. Sugarcane is still grown along the reaches of the lower Mississippi between Baton Rouge and New Orleans. Except for a few large refineries, the scenery is much the same as when Mark Twain described it in 1883:

'The great sugar plantations border both sides of the river all the way, and stretch their league-wide levels back to the dim forest walls of bearded cypress trees in the rear. Shores lonely no longer. Plenty of dwellings all along the way, on both banks, standing so close together, for long distances, that the broad river lying between the two rows becomes a sort of spacious street. A most homelike and happy region. And now and then you see a pillared and porticoed great manor house, embowered in trees.'

Rivers that flow into the Lower Mississippi are the Arkansas River, Red River, Atchafalaya River, which are detailed below:

Arkansas River

The 2,334km (1,450 mile) -long Arkansas River meanders through rolling plains and lush forests. It rises in the Rocky Mountains near Leadville, Colorado, flows east through Kansas, then southeast across a corner of Oklahoma, and bisects Arkansas before meeting the Mississippi. Numerous dams and locks control the flow as needed, due to extensive flooding (during the Great Flood of 1993, half the state of Arkansas was under water).

Atchafalaya River

The Atachafalaya River courses through 435km (270 miles) of south central Louisiana and out into the Atchafalaya Bay, on the Gulf of Mexico. It is bordered by the Atchafalaya Basin (the largest freshwater swamp in the world) and is home to a host of shrimp farms (portrayed in the Tom Hanks film *Forrest Gump*) and processing establishments.

Red River

Named for its reddish silt, the Red River is about 2,092km (1,300 miles) long, and the southernmost of the Mississippi's large tributaries. Rising high in

DID YOU KNOW...?

...that author and rivership pilot Mark Twain (real name Samuel Langhorne Clements) grew up in Hannibal, on the west bank of the Mississippi River? His father kept a dry goods and grocery store. *The Adventures of Tom Sawyer*, perhaps his most famous book in which he described pre-Civil War life, was published in 1876. It is set in a small Mississippi river town.

...that Louisiana was sold to the United States by France? It was, in 1803, after first being ceded to Spain in 1762.

...that the first bottle of Coca Cola was bottled in Vicksburg, Mississippi? The candy store where it was first sold (Biedenharn Candy Co.) is now home to the Biedenharn Coca-Cola Museum.

...that one of the most popular country songs, *Gentle on My Mind*, has a river connection? The song was written by banjo and fiddle player John Hartford, who, when not appearing in concerts all over the USA, piloted the steamboat *Julia Belle Swain* on the Illinois River.

...that mother-of-pearl button manufacture was a significant industry of the Upper Mississippi River region? Before the advent of plastic, men used to dredge mussels, or freshwater clams, and take them to camp sites along the riverbanks. The 'meat' was cooked out so that the shells could be cleaned and searched for pearls, which were then sold to button makers. Typically, round blanks were cut from the shells and then polished by tumbling them in solutions of acid and pumice. Holes were then drilled in the polished buttons, and designs – sometimes exquisite – were cut into them. They were then sorted, placed on cards and sold to general stores or clothing manufacturers.

...that flooding of the Mississippi sometimes occurs? Some may remember the 1993 flooding of the River Mississippi (known locally as the Great Flood of 1993), which caused severe hardship for many of the people that lived along its banks. It caused billions of dollars worth of damage, devastated many towns of the central Mississippi from Wisconsin to Arkansas, some of which are still abandoned.

...that the American south became known as Dixieland because of the French *dix* (the French word for ten) that appeared on $10 notes in Louisiana? These were notes issued by the Citizen's Bank of New Orleans prior to 1860, when *dix* was imprinted on the reverse side of notes used chiefly by the French-speaking residents of the region. Thus, the land of *Dixies*, or *Dixieland*, a

term that was first applied to Louisiana, and then to the whole South.

...that in the early days, steamboats lasted a mere 18 months on average? This was because they were made of wood and were often subject to collisions and fires.

...that the decorative feathers that spout from the funnels (stacks) of a steamboat are fashioned on the pattern of oak leaves? This is because oak timber, which is highly regarded for its strength and durability, was used for the construction of steamboat hulls. Symbolic of security, the oak acorn was widely adopted as ornamentation and appeared on the tops of steamboat booms, davits, flagpoles and masts.

...that the first 'showboat' was a floating theatre created by William Chapman Jr in 1831 and named the 'Floating Theater'?

...that Abraham Lincoln made money from steamboat passengers before he became a lawyer? In his youth, he watched steamboats disgorge passengers along the way – deck passengers who paid the least and had to wade ashore with their belongings at intermediate stopping points. He offered a service whereby he would row out to the steamboat in the river and bring them ashore for 24 cents. Lincoln was taken to court by the local ferry operator, who claimed that he was operating an unlicensed ferry. Lincoln won the case, however, because, as he so clearly stated, by definition, that a ferry crossed from one side of the river to the other, whereas he was only going halfway across the river (to pick up passengers) then going back to his starting point. It was this appearance in court that started him thinking about becoming a lawyer.

...that the city of Vicksburg, Louisiana, played host to the worst steamboat disaster in history? The death toll exceeded 1,500, rivalling that of the ocean-going *Titanic*. It happened shortly after the Civil War ended, when the side-wheeler *Sultana* was in Vicksburg undergoing a boiler repair. It had 376 passengers, bound from New Orleans to Cincinnati. However, on the fateful night of 27 April 27 1865, the captain allowed some 2,000 Union troops who were newly released from Confederate prisons to come aboard. Then, just as the steamboat pushed against the spring current to the north of Memphis, one of her four boilers exploded. The steamboat burned to the waterline within 20 minutes, and the men were swept away by the flooding river.

the plains of eastern New Mexico, it flows southeast across Texas and Louisiana to just northwest of Baton Rouge, then enters the Atchafalaya River, about 386km (240 miles) north of New Orleans. The Civil War features heavily in the region.

DESTINATION HIGHLIGHTS LOWER MISSISSIPPI: FROM NEW ORLEANS TO MEMPHIS

From south to north, these destination highlights represent ports typically visited on a combination of typical seven-day itineraries.

New Orleans, Louisiana (Mississippi River; Mile marker 96.0)

The river port city is located directly on the Gulf of Mexico, above the Mississippi on the Chickasaw Bluffs, where the borders of Arkansas, Mississippi, and Tennessee meet. It was named in honour of the Duc d'Orléans, Regent of France, and founded in 1718 by Jean-Baptiste Le Moyne, and is renowned as the starting place of jazz and for being the birthplace of jazz trumpeter and vocalist Louis Armstrong (1901–71). It is also known for its famous, annual Mardi Gras in February and for its Cajun cuisine and music, so a downtown visit to the French Quarter and Bourbon Street is a must.

Natchez, Mississippi (Mississippi River; Mile markers 363.3–364.2)

Founded in 1716, Natchez has always been an important and historic steamboat port. Named after an indigenous tribe that inhabited the east side of the Lower Mississippi River, it was one of the few towns spared by Ulysses S. Grant during the American Civil War (1861–5). As a result, more than 500 antebellum buildings, including more than 200 gracious homes, still exist; they are now on the National Register of Historic Buildings. Many of the homes reflect the wealth of this important location in the heart of the cotton belt.

Vicksburg, Mississippi (Mississippi River; Mile markers 435.8–437.2)

Often referred to as the 'Gibraltar of the South,' the siege of Vicksburg (which lasted for 47 days), during the Civil War was one of the fiercest battles of the war. The city, which lies on the Mississippi River at the mouth of the Yazoo River, was founded in 1817, and is rightly proud of its Vicksburg National Military Park (7 sq km/2.7 sq miles) and its battlefields and monuments, which form one of the best-preserved Civil War battlefields in America.

Baton Rouge, Louisiana (Mississippi River; Mile marker 229.4)

Baton Rouge is the State capital (founded in 1811) and an important port at the head of deep-water navigation on the Mississippi River. It became an important industrial and refining centre when the Standard Oil Company established a huge refinery there in 1909, and was reportedly the stomping grounds for some of America's most colourful political characters. Apart from the downtown area, you can also visit Houmas House, the epitome of an antebellum mansion with its colonnaded façade – and a fine example of Greek Revival architecture. The Old State Capitol building is an architectural treasure.

American Queen alongside in New Orleans.

Memphis, Tennessee (Mississippi River; Mile marker 736.0)

Memphis is America's third-largest inland port. But any mention of Memphis, and most people will immediately think of Elvis Presley, the King of Rock 'n' Roll, and Graceland Mansion – perhaps the most famous home in America's musical history. This is also Presley's burial place (he died on 16 August 1977), and you can visit it and tour its rooms including the Hall of Gold, Elvis's private office. The star started his career from a recording studio in Memphis, but was born in Tupelo, Missouri, on 8 January 1935, and moved to Memphis as a teenager.

Memphis received much attention when the civil-rights leader Reverend Martin Luther King Jr was killed on the balcony of the Lorraine Motel by a sniper's bullet. He was visiting Memphis in support of a 1968 sanitation workers' strike at the time. James Earl Ray was convicted of the murder. The motel room in which Dr King stayed is now a museum.

Also worth noting in Memphis is the Cotton Carnival, held annually in May.

DESTINATION HIGHLIGHTS UPPER MISSISSIPPI: FROM MEMPHIS TO MINNEAPOLIS/ST PAUL

St Louis, Missouri (Mississippi River; Mile marker 181.0)

The city of St Louis was founded in 1764 as a fur-trading post. Today it's a major transportation hub, the largest city in the state and 'Gateway to the West.' Its famed 192m (629.5ft) stainless-steel arch was built in 1965 and was designed by the Finnish American architect Eero Saarinen to commemorate St Louis's historic role as a Gateway to the West. The Mall of America (the largest shopping mall in the world) is located close by.

Hannibal, Missouri (Mississippi River; Mile marker 308.8)

Samuel Langhorne Clemens (better known as Mark Twain) grew up here. There are several bridges, but one in particular is of note: the Mark Twain Memorial Bridge, constructed in 1935. The city is full of other Mark Twain items, such as the Mark Twain Museum with monuments at almost every turn dedicated to him or one of his characters. Another famous locally born personality is Molly Brown, heroine of the *Titanic* sinking and the subject of the musical *The Unsinkable Molly Brown*, whose birthplace is preserved as a museum today.

Burlington, Iowa (Mississippi River; Mile marker 403.9)

Surrounded by limestone hills that resound with the myths and legends of the lore of North America's indigenous peoples (it was here that Chief Black Hawk began the Black Hawk War of 1832), the city has a historic district (Heritage Hills) that can be

The St. Louis Gateway Arch in St. Louis, MO.

experienced on a city tour that includes Crapo Park (pronounced 'Cray-po') and the Garrett-Phelps House (built by prominent banker William Garrett around 1851).

Davenport, Iowa (Mississippi River; Mile marker 484.0)

Legendary jazz cornetist, pianist and composer Bix Beiderbecke was born here, and every July the Bix Festival commemorates him. You can also visit the John Deere Pavilion with its displays of agricultural and farming techniques, vintage and modern farm equipment.

Dubuque, Iowa (Mississippi River; Mile marker 582.0)

Dubuque is named after Julien Dubuque (1762–1810), a French Canadian trader who in 1788 concluded a treaty with the Meskwaki (Mesquakie/Fox tribe) Indians giving him lead-mining rights. The Mississippi River Museum houses a national collection of river biographies, the National Landmark steam dredge *William B. Black*, the largest collection of historic vessels on the Mississippi, and the National Rivers Hall of Fame.

Scale replica of the Mississippi in Memphis.

Winona, Minnesota (Mississippi River; Mile marker 725.6)

Winona was built on a giant sandbar that was created by the meanderings of the Mississippi River. It was founded in 1851 by a steamboat captain, Orrin Smith, and quickly grew and prospered as a full-fledged river community. Today it's a thriving industrial and business centre. The headquarters of the Watkins Company (importers of spices and extracts), is full of Tiffany stained-glass windows.

Memphis, Tennessee (Mississippi River; Mile marker 736.0)

See page 295.

Wabasha, Minnesota (Mississippi River; Mile marker 760.3)

This summer resort, located about 127km (79 miles) southeast of Minneapolis/St Paul, offers a peaceful, tranquil setting in the midst of woody wilderness.

Minneapolis/St Paul, Minnesota (Mississippi River; Mile marker 839.0)

Located on the Mississippi River near the mouth of the Minnesota River, this mid-western city with its dual name has long been known for its moderation. Its name comes from the Sioux Indian word *Minne* (meaning 'water') and the Greek *polis*, (meaning 'city'). It was incorporated in 1856 and in 1872 the two cities merged to become Minneapolis. Today, Minneapolis is the commercial and industrial centre of an extensive agricultural region.

DESTINATION HIGHLIGHTS OHIO RIVER

Chattanooga, Tennessee (Tennessee River; Mile marker 433.0)

Founded in 1819, Chattanooga lies along the Moccasin Bend of the Tennessee River, close to the border with Georgia. Its main economy is derived from tourism, warehousing and distribution. A steep-incline railway ascends Lookout Mountain, and inside is a cave with a 44m (145ft) waterfall. At the top of the mountain gardens, odd stone formations form what is known as Rock City.

Nashville, Tennessee (Cumberland River; Mile marker 191.0)

Until 1963 Nashville was the capital of the State of Tennessee (the State Fair is held every year in September). Nashville has grown into the home of Country Music USA, and is the centre of a huge recording industry. Once a major river port and rail hub, it is now the home of the Grand Ole Opry country music stage show, which began regular radio broadcasts in 1925. The State Capitol Building was designed by William Strickland, the Philadelphia architect, along Greek classical lines.

Paducah, Kentucky (Ohio River/Tennessee River; Mile marker 934.5)

Located in southern Kentucky, at the confluence of the Ohio and Tennessee rivers, Paducah was originally named Pekin by the first settlers in 1821, then later renamed after Paduke, a Chickasaw Indian chief who lived in the area. The town became a city in 1856 and underwent rapid development during the 1840s and 1850s when the lumber industry flourished.

During the Civil War 42,000 Union soldiers boarded a military convoy consisting of 173 steamboats and 12 gunboats before sailing up the Tennessee River to Shiloh for battle in the American Revolution. The Museum of the American Quilters Society is here (you can put your 'mark' on a quilted pillow sham).

Kentucky – the Bluegrass State – is where 95 percent of all American Bourbon is created. It's made from 51 percent corn, plus rye and wheat, among other ingredients.

Cave-in-Rock, Illinois (Ohio River; Mile marker 881.0)

Now a state park, this location (actually a 17m/55ft -wide hole in the wall that penetrates 33m/108ft into the riverbank) was where river boatmen were lured, robbed and murdered by local pirates. Cave-in-Rock was later used by the infamous Harpe brothers' gang of outlaws as their operations base.

Henderson, Illinois (Ohio River; Mile marker 803.8)

Located in northeastern Illinois, Henderson was named after Richard Henderson, who laid out the town in 1797. John James Audubon, the artist and ornithologist, was the city's most famous resident. The Audubon Museum is filled with artifacts devoted to the surrounding region's wildlife. During the summer, the favorite activity is horse racing (thoroughbred and harness racing), on the Audubon Raceway.

Louisville, Kentucky (Ohio River; Mile marker 602.0)

Louisville, the largest city in the state of Kentucky, is pure horse country and home of the Kentucky Derby. You can visit Churchill Downs racetrack, and the adjacent Kentucky Derby Museum – the largest equestrian museum dedicated to a single horse race. In 1811, Louisville became the centre of attention when Nicholas Roosevelt, son of President Roosevelt – and a steamboat captain – docked the New Orleans in the city. By 1920 the city had become a major river port.

Madison, Indiana (Ohio River; Mile marker 558.0)

Madison is located in the southeastern region of Indiana. Incorporated as a city in 1838, it is today a living museum for 19th-century American architecture.

Cincinnati, Ohio (Ohio River; Mile marker 470.2)

Located on the Ohio River in southwestern Ohio, it is 24km (15 miles) away from the border with Indiana. The poet Longfellow referred to Cincinnati as the 'Jewel of the West', although the city was also known as Porkopolis due to the prominence of its grain and pork industries. Today it is known for its machine tools, soap and detergents, cosmetics, jet engines, automobile parts, and playing cards. The city, the third largest in Ohio (Cleveland and Columbus are larger), was responsible for building the majority of the 2,500 to 3,000 steamboats built during the 1800s. It's also known for its Cincinnati Zoo, founded in 1875 – the second oldest zoo in the USA.

The American Queen on the Ohio River in Cincinnati.

Gallipolis, Ohio (Ohio River; Mile marker 269.5)

Gallipolis, founded in 1790 by the Scioto Company and incorporated as a city in 1865, is located at highest point on the Ohio River in southern Ohio. The 'City of the Gauls' began as a speculation project that encouraged investors in France to purchase land in Ohio. It was settled by French colonists in 1790, and during the Civil War it was a principal centre for treating injured Union soldiers.

Marietta, Ohio (Ohio River; Mile marker 171.8)

Marietta, in southern Ohio, lies at the confluence of the Muskingum River and the Ohio River; it was the first capital of the Northwest Territory and an important trading stop for the steamboats. Today, its Ohio River Museum is dedicated to the steamboat era.

Pittsburgh, Pennsylvania (Ohio River; Mile marker 0)

Located in southwestern Pennsylvania, at the confluence of the Allegheny and Monongahela rivers (these unite at the point of the 'Golden Triangle', or business district, to form the Ohio River). Known as 'Steel Town USA,' Pittsburgh is where steamboating first began in 1811, when the New Orleans set off on its journey to the place after which is was named, reaching it four months later. When seen from the river, Pittsburgh seems mildly attractive; its Carnegie Museum of Natural History certainly is – Andrew Carnegie, the Scottish-born steel baron-turned-philanthropist, was, in his time hailed as the world's richest man). Steamboats arrive at the North Shore Dock, inaugurated in 2002.

The Pacific Northwest

The scenic grandeur, towering mountains, open landscapes and rich soil drew explorers and pioneers to the Pacific Northwest, and steamboat transportation was key to its development.

The Colombia and Snake rivers provide valuable lessons in the history of the pioneers of the rugged Pacific Northwest region and in the culture and traditions of the indigenous peoples of the United States.

Note that cruising in the Pacific Northwest is all about being outside. It's often wet, so do take some rainproof outerwear. The vessels will provide umbrellas when it rains.

Columbia River

Although the indigenous peoples of this region used the Columbia River for centuries, it was first charted by Captain Robert Gray, an American, when, on 11 May 1792, he crossed a sandbar into the mouth of the river aboard his vessel *Columbia Rediviva*.

Thomas Jefferson, the third president of a very young country, was eager to find the fabled Northwest Passage (a route to link the Atlantic and Pacific oceans, and to Europe and the Orient) before the British did. He pressed Congress to provide $2,500 to fund a 'Corps of Discovery' expedition, to be commanded by President Jefferson's private secretary, Meriwether

American Empress leaving Stevenson, Washington.

Lewis (30 years old at the time), and former army captain, William Clark (33 years old at the time).

The pair became known as Lewis & Clark. President Jefferson surmised that the Columbia River shared its headwaters with another big river, the Missouri, and thought that an overland expedition would be faster than a seagoing one. Lewis & Clark led their expedition across the continent and succeeded in reaching the Pacific Ocean, but proved that Jefferson's premise was incorrect; the Columbia River did not, in fact, meet the Missouri. They ended their exploration in 1811 at the port town of Astoria, named after the German fur trader Astor.

The Columbia River, which forms three-quarters of the northern boundary of Oregon, begins as a trickle in the high alpine meadows of Canada, and flows northwest through forests and desert canyons (the Rocky Mountain Trench) before turning sharply south to join the Snake River. The combined flows then cut through the Cascade Range to empty into the sea about 1,931km (1,200 miles) later, through a broad estuary.

The 19th century brought rapid changes that left their mark on the river. Pioneered by Lewis and Clarke (their reconstructed log winter camp and rainforest paths at Fort Clatsop, Astoria can still be seen today), the Columbia River is America's grand gateway to the West. In 1805 they canoed down the Clearwater and found an even bigger river – the Snake – at what is now called Lewiston, Idaho.

Snake River

As you cruise upstream, eight sets of locks on the Snake River allow small vessels to navigate to Clarkston, approximately 21m (68.5ft) above sea level. The confluence of the Snake and Clearwater rivers is in Clarkston, Washington State, over 724km (450 miles) from the sea. Clarkston is the twin city to Lewiston, Idaho.

The locks and dams provide vital hydroelectric power to the Pacific Northwest. Since the 1930s, several large power projects have been constructed along the Columbia River, including the Mica Dam (Canada), and the Grand Coulee Dam, Bonneville Dam, Dalles Dam and Chief Joseph Dam.

You'll experience a daylight transit of Columbia River Gorge, with its waterfalls and steep vertical cliffs created by volcanic activity. The gorge is the only sea-level route through the Cascade Mountain Range, which separates the dense forests of the coastal areas of Oregon and Washington from the dry rolling hills and wine country of Walla Walla. It holds federally protected status and is managed by the United States Forest Service.

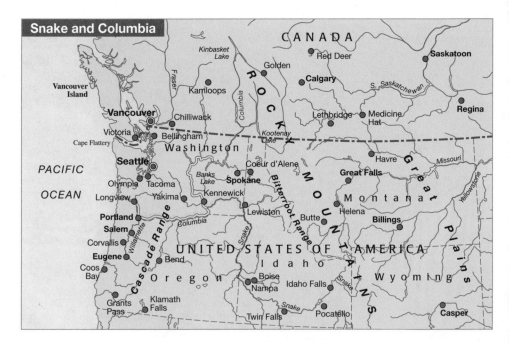

In order of ascendance, they are:

Astoria (sea level)
Bonneville (elevation 22m/72ft)
The Dalles (elevation 49m/160ft)
John Day (elevation 81m/265ft)
McNary (elevation 104m/340ft)
Ice Harbor (elevation 134m/440ft)
Lower Monumental (165m/540 ft)
Little Goose (elevation 194m/638ft)
Lower Granite (elevation 225m/738ft).

The Snake River is the largest tributary of the Columbia River, and joins it after a journey of just over 1,669km (1,037 miles). It combines the runoff of Wyoming, Utah, Nevada, Ida, Oregon and Washington states. It rises in the mountains of the Continental Divide close to the southeastern corner of Yellowstone National Park, then flows through Jackson Lake along the eastern base of the magnificent Teton Mountain Range, and enters Idaho through the Palisades Reservoir. It joins the Columbia River just south of Pasco, Washington.

Cruising to the end of the navigable section of the Snake River brings you close to Hells Canyon (North America's deepest gorge, and one of the deepest in the world), where you can view prehistoric petroglyphs. The largest tributary is the Salmon River, which joins the Snake River near the downstream end of the canyon. Hell's Canyon forms part of the Idaho-Oregon boundary, between the Seven Devils Mountains the Wallowa Mountains. It is 200km (124.8 miles) long with a maximum depth of 2,400m (7,874ft).

Excursions (some are at extra cost) include Visits to Stonehenge (a replica of the real one in Wiltshire, England), Hells Canyon, Multnomah Falls – the second largest (at 189m/620ft) in the USA – plus salmon fishing and canoe paddling.

DID YOU KNOW...?

...that the Columbia River and its tributaries have a watershed the size of France? More than 100 dams have been built along the river in the past 50 years, but to the detriment of the salmon population.
...that the model for the face of Sacagawea on the US "Golden Dollar", minted in 2000, is that of Randy'L He-dow Teton. The (then) 23-year old beauty (b.1976) also served as godmother to the launch of the now-defunct American West Steamboat Company's *Columbia Queen* (now *Louisiane*). She is a member of the Shoshone-Bannock Tribe and the Cree Nation that live in the Pacific Northwest.

...that in 1976 the Teton Dam collapsed, causing serious flooding of the Upper Snake River Valley?
...that over one million salmon and steelhead once migrated up the River Snake each year? They traveled up to 1,448km (900 miles) from the ocean to spawning grounds in the Idaho and Oregon mountains. However, in the 20th century, the salmon runs in both the Columbia and Snake rivers declined by about 90 percent, the dams being the principal culprit. The five varieties of River Snake salmon are: spring/summer Chinook, fall Chinook, sockeye, Coho (now extinct) and steelhead.

The Grand Saloon on *American Queen*

USA River cruise companies

Here we provide some background information on the three all-American companies with steamboats/riverboats, including the year in which each company was founded.

American Cruise Lines

The company, based in Guilford, Connecticut, was originally formed in 1974 by Charles Robertson, a renowned yachtsman who raced 12m (39ft) America's Cup yachts. The company now builds its riverships in its own small shipyard in Salisbury, Maryland, on the Chesapeake Bay.

The company operates stern paddle-wheelers (both real and replica steamboats) on the Mississippi River and the Columbia and Snake rivers in the US Pacific Northwest. Although there are many individual passengers, the vessel also attracts alumni, affinity and special-interest groups.

American Queen Steamboat Company

It was founded in 2012 as the Great American Steamboat Company by Jon Waggoner, Ted Sykes and a number of cruise industry investors including HMS Global Marine and started operating the steamboat *American Queen* as an inclusive product. The company, whose headquarters are in Memphis, Tennessee, changed its name to the American Queen Steamboat Company in 2016. Although there are many individual passengers, the vessel also attracts alumni, affinity and special-interest groups.

The company operates stern paddle-wheelers (both real and replica steamboats) on the Mississippi River and the Columbia and Snake rivers in the US Pacific Northwest, and has a passenger loyalty club (Steamboat Society of America).

French America Line

Founded in 2015, the company focuses on southern hospitality, with food menus created and overseen by Regina Charboneau, noted Creole chef. It is a 'drinks-inclusive' product, and also offers illy brand Italian coffees. Each cabin has an iPad preloaded with menus, excursion information and e-books. The company operates only on the Mississippi River.

American Cruise Lines' *Queen of the Mississippi* is seen leaving port in New Orleans.

AMERICA ★★★+

YESTERYEAR'S RIVERBOAT ERA TRADITIONS ARE MIXED WITH MODERN SURROUNDINGS.

Operator .... American Cruise Lines
Built 2016
Length (ft)..305
Former Names .... none
Passenger beds...185
Approximate cabin size (sq ft) 203-445
Even numbered cabins (port side) ....No
Rivers sailed... Mississippi

BERLITZ'S RATINGS		
	Possible	Achieved
Hardware	100	70
Accommodation	100	66
Cuisine	100	66
Service	100	65
Miscellaneous	100	68
OVERALL SCORE 335 points out of 500		

This replica steamboat (it's actually a riverboat) was built in American Cruise Line's own shipyard in Chesapeake, Maryland. It is registered in the US, is owned by US citizens, adheres to US Coast Guard safety regulations and has an all-American crew.

Presently, the largest vessel in the American Cruise Lines riverboat (replica steamboat) fleet, *America* has a rounded front, but a rather boxy exterior appearance at the stern, due to the fitting of the large red paddlewheel. There is a decent amount of open deck space at the stern, however, and the riverboat has a real calliope (steam organ).

There are six passenger decks (including an uppermost, open deck), two lifts (elevator) that goes to almost all decks, and a bow (front) landing ramp for use as a gangway for passengers and stores. Note that there is no medical facility, beauty salon or laundry, and the ceilings in the public rooms are quite low. However, Wi-Fi is free for everyone.

Public rooms include the Magnolia Lounge (a forward-facing observation lounge), a Paddlewheel Lounge (with aft views over the paddlewheel) and a Sky Lounge (also with aft views).

Daily educational events and themed entertainment paint a picture of life on the Mississippi in days gone

by. A pre-cruise hotel package is included with each cruise. For accommodation choice, there are eight cabin price categories (one of which is for solo occupancy), depending on the size and location you choose (these measure 27.9 sq m/300 sq ft, plus one Owner's Suite measuring 55.7 sq m/600 sq ft). All cabins have a river view (there are no 'interior' cabins).

Except for cabins on the lowest deck, most have floor-to-ceiling sliding glass doors leading to a small balcony, with old-style safety railings. Contrary to maritime tradition, even-numbered cabins are on the starboard side (they should be on the port side). Note that the cabins don't have a mini-fridge. Also, if you choose a cabin at the aft of the vessel, you may experience noise from the diesel engines and generators.

The dining room is located in the centre, on Main Deck. It seats all passengers in an open seating arrangement, so you can sit where you likr and with whomever you wish. The place settings are attractive, although there's not a fish knife in sight. If you have special dietary needs, make them known when you book. Complimentary beer and wines are served with lunch and dinner; free water and sodas are available around the clock. Breakfast can be served in your cabin (on the balcony, perhaps).

Service is provided by young, enthusiastic college-age waiters/waitresses. It is, however, quite casual, with little finesse. The cuisine is based mostly on Southern-style fare, with an emphasis on Cajun dishes, beef, fish and seafood, while desserts will typically include pecan pie, Key Lime Pie, and Mississippi Mud Pie (sweet potato pie). Presentation is plain and unstuffy. Complimentary beer and wines are served with lunch and dinner, free water and sodas are available around the clock. Breakfast can be served in your cabin (on the balcony, perhaps).

AMERICAN DUCHESS ★★★+
THIS BRIGHT RED STERN PADDLEWHEELER OOZES PURE AMERICANA TRADITIONS.

Operator .... American Queen Steamboat Company
Built 1995
Length (ft) 340
Former Names ....*Isle of Capri*
Passenger beds..166
Approximate cabin size (sq ft) 180-550
Even numbered cabins (port side) ....Yes
Rivers sailed.. Mississippi

BERLITZ'S RATINGS		
	Possible	Achieved
Hardware	100	72
Accommodation	100	73
Cuisine	100	67
Service	100	65
Miscellaneous	100	70
OVERALL SCORE 347 points out of 500		

American Duchess is little sister to *American Queen*. The hull was built as the casino boat *Isle of Capri* in 1995. It was acquired by the American Queen Steamboat Company before being stripped and totally custom built in 2017 in Morgan City, Louisiana. It is registered in the US, is owned by US citizens, adheres to US Coast Guard safety regulations and has an all-American crew.

The vessel, which was named in August 2017 by Marissa Applegate using a special bottle of Maker's Mark bourbon, has four passenger decks (the uppermost accommodation deck looks rather square and not at all handsome), a lift that goes to almost all decks, and a bow landing ramp for use as a gangway. The lower two decks have very high ceilings. There is no medical facility (but the vessel is seldom far from land), beauty salon or laundry.

The interior decor is an interesting mix of contemporary and traditional Americana (the entrance lobby has a 11m (36ft) -high ceiling with beautiful Austrian crystal chandeliers), and paintings, sculptures, pictures and historic artefacts reflect the heritage, culture and nature of the Mississippi.

The Auditorium is the centre of shipboard social gatherings and entertainment. Riverlorians bring the region to life, and each day, a copy of the next day's programme is delivered to your suite/cabin. Although there are many individual passengers, the vessel also attracts alumni, affinity and special-interest groups.

The cabins (the company calls them all 'suites') measure between 16.7 and 44.5 sq m (180–500 sq ft) and are decorated in a modern interpretation of classic riverboat style. What's unusual are 'loft cabins' – the first on any steamboat/riverboat in the USA. Note that the cabins do not have a mini-fridge and, if you choose a cabin towards the aft of the vessel, that the diesel engines and generators may be noisy.

The Grand Dining Room seats all passengers in one open seating, so you can sit with whomever you wish. Table settings have attractive place settings, although there are no fish knives. The cuisine is straightforward and unfussy. There is a vegetarian selection on each lunch and dinner menu, but if you have special dietary needs, make them known when you book. Wine and beer are complimentary with dinner. The wine list features mainly American wines (the red wine glasses are small).

Breakfast, lunch, dinner, afternoon tea and other snacks are provided daily. If you have special dietary needs, make them known when you book. Although breakfast items are basically the same each day, there's always an additional 'special of the day'.

The salad selections are good, as are the downhome, waistband-expanding desserts such as pecan pie, angel food cake, spiced pumpkin pie, and chocolate brownies. Due to limited storage space, some food items (such as bread rolls, croissants and ice cream, among others) are purchased from on-shore suppliers.

Aft is a Grill Room, for grilled items and BBQs. Forward on the port side is Baristas, which is for those all-important coffees.

Service is provided mostly by young, enthusiastic college-age waiters/waitresses. It is, however, quite casual, and there's little finesse.

AMERICAN EMPRESS ★★★+
THIS COMFORTABLE PADDLEWHEELER EMBODIES PACIFIC NORTHWEST GOLD-RUSH STYLE.

Operator .... American Queen Steamboat Company
Built 2003
Length (ft) 360
Former Names ....*Empress of the North*
Passenger beds 223
Approximate cabin size (sq ft) 150-410
Even numbered cabins (port side) ....Yes
Rivers sailed ....Columbia, Snake

BERLITZ'S RATINGS		
	Possible	Achieved
Hardware	100	70
Accommodation	100	68
Cuisine	100	67
Service	100	65
Miscellaneous	100	67
OVERALL SCORE 337 points out of 500		

Built in 2003 as *Empress of the North* at the Nichols Brothers Boat Builders in Freeland, Washington, this is an authentic stern-wheel-driven vessel, though not a steampowered one. Its name was changed by new owners, to *American Empress*. It is built in the US, is registered in the US, is owned by US citizens, has an all-American crew and complies with US Coast Guard safety regulations.

There are four passenger decks, a bow landing ramp for use as a gangway and two large smokestacks that can be lowered for low bridges. The vessel's two engines are named after Dolly Parton and Claudette Waggoner, wife of AQSC chairman John Waggoner, who smashed a large bottle of sparkling wine for the re-naming ceremony on 5 April 2014. Its aft paddlewheel is 10.7m (35ft) in diameter, 9.8m (32ft) wide, and can achieve a maximum of 15 rpm (revolutions per minute). The steam whistles come from an unknown steamer of the 1800s, and the wheel in the bridge is from the Seattle fireboat *Duwamish*.

The interior decor is pure Americana, and paintings, sculptures, pictures and artefacts feature the heritage, culture and natural history of Alaska and the Pacific Northwest. There are three bars, two lifts and a two-level Show Lounge (located forward) with a thrust stage, dance floor and large chandeliers.

The iconic Paddlewheel Lounge has a low ceiling, Victorian-style decor and views of the paddlewheel aft; it also includes a couple of bookcases.

There are several cabin types (including 'Loft Suites'), sizes and price grades; 105 (out of 112) cabins have a private balcony. The cabins measure between 14 and 38 sq m (150 and 410 sq ft). All have Victorian-style furniture, a Keurig coffee maker and mini-fridge.

Six 'suites' (technically these aren't suites as there's no separation between living and sleeping areas) have the best position, just aft of the navigation bridge. Be aware that the cabins towards the aft of the vessel – near the diesel engines and generators – can be noisy.

The bathrooms are plain. Two grades have small bathtubs, but most have only shower enclosures. Clarins (French) toiletry amenities are provided.

The artwork depicts scenes from the river and steamboat scenes from the 1800s.

The Astoria Dining Room has wedding white decor, but several pillars interfere with the layout. Dining is in an open seating, with dinner at 7pm. Regional Pacific Northwest cuisine is featured. If you have special dietary needs, make them known when you book.

The presentation is straightforward and unfussy. Vegetarian and heart-friendly meals are featured daily. Wine and beer are complimentary with dinner. Lemonade and iced tea are provided at every meal. The wine list focuses on Pacific Northwest wines.

Breakfast, lunch, dinner, afternoon tea and other snacks are provided daily. Although breakfast items are basically the same each day, there's also an additional 'special of the day'.

The salad selections are good, as are the down-home desserts such as pecan pie, angel food cake and chocolate brownies. Due to limited storage space, some items (such as bread rolls, croissants and ice cream, among others) may be purchased from on-shore suppliers.

For the always-hungry, popcorn and yoghurt machines are available 24 hours a day.

There is no medical facility, beauty salon or laundry, but there is a small shop (the Rivershipique) for movies to watch in your cabin; you can also borrow movies from the library without charge. Note that drinks prices are very high, and an additional per person charge is added to your cruise fare for port charges and ground handling fees. The dining room staff (servers) also acts as your cabin attendants.

The company has its own bus for shore excursions, and bicycles for passenger use are also carried.

Suggested crew gratuities are pooled and shared among all crew, while a 15 percent gratuity is added to all bar purchases.

AMERICAN PRIDE ★★★+
TRY THIS STERN PADDLEWHEELER FOR PACIFIC NORTHWEST CASUAL CRUISING.

Operator	American Cruise Lines
Built	2012
Length (ft)	295
Former Names	*Queen of the Mississippi*
Passenger beds	150
Approximate cabin size (sq ft)	203-445
Even numbered cabins (port side)	No
Rivers sailed	Columbia, Snake

BERLITZ'S RATINGS		
	Possible	Achieved
Hardware	100	70
Accommodation	100	64
Cuisine	100	68
Service	100	65
Miscellaneous	100	67
OVERALL SCORE 334 points out of 500		

American Cruise Lines' stern paddle-wheeler *American Pride* was the first riverboat to be constructed in 17 years, since *American Queen* made its debut in 1995. The replica steamboat was built in the US, is registered in the US, is owned by US citizens, adheres to US Coast Guard safety regulations, and has an all-American crew. The bright red stern-mounted paddlewheel weighs 23 tons. This small replica steamboat (it's actually a riverboat because it has diesel, not steam, engines) entered service in 2012.

American Pride has five passenger decks. There is no medical facility, beauty salon or laundry. In the public areas, there are various lounges/bars, one lift and a bow landing ramp for use as a gangway. The Cascade Lounge has panoramic forward-facing river views, while the Paddlewheel Lounge and sky Lounge both have paddlewheel-/aft-facing views. It was originally named during festivities in Nashville on 25 August 2013 in conjunction with the inaugural cruise. A one-night pre-cruise hotel stay and all transfers are included. Daily educational events and themed entertainment paint a picture of life on the Mississippi in days gone by. It originally operated cruises on the Mississippi River, but was moved to the Pacific Northwest in 2016 due to demand, and its name was changed.

Some 65 cabins have a (very) narrow private balcony, while over 20 have non-opening river-view windows. Contrary to maritime tradition, even numbered cabins are on the *starboard* side (they should be on the *port* side). Note that cabins do not have mini-fridges. Also be aware that if you choose a cabin towards the aft of the vessel, the diesel engines and generators can be noisy.

Most of the cabins are quite spacious (each is larger than 27.9 sq m/300 sq ft) and have hotel-style bathrooms, telephones, Wi-Fi, satellite television and room service. Some 12 cabins are designated for solo travellers.

Lecturers help to bring the region to life, and each evening brings a new edition of the next day's daily programme – delivered to your cabin. Although there are mostly individual passengers, the vessel also attracts alumni and affinity groups.

The Dining Room is in the centre of the vessel on Main Deck (the galley is aft) and seats all passengers in one seating, with attractive place settings. Regional Pacific Northwest cuisine is featured. The presentation is straightforward and unfussy, which is fine, but there are no fish knives. The staff also perform the duties of cabin attendants. Vegetarian and heart-friendly meals are also featured daily. The fresh baked rolls, pastries, pies and cookies are good, and lemonade and iced tea are provided at every meal.

The wine list contains mostly Pacific Northwest wines (all at extra cost), but the red wine glasses are small. The fresh baked rolls, pastries, pies and cookies, however, are good. Lemonade and iced tea are provided at every meal. For the always-hungry (and snack attacks at any time) popcorn and yoghurt machines are available 24 hours a day.

Note that drinks prices are high (a gratuity is automatically added) and port charges will be added to your cruise fare. Suggested gratuities to the crew are also high, but are pooled and shared among all crew.

AMERICAN QUEEN ★★★★
TWAIN'S CHARACTER LIVES ON ABOARD THE WORLD'S LARGEST PADDLEWHEEL STEAMBOAT.

Operator .... American Queen Steamboat Company	
Built 1995	
Length (ft) 414	
Former Names .... none	
Passenger beds 436	
Approximate cabin size (sq ft) 80-363	
Even numbered cabins (port side) .... Yes	
Rivers sailed .... Mississippi	

BERLITZ'S RATINGS		
	Possible	Achieved
Hardware	100	72
Accommodation	100	67
Cuisine	100	72
Service	100	67
Miscellaneous	100	74
OVERALL SCORE 352 points out of 500		

Mark Twain said: 'Someday, they'll build the biggest steamboat the world has ever known; and she'll be long, white and gleaming in the sunshine with her twin stacks. And that one shall be the *queen* of the Mississippi.'

The stern paddlewheel steamboat *American Queen* is just that. It debuted in June 1995, cost $65 million, *is* the largest steamboat ever built, and the 30th steamboat built for the long-defunct Delta Queen Steamboat Company. Built by the McDermott Shipyard in Morgan City, Louisiana, it has vintage tandem steeple-compounded, horizontal reciprocating steam engines from about 1930. They originally drove a steam dredge (named *Kennedy*) belonging to the US Army Corps of Engineers; it had been abandoned for many years when the former owners located it.

The engines have four steam cylinders (one high and one low pressure cylinder on each side of the paddle-wheel). 'Steeple compound' means that the steam is expanded twice within the engine with the two cylinders attached to each other. The high-pressure cylinders receive 'live': steam from the boiler to move their pistons down the cylinder bore. After the steam expands in the high-pressure cylinder, it is exhausted into the low-pressure cylinder; it then expands again and allows more work to be performed than in a single expansion engine.

Tandem pistons mean that the high- and low-pressure pistons are mounted on the same piston rod (in tandem). An engine that is double-acting is powered by the steam on both the outward and return strokes. This effectively doubles the number of cylinders, which in turn results in eight expansions

in each revolution of the paddle-wheel. The engine is placed horizontally rather than vertically, which distributes the weight over a larger area and helps reduce the vessel's draft in shallow water.

American Queen's stern paddlewheel weighs 45 tons, and has a 10.9m (35.7ft) -long shaft. It is 9.1 m (29.8 ft) wide and 8.5m (27.8ft) in diameter. When sailing under low bridges, the pilot house (navigation bridge) and twin, fluted funnels can be lowered hydraulically.

American Queen was originally named in New Orleans by noted American radio commentator Paul Harvey, but it was his wife, Angel Harvey, who smashed a giant bottle of tabasco sauce – the largest such bottle ever made – at the naming ceremony. The steamboat also features a calliope, or 'steam piano', driven by the steam engine.

Following the events of 11 September 2001, however, the steamboat was laid up. After a succession of other operators, a group of cruise and travel professionals purchased it in 2011, and a new company was born – the Great American Steamboat Company (renamed the American Queen Steamboat Company). *American Queen* was renamed by Priscilla Presley on 27 April 2012.

Although it was built in the 21st century, *American Queen* is pure Victoriana inside, a floating palace of fretwork and curlicues crowned with tall, fluted funnels – and a bright red paddlewheel.

There are six passenger decks, two lifts, plus bow landing ramps (gangways). Public areas include a Grand Saloon that spans two decks and is the centre of shipboard social gatherings and entertainment. Designed like a miniature opera house, it has a large stage with a proscenium arch and it has seating in individual chairs on the lower level; the upper level has eight 'private' boxes, and an aft seating section. There are two large chandeliers, and the shows are mostly pure Dixieland.

Other facilities include a Gentlemen's Card Room (but ladies are also welcome), with a television hidden behind a stuffed, mounted wild pig's head; the Ladies' Parlor, a demure Victorian room (lookout for Rhett Butler) with antique sewing paraphernalia, period silk dresses and other feminine items, plus a Porter mechanical music box in full working order (complete with perforated discs); and a Mark Twain Gallery, filled with 19th-century literary works (including a full 1894 *Encyclopedia Britannica*) located above the dining room with windows that look into its upper level.

The Chart Room has charts, piloting instruments, books on rivers (including a full set of Mark Twain *Author's National Edition* with author's signature produced by automatic writing), and four Mark Twain sayings on large brass plates set into an octagonal dome.

There's a small cinema for videos and popcorn in bags, and an Engine Room Bar (for sing-alongs). Front Porch (for casual eats, with indoor and outdoor seating) has a self-serve beverage and ice cream station. There's an open Sun Deck for scenery watching, a Calliope bar, with daily hot dogs, and a small room with basic exercise equipment.

The decor includes an eclectic mix of antique furniture and Victorian era trinkets, and easy-to-maintain replica furniture. Sadly, the outer decks have plastic chairs and tables, which just don't seem right for a steamboat trying to maintain traditions of the past.

Activities include daily 'riverlorian' talks – a vital part of the steamboating experience, calliope concerts, sing-alongs, engine room and galley visits, craft lessons, bingo (note that bingo numbers only go to 75 in the US – not 99 as in Europe), kite-flying and line-dancing lessons. A doctor is also on board.

A state trooper aboard *American Queen* carried the Olympic torch for 67.6km (42 miles) along the river from Paducah, Kentucky, to Mound City, Illinois, in 1996. A replica torch can be found in a cabinet in the Mark Twain gallery.

The dress code is casual during the day (tracksuits, shorts and polo shirts or T-shirts being popular), and a little less casual at night.

There are several accommodation categories, with many cabins (rather fancily referred to as staterooms) having river views, and sizes ranging from 7.4 to 32.8 sq m (80 to 353 sq ft). They have colourful bedspreads, wood and brass accents and wall-to-wall carpets, but few have a full-length mirror for dressing. Some cabins interconnect, some are wheelchair-accessible, and some have partially obstructed views, so check carefully before you book. Some are larger than others and have more features – hence the different categories and prices.

Many cabins have a bathtub with tiled surround; others have a large shower enclosure (all bathrooms feature a large washbasin, and space for personal toiletries). Bay windows feature in 22 cabins, while some have an additional washbasin in the dressing area; some cabins feature a third berth.

The accommodation is named after places or people associated with steamboating (examples included Molasses Run, Dog Tooth Bend, Licking River, Morgan City, Evangeline Oak, Cave in Rock and Wabasha). Bathrobes are not provided, and some vibration is evident in the aft cabins on the lowest deck.

The wedding-cake white JM White Dining Room is a stately two decks high on two sides (with large river-view picture windows and with wall-hung tapestries), and one deck high in the centre. It is decorated in true 1890s steamboat fashion. Windows from the Mark Twain Gallery on the deck above look into the port and starboard sections. There are two seatings for dinner, at tables for two to eight; typical dinner times are 5.30 pm and 7.45 pm.

The cuisine is pure Americana – with USDA prime beef, steak, fried chicken (said to have originated aboard the Mississippi steamboats), lobster, catfish and shrimp, and Southern-style (fried food), down-home cooking using regional ingredients.

The presentation is unfussy, and there's not a fish knife in sight. The salad selections are good, as are the down-home, waistband-expanding desserts such as pecan pie, angel food cake, spiced pumpkin pie and chocolate brownies. Due to limited galley and storage space, some food items (such as bread rolls, croissants and ice cream, among others) are purchased from on-shore suppliers.

Breakfast, lunch, dinner, afternoon tea and other snacks are provided daily. Breakfasts are similar each day, but with an additional 'special of the day', for example Southern-style crispy bacon, and pancakes with BBQ sauce. Vegetarian selections are on lunch and dinner menus. Special dietary needs should be made known when you book. Wine and beer are complimentary with dinner. The wine list features mainly American wines, but note that the red wine glasses are very small.

Service is provided by young, enthusiastic waiters/waitresses. It is, however, quite casual, with little finesse. Continental breakfast can be delivered to your cabin. On disembarkation day only a limited self-serve buffet is provided.

Outside on deck is a hot rocks grill, for grilled chicken, shrimp and spare ribs.

LOUISIANE ★★★+

THIS STERN PADDLEWHEELER OOZES DIXIELAND CHARACTER AND TRADITIONS.

Operator	French America Line
Built	2000
Length (ft)	218
Former Names	*Columbia Queen*
Passenger beds	150
Approximate cabin size (sq ft)	91–267
Even numbered cabins (port side)	Yes
Rivers sailed	Mississippi

BERLITZ'S RATINGS	Possible	Achieved
Hardware	100	68
Accommodation	100	66
Cuisine	100	66
Service	100	65
Miscellaneous	100	68
OVERALL SCORE 333 points out of 500		

This riverboat was originally designed and built in 2000 as a casino boat (sister to *Detroit Princess* – presently on Lake Charles, Louisiana). *Louisiane* was built in the US, is registered in the US, is owned by US citizens, adheres to US Coast Guard safety regulations and has an all-American crew.

There are four passenger decks, a lift that goes to almost all decks, and a bow landing ramp for use as a gangway. There is no medical facility, beauty salon or laundry.

The design is reminiscent of the 19th-century steamboats, and the interior decor is classic, elegant Americana.

Louisiane is a small vessel, with a limited number of multi-functional public rooms, including the Back Porch – an indoor/outdoor area with a wood floor, fine views and the Lewis & Clarke Lounge – which is like an anteroom to the Astoria Room (main lounge), for cocktails, hors d'oeuvres and conversation.

Regardless of the size or grade of accommodation you choose (there are seven price categories), you can expect a wood-panelled or wood-accented room, an armoire plus a chair, twin beds that convert to a king-sized bed (except for the solo stateroom),

TV, hairdryer, iron and ironing board (but, sadly, no one to do the actual ironing for you) and telephones with data ports.

Of the cabins (misleadingly called staterooms), the smallest is a dimensionally challenged 8.5 sq m (91 sq ft), while the largest measures 22 sq m (235 sq ft). Be aware that if you choose a cabin towards the aft of the vessel, that the diesel engines and generators can be noisy.

The bathrooms feature a shower (none has a bathtub), washbasin and toilet. Most cabins have double windows and semi-private verandahs or access to the open deck.

The Astoria Room is both the dining room and main lounge for social gatherings and evening entertainment; there is a bandstand/stage and wood dance floor and river-view windows on both sides. Dining is in an 'open seating' arrangement, which means that you can sit where you wish, with whom you wish, but dinner is early, at 6.30pm.

Breakfast, lunch, dinner, afternoon tea and other snacks are provided daily. Although breakfast items are basically the same each day, there's also an additional 'special of the day'. The presentation is straightforward and unfussy. Vegetarian and heart-friendly meals are also featured daily. Desserts include favourites such as Key Lime Pie and Mississippi Mud Pie (sweet potato pie). Note that the red wine glasses are small. Fresh baked rolls, pastries and cookies are often irresistible.

Illy coffee and a drinks-inclusive product make a cruise on this small vessel palatable. Also, a one-night pre-cruise hotel stay and transfers are included.

The price of drinks prices is high, and a 15 percent gratuity is automatically added.

QUEEN OF THE MISSISSIPPI ★★★+

DIXIELAND CHARACTER AND TRADTIONS THRIVE ABOARD THIS STERN PADDLEWHEELER.

Operator	American Cruise Lines
Built	2012
Length (ft)	295
Former Names	*American Eagle*
Passenger beds	150
Approximate cabin size (sq ft)	300-600
Even numbered cabins (port side)	No
Rivers sailed	Mississippi

BERLITZ'S RATINGS

	Possible	Achieved
Hardware	100	68
Accommodation	100	63
Cuisine	100	66
Service	100	65
Miscellaneous	100	68

OVERALL SCORE 330 points out of 500

This small replica steamboat (it's actually a riverboat because it is has diesel, not steam, engines) was built in the US, is registered in the US, is owned by US citizens, adheres to US Coast Guard safety regulations and has an all-American crew. The bright red stern-mounted paddlewheel weighs 23 tons.

There are five decks, a lift that goes to almost all decks, and a bow landing ramp for use as a gangway. There is no medical facility, beauty salon or laundry.

The Magnolia Lounge has panoramic forward-facing river views, while the Paddlewheel Lounge and Sky Lounge both have aft-facing views. The vessel was originally named *American Eagle* by Cheryl Landrieu (First Lady of New Orleans) during festivities in New Orleans in conjunction with the inaugural cruise. Its name was changed to *Queen of the Mississippi* in 2016.

Daily educational events and themed entertainment paint a picture of life on the Mississippi in days gone by.

Most of the cabins are fairly spacious (each is larger than approximately 28 sq m/300 sq ft) and have small, narrow balconies with sliding glass doors, hotel-style bathrooms, telephones, Wi-Fi, satellite television and room service. Several cabins are designated for solo travellers (a welcome addition). Contrary to maritime tradition, even-numbered cabins are on the *starboard* side (they should be on the *port* side). Note that cabins do not have a mini-fridge. Also, if you choose a cabin towards the aft of the vessel, note that the diesel engines and generators can be noisy.

The Dining Salon seats all passengers in one seating, with attractive place settings, although there are no fish knives. The staff also perform the duties of cabin attendants. Breakfast, lunch, dinner, afternoon tea and other snacks are provided daily (vegetarian dishes are also provided). If you have special dietary needs, make them known when you book. Complimentary beer and wines are served with lunch, and dinner, free water and sodas are available around the clock. Finally, you can taste some of those waist-expanding desserts such as Keylime pie and Mississippi mud pie.

QUEEN OF THE WEST ★★★+
YESTERYEAR LIVES ON ABOARD THIS SMALL PACIFIC NORTHWEST PADDLEWHEELER.

Operator	American Cruise Lines
Built	1996
Length (ft)	230
Former Names	none
Passenger beds	100
Approximate cabin size (sq ft)	49-280
Even numbered cabins (port side)	No
Rivers sailed	Columbia, Snake

BERLITZ'S RATINGS		
	Possible	Achieved
Hardware	100	64
Accommodation	100	62
Cuisine	100	66
Service	100	65
Miscellaneous	100	67
OVERALL SCORE 324 points out of 500		

Queen of the West was built in 1996 at the Nichols Brothers Boat Builders in Freeland, Washington (the same shipyard built *Empress of the North,* now named *American Empress*). It is an authentic stern-wheel-driven vessel, although not a steam-powered one. It entered service in 1995 and was the first overnight stern paddle-wheeler built in the west of the USA for over 80 years. Its red paddlewheel is three storeys high, 8m (26ft) in diameter and 9m (29ft) wide. For the technically minded, the maximum wheel revolutions are 21 rpm, which equals 17.25 knots at the centroid of thrust.

The exterior decks are painted blue, the superstructure is white. *Queen of the West* was built in the US, is registered in the US, is owned by US citizens, complies with US Coast Guard safety regulations and has an all-American crew.

There are four passenger decks, a lift that goes to almost all decks and a bow landing ramp for use as a gangway. There is no medical facility, beauty salon or laundry.

American Cruise Lines acquired it in 2009, enlarged several cabins and added more private balconies. The changes lowered the passenger capacity from 150 to 120, making the dining room, lounges and open decks more comfortable.

The interior decor is pure Americana and includes an elegant, white filigreed, spiral staircase. Artwork and photographs in hallways, cabins and public rooms feature classic stern paddle-wheelers of the past, the Lewis & Clark Expedition, the Oregon Trail Era and indigenous American peoples.

Bars and lounges include the Calliope Bar & Grill, which has a canopy-covered area that can be enclosed

during cooler weather. The calliope, with its single manual keyboard, is creamy white and resembles one of those electric organs popular in homes in the 1960s.

The single-deck-high Columbia Showlounge (main lounge) has windows on three sides.

The Wheelhouse Lounge is the late-night hangout. Outside on deck are white rocking chairs.

Lecturers help to bring the region to life, and each day brings a new edition of the daily programe, which is delivered to your cabin.

Suggested gratuities to the crew are high, but are pooled and shared among all crew.

All suites/cabins are decorated in turn-of-the-century steamboat-style, and all have river views (six suites and 22 other cabins have a private balcony), and all have flat-screen television, temperature control, an armoire (wardrobe) and small writing desk (except for four cabins designated as 'value' cabins). Luggage can be stored under the bed. Each has a gold-framed painting and photograph of some of the sternwheelers on the Pacific Northwest rivers in the 1800s. Maritime tradition aboard *ocean*-going ships dictate that even-numbered cabins should be on the port side (the same as the lifeboats), but aboard *Queen of the West* the odd-numbered cabins are on the port side, which is confusing to passengers used to the opposite. Note that if you choose a cabin towards the aft of the vessel the diesel engines and generators can be noisy.

The Lewis & Clark Dining Room, aft, has ornate decoration, with a historically accurate tin ceiling and river-view windows on two sides. Dining is open seating (you sit with whoever you wish), with dinner at 7pm.

Regional Pacific Northwest cuisine is featured. Its presentation is straightforward and unfussy (no fish knives again). Vegetarian and heart-friendly meals are also featured daily, such as Wallowa forest mushrooms and penne pasta. The fresh baked rolls, pastries, pies and cookies are very good, and lemonade and iced tea are provided at every meal. The wine list contains mostly Pacific Northwest wines (at extra cost), but the red wine glasses are small.

For the always-hungry (and snack attacks at any time) popcorn and yoghurt machines are available 24 hours a day.

SHIPS RATED BY SCORE

European Ships

Ship	Score	Rating	Ship	Score	Rating
AmaKristina	★★★★+	427	Viking Kadlin	★★★★	398
AmaViola	★★★★+	425	Viking Kara	★★★★	398
AmaStella	★★★★+	424	Viking Mimir	★★★★	398
Crystal Debussy	★★★★+	424	Viking Modi	★★★★	398
Crystal Ravel	★★★★+	424	Viking Nerthus	★★★★	398
AmaSerena	★★★★+	423	Viking Skirmir	★★★★	398
Crystal Mahler	★★★★+	423	Viking Tialfi	★★★★	398
Crystal Bach	★★★★+	422	Viking Vidar	★★★★	398
AmaPrima	★★★★+	421	Viking Vilhjalm	★★★★	398
AmaReina	★★★★+	421	Viking Beyla	★★★★	397
AmaSonata	★★★★+	420	Viking Delling	★★★★	397
AmaVenita	★★★★+	418	Viking Eistla	★★★★	397
AmaVerde	★★★★+	417	Viking Gefjon	★★★★	397
AmaBella	★★★★+	411	Viking Heimdal	★★★★	397
Scenic Jasper	★★★★+	411	Viking Hlin	★★★★	397
Scenic Opal	★★★★+	411	Viking Mani	★★★★	397
AmaCerto	★★★★+	404	Viking Ingvi	★★★★	397
Scenic Jade	★★★★+	404	Viking Lofn	★★★★	397
Amadeus Silver III	★★★★+	403	Viking Skadi	★★★★	397
Asara	★★★★+	403	Viking Tor	★★★★	397
Scenic Jewel	★★★★+	403	Viking Var	★★★★	397
Amadeus Provence	★★★★+	402	Viking Ve	★★★★	397
Crystal Mozart	★★★★+	402	Viking Vili	★★★★	397
Scenic Gem	★★★★+	402	Viking Astrild	★★★★	396
Amadeus Silver II	★★★★+	401	Viking Baldur	★★★★	396
Viking Herja	★★★★	399	Viking Bestla	★★★★	396
Viking Hermod	★★★★	399	Viking Buri	★★★★	396
Viking Hild	★★★★	399	Viking Gullveig	★★★★	396
Viking Rolf	★★★★	399	Viking Idi	★★★★	396
Viking Egil	★★★★	398	Viking Kvasir	★★★★	396
Viking Eir	★★★★	398	Viking Osfrid	★★★★	396

Ship	Score	Rating	Ship	Score	Rating
AmaCello	★★★★	395	Amadeus Brilliant	★★★★	381
AmaDante	★★★★	395	Emerald Sky	★★★★	381
AmaDolce	★★★★	395	Emerald Star	★★★★	381
Viking Embla	★★★★	395	S.S. Catherine	★★★★	381
Viking Jarl	★★★★	395	Amadeus Elegant	★★★★	379
Viking Lif	★★★★	395	Emerald Radiance	★★★★	378
Viking Rinda	★★★★	395	Savor	★★★★	376
AmaLyra	★★★★	394	Grace	★★★★	375
Viking Alruna	★★★★	394	Scenic Diamond	★★★★	375
Viking Magni	★★★★	394	Avalon Imagery II	★★★★	374
Amadeus Silver	★★★★	393	Viking Hemming	★★★★	374
Viking Alsvin	★★★★	393	Viking Torgil	★★★★	374
Viking Atla	★★★★	393	Thomas Hardy	★★★★	373
Viking Bragi	★★★★	393	Avalon Passion	★★★★	372
Viking Forseti	★★★★	393	Scenic Amber	★★★★	372
Viking Freya	★★★★	393	Scenic Sapphire	★★★★	372
Scenic Azure	★★★★	392	S.S. Antoinette	★★★★	372
Viking Idun	★★★★	392	Oscar Wilde	★★★★	371
Viking Odin	★★★★	392	Amadeus Royal	★★★★	370
Viking Aegir	★★★★	391	Avalon Tranquility II	★★★★	370
Viking Njord	★★★★	391	Scenic Ruby	★★★★	370
Amadeus Diamond	★★★★	390	Avalon Tapestry II	★★★★	368
Amelia	★★★★	390	Inspire	★★★★	368
AmaVida	★★★★	389	Avalon Illumination	★★★★	366
Anesha	★★★★	388	Emily Brontë	★★★★	366
Scenic Crystal	★★★★	388	Lord Byron	★★★★	366
S.S. Joie de Vivre	★★★★	388	Avalon Poetry II	★★★★	365
Joy	★★★★	387	Douro Serenity	★★★★	365
Emerald Dawn	★★★★	385	Amadeus Classic	★★★★	364
S.S. Maria Theresa	★★★★	385	Jane Austen	★★★★	364
Emerald Destiny	★★★★	385	Douro Elegance	★★★★	363
Emerald Sun	★★★★	384	Charles Dickens	★★★★	361
Scenic Pearl	★★★★	384	Amadeus Symphony	★★★★	360
Emerald Liberté	★★★★	383	Treasures	★★★★	360

Ship	Score	Rating	Ship	Score	Rating
Avalon Expression	★★★★	359	Thurgau Ultra	★★★+	330
Monarch Empress	★★★★	357	Excellence Royal	★★★+	329
Elbe Princesse	★★★★	356	A-ROSA Flora	★★★+	328
William Shakespeare	★★★★	354	River Venture	★★★+	328
Edelweiss	★★★★	353	A-ROSA Silva	★★★+	326
Excellence Princess	★★★★	353	River Splendor	★★★+	326
River Voyager	★★★★	353	Travelmarvel Sapphire	★★★+	326
Alina	★★★★	352	River Discovery II	★★★+	325
Avalon Artistry II	★★★★	351	Excellence Rhône	★★★+	324
Esprit	★★★+	347	Swiss Jewel	★★★+	324
Aurelia	★★★+	346	A-ROSA Viva	★★★+	323
Avalon Vista	★★★+	346	Brabant	★★★+	323
Miguel Torga	★★★+	345	Travelmarvel Diamond	★★★+	321
Avalon Visionary	★★★+	344	Travelmarvel Jewel	★★★+	321
Queen Isabel	★★★+	344	A-ROSA Brava	★★★+	320
Avalon Felicity	★★★+	343	A-ROSA Stella	★★★+	317
Monarch Baroness	★★★+	343	Sonata	★★★+	317
Sapphire	★★★+	343	Swiss Gloria	★★★+	317
Avalon Panorama	★★★+	342	Swiss Ruby	★★★+	317
Loire Princesse	★★★+	341	A-ROSA Aqua	★★★+	316
Monarch Queen	★★★+	341	A-ROSA Riva	★★★+	315
Ariana	★★★+	338	A-ROSA Luna	★★★+	314
Cyrano de Bergerac	★★★+	336	A-ROSA Mia	★★★+	313
Emerald	★★★+	336	Leonora	★★★+	312
Gil Eanes	★★★+	336	Antonio Bellucci	★★★+	310
Avalon Luminary	★★★+	335	Swiss Corona	★★★+	308
Avalon Affinity	★★★+	334	Thurgau Silence	★★★+	308
Avalon Creativity	★★★+	334	A-ROSA Donna	★★★+	306
Excellence Melodia	★★★+	333	Nestroy	★★★+	306
Excellence Queen	★★★+	332	Seine Princess	★★★+	306
Swiss Tiara	★★★+	332	A-ROSA Bella	★★★+	305
Excellence Allegra	★★★+	331	Beethoven	★★★+	304
Lafayette	★★★+	330	Regina Rheni	★★★+	304
Gérard Schmitter	★★★+	330	River Princess	★★★+	304

Ship	Score	Rating	Ship	Score	Rating
Serenade I	★★★+	303	Swiss Pearl	★★★	286
Maxima 1	★★★+	302	Botticelli	★★★	285
Serenade 2	★★★+	301	Infante Don Henrique	★★★	285
Filia Rheni II	★★★	298	River Art	★★★	285
Primadonna	★★★	298	Symphonie II	★★★	285
Prinzessin Isabella	★★★	298	Casanova	★★★	284
S.S. Beatrice	★★★	298	DCS Amethyst	★★★	283
Swiss Crown	★★★	298	Douro Cruiser	★★★	283
Belvedere	★★★	297	Select Explorer	★★★	283
Camargue	★★★	297	France	★★★	282
Douro Queen	★★★	297	Modigliani	★★★	281
Bellejour	★★★	296	Mona Lisa	★★★	281
Douro Spirit	★★★	296	Sans Souci	★★★	281
Bellefleur	★★★	295	Seine Comtesse	★★★	281
Excellence Pearl	★★★	295	Frederic Chopin	★★★	280
Serenity	★★★	295	Michaelangelo	★★★	280
Viktoria	★★★	295	Rhineprinzessin	★★★	280
River Royale	★★★	294	Excellence Coral	★★★	279
Bellissima	★★★	293	L'Europe	★★★	279
Princesse d'Aquitaine	★★★	293	Leonardo da Vinci	★★★	279
River Duchess	★★★	293	Switzerland	★★★	277
Vista Flamenco	★★★	293	Bijou du Rhône	★★★	276
River Empress	★★★	292	Switzerland II	★★★	276
Swiss Diamond	★★★	292	the B	★★★	276
River Countess	★★★	291	Bolero	★★★	275
River Queen	★★★	291	the A	★★★	275
Rousse Prestige	★★★	291	Van Gogh	★★★	275
Spirit of Chartwell	★★★	291	Fernao de Magalhaes	★★★	274
Swiss Crystal	★★★	290	Katharina von Bora	★★★	274
Vivaldi	★★★	288	River Aria	★★★	274
La Belle de Cadix	★★★	287	Vasco da Gama	★★★	274
Rhine Melody	★★★	287	Saxonia	★★★	273
Prinzessin Sisi	★★★	286	La Boheme	★★★	272
Royal Crown	★★★	286	Mistral	★★★	272

Ship	Score	Rating	Ship	Score	Rating
River Concerto	★★★	272	Der Kleine Prinz	★★+	211
Bizet	★★★	270	Koenigstein	★★+	210
Carmen	★★★	270	Sofia	★★+	209
Amadeus I	★★★	269	Arlene	★★+	208
Monet	★★★	269	Rousse	★★	200
Renoir	★★★	269	Danubia	★★	197
Victor Hugo	★★★	267	Poseidon	★★	193
River Rhapsody	★★★	266	Princess	★★	193
River Harmony	★★★	265	Statendam	★★	192
River Melody	★★★	264	Lady Anne	★★	189
Elegant Lady	★★★	263	Calypso	★★	185
River Adagio	★★★	262	Virginia	★★	182
Carissima	★★★	258	Amsterdam	★★	179
Johannes Brahms	★★★	258	My Story	★★	179
Princesse de Provence	★★★	257	Rotterdam	★★	173
Provence	★★+	246	Prinses Christina	★★	166
Douce France	★★+	244	Rhine Princess	★★	165
Verdi	★★+	244	Douro Princess	★★	163
Normandie	★★+	241	Azolla	★★	162
Prinzessin Katharina	★★+	241	Prinses Juliana	★★	158
River Allegro	★★+	236	Diana	★+	147
Olympia	★★+	235	Horizon	★+	145
Rex Rheni	★★+	234	Salvinia	★+	128
Rigoletto	★★+	233	Alena	NYR	NYR
Esmeralda	★★+	232	AmaLea	NYR	NYR
Da Vinci	★★+	228	AmaMagna	NYR	NYR
Bellriva	★★+	222	Elbe Princesse II	NYR	NYR
Alemannia	★★+	212	NickoVision	NYR	NYR
Rembrandt von Rijn	★★+	212	Robert Burns	NYR	NYR

USA Ships

Ship	Score	Rating	Ship	Score	Rating
American Queen	★★★★	352	American Pride	★★★+	334
American Duchess	★★★+	347	Louisiane	★★★+	333
American Empress	★★★+	337	Queen of the Mississippi	★★★+	330
America	★★★+	335	Queen of the West	★★★+	324

Credits

Photo Credits

123RF 52
1A Vista Reisen 151B
4Corners Images 6/7
A-Rosa River Cruises 106, 135B, 136T, 137B, 138B, 138T, 139B, 140T
Alamy 4/5, 98, 101, 102, 285
Alpina River Cruises 210T
AmaWaterways 117B, 118T, 119B, 119T, 120B, 120T, 121T, 123B, 123T, 124B, 124T, 125B, 125T, 126T
American Cruise Lines 302, 305, 309, 310
American Queen Steamboat Company 278/279, 280, 282, 287, 294, 297, 298, 300, 303, 304
APT 150T
Artmüller Wolfgang 199T
Avalon Waterways 16, 20, 36, 42/43, 107, 146T
AWL Images 1
Ayako Ward 7B, 18, 109
bertknot 167T
Bigstock 54, 66, 71, 72, 79, 85, 86
Blue on flickr 166B
Breeze River Cruises GmbH 116T, 219B
CEphoto, Uwe Aranas/CC-BY-SA-3.0 227B
Cha già José 240T
Christian Jansky 231B
Continental Waterways 203B
CroisiEurope 14, 40, 51, 76, 91, 93, 94, 97, 149B, 154T, 155B, 160B, 163B, 167B, 178B, 179B, 180B, 181T, 182B, 186B, 188B, 188T, 189B, 191B, 192T, 200T, 205B, 229T, 241B, 246B, 247T, 248T, 277T
Crystal Cruises 158B, 159B, 159T, 160T
David Frield 230B
DCS 161T
Dietmar Heinz 195T
Dimitar Denev 213B
Douglas Ward 7, 10, 15, 17, 21, 22, 23, 24TL, 24TR, 24ML, 24MR, 25, 26, 29, 30, 33, 34, 36/37, 38, 41, 47, 68, 104/105, 112, 136B, 148T, 153T, 158T, 164B, 165T, 166T, 173T, 175B, 187T, 189T, 197T, 234B, 244B, 246T, 251T, 260T, 262B, 266B, 276B, 286, 306
Douro Azul 204T, 232B

drayy 162T
Dreamstime 55, 63, 73, 90, 99, 100
Duca696 165B
Dunav Tours 168B, 218B, 219T
Elliott Brown 191T
Emerald Waterways 169B, 170B, 170T, 171B, 171T, 172B, 172T
Feenstra Rhine Line 132B, 134B
Fotolia 65
Fred. Olsen Cruise Lines 154B
French America Line 308
Frila 163T
Gate 1 Travel 193B, 194
geraldm1 185T
Getty Images 290, 292
Globus/Avalon Waterways 141B, 142B, 142T, 143T, 144B, 145B, 145T, 147T, 148B
Grand Circle Cruise Line 213T, 215T
Granger/REX/Shutterstock 284
Hamburg Seehandlung 144T
Hans-Rudolf Stoll 164T
helmut1972 - binnenschifferforum. de 195B, 275B
HRL European River Cruise Ventures 211B
Isiona River Equity AG 146B
iStock 48, 57, 60, 67, 75, 80
Jean Housen 128B
Jim Thorne 215B
Jonathan Bachman/Invision/AP/ REX/Shutterstock 301
KLUG Touristik 203T
Klugschnacker 184T, 220B
Lydia Evans/Apa Publications 95
Lüftner Cruises 126B, 127B, 127T, 128T, 129B, 129T, 130B, 131B, 131T
Mike Louagie/AmaWaterways 114/115
Mizu001 3ML
MS Mosel GmbH 143B
Nicko Cruises 151T, 153B, 180T, 196B, 200B, 206B, 228B
Nitram2805 185B
panta rhei pr gmbh 174B, 176B, 176T, 177T
Parchimer 193T
Phoenix Reisen GmbH 116B, 117B, 132T, 133T, 134T, 140B, 141T, 155T, 202T, 207B, 222T, 240B

pinguin1961 252T
Premicon 150B, 152B, 152T, 190B, 245B, 245T
Qsimple 199B
Quality Tours 162B
Rich Monroe 122T
Richard Palmer 209T
Rijfers River Cruises 204B
Riseday Holdings 202B
Riviera Travel 198T, 243T
Rolf Heinrich, Köln 118B, 122B, 130T, 133B, 135T, 137T, 139T, 147B, 149T, 157T, 161B, 173B, 182T, 183B, 186T, 187B, 192B, 196T, 197B, 198B, 201B, 205T, 206T, 207T, 208T, 209B, 210B, 216B, 216T, 218T, 220T, 224T, 226T, 227T, 228T, 230T, 232T, 235B, 235T, 238T, 241T, 248B, 250B, 251B, 252B, 254B, 255T, 262B, 264B, 264T, 265T, 266T, 267T, 268B, 268T, 269B, 270B, 271B, 271T, 272T, 273T, 276T
Saga Group Limited 179T
Scenic Group 19, 22B, 46, 223T, 223B, 224B, 225B, 225T, 226B
Scylla 169T, 174T, 183T, 190T, 221B, 236T, 236B, 237B, 237T, 238B, 239B, 239T
Select Voyages 157B, 229B, 277B
Shutterstock 121B, 156B, 156T, 168T, 217B, 295
SijBrands 247B
Sylvaine Poitau/Apa Publications 92
Tauck 181B, 184B, 221T
Thomas R Machnitzki 296
Thurgau Travel 243B, 244T
Tony Kliemann 208B
Trans River Line 201T
Twerenbold Service AG 175T, 177B, 178T
U by Uniworld 242B, 242T
Uniworld River Cruises 8, 9, 13, 35, 39, 83, 87, 113, 114, 211T, 212B, 212T, 214B, 214T, 233B, 233T, 234T
Vantage River Cruises 217T
Viking River Cruises 10/11, 62, 249B, 249T, 250T, 253B, 253T, 254T, 255B, 256B, 256T, 257B, 257T, 258B, 258T, 259B, 259T, 260B, 261B, 261T, 263B, 263T, 265B, 267B, 269T, 270T, 272B, 273B, 274T, 274B, 275T

Cover Credits

Front cover: AWL Images
Back cover: American Queen Steamboat Company, Scenic Group, Uniworld River Cruises, Ayako Ward

Berlitz/Insight Guide Credits

Distribution
UK, Ireland and Europe
Apa Publications (UK) Ltd
sales@insightguides.com

United States and Canada
Ingram Publisher Services
ips@ingramcontent.com

Australia and New Zealand
Woodslane
info@woodslane.com.au

Southeast Asia
Apa Publications (SN) Pte
singaporeoffice@insightguides.com

Worldwide
Apa Publications (UK) Ltd
sales@insightguides.com

Special Sales, Content Licensing and CoPublishing
Insight Guides can be purchased in bulk quantities at discounted prices. We can create special editions, personalised jackets and corporate imprints tailored to your needs. sales@insightguides.com; www.insightguides.biz

First Edition 2014
Third Edition 2018

www.berlitzpublishing.com

Author
Douglas Ward

Managing Editors
Sarah Clark/Rachel Lawrence

Copyeditor
Clare Peel

Picture Editor
Tom Smyth

Head of Production
Rebeka Davies

TELL US YOUR THOUGHTS

Dear Cruiser,

I hope you have found this edition of Berlitz River Cruising in Europe and the USA both enjoyable and useful. If you have any comments or queries, or experiences of cruising that you would like to pass on, or perhaps some ideas for subjects that could be included in the future, I would be delighted to read them. With your help, I can improve and expand the guide in future editions.

The world of cruising is evolving fast and certain facts and figures may have changed since this guide went to print, so if you have found any outdated information in these pages, please do let me know and I will make sure it is changed as soon as possible.

You can write to me by email at: shipratings@hotmail.com

Or by post to:
APA Publications
PO Box 7910
London SE1 1WE
United Kingdom

Thank you,
Douglas Ward

Index